IN THE SHADOW OF AUSCHWITZ

IN THE SHADOW OF

AUSCHWITZ

THE POLISH GOVERNMENT-IN-EXILE AND THE JEWS, 1939–1942

BY DAVID ENGEL

The University of North Carolina Press

Chapel Hill & London

© 1987 The University of North Carolina Press

All rights reserved

Manufactured in the United States of America

Library of Congress Cataloging-in-Publication Data

Engel, David.

In the shadow of Auschwitz.

Bibliography: p.

Includes index.

1. Jews—Poland—Politics and government.

2. Holocaust, Jewish (1939–1945)—Poland.

3. Poland—History—Occupation, 1939–1945.

4. World War, 1939–1945—Governments in exile.

5. Poland—Ethnic relations. I. Title.

DS135.P6E54   1987   940.53'15'039240438   86-24703

ISBN 0-8078-1737-6

For My Family

CONTENTS

ACKNOWLEDGMENTS

A while ago a colleague complained that his assistance had been profusely acknowledged in a book with whose thesis he held no quarter. Another colleague mentioned on the same occasion that he had once felt compelled to request that a publisher remove his name from the acknowledgments in a work that he found similarly exceptionable. Hence it seems fitting at the outset to thank these two gentlemen, who have warned me of the pitfalls in even so seemingly simple an endeavor as expressing gratitude. Of course, in accordance with what I take to be their preference, I shall not name them.

This work began as an independent venture. It did not originate as a doctoral dissertation, nor was it carried out as part of the activities of any research institute. Nevertheless, a number of people have in various ways lent their encouragement, assistance, and constructive criticism, and despite the risks in so doing, I shall name them (alphabetically): Arnold Band, Yehuda Bauer, Harold Borko, Saul Friedländer, Amos Funkenstein, Yisrael Gutman, Joanna Hanson, Marek Kahan, Jan Karski, Paweł Korzec, Shmuel Krakowski, Emanuel Melzer, Matityahu Minc, Antony Polonsky, Yoel Raba, and Count Edward Raczyński. I am grateful for the time and attention that these people have given me during the course of my work, and I hope that after this book sees the light of day, none will feel inclined to disavow association with it. Of course, the naming of these individuals in no way implies their agreement with the statements or interpretations that follow, which are entirely my own.

I also acknowledge with gratitude the conscientious assistance of the staffs of the archives, libraries, and research institutions whose holdings have provided the raw materials for this study—especially the Hoover Institution (Stanford, California), the Polish Institute (London), the Wiener Library (Tel Aviv), and Yad Vashem (Jerusalem). The Charles Brown Foundation and the Bernstein-Maslansky Fund generously responded to appeals for financial support, and I thank their directors, Irving Allen and Larry Barr. The Bureau of

Jewish Education of San Francisco provided technical assistance during the period of research at Stanford, which I also recall with thanks.

Yet for all of my debts to the people and institutions just named, my greatest and most consistent source of support and encouragement, in every sense, has been my family. Thus to Ronit, Karen, Michelle, Natalie, Shirley, and Harold Engel this book is dedicated.

Tel Aviv, 1985

NOTE ON NAMES AND TRANSLITERATION

Many of the people mentioned in this book have been called by several different versions of their names. For the sake of clarity and consistency, the following conventions have been adopted:

Jews who during the period treated in this study held official positions in Polish governing, administrative, or legislative bodies are referred to by their Polish names, whereas those who were associated primarily with Jewish organizations are referred to by their Hebrew or Yiddish names (thus Ignacy Schwarzbart rather than Yitshak, but Anshel Reiss rather than Anzelm). Only one version of a person's name has been employed throughout, even if over the years the primary focus of his activity changed (thus Yitshak Gruenbaum rather than Izaak, even for the years when he served as a deputy in the Polish Sejm). Hebrew names are transliterated according to the same scheme as all other Hebrew words and phrases (see below), even if a given individual's Hebrew name was generally pronounced with a Yiddish inflection (thus Noah Pryłucki rather than Noyekh). In some cases, the Latinized spelling most commonly used by the person in question has been retained (thus Szmuel Zygielbojm rather than Shmuel). This rule has been applied in all cases to surnames (thus Schwarzbart rather than Szwarcbart). Hebraized surnames adopted during or after the period treated in this book are not employed (thus Moshe Kleinbaum rather than Moshe Sneh). No names of either Jews or Poles have been Anglicized (thus Moshe rather than Moses, Stanisław rather than Stanislaus).

In most cases, professional titles or titles of nobility attached to individual names have not been used. Occasional exceptions have been made, especially for clerical and military titles when the information conveyed by them seemed relevant to the discussion. The British title of knighthood, Sir, has been employed throughout.

Place names are rendered according to the official language of the country in which they are located (thus Kraków rather than Cracow). Polish names are employed for all places located within Poland's

Note on Names and Transliteration

interwar boundaries (thus Wilno rather than Vilnius or Vilna, Lwów rather than Lviv or Lemberg). Exceptions are made in the cases of major cities, such as Warsaw and Jerusalem, whose English names differ significantly from their native-language forms.

Transliterations from Hebrew and Yiddish have been rendered according to the scheme employed in the publications of the Conference on Jewish Social Studies. No attempt has been made to systematize the transliteration of the few Russian titles and phrases that appear in the book.

IN THE SHADOW OF

AUSCHWITZ

INTRODUCTION

The Polish Jewish historian Paweł Korzec concluded his 1980 study of the politics of the Jewish question in interwar Poland with the provocative observation that "the manner in which Poland treated Polish Jews between the two world wars contributed to making the immense tragedy which was to befall them under the Hitlerite yoke possible."[1] This was perhaps the bluntest—though by no means the first—statement of a view widely held among Jewish students and survivors of the Holocaust, that responsibility for the wanton murder of 3 million Polish Jews must be assigned not only to the Nazi murderers themselves but also to those Poles who, it is alleged, at best looked on with indifference as their Jewish fellow citizens were stripped of their property, herded into ghettos, and marched in the end to the shooting pits and gas chambers. The comment suggests furthermore that this purported Polish response is to be attributed not, primarily, to the harsh conditions of the German occupation in Poland, in which assistance to Jews was, at least from 1941, a capital offense, but rather to the legacy of Polish-Jewish relations during the years of the Second Polish Republic, in which the Polish state and community had, according to the argument, vocally and unceremoniously excluded Jews from "that circle of persons toward whom obligations are owed, to whom the rules apply, and whose injuries call for expiation by the community," which sociologist Helen Fein has termed their "universe of obligation."[2]

This thesis has, to be sure, been hotly disputed. Some, expectedly, have attacked it on empirical grounds, denying altogether the existence of any Polish predisposition to regard Jews as beyond the set of those whose needs and interests the Polish state was intended to serve and arguing instead that whatever friction existed between Poles and Jews in the interwar years was mainly the result of the latter's unwillingness or inability to enter the mainstream of Polish society.[3] Others, while conceding that during the two decades before the outbreak of World War II strong anti-Jewish feeling was noticeable among segments of the Polish population, have maintained that the events of September 1939—and even more those surrounding the mass deportations from the Warsaw ghetto to Treblinka in the summer of 1942—effected a revolution in Polish consciousness, in which sympathy toward the Jewish plight became the dominant factor in determining the Polish people's behavior toward their threatened Jewish neighbors.[4] Proponents of both views, though differing in their assessments of Polish-Jewish relations during the interwar period, have emphatically denied all suggestions of Polish passivity —let alone complicity—in the face of the Holocaust and have adduced a lengthy list of examples of Polish aid to Jews during the war, often offered at risk of life, in support of their contention.

The debate exists as well on the level of interpretation. One recent comment on the problem has warned that "it is all too easy to be wise after the event, and to suggest that the [Jews'] tribulations of 1918–1939 were a preamble to the ensuing tragedy [under the Nazis]," implying that the entire question of Polish attitudes toward Jews, whether before or during the Second World War, is largely irrelevant to understanding how Polish Jewry perished in the Holocaust. "The Nazis' 'Final Solution,'" the same writer has argued, ". . . was no mere pogrom on a grand scale; it was a calculated act of genocide executed with the full authority of the German state, a mass murder committed in full accordance with the dictates of the Nazis' unique, and alien ideology." According to this view, although "the survivors were all too few, . . . in the circumstances, it is hard to see how it could have been otherwise."[5] On the other hand, a far-reaching sociological analysis of the Holocaust has concluded that differences in the percentage of victims of the final solution in the various countries under Nazi occupation "can best be understood by first accounting for the level of previous antisemitism, which predisposed states to high cooperation with the drive to exterminate the Jews."[6] If, then, this argument suggests, the Germans murdered a greater proportion of Polish Jews than of Jews of any other land in which the Nazi killing machine was set in motion, this situation is attributable first of all precisely to the heritage of antipathy left by the experience of the previous twenty years.

Yet for all that has been written on the subject thus far, the discussion remains remarkably unsatisfying. On the one hand, the mere recounting of instances—however numerous—in which Poles offered succor and shelter to Jews tells no more about the overall tenor of relations between the two groups than would a similar list—easily composed—of instances of Polish cooperation in Nazi anti-Jewish actions.[7] Clearly, such examples must be placed within the context of the entire range of Polish responses to the Jewish situation throughout the war years before their significance can be properly evaluated.[8] Nor is there great insight in dismissing the entire problem as inconsequential by exploiting the indisputable fact that the German occupiers had in mind for Polish Jews a far different fate than was ever intended them by even the most rabid Polish antisemite. Of course it must not be forgotten that the murder of Poland's Jews was committed by Germans, not by Poles; and it is a moot question whether any amount of Polish assistance to Jews would, on the macroscopic level, have altered the outcome of the Nazis' annihilation campaign to any statistically significant extent. But it must also not be forgotten that at the time of the events under discussion those Poles who were called upon to respond to what was happening to their Jewish fellow citizens did not enjoy the benefit of hindsight from which to judge the eventual statistical consequences of their actions. No doubt most of the forty thousand or so Polish Jews who survived the war in hiding among Poles or under cover of the Polish forest owed their lives to the willingness of Polish non-Jews to aid them. But if so, it is also meet to inquire how many more Jews owed their deaths to the unwillingness of other Poles to do the same thing. There can be no question that between 1939 and 1945 Polish attitudes toward Jews were of the greatest consequence for tens—perhaps even hundreds—of thousands of human beings.

On the other hand, those who have posited a high degree of continuity between Polish-Jewish tension in the interwar period and the eventual annihilation of Polish Jewry in the Holocaust have not yet shown precisely how specific interwar attitudes affected Polish behavior toward Jews during the war years. Though it may indeed be possible to demonstrate a statistical correlation between the level of antisemitism in a particular country during the late 1930s—assuming that such a thing can be accurately measured and graded—and the losses sustained by the Jews of that country between 1939 and 1945, this still does not explain why such a correlation should exist. It is not at all obvious, for example, that the German occupation should not have aroused a feeling of solidarity among all of the victims of

Nazi oppression, in Poland and elsewhere. Nor does it follow that the absence of a sense of obligation toward Jews among the Polish community had necessarily to lead to widespread Polish indifference to or satisfaction with the Jewish plight. Even if it is granted that most Poles did not regard themselves as their Jewish brothers' keepers, this still does not mean that they could not have made a calculated decision to assist the threatened Jews because they believed it to their advantage to do so. The question of self-interest, as much as that of "value consensus," has to be addressed if the behavior of Poles toward Jews during the Holocaust is to be understood.

The calculus of self-interest need not apply only to individuals who perform a given action in expectation of personal pecuniary gain. It can also apply to a collectivity pursuing more general, less tangible goals. The Polish community during the Second World War sought above all the restoration of its independence within the borders of the prewar Polish state—an objective that, as it turned out, was at best only partially fulfilled. It seems appropriate, then, within the context of the debate over the character of wartime Polish-Jewish relations, to ask to what extent the leaders of the Polish community believed that this goal might be advanced by aiding the Jews in their struggle against the Nazis. Indeed, on the surface at least, there appear to have been good reasons why they might have so believed. The expropriation, isolation, concentration, and—eventually—murder of the Jewish population was an integral feature of German policy in occupied Poland. Hence any blow struck against these actions was in a sense also a blow against the occupying regime as a whole, and more specifically against the possibility that the fate of the Jews might eventually be visited upon the Poles as well. Conversely, passivity in the face of Nazi anti-Jewish actions could have been regarded as tantamount to acquiescence to a central aspect of the occupation, contributing in turn to a weakening of Polish resistance overall. What is more, a people fighting to regain its freedom stands to benefit from the support of dedicated allies and certainly cannot afford to alienate any who might conceivably fill such a role. In this sense, the assistance of Jews, both within the occupied homeland and abroad, might well have been valued by Polish leaders; and they might reasonably have assumed that the greater the Polish contribution to the Jewish struggle, the more the Jews might feel obliged to reciprocate.

Such reasoning is, of course, altogether hypothetical, taking no notice of the actual situation's details or complexities. It is, nonetheless, credible; and in any event thoughts similar to these were discussed and debated by Polish leaders, both explicitly and implicitly, on several occasions during the course of the war. Such deliberations obviously were of crucial importance in shaping the relations between Poles and Jews in the shadow of Auschwitz. It seems important, then, not only to trace the course of these discussions and to ascertain their outcome, but to reconstruct, to the extent that the available documentation allows, the thinking by which the leaders determined whether and to what extent assistance to Jews coincided with the Polish national interest. More specifically, it seems valuable to set the influence of prewar conceptions of the Jewish question in Poland against that of more immediate, practical considerations in guiding the Polish leadership in its resolution of the problem. In this fashion it may in turn be possible to clarify the nature of the connection between the tenor of Polish-Jewish relations during the period between the two world wars and Polish responses to the Nazi Holocaust.

The study that follows examines the thinking on Jewish-related matters of that segment of the Polish leadership which conducted the struggle for the renewal of Poland's independence within its prewar borders from a position of exile outside the occupied homeland. The decision to concentrate upon the government-in-exile rather than upon the underground leadership in Poland itself was taken for a number of reasons.[9] In the first place, the underground was formally subordinate to the exile regime, which represented the legal continuation of the Polish Republic in the eyes both of the Polish community and of the nations of the world. Obviously, because of the physical separation between the two centers—not to mention the conditions of war and occupation that impeded communication between them—the ability of the government-in-exile to direct the day-to-day operations of the underground was limited. The government did, nevertheless, control the general formulation of Polish policy, both toward the occupying forces and in the international diplomatic arena. It also exercised considerable moral authority over the underground leaders, and through them over the Polish community as a whole. The attitudes of the government-in-exile thus stood to exercise critical influence over the Polish population's behavior toward its Jewish neighbors.

The government-in-exile was, moreover, the principal vehicle through which news of the condition of Polish Jewry could be relayed from underground sources in Poland to the governments of the Allied and neutral nations, to Jewish organizations throughout the world, and to the Western public at large. All of these, like the Polish underground and community as a whole, were potential sources of aid to the threatened Jews. Their perception of what was happening to Jews under Nazi rule—in particular, from mid-1942 on, their willingness to believe the news that Jews were being systematically murdered en masse—was conditioned in no small measure by the government-in-exile's decisions about how information received from the homeland was to be passed on. In addition, the government-in-exile, as the recognized legal representative of Polish Jewry (as of all Polish nationals) in the eyes of the Allied and neutral nations, was uniquely able to intervene with the governments of these countries and to sound the cry of help on behalf of its Jewish citizens. It is true that its influence in this regard was not great, and it may well be that no amount of Polish pressure would have significantly changed those governments' own Jewish policies; but there was virtually no possibility that another nation would take action in defense of Polish Jewry if the Polish government did not at least request, let alone demand, that it do so. In this respect, too, at least as far as it could tell at the time, the government-in-exile—if not through action in the diplomatic sphere then certainly through failure or unwillingness to act—was in a position to affect the fate of Polish Jewry profoundly.

The fact that the government-in-exile was able to maintain contact with Jewish organizations in the West was significant from another perspective as well. In the occupied homeland, German policies severely impeded communication between Poles and Jews, so that opportunities for both sides adequately to explore possible bases for formal, long-term cooperation were lacking. Nor, under the conditions of occupation, was there much chance for Jews to contribute actively and obviously to the Poles' struggle for liberation. Underground leaders as a result had a much narrower basis from which to evaluate the practical benefits to their own cause likely to result from aiding Jews than did those in exile, who could and did consider carefully the various ways in which Jews, not only in Poland but throughout the world, might help the government achieve its basic objectives. Therefore it is easier to estimate fairly for the exile government than for the homeland leadership the relative effect of calculations of Poland's national self-interest upon behavior toward Jews. Besides, the determination of national self-interest is in any case primarily the responsibility of government. As long as the Polish community's recognized instruments of government were located abroad, the underground leadership was not forced to consider the problem of Polish-Jewish relations in all of its ramifications.

Curiously, though, for similar reasons, it is also easier to evaluate the relative effect of prewar values and attitudes toward the Jewish question upon government actions than upon those of the underground. The exile regime sought from the outset to represent itself as a radical departure from the governments that had ruled Poland since Marshal Józef Piłsudski's 1926 coup d'etat, and especially from those which had held power following the marshal's death in 1935. These latter governments had, among other things, pursued a Jewish policy that clearly legitimated the Jews' exclusion from the Polish universe of obligation. Did the government-in-exile's commitment to a break with the immediate prewar legacy include this aspect of Polish policy as well? This was a question with which the government was forced to wrestle virtually from the beginning of its existence, largely because of pressure brought to bear upon it by Jewish organizations in the West. The underground, in contrast, was under no such pressure, either internal or external, to face the issue in a principled fashion. Thus the political controversies engendered by the Jewish question in interwar Poland were played out during the war years more in exile than in the occupied homeland.

For all of these reasons, it seems sensible to begin an investigation into the responses of the Polish leadership to the Holocaust of Polish Jewry with an examination of the Jewish policies of the Polish government-in-exile.

Initially it was intended to present the complete results of this study in a single volume encompassing the entire period of the Second World War. However, the immense quantity of documentary material that must be presented and analyzed in order to treat the subject fully, fairly, and accurately has made it necessary, in order to keep the work within manageable dimensions, to close the present volume at the end of 1942. It was then, on 10 December, that the Polish government issued the diplomatic note that brought for the first time formally "to the knowledge of all civilised countries" the horrible news that "the German authorities aim with systematic deliberation at the total extermination of the Jewish population in Poland."[10] The actions of the government-in-exile in the wake of this declaration will await separate analysis in a second volume.

In the event, the note of 10 December does represent a sort of caesura in the development of the government-in-exile's relation to the Jewish situation: its publication marked the government's first public acknowledgment that the Jews of Poland were confronted with a special peril greater even than that faced by the Poles, and as such it gave the issue of assistance to Jews a far greater urgency than it had ever before possessed. This greater urgency was primarily the result of greater visibility given the Jewish plight in the West from late 1942 on, a development to which the Polish note contributed significantly. The government-in-exile had, however, been in possession of fairly detailed information concerning a German plan to destroy all of Polish Jewry physically for at least six months before the declaration's issue. It was during this interval that the government first became acutely aware that its assessment of its interests and obligations vis-à-vis its Jewish citizens was a matter of life and death for a large number of people. As it happened, though, such an assessment had already been fully formulated during the first three years of the war, on the basis both of underground reports on the nature of Polish-Jewish relations in the homeland and of the government's ongoing interaction with Jewish organizations in the West over its general attitudes toward solving the Jewish question once Poland was liberated. Out of these two sources the government-in-exile had constructed fairly clear guidelines concerning the degree to which it ought to sponsor and defend Jewish interests. Although such guidelines were never committed to writing in a single comprehensive statement, they do emerge conspicuously from the copious documentary evidence to be found in the government-in-exile's archives.

The development of these guidelines, essentially complete by the end of 1942, is the principal theme of the chapters that follow. This study aims to establish as precisely as possible what those guidelines were, to describe the manner in which they were implemented during the first three years of the war, and to explain, as fully as the available documentation allows, the thinking behind their adoption. In the pursuit of this last aim, special notice will be taken of the influence of prewar Polish attitudes toward the Jewish question upon the government-in-exile's formulation of its own position.

One final word of caution is necessary. There seems to exist at times an almost irresistible temptation—as the opening paragraph of this introduction will attest—to follow statements of fact about Polish actions or inactions on behalf of Jews under Nazi rule with evaluative statements about the nature and extent of Polish moral responsibility or nonresponsibility for the Holocaust. The latter term of this combination indeed defines a weighty and compelling problem, and it ought to be obvious that any consideration of it must rest solidly upon knowledge of the former. Yet whereas the former lies clearly within the historian's professional bailiwick, the latter, strictly speaking, does not. This does not mean, of course, that the historian cannot form an opinion on moral responsibility as a result of his investigation of facts; but in the last analysis his professional historical training and expertise lend his moral judgment in the matter no greater authority than that of any intelligent, sensitive, informed human being. Thus in what follows there is no attempt to assign responsibility for the Holocaust to any except those directly involved in the mechanism of murder. On the other hand, if readers are helped as a result of this historical inquiry to approach the moral problem with a greater degree of factual awareness and insight into the situation's complexities, the work will have served a significant purpose.

BACKGROUND
The Prewar Legacy

"The Polish community must know," wrote Bishop Józef Kruszyński of Włocławek in a pamphlet published on the press of his diocese in 1921, "that the Jewish question hangs over it like the sword of Damocles."[1] His trepidation before the sword was widely shared. During the brief existence of the Polish Republic, born in the aftermath of the First World War and crushed in the maelstrom of the Second, Polish Jewry was made the object of such intense public scrutiny that to many it seemed the country's most pressing political problem. Even on the brink of the Nazi invasion of September 1939, Polish government officials and political leaders continued to insist that the precipitous deterioration in Polish-German relations not be permitted to hamper efforts to remove a large portion of the Jewish population from Poland. As Polish Foreign Minister Józef Beck explained, "The fact that in consequence of grave international developments discussion of the Jewish problem has receded into the background does not in any way mean that the Jewish question has ceased to represent for Poland . . . a significant problem needing to be solved now."[2]

How did the Jewish question come to be invested with such importance in Polish political life? Franciszek Bujak, a professor at the

University of Kraków who at various stages in his career maintained close ties with the Polish National Democratic and peasant movements, pointed in 1919 to three facts that, to his mind, made the Jewish problem "one of the most vexatious . . . which the Polish state is facing at the moment of its creation . . . : the high percentage of the Jewish population in the territories of the Polish state, the development of the Jewish national spirit . . . , [and] the great part played by the Jews in the world's politics."[3] His enumeration succinctly limned the contours of the public debate over Polish Jewry as it was conducted throughout the years of Poland's independence.

The first official Polish census, taken in 1921, identified in the country 2,855,318 Jews, some 10.5 percent of the more than 27 million inhabitants of the new state. Ten years later the number of Jews had climbed to 3,113,933, although their relative proportion had fallen to 9.8 percent.[4] Nowhere else in the world did Jews form such a high percentage of the total population. With numerical concentration naturally came high visibility as well. A Polish Foreign Ministry official calculated in 1937 that there were in the neighborhood of nine Jews residing upon each square kilometer of Polish soil, compared with one-half Jew per similar measure in the United States.[5] The implication of such a remark, of course, was that sheer numbers made Poland's Jewish problem unique and that solutions that might have been found satisfactory in other lands could not necessarily be transplanted with success to the Polish context.

What was vexatious, however, was less the total number of Jews than the anomalous distribution of their residences and occupation when compared with that of non-Jewish Poles. Among the predominantly rural Polish population, Jews stood out as a highly urbanized group, of whom the vast majority earned their livings in commerce or manufacturing.[6] This fact in turn led to the widespread belief that commerce and manufacturing in Poland had become virtual Jewish monopolies. The perception corresponded to reality only in part. Although Jews were, to be sure, disproportionately represented in these activities, non-Jews participated in them as well, and the concentration of Jews in trade and industry was for the most part on the decline.[7] Nevertheless, the notion that these pillars of Polish economic life had somehow been abandoned to Jewish control continued to exert a powerful influence upon Polish politics throughout the years of Poland's independent existence.

But why should this idea have been a cause for alarm? An explanation frequently offered by Polish writers on the Jewish question during the interwar years pointed to demographic trends that, it was argued, if left to proceed uncorrected, would result in the dislocation of a broad segment of Polish society. Poland's rural population had been increasing rapidly from the late nineteenth century, to the point where the land could no longer support all who sought to derive sustenance from it.[8] On the other hand, Polish industry had grown but slowly, and it had been unable to absorb the surplus population from the countryside. The result had been a continuing influx of displaced agricultural workers into the cities and towns, where, despite their hopes, they had been unable to find satisfactory employment. What they had found, though, was an urban economy seemingly dominated by Jews. Jews thus appeared to form "a barrier inhibiting the flow of the rural population into the cities."[9] Before Poland could prosper, many Polish writers concluded, the barrier needed to be removed.

This argument was employed to explain, among other things, the anti-Jewish boycott organized by the Polish National Democratic Party (Endecja) in 1912.[10] In this case, which attracted a measure of international protest, Polish leaders were able to contend that their actions were taken not out of any deep-seated antipathy toward Jews, but because they were necessary in order to preserve Poland's social health.[11] They were able in addition to maintain that whatever manifestations of antisemitism might appear in Poland could be understood primarily as a spontaneous expression of the ordinary antagonism between economic competitors.[12]

However, on critical examination, the demographic argument appears to offer little real explanation for the centrality of the Jewish question in Polish politics throughout the interwar years. To be sure, the struggle for livelihood in independent Poland was a real one, and clashes between Jews and non-Jews over employment or business opportunities were in evidence; but on the whole Jews emerged from their confrontation with the growing Polish bourgeoisie and proletariat on the losing side. The larger mechanized factories, which with the passage of time accounted for an ever-increasing share of industrial production, tended to prefer Polish to Jewish employees.[13] At the same time, the growth of urban markets, their increasing exploitation by modern capitalist enterprises, and the rise of Polish producers' and consumers' cooperatives helped to undermine the economic standing of the Jewish petty trader.[14] The situation prompted Morris Waldman of the American Jewish Joint Distribution Committee to remark on returning from a visit to Poland in 1927 that "whatever growth and development may take place in the industrialization of Poland is likely to prove . . . a further misfortune for the Jews."[15] The Jewish position was rendered still more precarious by the government's adoption in 1920 of a policy that discriminated de facto against Jews in awarding concessions in the state-held tobacco, liquor, salt, match, public transportation, and communications monopolies.[16] By the late 1930s close to 30 percent of Polish Jews were receiving some form of economic assistance from Jewish communal funds.[17] It thus seems difficult to maintain that Jews posed a significant barrier to the absorption of displaced Polish peasants in commerce and industry. If absorption continued to be a difficulty, other factors appear to have been more responsible.

It appears, too, that other factors were more responsible for the constant evocation of the skewed occupational distribution of Polish Jewry as a political problem of the first order. Bujak offered a clue to one of these factors in his 1919 tract on the Jewish question when he noted how the Polish people had come to realize that their continued dependence upon a non-Polish merchantry "would reduce them to dependence on a foreign element and cripple them economically and politically."[18] Evidently, what was at stake for him in the issue of Jewish occupational distribution was Poland's economic independence, which was, to his mind, the essential basis upon which Poland's political independence would ultimately rest. Here Bujak rooted himself in one of the fundamental axioms of Polish nationalist thought of all ideological shadings:[19] the notion that a necessary prerequisite to the reconstitution of an independent Poland was the conquest of commerce and manufacturing by a native Polish commercial and industrial middle class and urban proletariat. The Polonization of trade and industry was for Polish nationalists of virtually every stripe not only a matter of the Polish community's social and economic well-being but also an essential component of the movement for national rebirth.[20] Similarly, it seems that the vocational structure of Polish Jewry became a political problem not so much because Jews competed with Poles for positions in trade and industry as because they occupied such positions at all. The call to free Polish commerce from "foreign [i.e., Jewish] domination" appears to have been voiced largely independently of the demographic pressures that aroused a Polish demand for urban employment.

Such a call, though, contained the hidden assumption that Polish Jewry, whose continuous presence in Poland could be traced at least to the twelfth century, constituted in fact an alien element whose concentrated involvement in trade and artisanry necessarily contradicted the Polish national movement's aim of economic independence. This was an assumption that Poles appear to have had some difficulty explaining, especially to observers from those Western countries that had during the previous century endeavored to integrate their own Jewish populations into the mainstream of their public and social life. To be sure, Jews were on the whole highly visible in Poland as a distinct ethnic group, marked off from the Polish community not only by occupation but also by a range of cultural characteristics, including religion, language, dress, cuisine, and personal names. These differences were widely interpreted by Poles as signs of a perverse foreignness and of willful dissociation from the Polish community.[21] Yet this differentness did not imply logically that through the pursuit of their traditional occupations Jews could not contribute to the economic well-being of a Polish state that included them as equal citizens. In order to establish this contention, Polish writers on the Jewish question throughout the interwar period were bound to consider at length, in addition to demographic arguments, the nature of Jewish "separatism"—or, to use Bujak's phrase, "the development of the Jewish national spirit," the second of the three roots of the Jewish problem's vexatiousness.

The catchword "separatism" was commonly employed to denote the demand, consistently voiced by spokesmen for Polish Jewry, that the new Polish state recognize its Jewish citizens as members of an autonomous national corporation invested with the power to select its own leadership, to establish and administer its own state-supported religious and social institutions with a minimum of government control, and to operate a system of elementary and secondary schools with Yiddish or Hebrew as the language of instruction and the history and literature of the Jewish people as integral parts of the curriculum.[22] This demand, together with the corollary that Jews be permitted to employ their native languages for official purposes, was a basic one for Polish Jewry, largely because it adumbrated the notion that the new Polish state ought to exist to serve the collective needs and interests not only of the Polish community but also of the various ethnic minority groups that together accounted for one-third of the new state's population.[23] This concept of Poland as a "state of nationalities [*państwo narodowościowe*]," as opposed to a "nation-state [*państwo narodowe*]," was roundly rejected by the Polish right and center, while the left in theory espoused a variant of it largely for tactical purposes.[24] Insofar as it implied the recognition of Polish Jewry's right to communal autonomy, it was spurned all along the political spectrum.[25]

To the West the Poles endeavored to found their rejection of autonomy for Jews upon principles of egalitarian democracy: granting autonomy would create "two classes of citizens, condemned to eternal discord, one representing [the] 86% of the Christian citizens with normal rights, the other the 14% [*sic*] of Jewish citizens enjoying special privileges in addition to normal rights."[26] Actually, however, it appears that the reasons ran deeper: most Poles seem to have perceived the Jewish demand as yet another indication of the long-standing refusal of Polish Jewry to acquiesce loyally to the prospect of Polish sovereignty and to identify itself with Poland's national goals. When on 25 February 1919 the issue of Jewish autonomy was first raised for discussion in the Constituent Sejm (an elected assembly charged with drafting a constitution for the new state), the National Democratic leader Wojciech Korfanty admonished against the creation of a Jewish "state within a state," for fear of strengthening the "anonymous [world Jewish] power" that had purportedly resisted with all its might the rebirth of Poland's political freedom.[27] In a similar vein Bishop Kruszyński warned that "the present efforts of Jewry [to obtain the status of a national minority] run entirely counter to our national interest," because they "postulate the notion of a Judeo-Poland."[28] And Bujak cautioned that "under certain conditions a Jewish national autonomy might easily lead to the most fatal consequences for the Polish state."[29] It seems that many Poles were convinced that Jews were irreconcilably hostile to Polish independence and, what is more, that they might conceivably reach a position where their hostility could bring down the Polish Republic.

The perception of Jewish enmity to the Polish national cause had its roots in the so-called *Litwak* immigration of the three decades prior to the First World War. Since 1881 successive waves of anti-

Jewish violence in Russia had led some 250,000 Jews, many of whom had managed to acquire a veneer of Russian culture, from the eastern provinces of the Pale of Settlement to search for refuge in the cities of Congress Poland. By the outbreak of war, these *Litwaki*, as they had come to be known,[30] had managed to engender in certain Polish nationalist writers a suspicion of Jews in general as enthusiastic Russifiers or even, some contended, willing agents of the tsarist regime.[31] Curiously, though, the *Litwaki* were also perceived as bearers of the Jewish national idea who had implanted the notions of separatism and corporate autonomy among a Polish Jewry that had hitherto been prepared to seek integration into the Polish community.[32] The common denominator between the two alleged effects of the *Litwak* incursion was clearly antipathy to the Polish national movement. Jewish separatism thus became linked to a fundamentally anti-Polish attitude.

Ironically, though, the same conclusion could also be reached from an altogether opposite premise: that Jews were not a Russifying element in Poland at all, but actually a Germanizing one. Such a proposition was suggested first of all by the fact that most Polish Jews were the descendants of earlier eastward migrants from Germany, as well as by the continued attachment of Polish Jewry to the Germanic-based Yiddish language. Since the demand for Jewish autonomy was more often than not tied to the use of Yiddish as the language of Jewish communal life, the anti-Polish character of the autonomy idea could again easily be inferred.[33] The experience of World War I, in which German Jewish leaders rashly proposed that a Polish Jewry guaranteed national autonomy by the occupying Central Powers would willingly serve as the advance guard of German policy in Eastern Europe,[34] seemed to many Poles to establish the truth of this inference beyond doubt.[35] Surveying from his essentially pro-Allied perspective the role played by Jews during the war, Endecja founder Roman Dmowski concluded that enthusiasm for the autonomy concept had driven Jewry willy-nilly into a conspiracy with Germany and Austria to prevent the independence of Poland at any cost. Jews and Poles appeared to him—and to many others—to be locked in mortal combat; Jews intended to turn Poland into their new Palestine and the Poles into the modern equivalent of Canaanite slaves.[36]

Polish nationalists had no doubt, too, that Jews were quite capable of achieving their purported goal. Bujak noted "the great part played by the Jews in the world's politics" as the third reason for the Jewish question's centrality in Poland; and indeed, the fear that Jewish influence abroad might be decisive in determining the country's fate became a leitmotif of Polish discussions of the issue during the early years of Polish independence. Such a possibility was brought into especially sharp focus at the close of the First World War, when Poland's political future rested largely upon the disposition of the victorious Allied powers assembled at Versailles and the Polish image in Western public opinion had been severely damaged precisely because of the volatile relations between Poles and Jews. In the wake of the breakdown of responsible authority in Poland in November 1918, Poles—their emotions fanned by charges of Jewish complicity not only with Germany and Austria but with Ukrainian nationalists and the Russian Bolsheviks as well[37]—had embarked upon a wave of pogroms throughout much of Galicia and also in other parts of Poland.[38] News of these riots reaching the West made the situation of Polish Jewry a focus of international attention. Protest meetings were organized in major cities across Europe and America, and the governments of Britain, France, and the United States discussed the matter at the diplomatic level with official Polish representatives.[39] During 1919 all three powers dispatched special governmental commissions of inquiry to Poland to probe the extent and causes of the anti-Jewish violence.[40] The issue of Polish-Jewish relations was also raised at the Paris Peace Conference in the context of the discussions over the creation of an independent Polish state. The Committee of Jewish Delegations at the Peace Conference, which had been organized on 25 March 1919 for the purpose of bringing before the Allies matters of primary concern to Jews throughout the world, played a central role in encouraging the Western powers to include international guarantees for the rights of Polish Jewry as an essential element in the disposition of the Polish question.[41]

The outcome of the discussions at Versailles was the conclusion between the Allies and the newly created Polish state of the so-called Minorities Treaty of 28 June 1919. According to this agreement, Poland was to guarantee that all inhabitants of its territories would enjoy full and equal rights as Polish citizens, without regard to their religious or ethnic identity. Poland further obligated itself to ensure that all members of ethnic minorities would be able freely to employ their native languages for public purposes and that in areas largely inhabited by non-Polish-speaking populations, the public elementary schools would offer instruction in the language of the minority pupils. Two provisions of the agreement made specific mention of the Jews: Article 10 provided that Jewish communities should receive public funds for the organization of Jewish schools, and Article 11 enjoined Poland from requiring Jews to perform civic functions on Saturday, the Jewish Sabbath.[42] The signing of the treaty was a source of great satisfaction to Jewish leaders, both in Poland and throughout the world.

The Poles expressed a different attitude. To them, the agreement had been concluded under duress, forced upon them by the Allies as a virtual condition of their independence; as such, it represented an affront to Poland's sovereignty and placed an unwarranted limitation on the state's ability to arrange its internal affairs as it saw fit.[43] Not surprisingly, the role of the Jews in the genesis of the treaty was singled out for special condemnation. Wincenty Witos, leader of the centrist Piast Party, largest of the political groups representing the Polish peasantry, told the Constituent Sejm on 31 July 1919 that in their advocacy of the agreement Jews had deliberately sought to disgrace the Polish people; he promised that the "special privileges" granted them by the treaty would be revoked the moment "foreigners" ceased "to run things in our home."[44] To Polish Premier Ignacy Jan Paderewski, the inescapable conclusion to be drawn from the imposition of the Minorities Treaty upon Poland was that Jews had successfully exerted international influence in order to turn the country into a virtual binational state, in which Poles were obliged to share with them their hard-won sovereignty on an equal basis.[45] Other Polish nationalist spokesmen railed bitterly against the "inflammatory propaganda" appearing in Western newspapers about the pogroms, which had, they claimed, not only inspired the Minorities Treaty but also proved the existence of "organized and well-financed endeavors to assist Jewry by destroying the dearly-won freedom of Poland."[46] In short, the ability of Polish Jews, in concert with their coreligionists abroad, to arouse the nations of the West to serious action on their behalf convinced large numbers of Poles that Jews represented a powerful and especially dangerous internal enemy. Bishop Kruszyński's words expressed what appears to have been a prominent attitude among Poles: "Almost the whole of Jewry is thoroughly hostile toward us, and that hostility serves . . . to undermine our independent existence at its very dawn."[47]

_____

The fear of the Jewish enemy, inexorably hostile to the very idea of Polish sovereignty, reflected what seems to have been a basic Polish insecurity over the durability of the nation's independence. Indeed, in Poland's precarious geopolitical situation during the interwar years, a certain apprehension was not only unavoidable but, as events were to prove, even well-advised. The country was bordered to the east and west by powers—the Soviet Union and Germany—at whose expense significant territories had been awarded the new Polish state and who had in consequence made revision of their boundaries with Poland one of their principal foreign policy objectives. Slightly over a century before these powers, *mutatis mutandis*, had conspired to destroy Poland's political freedom, and Poles could never entirely escape the dread of an eventual fourth Polish partition. In the event, in September 1939, such a partition was actually carried out.

This state of affairs no doubt encouraged Poles to suspect the loyalty of their non-Polish fellow citizens. It seems strange, though, that among the four principal ethnic minorities that together accounted for one-third of the Republic's population, Jews should have been perceived as especially threatening. In the case of each of the other groups—Ukrainians, White Russians, and Germans—some logical (if not always factual) justification existed for associating them presumptively with German or Soviet revisionist demands. With regard to the Jews, in contrast, no obvious logical basis for such a presumption could be found. Jews possessed no compelling reason, a priori, for preferring either German or Russian to Polish hegemony. Attempts by Poles to adduce such a reason through facile association of linguistic habits with political loyalties led only to the conclusion that Jews were simultaneously Russifiers and Germanizers, a contradiction that indicated merely the concern of the Polish national movement for justifying the presence of strongly held anti-Jewish feelings within it.

By the same token, though, Jews possessed no compelling reason a priori for preferring Polish to German or Russian hegemony. Polish

Jewry as a group—like many of those peoples of Eastern Europe whose political heritage had included a protracted period of existence as an ethnic minority within a multinational empire—was marked by a high degree of internal cohesiveness and national consciousness, which made the Jewish group itself the principal focus of the individual Jew's identification and loyalty. This particularistic attitude was reinforced by the divergence in social structure between the Jews and the other peoples among whom they lived. Polish Jews were engaged in a formidable day-to-day struggle to secure the means of their livelihood—and, at times, even their bodily safety—under conditions markedly different from those affecting the surrounding non-Jewish population. Jews therefore tended to consider the question who should rule the Polish territories first of all from the perspective of their own battles for ethnic, economic, and physical survival.[48] Of primary importance was not the national character of the governing authority so much as its political and social orientation. In theory, at least, Jews were prepared to support almost any regime that guaranteed their security and civic equality and that recognized their right to maintain their integrity as a particular historic community.

This willingness did not, however, despite the Jews' awareness of their negative standing in the eyes of much of the Polish national movement, necessarily imply Jewish hostility to the idea of Polish independence. In reality, a very different attitude was noticeable, especially in the lands of the Russian partition, in the decade preceding the creation of the new Polish state. During this period Polish nationalists, taking advantage of the forum provided them following the 1905 revolution by the establishment of the Russian State Duma and the campaigns for election of delegates to it, began vigorously to demand home rule for Poland under the dominance of the Polish nation. In this situation Jews throughout the empire began to consider their own reactions to such a possibility. To be sure, they were on the whole most anxious over the indications of antisemitism that they perceived within the Polish national movement, particularly after the Polish caucus in the Third Duma supported the imposition of restrictions upon Jewish participation in the proposed organs of urban self-government in the Congress Kingdom.[49] But nevertheless, for all of the bitterness expressed by Jewish spokesmen over this explicit Polish rejection of the principle of Jewish civic equality, only a handful suggested that Jews actively attempt to frustrate Polish efforts to achieve territorial autonomy.[50] More common was the approach taken by a group of prominent Jews from Minsk, who, in the name of the principles of democracy and the equality of nations, adopted a resolution affirming the concept of urban self-government in Poland, provided the enabling legislation allowed for no restrictions of an ethnic or religious nature.[51] In a similar vein, Yitshak Gruenbaum, the foremost spokesman of the Zionist movement in Congress Poland, went so far as to argue that Polish support for anti-Jewish restrictions actually demonstrated the vital interest of Polish Jewry in the success of the Polish drive for autonomy. "Between the lines [the Poles] are hinting to us," he wrote, "that were the governing authority in Polish hands, they would not restrict our rights, but would merely do as the English and Americans have done, and prevent the entry of [foreign] Jews into their country." He concluded that Jews must continue to struggle for a self-governing Poland that would recognize Jewish civil and national rights.[52]

To be sure, this attitude was not motivated by any special Jewish love for the Polish cause per se. It reflected rather a resolution adopted in 1906 at the Third Conference of Russian Zionists in Helsingfors (Helsinki), demanding the overall democratization and decentralization of the Russian regime and affirming Zionist identification with the struggles of all of the empire's territorial minorities for a greater degree of home rule.[53] Weakening the hold of the tsarist regime, under which Jews had been oppressed as nowhere else in Europe during the preceding decades, had become from the turn of the twentieth century a primary goal of Jewish—not only Zionist—political activity throughout the empire, including the Congress Kingdom. Since the establishment of an autonomous Poland would necessarily imply the existence of restrictions upon the imperial power, it appeared to be in the Jewish interest to work toward such a goal, whatever the attitude of the Poles toward more particularistic Jewish political objectives.[54] Here the practical expression of Jewish political particularism was determined not by the behavior of the Poles in isolation but by a careful weighing of actual alternatives.

Considered rejection of an explicitly anti-Polish course, even in the face of profound pessimism about the prospects for fruitful Polish-Jewish cooperation, was observable, too, in Austrian-ruled Galicia, although the tenor of Jewish attitudes was different from that which prevailed in Russian Poland. Since 1867 the province had functioned as an autonomous dominion within the reorganized Habsburg Empire, in which Poles, with the backing of the imperial regime in Vienna, formed the dominant national group. This experience had provided Jews with an extended opportunity to observe how Poles in positions of power behaved with regard to Jewish political goals. For the most part, Jews were not happy with what they saw,[55] but there was little that they could do to change the situation. The only conceivable alternative—an alliance between Jews and the Ukrainian majority of East Galicia that would press for the recognition of the national rights of both groups[56]—was impractical, not only because of the preference of most Jewish leaders for Polish culture over Ukrainian, but also because, except in limited instances, such an alliance had no chance for success.[57] As both the Ukrainians and the Jews saw their particularistic ambitions frustrated by Polish hegemony, some Jewish leaders, especially in East Galicia, developed a certain sympathy for the Ukrainian national movement; but the relative weakness of the Ukrainians in comparison to the Poles mitigated any inclinations toward open identification. In general, Galician Jews strove to avoid taking any stand that would antagonize either of the other two principal ethnic groups in the province.[58] Like the Jews of Russia, they affirmed, in their own interest, the basic principles of the equality of all nations and their right to self-determination. Where, however, political conditions in Russia drove Jews toward a definite, if reluctant, pro-Polish orientation, in Galicia they demanded an approach of benign neutrality toward the Polish cause.

In neither region, though, was there any significant attempt by the Jews of Poland to interfere with the creation of an independent Polish state at the close of World War I. On the contrary, by the spring of 1918 all major Jewish political organizations in Poland had sensed it discreet to support publicly the establishment of Polish sovereignty at least over the territories in which Poles formed a majority of the population.[59] This does not mean that Jews, both in Poland and throughout the world, did not greet with considerable trepidation the prospect of seeing a Jewish community of well over 2 million subjected to Polish rule;[60] it simply appeared obvious, as Gruenbaum explained, that "whatever the final outcome of the . . . World War, Poland—in whole or in part, one way or another—will become once more an independent state."[61] Even before the Polish Republic had been proclaimed, the leadership of Polish Jewry appears to have concluded that all future struggles for security, equality, and autonomy would need to be conducted with regard to a Polish ruling power.[62] The fundamental axiom of Jewish politics was henceforth to be that most succinctly enunciated by the Folkist leader Noah Prylucki at a meeting of the Warsaw City Council in September 1916: "From the perspective of our state identity we are Poles, but ethnically and culturally we are Jews and wish to remain so."[63]

On the other hand, Jewish leaders appear on the whole to have distinguished between the notion of Polish sovereignty as such and its extension over territories inhabited primarily by non-Poles. In the months following the war's end, as Polish territorial ambitions came into conflict with the aspirations of the Lithuanian, Ukrainian, and White Russian peoples for independent states of their own, Jews inhabiting the lands under dispute were caught, often literally, in the crossfire. Such a situation demanded, of course, that Jews exercise the utmost caution in their political pronouncements; in any case, a declaration clearly favoring the Polish side was out of the question. However, the Jewish reticence to identify with the Polish view of the new Poland's proper boundaries seems to have been motivated as well by a perception that the Poles were attempting to become a new imperial power in Eastern Europe. A number of Jewish spokesmen who commented on the Polish struggle with the rival national groups used the occasion to reemphasize their commitment to the principle of national self-determination.[64] Gruenbaum even went so far as to decline a direct request from Head of State Marshal Józef Piłsudski to conduct pro-Polish propaganda among the Jews of Wilno, citing his lack of authority to intervene in Wilno Jewry's internal affairs.[65] In a similar vein, the Bund, despite strong pressure from the Polish Socialist Party, refused to endorse Poland's declaration of war upon the Soviet Union in 1919, thereby rejecting implicitly the Polish objective of eastward expansion.[66] At the root of this attitude evidently lay the conviction that an imperial Poland, founded upon the subjugation of non-Polish peoples, would not be likely to uphold the right of Jews to civic equality and national autonomy and might even force them into the role of an instrument for thwarting other groups' national aspirations. The Galician Zionist leader Yosef Tenenbaum expressed this concern succinctly in an essay on the Jewish question in Poland prepared in conjunction with the Versailles conference: "Poland must not be a national imperialist state, but a state of free nationalities, a Fatherland for all of the peoples who live under its flag, a Fatherland also for the Jews."[67]

Undoubtedly, the reserved Jewish attitude toward Poland's territorial claims heightened Polish suspicions of Jewish loyalty and thus sharpened the tension between the two groups at the outset of Poland's independence. In the eyes of many Poles, anything less than unqualified support for the maximalist territorial position was regarded as rejection of Polish sovereignty, for it indicated that Jews were not prepared to leave decisions of overriding national importance to the Polish community alone.[68] Nonetheless, most Jews would not consider relinquishing the conduct of an independent national political program. The impact of the postwar pogroms, added to the more general economic and cultural exigencies of Jewish life in Poland, made achievement of autonomous national status within the new Polish state appear to most Polish Jewish leaders nothing less than a matter of survival.[69] Many, as a result, were even willing to see their relations with the Poles placed on a veritable war footing over this issue. Yitshak Gruenbaum, for one, showed no compunction about describing those relations in military terms: "The Polish community and its parties, its press and literature, the law and the governing power [on the one hand], and the Jewish community with its separate parties [on the other], stand arrayed against each other, battle lines drawn."[70]

Polish nationalists, for their part, employed military metaphors as well. According to Andrzej Niemojewski, a leading Polish journalist, the Polish people stood in mid-1919 "on the eve of a civil war with the Jews."[71] Thus, from the Polish perspective, the Jewish question reduced itself to a matter of controlling as completely as possible the threat posed by this enemy within. Exercise of this control meant, first of all, that the Polish community needed to take concerted action to limit Jewry's ability to strengthen its position in the country as a distinct national group. Polish political parties and governmental officials argued among themselves throughout the interwar period about the most appropriate and effective manner of accomplishing this primary goal, with the parties of the left generally more willing than those of the right to acknowledge that as individuals Jews might enjoy an equal share in the benefits of Polish statehood; but the goal itself appears to have been a matter of almost constant national consensus. Though the dominant strategy varied depending upon changes in Poland's internal and external political situation, the end of weakening Jewry as a group to the maximum extent possible was pursued with vigor by virtually all segments of the Polish body politic. What is more, in working toward this end, measures were often taken that also adversely affected the political and social standing and economic well-being of large numbers of Jews as individuals.

The state contributed to the campaign against the internal Jewish enemy by systematically attenuating the guarantees of civic equality and collective rights for Jews contained in the Minorities Treaty and in the Polish constitutions of 1921 and 1935. Even before the elections to the Constituent Sejm in 1919, the Polish authorities introduced administrative measures that prevented many Jewish residents of Poland from enjoying the rights of Polish citizens and that severely limited the extent to which Jewish political parties could maintain an effective parliamentary representation of their own.[72] Jewish officers and soldiers who had served in the Polish legions together with Piłsudski, or who had volunteered for service against the Soviets, were subjected to a concerted campaign to remove them from the armed forces, culminating in August 1920 in the incarceration of a large number of them in the military internment camp at Jabłonna—on the grounds that they had actively collaborated with the Bolshevik enemy.[73] Jewish employees in state-owned enterprises were on occasion threatened with dismissal if they failed to report for work on Saturdays.[74] In 1924 the government ordered the directorate of the Jewish community of Warsaw to conduct its business, in contrast to its customary practice and in opposition to the terms of Article 7 of the Minorities Treaty, exclusively in the Polish language.[75] A law enacted in 1928 officially limited the jurisdiction of the Jewish communities to religious functions, effectively denying them the control over education promised them at Versailles.[76] State support for Jewish education was regularly withheld, until by 1934 not a single Jewish school in Poland was receiving public funds.[77] Until 1931 the Polish parliament refrained from abolishing those anti-Jewish restrictions imposed by the former partitioning powers that had remained legally in force following the establishment of Polish independence.[78] And in 1936 the government, ostensibly on economic and humanitarian grounds, enacted legislation severely restricting the kosher slaughtering of meat.[79]

Much legislation in the economic field also affected Jewish interests adversely—often, it seems, by design. A law requiring all businesses to close on Sunday, enacted in 1919, placed at a severe competitive disadvantage the approximately one-third of the adult Jewish population who, in strict observance of the religious prohibition of all labor on the Jewish Sabbath, conducted no business on Saturday as well.[80] Discriminatory hiring practices kept Jews from obtaining concessions in state-owned industries and restricted Jewish access to employment in the public sector.[81] The tax burden imposed by successive governments, especially during the period of the Piłsudski dictatorship (1926–35), tended to fall most heavily on the urban population, and thus disproportionately on the Jews.[82] A moratorium on peasants' debts decreed in 1932 brought ruin to many Jewish merchants who had allowed their rural customers to purchase from them on short-term credit.[83] In the same year the state ordered all artisans to pass licensing examinations, conducted exclusively in the Polish language, in order to be permitted to ply their trades, thus effectively separating the many Jewish handworkers who had never received a Polish education from their source of livelihood.[84] By 1936 the government was openly condoning, and to an extent even actively encouraging, a boycott of Jewish businesses. Prime Minister Felicjan Sławoj-Składkowski told the Sejm on 4 June that Poles ought "by all means [*owszem*]" to engage in an economic struggle against the Jews.[85] Two months later, in a blatant effort to facilitate the identification of Jewish stores for boycott purposes, the government ordered all enterprises to post the names of their proprietors as listed on their birth certificates.[86] Jews who attempted to confront pickets placed in front of their establishments were charged with the crime of "insulting the Polish nation" and made liable to prison terms of up to one year.[87]

The battle against the Jewish enemy was waged in the schools and colleges as well. Polish universities began imposing restrictive quotas for Jewish students in 1924, and over the next fifteen years the percentage of Jews among the students in institutions of higher learning in Poland declined from 24 to 8.[88] The government consistently refused to take action against the numerus clausus, claiming respect for the principle of university autonomy.[89] In fact it practiced discrimination itself, by admitting only limited numbers of Jews to state-sponsored trade schools.[90] Polish authorities placed a further obstacle in the way of Jews seeking entrance to the free professions by refusing to recognize the validity of many diplomas earned at foreign universities.[91] Moreover, those Jews who succeeded in gaining admission to Polish institutions of higher learning found them rife with antisemitism. From 1931 on universities throughout Poland experienced periodic outbreaks of anti-Jewish violence, and from 1934 on Polish students attempted to force Jews to segregate themselves in so-called ghetto benches in the lecture halls.[92]

From the universities, anti-Jewish violence spread outward; the years 1935–38 witnessed a renewed wave of pogroms. Although estimates of the extent of the violence vary, it seems certain that scores of Jews lost their lives and hundreds more were wounded.[93] The government's attitude toward this new turn in the fight against Jewry was ambivalent. In contrast to their affirmation of economic warfare and legal and social discrimination, it is by no means certain that the state authorities encouraged these riots, or even that they were pleased over their occurrence. The formal statements of government officials and leaders of the ruling Sanacja Party during the pogrom wave, even those intended exclusively for internal consumption, regularly expressed disapproval of physical abuse as a weapon in the struggle against Jewry.[94] And to be sure, it is hardly likely that an authoritarian regime which, following the death of its architect, Piłsudski, in May 1935, feared most the challenge to its hegemony from the antisemitic right, would champion lawlessness of large proportions in the name of a cause associated primarily with its strongest political opponents. Yet although it possessed means of coercion that would have permitted it to nip the mounting tide of violence in the bud, the government appears to have refrained from employing them actively. Cases were noted in which police waited for several hours before taking action to control the disturbances, and in some instances the police did not intervene at all. Official investigations tended frequently to attribute the riots to Jewish provocation, and court sentences against rioters, when imposed at all, were on the whole light.[95]

For their part, Jews could mount nowhere near as effective an arsenal in the service of their objectives. As Gruenbaum had noted, the primary force at the disposal of the Jewish community was the network of Jewish ethnic political parties, which collectively enjoyed the support of the large majority of Polish Jewry. During the 1920s these parties assumed the major responsibility for protecting Jewish interests against Polish attacks, as well as for carrying on the positive struggle for national autonomy. In the elections to the Constituent Sejm of 26 January 1919, Jewish lists, despite the encumbrances placed by the authorities on Jewish participation, garnered almost half a million votes—some 10 percent of the total—although as a result of gerrymandered electoral districts they returned only 11 out of 394 delegates.[96] The very nature of the assembly's task required these eleven elected Jewish representatives to stand at the center of the battle over Jewish political demands. And at the outset there was reason to expect that despite their relatively small number, they would be able to wage an effective fight. In the new state's multiparty parliamentary system, based upon proportional representation and interparty coalitions, even the smallest factions were sometimes in a position to affect the disposition of proposed legislation, and thus to extract concessions in return for their votes.

In fact, the Jewish caucus in the Sejm found itself in just such a position virtually at the outset of the assembly's deliberations, when a contest developed over the election of a deputy to the post of speaker of the House (*Marszałek Sejmu*). Following an inconclusive first ballot, the majority of the Jewish caucus chose to enter into an agreement with Endecja, by which Jewish support for the Endek nominee would be rewarded with the appointment of a Jew to the Sejm's all-important Constitutional Committee. On the second ballot the candidate of the right, Wojciech Trąmpczyński, was elected over the peasant leader Wincenty Witos, the common candidate of the center and left, by 155 votes to 149. The Jewish vote had made the difference, and Yitshak Gruenbaum took his seat on the Constitutional Committee, as arranged.[97]

Yet even at this early stage a fundamental dilemma was apparent, which was ultimately to undermine the effectiveness of the Jewish parties as weapons in the Polish-Jewish battle. The decision to align in a parliamentary division with Endecja, the most hostile of all Polish political parties toward Jewish interests, was certainly not to be taken lightly. Gruenbaum, in fact, had opposed it, arguing that in the long run Jewish interests would best be served by a close alliance with the parliamentary left. In reply, the maneuver's chief advocate,

Ozjasz Thon, maintained that in the matter of selection of the Sejm's presiding officer no Jewish interest was directly involved, and that a show of goodwill toward Endecja would result not only in a key committee appointment for the Jews but perhaps even in a certain tempering of the party's harsh anti-Jewish stance.[98] These arguments, though, held implications far beyond the immediate situation. They represented two differing general conceptions of how the Jewish political parties ought to conduct their parliamentary affairs. One held that the Jews should identify themselves exclusively with those groups who were least hostile toward the concept of a "state of nationalities," thereby placing themselves in more or less permanent opposition to a right-center majority unalterably wedded to the single nation-state idea, whereas the other advocated a conciliatory approach, based upon cooperation with the governing coalition, in the hope of building for the Jews a reservoir of goodwill that might eventually lead to legislation favorable to Jewish interests. The former position was represented most prominently by Zionists from Congress Poland (the Bund held a similar attitude, but it was never able to elect a representative in any national election); the latter by Zionists from Galicia and, with substantial differences of emphasis, by Agudas Yisroel.[99]

The actual behavior of the Jewish political leadership, at least before Piłsudski's coup, oscillated between these two poles. For the first eighteen months of the term of the Constituent Sejm, and particularly during the premierships of Leopold Skulski and Władysław Grabski (December 1919–July 1920), the strategy of conciliation appeared more promising. Polish authorities, noting the unfavorable publicity that the country had received in the Western press as a result of the postwar pogroms, and concerned lest their anti-Jewish image prove an obstacle to the negotiation of a badly needed loan from the Allied powers, were interested at the time in erecting a facade of Polish-Jewish cooperation, behind which their basic hostility to Jewish aspirations could be camouflaged. To this end, first Skulski and then Grabski had sponsored an initiative for a parliamentary alliance between the government and the Jewish caucus. Talks between the two sides were arranged, under the mediation of the Polish-born German Jewish writer Alfred Nossig. Following Grabski's resignation on 24 July 1920, however, the negotiations collapsed, and the majority of the Jewish Sejm representation swung to the strategy of opposition.[100] During the debates over the drafting of the constitution, the Jewish caucus steadily supported the opposition parties of the left, and in certain instances its stand may have helped to force compromises upon the right-center majority.[101]

The strategy of opposition was reflected also in the formation, largely at Gruenbaum's instigation, of a combined Bloc of National Minorities prior to the 1922 elections, the first held under the new constitution. This fusion of German, Jewish, Ukrainian, White Russian, and Great Russian electoral lists was predicated upon the assumption that all of the national minorities shared an overriding common interest in resisting the exclusivist pretensions of Polish nationalism; it was thus conceived from the start as a means of bolstering the parliamentary opposition. Indeed, the appeal it demonstrated at the polls, capturing 20 percent of the seats in the lower house of the new legislature (which retained the name Sejm) and 24 percent in the upper house (Senat), made it a political force of considerable importance. The strength of the Jewish faction within the bloc was also impressive—thirty-five mandates in the Sejm, twelve in the Senat. On the other hand, as proponents of conciliation among the Jewish leadership had warned, the bloc was roundly condemned by all of the Polish political parties, most of whom saw in it an expression of hostility toward Polish rule. In the wake of its creation, all of the minorities, and especially the Jews, felt the sting of a backlash from enraged Polish nationalists.[102] When, in the first serious contest of strength in the new parliament, the bloc played a critical role in electing the left-wing peasant leader Gabriel Narutowicz to the office of president of the Republic over the candidate of the right, Count Maurycy Zamoyski, Endecja labeled Narutowicz "the president of the Jews" and launched a campaign for his removal from office, accompanied by large-scale protest demonstrations in Warsaw. Seven days following his election, the president was shot to death by a Polish nationalist fanatic.[103]

The murder of Narutowicz offered a morbid illustration of one of the difficulties inherent in the strategy of opposition: the heightened antagonism that any such behavior invariably aroused among Poles. Proponents of conciliation among the Jewish leadership also challenged the specific tactic of a minorities bloc, questioning whether a true community of interest existed between the highly urbanized Jewish community and the predominantly agricultural territorial minorities of the eastern provinces. Indeed, conflicts among the various ethnic groups came quickly to negate the possibility that the bloc could effectively function over the long term as a united opposition force.[104] The result was a renewed interest among Jews in the conciliatory approach, which led by July 1925 to the conclusion of a formal compact (*ugoda*) for parliamentary cooperation between the Jewish caucus and the second government of Władysław Grabski. The agreement contained forty-two points, according to which the government obligated itself to take steps to end all forms of anti-Jewish discrimination in the economic, political, cultural, and religious fields.[105] In return, Leon Reich, chairman of the Jewish caucus, declared at a meeting of the Polish cabinet that "the Jewish parliamentary representation stands firmly behind the inviolability of Poland's frontiers, the paramount interests of the State, and the need for internal consolidation."[106] However, the government soon demonstrated its unwillingness to follow through with its end of the bargain, and on 20 October the Jewish caucus officially moved back into opposition.[107] By this time, though, the Jewish faction had alienated its former partners in the minorities bloc, who regarded the *ugoda* as an act of treachery. The Piłsudski coup of May 1926 thus found Jewry virtually isolated within the Polish political arena.

The failure of both approaches to parliamentary behavior during the years prior to Piłsudski's seizure of power left the Jewish political leadership in a quandary. Piłsudski appears to have apprehended the Jews' dilemma readily; in any case, his overtures to Jewry following his accession, combining promises to suppress overt manifestations of antisemitism with consistent condemnation of Jewish particularist attitudes, shattered whatever sense of unity had hitherto prevailed among the Jewish parties and split the Jewish leadership into a multitude of mutually antagonistic factions.[108] Before the elections of 1928, Agudas Yisroel and the Folkspartay had for all practical purposes disbanded their separate electoral lists and entered the government-sponsored Nonpartisan Bloc for Cooperation with the Regime (*Bezpartyjny Blok Współpracy z Rządem*—BBWR); the Zionists of the former Congress Poland, under Gruenbaum's leadership, had joined a reconstituted minorities bloc; whereas the Bund and the Galician Zionists had chosen to continue on their own. The outcome of this fragmentation was disastrous to Jewry as an organized force in Polish politics: Jewish representation fell in the Sejm from thirty-five to fifteen mandates (seven through the minorities bloc, six for the Galician Zionists, two through BBWR) and in the Senat from twelve to six.[109] Even more ominous was Piłsudski's success in significantly curtailing the influence of parliament as a factor in the formulation of state policy. In consequence of these changes, the prospect that the Jewish political parties would ever be able to secure Jewish group goals through the application of parliamentary pressure began by the late 1920s to appear less and less encouraging to ever-growing numbers of Jews. The battle that Polish Jewry had willingly joined at the outset of Polish independence now seemed in danger of being lost. Disillusionment with politics was felt even among the Jewish leadership. The Jewish Sejm representative Jakób Wygodzki, for one, openly expressed doubts about the efficacy of the entire Jewish political campaign: "The concrete results of this struggle," he declared in 1929, "amount to zero."[110]

There was, however, another weapon available to Polish Jewry in its war. This was the concern of Jews throughout the world for the fate of Europe's largest Jewish community and the sympathy for it that it had been able to arouse in Western public opinion. Even before World War I, some Jewish leaders had realized that the Polish national movement was strongly dependent for its success upon public sympathy in Europe and the United States, as well as upon the support of the major powers, and that such dependence might be exploited—given a Western public that since the Kishinev pogrom in 1903 had become sensitized to the predicament of East European Jewry, and Western governments concerned by the specter of a flood of Jewish immigrants fleeing persecution—to win Polish concessions for Jewish political demands.[111] By the end of the war, it appears to have been widely agreed among Jewish spokesmen, both in Poland and throughout the world, that the exercise of international pressure upon Poland to recognize Polish Jewry's right to civic equality and national autonomy was to be encouraged. For the most part, Jewish spokesmen who initiated contact with Western leaders insisted that their actions not be interpreted as expressions of opposition to Polish statehood and confined their requests to the enactment of international guarantees of Jewish individual and collective rights.[112] Along these lines various drafts of a charter of Jewish rights in Poland were placed by Jewish interests before the Versailles conference.[113]

Actually, however, the Minorities Treaty that ultimately issued from the conference fell far short of most Jewish demands. In particular, it failed to recognize Jews and other minorities as "distinct public corporations" entitled to proportional representation in state and local governing bodies and to a proportional share of state and local budgets for religious, educational, charitable, and social functions—all provisions that the Jewish delegates at Versailles had seen as essential to their campaign for national autonomy. Although the treaty was greeted favorably by the political leaders of Polish Jewry, the international arena seemed to them, at least at the outset of Poland's independence, a less promising forum than the Polish parliament for waging the Jewish war.[114]

Nevertheless, at least until the mid-1930s, concern for Poland's image in the West does appear to have had a restraining effect upon successive Polish governments in planning their sorties against the Jewish enemy. They viewed the adoption of the Minorities Treaty as a demonstration of international Jewish power, and if its imposition upon Poland outraged them, it also pointed to potential dangers in the adoption of too aggressive an anti-Jewish policy. Evidently this was the principal consideration underlying the efforts in 1920 and 1925 to reach a formal agreement with the Jewish political leadership. It also appears to have informed Piłsudski's handling of incipient swells of anti-Jewish violence in 1929 and 1931, when swift and determined action by the police, courts, and government ministries defused potentially explosive incidents in Kielce, Lwów, Poznań, Wilno, Kraków, and elsewhere.[115] Polish diplomatic officials abroad reinforced the wisdom of this policy, noting press coverage praising the government's approach to the situation, as well as action by Jewish organizations intended to make certain that the authorities were clearly dissociated from the rioters in the public mind.[116]

Yet the same thinking does not appear to have guided Piłsudski's successors as they confronted the mounting tide of anti-Jewish violence following the marshal's death. Indeed, government policies, even during the final year of Piłsudski's life, revealed far less sensitivity than before to Western opinion on the situation of Polish Jewry. This change was no doubt related to the reorientation in Polish foreign policy introduced by Józef Beck following his assumption of the foreign affairs portfolio in 1932. Under Beck, Poland deemphasized the centrality of its traditional ties with France and concluded instead, on 26 January 1934, a ten-year nonaggression pact with Nazi Germany. Convinced that Germany—which had hitherto, in the name of the German minority in Poland, lodged frequent complaints against the Polish government over alleged violations of the Minorities Treaty—would now offer no obstacle, Beck had felt sufficiently bold to declare before the League of Nations on 13 September 1934 that Poland would no longer submit to League supervision of its handling of minority affairs.[117] The Polish government had braced itself for severe criticism in the British, French, and U.S. press, but to its surprise it found the reaction from all sides to be mild and, even where adverse, fleeting.[118] No doubt largely as a result of this benign response, many Polish officials came to believe that, with proper presentation, the nations of the West could be made to see the Jewish question from the Polish point of view.[119]

At the same time, domestic pressures were forcing the regime to prosecute the battle against the Jews more boldly. Beginning around 1933 the Polish community as a whole began to display a growing propensity for radical action leading to a permanent solution of the Jewish question. The rise of Hitler to power in Germany may have played a role in this change by lending antisemitism legitimacy in the public eye.[120] From 1933 on a growing antisemitic pamphlet literature preached the doctrine that Jews not only were incapable of making any positive contribution to Polish life but were compelled by their religious tradition or racial characteristics to strive to undermine their Polish hosts at every turn. Many of these works surveyed the history of Polish-Jewish relations, in order to prove that while Poles, through their inborn sense of compassion and naiveté, had thrown open the gates of their land to Jews persecuted throughout the world, the Jewish refugees had consistently exploited Polish generosity, concerning themselves exclusively with their own profit, until they had brought Poland to a state of economic and cultural ruin.[121] Such ideas were echoed, albeit with somewhat less vulgarity, in the writings of respected men of letters such as Stanisław Cat-Mackiewicz and Władysław Studnicki, and of political leaders such as Roman Rybarski. Studnicki, a professor at the University of Wilno, wrote a lengthy essay on Polish-Jewish relations, in which he spoke of the need for "dejudaizing Poland."[122] Rybarski, chairman of the Endek caucus in the Sejm, even went so far as to devote a chapter to the Jewish question in what purported to be a serious statement on the future of the Polish economy, concluding that "the role of the Jews in our economic history . . . has been without exception harmful" and calling upon Poland to "relieve itself of this Jewish burden."[123]

Such writings appear to have contributed decisively to the weakening of certain psychological barriers that had hitherto checked the Polish community from working single-mindedly toward the outright elimination of the Jews from Poland. Although the premise that Jews constituted a hostile and subversive element that needed to be prevented from exercising influence over any aspect of Polish life had from the outset of Polish independence been accepted by many Poles, enthusiasm for vigorous action aimed at driving the bulk of Jewry from the country had evidently often been tempered by the belief that despite their hostility, Jews continued to perform vital economic functions.[124] Moreover, the parties of the Polish left, though sharing the fundamental fear of the Jewish internal enemy, appear often to have felt constrained by principle to dissent from certain anti-Jewish measures taken by successive governments.[125] By 1935, however, many of these scruples and inhibitions seem to have been overcome. In that year the recently formed united Peasant Party (Stronnictwo Ludowe), which included significant leftist elements, formally declared its "aim to solve the Jewish problem through the emigration of Jews to Palestine and to other places."[126] Significant elements within the Polish Socialist Party (PPS) also began to take the position that the Jewish problem in Poland could not be resolved without large-scale Jewish emigration from the country.[127] Thus following Piłsudski's death none of the major Polish parties was prepared to state unequivocally and in one voice that further coexistence between Poles and Jews upon Polish soil was possible or even desirable.[128] No doubt popular hatred of Jews, fanned by antisemitic agitation and vividly expressed in boycott and pogroms, deterred even those parties ostensibly committed to democracy and personal freedom from defending forthrightly the basic right of Polish Jews to continue to reside in their country of citizenship.

In such circumstances—with popular anti-Jewish violence threatening to become a tool in the hands of the right-wing opposition to the regime, with the left no longer offering effective opposition to the intensified anti-Jewish onslaught, and with foreign opinion appearing less a cause for concern than ever before—the government evidently felt constrained to take up the chant for the mass exodus of Poland's internal enemy. In this fashion it apparently hoped to channel mounting popular anti-Jewish pressure in a direction that would buttress, rather than undermine, its authority. Thus in late 1935 Beck created a new department at the Foreign Ministry, charged specifically with developing a program for peaceful, orderly, mass Jewish emigration from Poland. From then until the outbreak of war, the concept of peaceful, orderly emigration stood at the center of the regime's approach to Jewish affairs.[129]

The idea of peaceful emigration depended for its success first of all upon the existence of foreign territories willing and able to absorb the bulk of a community over 3 million strong. The search for such territories necessarily led to the major European colonial powers and required that Poland explain to them why they ought to open their overseas dominions to mass settlement by Polish Jews. Here there was irony of the first order: the country that for fifteen years had railed against the Minorities Treaty as unwarranted interference in a purely domestic matter now declared the Jewish question to be "essentially an international one," to which "a radical settlement . . . [could] only be reached by agreement among several states."[130] There was irony also in the fact that a policy predicated in part upon decreasing Western concern for the situation of Polish Jewry could be made or broken by the skill of Polish diplomats in rearousing such concern in a manner favorable to Polish interests.

The approach to the West taken by the Polish government contained two principal elements. First, it sought to place a major portion of the responsibility for the existence of a Jewish problem in Poland upon the nations of Western Europe themselves. This point was made unequivocally in a resolution proposed by the Polish League of Nations Federation to the International Federation of League of Nations Societies in January 1938. "The preponderance of Jews . . . in Poland," the resolution stated, "is the result of pogroms and massacres practised against the unfortunate Jewish nation from the eleventh to the fifteenth century and of the liberal welcome accorded to those exiles in Poland." Therefore, the document continued, "Poland has the right to demand that the Western nations, who, by their bygone policy, were responsible for the disproportionate influx of Jews into Polish territory, should sympathetically collaborate in an attempt to solve the Jewish question." The resolution concluded by stating that "it is the duty of such countries to help Poland by facilitating access to suitable colonial territories, by giving the whole of Palestine to the Jews . . . , and by allowing Polish Jews to enter their territories from which in years past all Jews were expelled."[131]

Second, the Polish case for an international solution to the Jewish question stressed the danger that failure to locate outlets for orderly Jewish emigration might well jeopardize both the physical safety of Polish Jewry and the future stability of the current Polish regime. Here Polish diplomats laid emphasis upon the demographic and economic aspects of the Jewish question, noting that "the Polish nation will never tolerate a foreign element in its urban population in such a high proportion as the present proportion of the Jews" and that "the excessive share of the Jews in commerce and industry . . . leads to antisemitic movements in the cities and towns."[132] Polish diplomats expressed concern to their Western counterparts over how long the government could be expected to control popular anti-Jewish hostility. In a meeting with the American ambassador in Warsaw, Anthony Drexel-Biddle, Beck remarked that although the authorities perceived the need for suppressing violence against Jewish property and were capable of doing so, they also recognized the depth of popular feeling and felt compelled to take it into account in looking at the Jewish question.[133] Carrying this train of thought one step further, Beck instructed the Polish ambassador in London, Edward Raczyński, to impress upon the British government that any delay in solving the Jewish question peacefully would likely strengthen the hand of those elements in Poland who would sooner drive the Jews from the country by force.[134] Were this to happen, Raczyński warned the British Foreign Office's Central European Affairs chief, William Strang, "the Polish Government would inevitably be forced to adopt the same kind of policy as the German Government, and indeed to draw closer to that Government in its general policy."[135] Otherwise, in the words of the proposed resolution to the Federation of League of Nations Societies, "the ultra-nationalist elements [could] exploit this state of affairs as a pretext for creating a totalitarian regime."[136]

Such warnings, however, made little impression; outside of the agreement of the French government to permit a Polish expedition to explore the feasibility of Madagascar as a site for Jewish resettlement,[137] no progress was achieved. Despite repeated attempts, Poland was unable to bring its emigration program before the International Conference on Refugees meeting at Evian, France, in July 1938, or before the Intergovernmental Committee on Refugees established in its wake. Similarly, Polish pressure had no effect upon British immigration policy regarding Palestine. The unavoidable fact was that the Polish government had chosen to build its approach to the Jewish question around the notion of Jewish emigration precisely at the time when the number of potential destinations for Jews had dwindled to virtually none.

Most likely Polish Jews observed these developments with mixed emotions. On the one hand, Jews clearly had an interest in the success of the Polish attempt to make the Western powers take notice of their situation. As early as 1932 Gruenbaum had argued that in the face of the onslaught of Polish antisemitism only the united effort of Jewish communities throughout the world in arousing Western sympathy could offer the suffering Jews of Poland any chance of relief: "We must prove to the world and to ourselves," he exhorted, "that we are still to be reckoned with."[138] As a step in this direction, Polish Jews had taken an active role in the movement to create a World Jewish Congress, which would act as a quasi-official representative of the entire Jewish people in the international arena.[139] Indeed, when such an organization was finally established in 1936, the situation of the Jews of Poland occupied a major portion of its attentions. Yet this body too was unsuccessful in rearousing international concern for Polish Jewry's plight, a fact that had become apparent to some Jewish leaders at least by 1938. Commenting upon the Evian refugee conference then in progress, a writer for the official organ of the World Zionist Organization expressed his regret that the scope of the deliberations had been limited to Germany and Austria and that the sufferings of "six million Jews in distress without escape, on the very edge of the abyss, in Eastern and Central Europe," had not been properly grasped by the delegates of the more than thirty nations assembled at the French resort town.[140] In this situation the failure of the Poles to make the Western powers pay attention to the Polish Jewish plight must have been disconcerting to many Jews.

Moreover, by this time large numbers of Polish Jews clearly wanted to leave the country. In 1933 the number of Jewish emigrants was double that of the previous year; by 1935 the number had doubled again. During these years Jews accounted for half of all those leaving Poland. Although there was a sharp drop in Jewish emigration beginning in 1936, it was attributable not to any lesser desire to escape but to the tightening of restrictions upon entry into Palestine, the destination of over two-thirds of the migrants.[141] Those Jews who wished to emigrate thus had a definite stake in the outcome of the Polish efforts to locate destinations for their resettlement, and in this sense they could not but have been disheartened at the government's lack of positive results.

On the other hand, it seems that most Jewish leaders feared the success of the Polish venture even more than they feared its failure. In 1937 the Central Committee of the Bund issued a statement roundly condemning the government's emigration program and insisting that the mass of Jews had no interest in leaving the country.[142] Similar positions were taken by the Folkists and by Agudas Yisroel.[143] As these parties had long waged a fierce ideological battle with the Zionists on behalf of the notion that the solution to the Polish Jewish problem was to be found in Poland rather than in a Jewish national home overseas, their opposition to official emigration schemes was not surprising. Yet even among Zionists, the question of how to respond to the government's new policy proved a source of sharp controversy. Many leaders expressed concern that the slightest hint of cooperation with the government in its efforts, including even those in support of the Zionist program in Palestine, might be interpreted as an admission that, as the Polish right had maintained all along, Jews were in fact both an alien and a superfluous element in the land of the Poles. This admission, in turn, they feared, could be employed by antisemites as a pretext for augmenting anti-Jewish violence, or even by the government itself as a justification for stepping up the political and economic struggle against Jewry.[144] Thus the mainstream of the Polish Zionist movement did not look upon the government's activities in the international arena with favor.

The only organized Zionist support for the emigration concept came from the breakaway Revisionist faction, led by Ze'ev Jabotinsky, who as early as 1931 had spoken of the need for Zionists to ally themselves with countries interested in decreasing their Jewish populations in "a concerted attack upon the League of Nations, England, and world public opinion."[145] The Revisionists, who espoused a doctrine of aggressive Jewish nationalism emphasizing military training, strict internal discipline, and the achievement of a Jewish state in Palestine by force of arms, held that Polish antisemitism was ineradicable as long as Jews remained in the country in such large numbers, and called therefore for the "evacuation" of 750,000 Jews from Poland over a ten-year period.[146] Believing that organized emigration on such a large scale could not be accomplished without the active assistance of the state authorities, they were prepared to work hand in hand with the Polish government toward fulfilling their goal. Because of this attitude, as well as because of their willingness to relegate the struggle for Jewish civil and national rights in Poland to a relatively low level of priority, the Revisionists were looked upon in Polish ruling circles with particular favor and regularly benefited from the assistance—and even, on at least one occasion, from the financial support—of government agencies.[147]

The government proved unable, however, to entice the mainstream Zionist leadership into cooperation. The Jewish Agency for Palestine, the official body responsible for organizing immigration to the Jewish national home, refused a formal Polish request to allocate 50 percent of its available quota of immigration certificates to Polish Jews.[148] In 1938, following the failure of the Evian conference to take up the problem of Polish Jewry, some individual Zionists were co-opted by the government onto a Committee for Jewish Colonization, whose task was to impress upon Western diplomatic circles the dire consequences likely to result from continued international inaction; but these people were sharply criticized by most of the Zionist leadership.[149] This criticism in turn no doubt weakened even further Poland's case before the Western powers, for without the backing of the Jewish movement whose ideology rested upon the postulate of resettlement, the notion that the Jewish problem could be solved through peaceful, voluntary emigration must have appeared highly dubious. Thus, as pressures within Poland mounted, international concern for the fate of Polish Jewry appeared to both Poles and Jews an ever-less-likely source of salvation.

For Polish Jews, the realization that neither the domestic nor the international political arena held out significant hope for the improvement of their position resulted in a far-reaching crisis. The Zionists, long the dominant force in Polish Jewish politics, began to feel serious disaffection among their rank and file. This discontent was expressed largely through growing Jewish support for more radical political movements, both of the right and of the left. The Revisionists steadily expanded their infrastructure throughout Poland during the 1930s,[150] while at the other end of the political spectrum the Bund emerged in the latter half of the decade as the dominant Jewish party in Warsaw, Łódź, Lublin, Wilno, and other major Jewish centers.[151] In most cases, affiliation with these groups was more likely an expression of loss of confidence in the mainstream Jewish leadership than an identification with the unique features of their political programs. The 1930s appear to have witnessed a mounting preference among Jews for nonpolitical over political approaches to their day-to-day struggle for survival. During the decade economic self-help, public protest, and physical self-defense assumed greater importance as means by which Jews sought to respond to their situation. Local and national committees were formed to assist Jews seeking employment, to provide vocational retraining and financial aid for Jews who had lost their jobs or businesses, and to offer moral and monetary support to Jewish merchants affected by the anti-Jewish boycott.[152] In the face of the rising tide of anti-Jewish legislation and violence, ever-growing numbers of Jews, representing virtually all segments of the community, participated in protest strikes and public demonstrations of Jewish solidarity.[153] Increasingly, too, threats and instances of violence were met by organized Jewish militias and patrols, aided at times by sympathizers from among Polish socialists and communists.[154]

These activities were undoubtedly appreciated by the broad masses of Polish Jews, whose morale was raised by participation in active attempts to foil the schemes of their adversaries. In the long run, however, they could have only a palliative effect. In no sense were they likely to moderate either the tension between Poles and Jews or the government's unwillingness to take firm action in defense of Jewish rights. Indeed, it was clear that under the conditions prevailing in Poland in the late 1930s, the struggle of Polish Jews for a secure existence upon Polish soil, whether as individuals or as members of an autonomous national community, had virtually no chance for success. The significance of Jewry as a political force had been reduced to nil, its economic strength decimated. And for all but a relatively small number, there was no possibility of escape.

By 1939, however, Jewish leaders realized that the Poles and the Polish government might no longer constitute the main threat to their security. The deterioration in Polish-German relations and the specter of approaching war reopened, in a sense, the old question of who would rule the Polish territories, and in the situation at hand, there could be no doubt where Jewish interests lay. On 28 March 1939 the Central Committee of the Zionist Organization of Congress Poland issued a declaration expressing the readiness of Polish Jewry to sacrifice its blood to preserve the integrity of Poland's borders. On the same day, both Zionist leader Apolinary Hartglas and Bund spokesman Wiktor Alter affirmed that Polish Jews would take up arms in Poland's defense.[155] On 19 June the Polish Jewish journalist Henryk Szoszkies, speaking at the New York World's Fair on behalf of a committee representing all Zionist factions and Agudas Yisroel, assured his audience that "when Poland will find it necessary to issue a call to arms, the Jews of my country will stand ready to take the field along with all their countrymen and to give their life and blood for the preservation of Poland's independence."[156] During the previous two days, Szoszkies had been instrumental in persuading the American Federation of Polish Jews to adopt a resolution promising "moral and material assistance to Poland . . . against the wave of Nazi imperialism."[157] The Polish consul-general in New York, Sylwester Gruszka, noted in a report to his embassy in Washington that for the first time in years the annual meeting of the federation had been conducted in an atmosphere "entirely sympathetic to Poland."[158]

Such expressions of loyalty do not, however, appear to have exerted any significant influence on Polish thinking about the Jewish question. The government continued to press on with its emigration program. In April 1939 Beck, who had come to London to obtain guarantees of military assistance from Britain in the event of a German invasion, insisted on devoting a portion of his discussions with British leaders to the problem of Jewish overseas resettlement.[159] On 10 June Raczyński followed Beck's intervention with a memorandum to the British Foreign Office, complaining that the British government's White Paper of May 1939, which set strict quotas for Jewish immigration to Palestine, had "exercise[d] an adverse effect on Poland's vital needs for emigration outlets."[160] The Polish government's frustration with the lack of any positive international response to its program was patent. Because of this situation, there is reason to believe that eventually the regime might have succumbed to public pressure and become itself an active sponsor of anti-Jewish violence. One of the conclusions that the government drew from the limitation of the scope of the Evian conference to refugees from Germany and Austria was that only countries that pressured their Jews to emigrate against their will were rewarded with a measure of international attention.[161] Accordingly, the regime's political front movement, the Camp of National Unity (Obóz Zjednoczenia Narodowego—OZN or OZON), began in 1939 to display a markedly more aggressive attitude toward the ongoing struggle against the Jewish adversary.[162] On 23 July 1939, only five weeks before the German invasion, the regime's quasi-official newspaper, *Gazeta Polska*, warned the Polish people that although Jews might appear to be rallying to the country's defense in a time of crisis, they were expressing merely their aversion to Nazism's anti-Jewish orientation, not their love of Poland.[163] Jewry was still perceived as a dangerous enemy, and any government that sought to represent the Polish nation needed to defend it not only against the German but against the Jewish threat as well.

DECLARATIONS

Incidents of agitation and popular violence against Jews were recorded even following the conclusion of the Ribbentrop-Molotov agreement of 23 August 1939, when reservists had been mobilized and war appeared imminent to all.[1] Nevertheless, though Jewish spokesmen continued to lash out against the Polish antisemites, the signing of the pact between Germany and the Soviet Union sealed their conviction that the well-being of Polish Jewry depended upon Poland's ability to withstand the military threat.[2] Hence the German invasion on 1 September 1939 elicited firm expressions of patriotism from Poland's Jewish population. In the first days of the war, the president of the Warsaw Jewish community board appealed to his fellow Jews "to show their readiness to make every sacrifice for the defence of their country and to prove their loyalty as citizens."[3] The Jewish parliamentary caucus solemnly promised at a special emergency session of the Sejm that Jews would work "without reservation" for a Polish victory.[4] There were more tangible demonstrations of Jewish ardor for the Polish cause as well, even apart from the sacrifices of the Jewish soldiers who took to the battlefield in the September campaign.[5] The Jews of Warsaw, for example, volunteered in large numbers to dig shelter trenches to protect the city's residents from air attack.[6]

Feelings of sympathy and support for Poland were displayed by Jews throughout the world as well. In England the *Jewish Chronicle* expressed its "deep admiration and respect for the courage and fortitude" of the Polish people,[7] while the *Zionist Review* assured its readers that "the Polish nation will live once again enjoying freedom and independence in a normal existence of statehood."[8] In the United States the Yiddish-language daily *Der Tog* urged its readers to forget past Jewish grievances against the Polish government and to recall that "throughout the past 150 years Poland's freedom has been firmly bound to the progress of the democratic spirit."[9] In Palestine *Davar*, the influential voice of the Jewish labor movement, praised the Polish people, who had "fought like lions for their capital and for their freedom,"[10] and the independent daily *HaBoker* expressed the solidarity of the entire Jewish settlement in Palestine with the Polish nation.[11]

Some Jewish leaders also sought to follow up such pronouncements with concrete action. In the earliest weeks of the war, Rabbi Stephen Wise, president of the American Jewish Congress, and Henry Montor, executive director of the United Palestine Appeal, approached Poland's ambassador to the United States, Jerzy Potocki, with an offer to place the considerable fund-raising and public relations expertise of their organizations in the service of Polish efforts to mobilize American popular support. On 15 September 1939 Montor presented Potocki with a detailed program for the conduct of pro-Polish propaganda, utilizing all available American media, and advised the ambassador of his readiness to help with its implementation.[12] In France a group of Polish Jewish expatriates established a Center for Polish-Jewish Collaboration, "with the goal of bringing all Jews of Polish origin together . . . [to work toward] the restoration of the state." This organization proposed to exploit the contacts of its members with Polish Jewish businessmen in Canada and South America in order to raise funds for propaganda activities in Allied and neutral countries, as well as to provide the Polish army-in-exile then being formed on French soil with food parcels, warm clothing, and medical supplies.[13]

There were, of course, sound practical, particularistic reasons for such behavior. A Hebrew teacher from Warsaw, Haim Kaplan, who left a detailed day-by-day account of his experiences in the Polish capital under Nazi occupation, explained in his diary entry for 1 September 1939 that "wherever Hitler's foot treads there is no hope for the Jewish people." It thus seemed obvious to him "that the Jews show their devotion to the fatherland in a demonstrative fashion."[14] Yitshak Gruenbaum, too, noted that "this time the Jews are not fighting only . . . Poland's war; they are also fighting their own war against the enemy of their people."[15]

Yet there are indications that, apart from calculations of self-interest, many Jews throughout the world genuinely empathized with Polish suffering and looked upon the Poles' struggle as fundamentally identical with their own. The influential Palestinian journalist Yitshak Lufbahn, for one, noted that the German invasion, precisely because of the specific danger it presented to Polish Jewry, had reawakened among Jews a sense of their common destiny with the Polish people—a sense that, though temporarily overshadowed by the adversity of the previous two decades, had led during the previous century to active Jewish participation in the movement for Polish liberation. "Until the last World War," Lufbahn observed, "there were two nations of significant cultural potential against whom history, which owed them their existence as free peoples, had rendered perverted judgment—these were the Jewish nation and the Polish nation." Though he minced no words in castigating what seemed to him the Poles' misapplication of the freedom granted them at Versailles in their treatment of their Jewish fellow citizens, he continued to believe that the existence of an independent Poland, like the existence of an independent state for the Jewish people, remained a historical necessity. Thus, he declared, "to the Polish people in their humiliation and degradation we come as brothers in time of trouble; we who ourselves lament and grieve so loudly over the terrible blow that has fallen upon the House of Israel in Poland feel a human need to offer this nation a few words of consolation . . . : 'Poland is not yet lost.' "[16]

For all such comforting expressions, however, the bitterness engendered by the experiences of the immediate past was not easily overcome. Montor wrote to Wise at one point that in light of "the past anti-Semitic record of some Government officials and the 'policy' of the Government itself for [*sic*] the forced emigration of Jews," he approached his dealings with the Polish authorities with considerable reservations.[17] Kaplan, too, betrayed a definite sarcasm when he noted in his diary the suddenness with which the Poles had been transformed into a symbol of freedom and progress. "The time is not long past," he observed, "when Hitler was their prophet, . . . particularly in regard to the Jews."[18] Thus, though Jews certainly perceived themselves, under the circumstances of the present war, as the natural allies of the Polish people, they appear for the most part to have entered into this alliance reluctantly. Many, like Lufbahn, calmed their misgivings with the hope that the Poles' tribulations would have a cathartic effect and that the nation, once liberated, would govern its land "upon foundations of justice, equal rights, and freedom of existence" for all of its national minorities.[19] Others were less sanguine. In the weekly journal that Lufbahn edited, a pseudonymous writer contended that Polish antisemitic behavior during the interwar years had been an accurate reflection of the character of the Polish people. He saw consequently little likelihood of substantially improved Polish-Jewish relations even after the eventual defeat of the Nazis.[20] Similarly, Montor wondered why Wise seemed so insistent on displaying Jewish goodwill toward the Polish cause when there seemed so little chance of its eventual reciprocation.[21]

The earliest reports on Polish attitudes toward Jews in the wake of the German invasion that appeared in Jewish news organs did not, taken as a whole, clearly support either the optimistic or the pessimistic tendency. Much was made, on the one hand, of a statement attributed to the staunchly anti-Jewish Sejm deputy Aleksander Prystor praising Jewish efforts in the defense of the country. This remark was supposed to indicate a change in the way many Poles were currently viewing Jews.[22] Similarly, Shmuel Margoshes, the editor of *Der Tog*, believed on the basis of items appearing in his newspaper that Polish leaders had embarked upon a serious campaign to suppress antisemitism.[23] On the other hand, the daily bulletin of the Jewish Telegraphic Agency carried notices of Polish consular officials in France and Romania engaging in systematic discrimination against Jewish Polish nationals residing in those states, and of Polish refugees in the latter country boycotting Jewish businesses.[24] Jewish refugees arriving in Romania or in the West from German-occupied Poland also complained of Poles participating in anti-Jewish pillage following the completion of the Nazi conquest.[25]

Hence it happened that Jewish leaders throughout the world came to attach decisive importance to the nature of the new Polish government-in-exile being formed in France as a device for perpetuating the sovereignty of the Polish nation in the aftermath of Poland's battlefield defeat. The tone set by this body with regard to Polish-Jewish relations during wartime and after liberation—particularly the degree to which it proved itself committed to a clear break with the prewar regime's approach to the Jewish question—was believed by Jews throughout the world to be a critical factor in shaping the future of Europe's largest Jewish community.[26] For this reason, it stood to play a determinant role in governing the depth and persistence of specifically pro-Polish—in addition to anti-Nazi—sentiments among Polish and world Jewry. The exile government and its members thus became from the start the objects of intense Jewish scrutiny, and the Jewish question was among the first issues that they were forced seriously to confront.

The government-in-exile, formally constituted in Paris on 2 October 1939 under the presidency of Władysław Raczkiewicz and the premiership of Władysław Sikorski,[27] did indeed present itself as a departure from the immediate prewar regime. Its leading personalities were drawn either from the ranks of the opposition parties under Piłsudski or from among nominal Sanacja supporters who since the marshal's death had been kept from the inner circle of power.[28] In accordance with the political credo of these newly ascendant forces, Raczkiewicz agreed, shortly after assuming the presidency, to renounce his constitutional privilege of governing without the consent of his cabinet, thereby abrogating one of the principal features of the Piłsudski-inspired constitutional revision of April 1935 and placing the new regime, in contrast to its predecessor, upon quasi-parliamentary foundations.[29] In subsequent weeks both Raczkiewicz and Sikorski issued periodic declarations pledging the establishment in postwar Poland of a liberal democratic political order, in which the principles of equal rights, the rule of law, and merit as the sole basis for advancement in public service would be scrupulously observed.[30] In addition, the new leaders sharply criticized the prewar government for failing to perceive the German threat to Poland's security and for neglecting to prepare the country's military and economic

resources to withstand the invasion of a foreign army.[31] The appointment of Sikorski—a general who, though technically remaining on
active military service throughout the Piłsudski years, had been re-
lieved by the marshal of all command responsibilities in 1928—not
only as prime minister but as commander-in-chief of the Polish
Armed Forces as well symbolized the new government's official dis-
avowal of the legacy of the former Sanacja leadership.

Nonetheless, there seems to be good reason to question whether
such democratic expressions were offered more out of conviction or
out of expediency. Certainly the new government could not have
acted much differently. The Nazi invasion had thoroughly discredited the pro-German, anti-French orientation that had been the hall-
mark of Beck's tenure as foreign minister in the eyes of the Polish
people, and the relative ease with which the Polish defenses had
been overcome had exposed the country's lack of military prepared-
ness to plain public view. Thus no government that was not composed of individuals untainted by the September disaster and that
did not repudiate the heritage of Piłsudski and his successors could
hope to enjoy the confidence of the Polish nation or claim to speak
on its behalf.[32] Similarly, any Polish government wishing to be recognized by Britain and France as a bona fide ally of the forces of democracy—and without such recognition no exile government could possibly hope to function—needed not only to feature past opponents of
Beck's approach to foreign affairs but also to renounce Sanacja's anti-
parliamentary proclivities.[33]

But although the credentials of the new government's leaders, particularly those of Sikorski himself, as francophiles of long standing
were for the most part beyond reproach, their record as liberal demo-
crats, in the sense that the term was understood in the West, was less
clear. The government was dominated by the sort of right-center coalition that Sikorski had evidently long regarded as the proper locus
of political power in Poland.[34] This group was committed to the notion of the state as the defender of the Christian religion and of the
national traditions of the Polish community, and for all of its concern
with parliamentary prerogatives, it favored a strong executive authority whose responsibility to the public would not unduly impair
its freedom of action.[35] Effective popular controls upon the government were absent: the National Council (Rada Narodowa) summoned by Raczkiewicz on 9 December 1939 and often referred to as

Poland's "parliament-in-exile" was actually no more than an advisory body, enjoying no legislative authority, to which the government was in only the most limited sense responsible.[36] Moreover, especially during the first year of its existence, the government proved reluctant to be guided by the expressed desires of the emerging underground movement in the occupied homeland concerning the relationship between the so-called secret state in Poland and the exile authorities.[37] Evidently—and understandably—the prerogatives of parliament diminished in importance in the eyes of Poland's new leaders once they had passed from opposition to power. In this respect, at least, the Sikorski government may have had more in common with its Sanacja predecessor than it cared to admit.[38]

This tension between the need for the government-in-exile to cultivate a liberal democratic image in Western public opinion and the apparent lack of an unequivocal personal commitment to democratic values by many of its members was evident in the government's approach to the Jewish question. The prewar regime's treatment of Jews, as of minorities in general, was regarded in the West as one of the most prominent signs of its illiberal character, and its successor was clearly anxious to avoid being perceived as gratuitously anti-Jewish.[39] Thus, in an early official declaration of principles, the prime minister announced that the sole purpose of his government was "the rebirth of a great and sovereign Poland that will be equally just for all its citizens."[40] Two months later he publicly promised the national minorities "justice, free national and cultural development, and the protection of the law."[41]

However, most of the exile government's leaders came to their new tasks with records indicating that they could be influenced by anti-Jewish prejudice. Sikorski himself, during his previous tenure as premier from December 1922 to May 1923, had actually managed to provoke the Jewish parliamentary caucus into joining Endecja in refusing his government a vote of confidence, both by tacitly denigrating Jewish loyalty to Poland and by explicitly stating his view that decisions affecting the future of the Polish state should be left to the "Aryan Christian majority."[42] Now he included among his official advisers men widely regarded in Jewish circles as antisemites, among them Information Minister Stanisław Stroński, who during the early years of independence had warned vigorously of the Jewish danger to the Polish state;[43] Finance Minister Adam Koc, founder of the

Sanacja front organization OZON, a group whose "Thirteen Theses on the Jewish Question" of May 1937 had concluded that "the Jewish element weakens the normal development of Polish national and state forces";[44] Minister without Portfolio Gen. Józef Haller, whose legions were known for their assaults upon Jewish communities during the Polish-Soviet war; and Minister without Portfolio Marian Seyda, former publisher of the periodical *Orędownik*, notorious among Polish Jews for its Jew-baiting. Considerable influence within the regime was wielded also by Gen. Kazimierz Sosnkowski, Raczkiewicz's designated successor as president, who was responsible for the internment of Polish Jewish soldiers in the detention camp at Jabłonna in 1920. Prominent as well were men who, although not commonly associated with anti-Jewish tendencies in interwar Poland, generally approved of the approach to the Jewish question taken by Piłsudski's successors. Among these were Raczyński, a protegé of Beck and architect of the strategy by which his chief renounced the Minorities Treaty in 1934, who remained throughout the war in the post of ambassador to the Court of St. James,[45] and Józef Retinger, Sikorski's personal secretary, who in 1941 was to explain to the British public that Poland was "a country which desires to develop normally but is hindered from doing so by the high percentage of Jews in its demographic organism."[46] On the other hand, Raczkiewicz, Foreign Minister August Zaleski, Interior Minister Stanisław Kot, and Labor Minister Jan Stańczyk were not regarded as having been overtly ill-disposed toward Jews during their previous careers. Indeed, Raczkiewicz was known in Jewish circles for his opposition to the 1936 law restricting the kosher slaughtering of meat, as well as for actions that he took to suppress a pogrom while serving as governor of the province of Pomorze.[47]

For the majority of the members of the Sikorski government, though, the Jewish question represented a formidable test of professed democratic sentiments. In light, too, of the widespread Jewish anxieties over the durability of the alliance that the German invasion of Poland had seemingly forced upon Poles and Jews in spite of themselves, Jewish leaders in the West and in Palestine were eager to discover as quickly as possible whether the test would be successfully stood. Here, too, initial indications were mixed. The personnel of the new government was a source of concern throughout the Jewish world, although for the most part Jewish public statements on this matter showed surprising restraint in scoring the dubious record on Jewish issues of such as Sikorski, Stroński, and Koc.[48] Also disquieting were things like the appearance of articles bearing uncomplimentary stereotypic references to Jews in the government's semiofficial organ, *Głos Polski*; government sponsorship of a memorial ceremony for Roman Dmowski; reports of physical violence by Polish soldiers in France against Jews who had volunteered for service with the Polish forces; and the appointment of Stanisław Cat-Mackiewicz to the Polish National Council.[49] The ledger was balanced, as it were, at least to some extent, by the inclusion of two Jews, PPS leader Herman Lieberman and Zionist activist Ignacy Schwarzbart, in the National Council, together with the appointment of another Jew, the Zionist Henryk Rosmarin, to head the Polish consulate in Tel Aviv. Jews were further encouraged by Sikorski's attendance at a special Paris synagogue service held to honor the Jewish victims of the Nazi invasion of Poland, by the action of the Polish consulate in Brussels in reinstating the citizenship of some four hundred Polish Jewish émigrés who had been rendered stateless by the Polish citizenship law of 1938,[50] and by a statement attributed to General Haller castigating the prewar regime's handling of Jewish matters and promising that the Poles had learned from their past mistakes.[51]

All of this appears to have made it difficult for Jewish leaders to determine just how they felt about the new Polish regime. Such confusion was apparent at a meeting of the Board of Deputies of British Jews held on 18 February 1940, at which outgoing board president Neville Laski expressed "great doubts" concerning the Sikorski government's attitude toward the future of the Jews in postwar Poland, while Leonard Stein, chairman of the Joint Foreign Committee of the board and the Anglo-Jewish Association, noted optimistically that "there were substantial elements behind the new Polish Government who genuinely desired the reconstruction of Poland on a more truly liberal basis than the Poland of the recent past."[52]

The awkwardness of situations such as this one prompted Jewish leaders, especially in Britain, to press the Polish government for an unequivocal authoritative declaration repudiating the Jewish policies of the prewar regime and promising unqualified respect for the civil rights of Jews in the Poland that would arise after the Nazi defeat. Jews were somewhat disquieted that none of the government's statements during the first months of the war regarding its vision for the future liberal democratic Poland had mentioned specifically the status of Polish Jewry.[53] The former Warsaw correspondent for the *Jewish Chronicle* noted in November 1939 that Jewish doubts concerning the government's intentions "possibly prevent the establishment between Poles and Jews working abroad for Poland's rebirth of the necessary positive and frank spirit of cooperation which was built up between Jews and Poles working for Poland's defence at home during the war." He added that under these circumstances, "the best policy for the new Polish leaders would be to come out with a clearly-defined statement" that would leave "no more room for vagueness and uncertainty."[54] Over the following months this advice was repeated often, both in the Jewish press and, more important, in private meetings between Jewish and Polish leaders.[55]

The Jewish appeal for a declaration, however, was consistently rebuffed by the Polish authorities throughout the first year of the war. Officially, the Poles explained their unwillingness to accede to the Jewish request with the formula that "the Polish government has repeatedly and publicly expressed its positive attitude toward the Jewish minority" and that in consequence there was no need for any additional statement.[56] This explanation was rejected by Jewish leaders, especially those in Britain, who responded to the Polish denial by voicing their demand ever more aggressively.[57] The willingness of the Polish government to issue a formal declaration on Jewish rights thus became during the first year of the war the primary bone of contention between Jews in the West and the new Polish regime. As such it came also to serve as a focus about which the more basic feelings of each side toward the other were defined and crystallized.

In a sense, the Polish attitude toward the declaration was surprising. The government-in-exile represented a country under occupation by two foreign powers, Germany and the Soviet Union, of which only the former was officially regarded by the Western Allies as their enemy. Nevertheless, it was the government's announced aim to seek restoration of Polish sovereignty within the country's entire prewar boundary.[58] This was an objective that the Allies could be counted upon to support firmly only with regard to the lands under German occupation; regarding the Soviet-held territories, the Poles were acutely aware of Allied hesitancy over their demands.[59] Moreover, the means by which the Polish government, as the representative of an overrun nation dependent for its existence upon French and British goodwill, could expect to influence the course of Allied diplomacy were severely limited. Thus, even beyond the ordinary exigencies of wartime propaganda, the Poles were sorely in need of Western spokesmen for their eastern frontier claims.

Apparently, at least during the early months of the war, an influential segment of organized world Jewry was prepared to consider playing such a role. In March 1940 representatives of the American Jewish Congress and the World Jewish Congress informed the Polish consul in Tel Aviv, Henryk Rosmarin,[60] that their organizations were about to launch an anti-Soviet propaganda campaign throughout Western Europe and the United States.[61] This intention reflected a profound disquiet in most Jewish circles over the Ribbentrop-Molotov pact and the Russian invasion of Poland: the latter was typically denounced in the Western and Palestinian Jewish press as an act that impaired the effort to defeat Nazi Germany.[62] Rosmarin was convinced, on the basis of his close contact with the Jewish settlement in Palestine, that Jewish leaders could easily be persuaded to link these sentiments with a demand for the return of the Soviet-occupied zone to Polish sovereignty, and he reported to the Polish Foreign Ministry's director-general, Jan Ciechanowski, that he had begun intensive efforts in this direction. Ciechanowski in turn was sufficiently impressed with Rosmarin's concept to forward his memorandum to the Polish ambassadors in London, Washington, and Paris, with the recommendation that "in view of the many possibilities which the international Jewish organizations possess in this area," the Jewish lead be followed in presenting the Polish case against the Soviets.[63] At the same time, the Nationalities Department of the Polish Ministry of Information independently arrived at a similar conclusion, as, from a different perspective, did Adam Ciołkosz, a PPS representative on the National Council.[64]

In this context, an official Polish gesture toward Jewish sensibilities, in the form of a declaration promising respect for Jewish civic equality in the future Poland, might have done much to cement the sort of active Polish-Jewish cooperation envisioned in at least some Polish political and administrative circles. Ciołkosz even explicitly recommended the issuance of a declaration along the lines called for by Jewish spokesmen in conjunction with efforts to enlist the assistance of the Bund's U.S. branch in organizing pro-Polish propaganda in the United States.[65] By expressly refusing to issue such a declaration, the Polish authorities, ignoring the cardinal principle stressed in the Nationalities Department memorandum that urged scrupulous avoidance of actions that might antagonize Jews, alienated a group from whose efforts in international propaganda they might, perhaps, have benefited.

How, then, should the Polish attitude toward a declaration on Jewish rights be understood? Although the archival record reveals few direct, candid communications on the subject among Polish officials, it is possible, from a mass of indirect documentary evidence, to detect a tangled mixture of perceptions, feelings, and political calculations that, in the minds of government leaders, must have outweighed any possible advantage that such a gesture toward Jewry might have brought.

In the first place, though Polish officials were clearly perturbed by the persistence of the demand for a declaration and by the complaints about alleged incidents of anti-Jewish behavior on their part that prompted it, there is little to suggest that during the early months of the war they regarded such expressions by Jews in the West as any more than minor irritants. Raczyński, who from his post in London stood closest to the principal center of agitation and whose evaluations of the situation thus carried significant weight with his superiors, cautioned Zaleski—in a memorandum of 22 January 1940 describing what the ambassador perceived to be the overwhelmingly hostile tone of British Jewish leaders and of the British Jewish press toward Poland—not to overestimate the significance of this allegedly anti-Polish propaganda, which he described as "transitory."[66] This comment was telling, for it reflected Raczyński's apparent conviction—rooted, perhaps, originally in the lack of strong Western protests over the abrogation of the Minorities Treaty—that the governments of the West were not overly concerned with the problems of Polish Jewry and that they were thus unlikely to take any substantive action on its behalf.

But if this was the case, then there was also little likelihood that the Allies could be induced to any meaningful degree to look more favorably upon Poland's eastern border demands through exposure to complaints about the ill-treatment of Polish Jews under Soviet occupation, complaints that Rosmarin, Ciołkosz, and the Nationalities Department had suggested could be made the basis of the envisioned Jewish anti-Soviet, pro-Polish campaign. This, evidently, was the thinking that prevailed among Polish policy makers, for there is no evidence to suggest that consideration of enlisting Jewish aid in the diplomatic struggle over Poland's future eastern border ever went, at least during the first year of the war,[67] beyond the action taken by Ciechanowski.[68] There seemed from this perspective little reason to make any political concessions to Western Jewry, if a propaganda campaign of dubious potential effectiveness and cessation of petty sniping in the Jewish parochial press were all that Western Jewry could offer in return.

Furthermore, Polish officials were acutely aware that the demand for a declaration was being voiced for the most part not by Jewish citizens of Poland but precisely by organizations of Western Jews.[69] Indeed, the most forceful representations on behalf of such a statement were made by the London *Jewish Chronicle* and by the incoming president of the Board of Deputies of British Jews, Selig Brodetsky. The involvement of Western Jews in what the Poles regarded as an internal Polish matter appears to have been deeply resented within Polish government and diplomatic circles. The acting Polish chargé d'affaires in France made this point clearly in a meeting with Ignacy Schwarzbart, a veteran Zionist from Kraków who represented Jewish interests in the Polish National Council, on 26 March 1940. Continued expressions of alarm by Jewish bodies in the West over the future of Polish-Jewish relations, the Polish official warned, would merely produce an anti-Jewish backlash among the Poles, leading to a vicious circle of mutual recrimination and animosity.[70] Evidently the Polish authorities recalled the diplomatic situation at the close of the previous world war, when international Jewish pressure had been instrumental in binding Poland to the Minorities Treaty. Not surprisingly, in view of the important role played by the struggle against the treaty in his earlier career, Raczyński was especially bothered by this association. In a second memorandum to Zaleski of 22 January 1940, the ambassador admonished the foreign minister that any specific statement by the government on Jewish rights was liable "to form the basis for further [Jewish] action" aimed at "tying us to a new form of obligations toward the minorities."[71]

Unlike the rationally negative assessment of the political rewards that the Polish regime was likely to derive from active cooperation with organizations such as the World Jewish Congress or the Board of Deputies, this latter argument seems to have been primarily emotional in nature. This explains, perhaps, the fundamental inconsistency between the two positions. If Raczyński, for one, indeed believed that Jewish complaints about the Polish government's approach to the Jewish question were not likely to cause the government any tangible political damage, then he did not need to be overly concerned about renewed Jewish agitation for a Minorities Treaty. And even if the reawakened specter of this symbol of world Jewry's abiding ill will toward the Polish cause and its ability to influence international perceptions of the Polish question did not permit him, or other Polish officials, to shake entirely the fear of Jewish power, despite their ongoing empirical sense of Jewish powerlessness, it did not logically follow that a declaration of the sort demanded by Jewish spokesmen would have left the Poles more vulnerable to future pressures for a new covenant. On the contrary, the government's continued refusal to affirm on its own the rights of Jews in the future Poland could only have lent credibility to the anticipated Jewish case for international guarantees of their status, whereas acquiescence to the call for a declaration might have helped to underwrite the regime's coveted liberal democratic image in the eyes of the Allies and thus perhaps to remove at least a measure of wind from the sails of any future move to revive the concept of a minorities pact. If Raczyński (and, no doubt, other Polish leaders as well) nonetheless saw the threat of such a move as all the more reason to resist the idea of a declaration, it may well be because the echoes of its first stirrings among British Jewry filled him with such revulsion that he simply could not contemplate the full ramifications of the situation with the necessary detachment and equanimity. The legacy of Poland's fifteen-year struggle against the bête noire of the Minorities Treaty suggested a clear and compelling conclusion: by speaking once again of the need for international guarantees of Polish Jewry's security, Jews had made it clear that they remained at bottom enemies of Poland whose aims vis-à-vis the Polish government must therefore be resisted at every turn.

The perception of Jewry as a whole as an implacable foe was reinforced, too, by testimonies of refugees and by reports reaching the government through underground channels from the occupied homeland itself. From at least as early as November 1939, the Polish authorities in France began to receive word that, although Jews may have stood resolutely alongside the Poles during the September battle against the German invaders, they had, in contrast, welcomed the Soviet aggressors with open arms.[72] Subsequent communications went so far as to claim active complicity between Jews and Russians, portraying the former as a privileged class, employed by the Soviets as the primary instrument for suppressing Polish and Ukrainian resistance and consolidating their rule in the newly occupied territories.[73]

The general outlines of this picture were confirmed by an eyewitness account of the situation of Polish Jewry delivered personally to Interior Minister Stanisław Kot in Angers by a courier from the underground, Jan Karski, in February 1940.[74] This document contained perhaps the earliest detailed discussion of the relations among Poles, Jews, and the two occupying powers received by the government, and as such it was to exercise a critical influence upon the thinking of Polish leaders with regard to the Jewish question. Karski, who in late 1939 had crossed the demarcation line between the German and Soviet zones of occupation with a group of Jews fleeing eastward and had established contacts with Polish underground figures in Lwów,[75] reported that the Jews had "taken over the most critical political-administrative positions" within the Communist cells created by the Soviet authorities in the captured territories, that they had come to play "quite a large role in the factory unions, in higher education, and . . . in commerce," and that "above and beyond even all this they are involved in loansharking and profiteering, in illegal trade, contraband, foreign currency exchange, liquor, immoral interests, pimping, and procurement." He also noted that "cases where they [the Jews] denounce the Poles . . . , where they falsely defame the relations [between Poles and Jews] in former Poland," were "quite common, more common than incidents which reveal loyalty toward Poles or sentiment toward Poland." Although he was careful to point out that these were generalizations that could not be applied to all Jews, and that in particular "the intelligentsia, the wealthiest Jews, and those of the highest level of culture . . . think of Poland often with a certain fondness and would happily greet a change in the present situation [leading to] the independence of Poland," he concluded that on the whole, Jewish behavior toward the Soviets was a cause of bitterness and disappointment among virtually all Poles.

In any event, this portrayal represented an unwarranted extrapolation from a fundamental kernel of truth. The Jews in the regions east of the Ribbentrop-Molotov line did indeed, by and large, greet the invading Soviet forces not as conquerors but as liberators. Their reason, however, in contrast to what most Poles came quickly to believe, was not so much an inherent Jewish antipathy toward Polish sovereignty as a sense that the Russian action had prevented the subjugation of all of Poland by the Germans. The Soviet invasion had been launched more than two weeks after the initial German attack, when the outcome of the campaign had already become clear. Indeed, on the day following the launching of the Soviet invasion, the Polish government itself decided to seek refuge in Romania, thereby tacitly abandoning the military defense of the homeland. The news of the quick collapse of the Polish Army before the German onslaught and the apparent abjuration of active resistance by the country's political leaders aroused obvious fears among Polish Jews, who, even if they could not yet anticipate the horrors that were to befall them in the near future, were well aware of Nazi doctrines regarding the Jewish question and of the manner in which the Hitler regime had treated German Jews for the previous six years. Their fears were amplified, moreover, by tales of wanton brutality and viciousness carried by the stream of refugees fleeing eastward in the face of the German advance. In this context, the incursion of the Soviet forces into Polish territory and their initially benign attitude toward virtually all segments of the local population appeared to most Jews an act of salvation, and they responded with the special gratitude due the rescuer from danger.[76]

This was, however, the only way in which most Jews benefited from the new Soviet regime. With the formal annexation of the captured territories shortly after their surrender and the replacement of the military with a civilian authority, the conquerors embarked upon a program of rapid Sovietization that undermined the socioeconomic structure of the predominantly bourgeois Jewish community. Strong measures were taken, too, to restructure Jewish cultural and educational institutions in line with the ideological dictates of the new ruling power. And on the political level, Jews were in fact severely underrepresented in the administrative cadres and in the workers' councils created by the Soviet government in the newly acquired provinces. The notion that Jews as a group possessed, in Karski's words, "a certain power of both a political and an economic nature" that made them feel "at home" with the new regime was patently false.[77]

The falsity of this idea did not, however, prevent its becoming a virtual axiom among the Polish population under Soviet rule. The long-standing popular Polish image of Jews as russophiles and Bolsheviks, coupled with the specific memory of charges of Jewish treachery during the Polish-Soviet clashes of twenty years previous, lent it a measure of credibility that no objective explication of the situation could overcome. And if objective "proof" of Jewish-Soviet complicity were needed, it could easily be deduced from the large numbers of Jewish refugees attempting to escape from the German into the Russian zone, in contrast to the prevailing movement of Polish refugees from east to west.[78] Thus there developed among Poles in the annexed Soviet territories a violently anti-Jewish atmosphere reminiscent of the pogrom mentality of the early years of Polish independence. As Karski noted, "The Poles . . . wait for the moment when they will be able . . . to take revenge upon the Jews . . . ; the overwhelming majority (first among them of course the youth) literally look forward to an opportunity for 'repayment in blood.' "

Whether the Polish authorities in exile were significantly shaken by the reports of Jewish collaboration with the Soviet occupiers is doubtful.[79] Nevertheless, the news must have suggested to them the need to view with a fair amount of hesitancy the proposition that world Jewry might be enlisted as an ally in the battle against Russian territorial designs. Even more, Karski's comments about the state of Polish-Jewish relations in the Soviet zone must have conveyed the impression that any favorable declaration by the government regarding Jewish rights in postwar Poland would cause it to lose credibility with the Polish community in the homeland. This conclusion was undoubtedly strengthened by intelligence issuing from the German zone, which depicted widespread sympathy among the Poles there with the conquerors' approach to the Jewish question.[80] Here, too, Karski's testimony left no doubt that broad strata of the Polish populace had found in antisemitism a common ground with the German occupiers, and in the anti-Jewish measures enacted by the Nazi regime a significant consolation for the subjugation of their country to foreign rule. As the courier bluntly explained, "The Jews pay and pay and pay . . . , and the Polish peasant, laborer, and half-educated, stupid, demoralized wretch loudly proclaim: 'Now, then, they are finally teaching them a lesson.'—'We should learn from them.'—'The end has come for the Jews.'—'Whatever happens, we should thank God that the Germans came and took hold of the Jews.'—etc."

To be sure, Karski and other underground informants noted the potentially grave danger to the Polish cause that issued from this state of affairs. Karski observed in his report that the ability of the Nazis to make of the Jewish question "something akin to a narrow bridge upon which the Germans and a large portion of Polish society are finding agreement . . . threatens to demoralize broad segments of the populace, and this in turn may present many problems to the future authorities endeavoring to rebuild the Polish state." In such a situation, the courier believed, the government-in-exile could not allow itself to sit idly by; in particular, he suggested that the government find a way actively to encourage the Poles in the homeland to join together with Polish Jewry in a common front against the Nazis.[81] And yet he felt constrained at the same time to concede that "the establishment of any kind of broader front would be beset with very many difficulties from the perspective of wide segments of the Polish populace, among whom antisemitism has by no means decreased." Against the background of these comments, the anxiety of the Polish exile authorities over their standing in the homeland and the influence of this anxiety upon their decision-making process are thrown into vivid relief. Though the issuance of a declaration on Jewish rights and its subsequent transmission to the underground in Poland might, it seems, have represented a significant step in a government effort to counteract an important Nazi tactic for solidifying the German occupation, the government, fearful of alienating what its own intelligence revealed to be a highly antisemitic constituency, could not see its way clear to take that step. It appears that the axiom of interwar Polish politics which taught that a primary task of any Polish government was to defend the Polish populace not only against the German and Russian threats to Poland's independence but against the Jewish threat as well remained in force even after both the military and the internal political upheavals of September 1939.[82]

On the other hand, no matter how the regime's leaders might have regarded Karski's assertion that "the acceptance of a passive attitude toward the current state of affairs threatens to demoralize the Polish populace," it was certain that, for the sake of Poland's image in the West, they could not allow the Poles to be presented as supportive in any way of any aspect of the Nazi regime. Thus, as a precaution against the eventuality that news of the prevailing attitude toward Jews among the Poles of the occupied homeland might filter through to Western outlets, Polish officials, probably in the Interior Ministry, arranged for the preparation of a decoy version of the Karski report, which, through skillful editing of the original text, actually managed to leave the impression that the entire Polish nation was united in its opposition to Nazi anti-Jewish measures. In place of Karski's assertion that "the broad masses of the Polish population" display an "attitude toward the Jews [which] is overwhelmingly severe," for example, the alternate version announced that "the attitude of the Poles toward the Jews has changed [from what it was before the war] . . . under the influence of what is happening [now]," and that "in many cases Poles display visible sympathy for the Jews" in actions that "often . . . end up *badly* for those who bare their heart." It also stated that "the present situation in the country is bringing forth" that common anti-Nazi front whose establishment Karski regarded as difficult precisely because Polish prewar attitudes toward the Jews had in fact not changed at all.[83] This carefully doctored mutation, which nonetheless retained all of the passages condemning the alleged Jewish misbehavior under the Soviet regime, appears to have formed the basis for the manner in which the government officially represented the situation of Polish Jewry during the first year of the war.[84]

At the same time, the Sikorski government—for all of its professed aversion to the ways of its Sanacja predecessor, and despite its express commitment to "free national and cultural development" for minorities—shared the prewar regime's preference for mass emigration as the ultimate solution for Poland's Jewish problem.[85] This, of course, should not be surprising, in light of both the pervasiveness of the emigration concept in prewar Polish politics and the personal backgrounds of many of the government's central figures. During the first year of the war the steady flow to the government of underground reports indicating widespread anti-Jewish feeling among the Polish population undoubtedly served to strengthen the conviction that continued peaceful coexistence between Poles and Jews on Polish soil was impossible. Roman Knoll, a former Polish ambassador to Berlin who was later to assume a key position in the government's political delegacy to the underground (Delegatura Rządu w Kraju), dispatched a lengthy memorandum from Warsaw to the Polish Interior Ministry in Angers in March 1940, in which he flatly indicated that the Polish people would never tolerate a return after the war to the status quo ante with regard to the Jewish question, and that only a territorial solution along lines envisaged by the Zionists could save Poland from the necessity of extirpating its Jewish population by violent means. "No longer," he wrote, "do we face a choice between Zionism and the former state of affairs; the choice is rather—*Zionism or extermination.*" Knoll, who evidently did not perceive the essential connection between Zionism and Palestine which by that time had become a basic feature of the Jewish national movement, then proceeded to outline a program of massive Jewish resettlement under Polish patronage on the northern shore of the Black Sea, with the city of Odessa made over into a Jewish port. This, to him, was the only realistic exordium for the disposition of Poland's future Jewish problem, given the depth of anti-Jewish hostility in the homeland.[86]

Knoll's suggestion, despite its hopelessly romantic supposition that an area for mass Jewish colonization under Poland's auspices could be carved out of prime Soviet territory, quickly captured the imagination of, among others, Interior Minister Kot. Kot was not known for any personal hostility toward Jews;[87] nevertheless, he apparently saw in the Black Sea scheme an escape from a dilemma in which Poland had been placed by virtue of its alliance with Britain. Though before the war, largely in an attempt to cultivate voluntary Jewish cooperation, the Polish government had included support for Zionist demands in Palestine as an integral part of its emigration program, it was now, in consequence of Britain's firm opposition to those demands, precluded from continuing to do so.[88] In his memorandum, however, Knoll had listed numerous advantages of the Black Sea region over Palestine as a target for Jewish settlement, to the point where Kot seems to have believed that he could actually swing organized Zionist support to this scheme. The minister even made so bold as to broach the matter openly to Selig Brodetsky and Leonard Stein at a meeting in Angers in April 1940. They, not surprisingly, rejected the suggestion out of hand, underscoring that Zionists of every persuasion regarded Palestine as the only legitimate target for mass Jewish settlement.[89] Shortly thereafter, Brodetsky threatened to embark upon a propaganda campaign among U.S. Jews in the hope of dissuading the Polish government from this plan.[90]

Though in the wake of Kot's discussions with the Anglo-Jewish leaders mention of the Black Sea idea was suspended as politically inadvisable, government officials continued in their attempt to lay the groundwork for a mass exodus of Jews from Poland following the conclusion of hostilities. In this regard they were especially interested in cultivating contacts with the Revisionist wing of the Zionist movement, which alone among Jewish political groups in prewar Poland had been prepared to cooperate with the government in working toward this goal. As early as 20 January 1940, Raczyński urged Sikorski to develop a personal acquaintance with the Revisionist leader Jabotinsky, and during subsequent months the Polish Foreign Ministry offered advice and assistance to Revisionist activists of Polish nationality, particularly to those seeking entry into the United States for the purpose of conducting propaganda.[91] Retinger, too, praising the Revisionists as "the most dynamic group within Jewry," established in April 1940 an ongoing link with Abraham Abrahams, head of the Revisionist New Zionist Organization's Political Department in London.[92]

Of course, these Polish leaders were aware that Revisionist political plans were every bit as closely tied to the future of Palestine as were those of the mainstream Zionists, and they did not raise with this group any concrete settlement scheme. However, precisely because the Revisionists were committed in advance to the emigration concept, they were not likely to press the Polish government for a declaration on Jewish rights in postwar Poland or to devote undue attention to alleged instances of Polish antisemitism. On the contrary, Jabotinsky expressly indicated in a published article that "it is pointless for us to demand that the Polish government-in-exile make declarations on matters [such as the Jewish question] that can be resolved only in reborn Poland," and stated emphatically that in his view the Polish government was morally obligated "to warn the Allies that Poland cannot bear the burden of solving an international problem such as that of Polish Jewry by itself."[93] Hence Abrahams told Retinger at one of their early meetings that to his mind Revisionist goals dovetailed completely with Polish needs and that in consequence his organization was prepared to adapt its propaganda activities to the desires of the Polish government. In return, according to Abrahams, the Revisionists desired Polish assistance in their efforts to recruit and train a volunteer Jewish army in North America to fight for the Allied cause. This also happened to be a project that interested a number of Polish officials, not only because the government-in-exile planned to raise a similar force among Polish emigrants in the Western Hemisphere, but also because it raised the hope that the government might eventually be able to have the Jewish legions attached to the Polish Army, thereby increasing the ranks of those fighting for Poland's freedom.[94]

The significance of these early discussions between Polish officials and Revisionist representatives seems, however, to have lain less in the direct results that followed in their wake (these were in fact minimal) than in the indirect role they may have played in crystallizing Polish government thinking about the Jewish question as a whole. Because the Revisionists had already resigned themselves to the notion of immediate mass emigration as the only feasible solution to Poland's Jewish problem, they had been able, unlike the mainstream Zionists who dominated organized British Jewry, to accept the notion that the Polish government, no matter what its internal political orientation, might be enlisted as an ally in their cause. This fact could only have underscored in the minds of the Polish authorities an argument that had been most recently enunciated by Knoll, that through sponsorship of Jewish resettlement Poland could be made to appear as a champion of the movement for Jewish national rebirth, and thus potentially gain Jewish sympathy for the Polish national cause in return.[95]

By the same token, the idea was current among Polish officials that Polish Jews who had already resettled in Western countries were on the whole more understanding of Polish attitudes toward the Jewish question, and hence potentially more favorably disposed toward Poland in general, than were the Jews of the West. Retinger, for one, was most impressed by the demonstrations of loyalty toward Poland that he observed in the activities of the Federation of Polish Jews in Great Britain. Because of this attitude he pronounced himself strongly in favor of the existence of a vigorous Polish Jewish emigrants' organization in England, "first of all because the defense of Polish Jewish interests would be brought together in their hands [rather than in those of the English Jews], and [the danger of] an eventual international forum concerning Poland's domestic policies would be averted."[96] Indeed, many Poles seem to have been convinced that the demand for a declaration on Jewish rights represented exclusively the thinking of Western—not of Polish—Jews, and that as such it could be circumvented altogether through appropriate political maneuvers. It was noteworthy in this context, too, that even Schwarzbart, who had long been a foe of successive Polish government attempts to foster mass Jewish emigration and who possessed close ties to the World Jewish Congress and to the World Zionist Organization, refused to associate himself with the call for a declaration and, while emphatically reminding the National Council of the need to make actual the principle of civil and social equality for Jews in postwar Poland, refrained from publicly criticizing the government over the incidents that had aroused so much Jewish ire in the West.[97] Polish officials who spoke with him gained the impression that Schwarzbart could eventually be made to see the Jewish question from the Polish point of view.[98]

Such observations served to strengthen the conviction of the Polish authorities that whatever the difficulties inherent in its implementation, the concept of mass emigration as the proper solution to the Jewish problem in their country remained worth pursuing. Even the adverse reaction of Brodetsky and Stein to the Black Sea scheme as presented by Kot was interpreted more as a dismissal of the proposed target than as a rejection of emigration altogether. Polish political leaders continued to hold out hope that Jews throughout the world could eventually be won over to the emigration idea and that Jewish agitation over alleged Polish antisemitism would be mitigated as a result. And even if Western Jewish organizations were to continue their agitation and were eventually to succeed in inducing the Allied governments to reproach the Polish government for its refusal to issue a declaration on Jewish rights—a prospect that at the outset of the war did not appear likely—the Polish government could quickly counter that the organized voice of Polish Jews had never asked for such a declaration. The government thus regarded itself as well insulated against the hostile jibes of such as the Board of Deputies and the *Jewish Chronicle*.[99]

Thus, when Polish policy makers examined the problem of the government's relations with the Jews of the free world during the first nine months of the war, they found no compelling reason to accede to the demand for a declaration on postwar Jewish rights, and several compelling ones to resist. With the fall of France in June 1940 and the government's subsequent transfer to London, though, the balance of forces in this political equation was decisively altered. Within three months of its reorganization across the English Channel, the government was to conclude that its perceptions of the attitudes of Polish Jews in the West and of the political influence of world Jewry had been in error and that the issuance of a declaration on Jewish rights had become a public relations necessity.

The transfer of its seat to London forced the Sikorski government to function within a set of political parameters quite different from those which had prevailed in France. Sikorski's reputation as a francophile had bestowed upon his regime no small amount of credit in the eyes of the French authorities, who in consequence had sought only minimally to supervise its internal operations. In Whitehall, however, as well as among the British public at large, the Polish government-in-exile does not appear to have been held in any comparable degree of esteem. Such, at least, was the message bluntly conveyed by Frank Savery, the British Foreign Office's principal Polish expert, in a candid exchange with the secretary-general of the office of the Polish prime minister, Adam Romer, held slightly over a month following the Polish government's reorganization on British soil. The British, according to Savery, had been alienated by what they perceived as the Polish cabinet's right-of-center orientation and saw in Sikorski a would-be autocrat whose concentration in his own hands of the twin functions of prime minister and commander-in-chief belied his stated commitment to those democratic ideals in whose defense Britain purported to have entered the war. Savery even went so far as to suggest that Sikorski be replaced as premier by Zaleski, with the general retaining only his military position.[100]

The Polish authorities' own investigations of British public and official opinion seemed independently to substantiate Savery's claims in large measure. Indeed, they had been concerned about their negative public image in England and its possible political repercussions ever since the first month of the war, when the appearance of an article by former Prime Minister David Lloyd George in the *Sunday Express* praising the Soviet invasion of eastern Poland as an act of liberation had created a storm at the Polish Embassy in London.[101] Now, in August 1940, the publication of a volume of articles on British war aims by eleven members of Parliament brought home to the government the manner in which the prewar regime's record on the minorities question could penetrate legislative circles and in turn be exploited in support of "projects for the future downright dangerous to Poland."[102] In October 1940 Jan Ciechanowski noted that British public opinion was moving steadily in a direction unfavorable to Poland over the issue of the eastern border.[103] By that time, too, the Polish Foreign Ministry was growing increasingly apprehensive over British overtures to the Soviet Union based upon formal recognition of Russia's de facto control of the territories that the Red Army had occupied since the beginning of the war.[104] Against this background, the need for the government-in-exile to bolster its image as a liberal regime that repudiated the Sanacja legacy, especially on the minorities question, was clear.

It also became obvious to the government that it had underestimated the degree to which Jewish allegations of Polish antisemitism could harm its standing with its British patrons. Polish Jewish soldiers arriving in England from France in July 1940 brought a host of complaints before various Jewish leaders in London, concerning not only their treatment in the ranks in France but also alleged anti-Jewish discrimination in assigning places on evacuation transports to Britain.[105] Their outcries quickly reached the Jewish press, together with charges that Jewish soldiers billeted in the Polish transit camp at Fulham were being subjected by their non-Jewish comrades to harassment and abuse.[106] To be sure, similar stories had appeared during the months when the Polish forces had been stationed in France, but with the army's removal to Britain they acquired for the British public a new immediacy. British Jews now began to ask their own government whether it intended to allow its Polish "guests" to engage in activities that, they claimed, violated both the canons of British public morality and the principles in whose name the war was ostensibly being fought.[107] Such questioning was intensified with the appearance in London of a new, outspokenly rightish newspaper, *Jestem Polakiem*, whose articles were felt by many Jews frequently to carry an anti-Jewish undertone and whose early numbers featured contributions by government ministers Seyda and Haller. In contrast to the situation in previous months, however, concern over the possible persistence of prewar Polish attitudes toward the Jewish question within the new government did not remain confined to Jewish circles. On 20 August 1940 the *Evening Standard* published an editorial excoriating what it termed the "anti-Semitic character" of *Jestem Polakiem* and decrying Seyda's association with it. "Some Polish leaders who have come to this country do not appear to understand the convention of the land with which they are allied," the British newspaper wrote; "they stand condemned by the mass of the English people."[108] The next day the subject of Polish-Jewish relations in the Polish Army was raised in the House of Commons during debate over the Allied Forces Bill, a proposal to grant quasi-extraterritorial status to the armed forces of the overrun Allied powers that had sought the hospitality of the British government for their exile administrations. In the course of the discussions, Labour MP Josiah Wedgwood charged that in France Jewish refugees from Poland had been impressed into the Polish Army, where, in his words, "they did not find themselves welcome." He further commented, in a remark about which the Polish government took sharp offense, that "the feelings of Poles toward Jews can only be paralleled by the feelings of Germans toward Jews." Another Labour MP, Sidney Silverman (who in addition served as a vice-president of the British Section of the World Jewish Congress), also expressed misgivings over the bill in light of alleged incidents of anti-Jewish behavior among Polish soldiers that had recently been brought to his attention. He requested that the War Office pledge to see to it that the Polish authorities take "every step in their power . . . to prevent recurrence of undesirable incidents . . . and to promote the friendly comradeship which ought to exist between people fighting for the same purposes in the same army." Sir Edward Grigg, the joint undersecretary of state for war, who had presented the bill before the House, replied that he found Silverman's proposal "absolutely fair and reasonable."[109]

The public and parliamentary attention accorded both the appearance of *Jestem Polakiem* and the question of the status of Jewish soldiers in the Polish forces, and, in particular, the effect that this attention appeared to exert upon the British government, proved a source of concern to the Polish authorities. A report to the government on the Commons debate over the Allied Forces Bill noted that the problem of Polish-Jewish relations had caused the particular situation of the Polish Army to come under an inordinate amount of scrutiny.[110] Another report from Sikorski's file indicated that "the activity of the periodical *Jestem Polakiem* in England has become a factor impeding the work of the Polish Government . . . in its relations with England."[111] Henryk Strasburger, the Polish treasury minister, feared that the British government would eventually conclude that the publication of *Jestem Polakiem* was in essence made possible, whether directly or indirectly, by the credits Britain had granted the Polish government and that it might be moved as a result to curtail future financial assistance.[112] A group of Polish journalists, including one member of the Polish National Council, warned Sikorski that the publicity over *Jestem Polakiem* had interfered with their efforts to develop friendly and productive working relationships with their English counterparts and that it was likely in consequence to hinder the conduct of pro-Polish propaganda in Britain.[113]

The seriousness of this situation was not lost on the Poles. However, there seems to have been much disagreement, including considerable individual vacillation, about how the government should respond. Sikorski appears actually to have anticipated some of the difficulties over the treatment of Jews in the Polish forces; already on 5 August, perhaps in an attempt to deflect expected criticism, he issued an order to all Polish troops "strictly forbid[ding them] to show soldiers of Jewish faith any unfriendliness through contemptuous remarks or anything humiliating to human dignity" and promising that "all such offences will be severely punished."[114] Others, however, were convinced that the charges of anti-Jewish discrimination and harassment in the Polish military units were unfair and needed to be forcefully rebuffed. A memorandum prepared for Sikorski the day following the issuance of the order argued that the British authorities had obtained a distorted impression of the situation in the ranks precisely because of willful, organized Jewish efforts to evade service in the Polish Army and to discredit the good name of Poland.[115] Evidently the prime minister was moved by this suggestion, to the point where he began to see in repeated calls for the establishment of proper interethnic relations in the armed forces a threat to his regime's standing in the eyes of the British government. When, toward the end of August, Schwarzbart introduced at a meeting of the Military Committee of the National Council a resolution concerning the necessity for feelings of brotherhood to prevail among all Polish soldiers, Sikorski is reported to have lobbied actively for its defeat. To one delegate he is said to have remarked angrily, "I am treating the Jews like a soft-boiled egg, but it is to no avail."[116] It seems, then, that in a sense Sikorski did not wish to see the National Council formally endorse the essence of the order that he had issued only a short time before.

Similar ambivalence was noticeable in the government's thinking about *Jestem Polakiem*. Labor Minister Stańczyk, a socialist, strongly condemned the paper as antidemocratic and antisemitic and demanded that it be banned outright. Not surprisingly, his demand fell upon deaf ears.[117] Sikorski at first favored government suppression of all Polish political publications other than the officially sponsored *Dziennik Polski* and *Polska Walcząca*, on the grounds that periodicals issued by particular parties or ideological groups imperiled the sense of national unity so necessary under conditions of occupation and exile.[118] Even this position, though, found little support among the other members of his cabinet. Seyda, predictably, strongly resisted the premier's suggestion, stating that the character of *Jestem Polakiem* had been severely distorted by the British press and recommending that steps be taken to improve the paper's public image, especially in the matter of its attitude toward Jews. In this opinion he enjoyed the support of Information Minister Stroński, who had in fact already begun to undertake action along these lines.[119] The manner in which the information minister approached this task, however, left the success of his mission in doubt from the start. At a cabinet meeting he resolutely declared, "Our conscience with regard to the Jews is completely clear, and anyone who assails us for antisemitism is a provocateur." He further decried the existence of a situation in which "certain Jewish circles regarded English soil as the proper ground for settling accounts with Polish nationalists."[120]

This became the spirit that was to typify Polish public reactions to the *Jestem Polakiem* affair. The editor of the paper, apparently in earnest, told a *Daily Herald* correspondent that he and his staff could not fairly be accused of anti-Jewish bias, even though they had published articles deploring the large percentage of Jews in commerce and the free professions in Poland and blaming Jews in large measure for the moral decay of France that had preceded its military defeat. After all, he claimed, in other articles the paper had criticized non-Jews with equal vigor. When the *Daily Herald* did not print the story, some government officials regarded it as a propaganda setback.[121] Similarly, *Dziennik Polski*, which was published under Stroński's supervision, reprinted an editorial from the *Catholic Herald* condemning the *Evening Standard*'s attack upon the alleged antisemitism of *Jestem Polakiem* as "no less an attempt to interfere with Poland's independence than German tactics."[122] Sikorski seems to have been embarrassed by this editorial, but he was unable to control the situation. Though he repeatedly assured British officials that publication of *Jestem Polakiem* had been suspended, the newspaper continued to be distributed openly until it died a natural death in mid-1941.[123]

In practical terms, then, the preponderance of Polish government opinion in August 1940 tended to favor active defense against British criticism of the tenor of Polish-Jewish relations over attempts to sidestep it through ostensible acceptance and promises that the situation would improve. It was, as a result, not at all surprising that when the Board of Deputies and the *Jewish Chronicle* renewed at this time their demand for an official Polish declaration on Jewish rights, the call would once again be rebuffed.[124] Apparently the government, despite its acute perception of the weakness of its standing with British public and official opinion and of the significant role played by the Jewish question in creating this state of affairs, continued at this point to believe that the possible advantages of such a declaration were outweighed by its liabilities.

The issue, in fact, was mooted, albeit obliquely, at a meeting of the government's Political Committee on 24 August, in the course of discussions over Sikorski's call to publish in the West a comprehensive outline of the principles guiding Polish foreign policy in wartime. In a draft paper that he had submitted to the other ministers a week previously, the premier had included a statement rejecting the Soviet claim that the annexation of Poland's eastern provinces should be regarded as an act of liberation of the non-Polish peoples who lived there and pledging that the reconstituted Polish state would guarantee these minorities "full national rights." When this provision came up for debate, Seyda strongly objected, arguing that such a "loose phrase" offered in an "offhand fashion" would effectively commit Poland in advance to a specific solution of "this vitally important issue." He further stipulated that even if such a guarantee were to be issued, care should be taken to avoid giving the impression that it applied also to Jews. These objections were supported, somewhat surprisingly, by Zaleski and Stańczyk. Though the latter had previously suggested the idea of "guaranteeing the White Russian, Ukrainian, and Jewish minorities the farthest-reaching national rights in the reconstituted Poland," he subsequently assented to Seyda's stipulation that the situation of the territorial minorities could not be equated with that of the Jews. The former rejected the adoption of any stand on the minorities question that might be formulated under the pressure of the moment "solely for foreign propaganda use." Specifically, he termed the Jewish question "exclusively a question of foreign policy," thus implying that the government should refrain from discussing it within the context of a possible domestic interethnic settlement.[125]

It seems that a hidden assumption underlying the deliberations at this meeting was that any declaration issued for propaganda purposes concerning the status in postwar Poland of the minorities in general, or of the Jews in particular, could not help but be insincere. That government thinking on the Jewish question continued now, as it had prior to the removal to England, to run along lines very different from those which any propagandistically valuable declaration might have suggested was graphically revealed in a position paper on the subject presented to Sikorski on 4 September. This memorandum began from the premise that "Poland is a Catholic country, and the Poles in that country have the right to be complete masters in deciding their own fate and that of the state." Only when Jews accepted this premise, according to the document, could their right to "full freedom in the areas of religion, language, culture, and association" be recognized. In practice, the paper noted, this meant that "Jews, who in Poland constitute a limited percentage of the population, may not play a decisive role in the economic life of the state, as this would place them in a privileged position and would be in conflict with state interests and, even more, as this would have sooner or later to become the source of an inexorable struggle between Polish and Jewish elements." The memorandum, in fact, not only continued to see in the removal of Jews to Palestine a primary element in the eventual solution of the Polish Jewish problem, but even went so far as to maintain that "the Polish Government must insist that Jewish emigration . . . not bring about the export of capital in such excessive measure as would of necessity redound to the detriment of the country's economic situation."[126]

The government implicitly understood, of course, that such sentiments could not be permitted at the moment to pass beyond the confines of its own inner circle; they echoed too strongly the attitudes of the discredited prewar regime and would almost surely be interpreted in the British press as antisemitic and antidemocratic. Apparently, though, in choosing the strategy of active defense against attacks upon their handling of Jewish affairs, the Polish authorities hoped in the long run to persuade the British public that these ideas, as well as other provocative statements about Jews that appeared in the pages of *Jestem Polakiem*, did not necessarily imply government antipathy a priori to all Jews. In particular, the government seems to have wished to show that such statements did not imply that Jewish soldiers in the Polish Army who quietly did their duty would not be treated on the same basis as other members of the ranks, and these sentiments, in the government's view, ought therefore not to be regarded as inconsistent with the proclaimed ideological war aims of the Allies.

Initial public responses to this approach were not on the whole encouraging. Press attacks upon *Jestem Polakiem* continued in a fashion frequently reaching the level of personal vituperation, with Seyda, in particular, branded as "the Polish Julius Streicher."[127] The newspaper also continued to be discussed in Parliament, and the British ambassador to the Polish government, Sir Howard Kennard, felt constrained to take up the matter with Sikorski in person.[128] Nor did it appear that the public was prepared to believe that Jews entering the Polish forces had no reason for anxiety over the treatment they would receive. Rather, the view of the *Jewish Chronicle* that "it would be wholly insufferable if those very [Jewish] Poles who had had to leave their own country because it had been made impossible for them to live in it, were compelled to serve in an army which is fighting to restore a country that never wanted them—and which, in fact, has so far failed to inspire confidence that it will have anything better to offer in restored Poland"—seems to have won considerable public sympathy.[129] In response to such Jewish concerns, the press and Parliament began to raise the demand that the Polish military authorities be denied the power to conscript Polish nationals resident in Britain and that Allied citizens fit for military service be afforded the option of fulfilling their obligations in the British Army.[130] Such a provision was, in fact, eventually enacted into law in the Allied Conscription Act of 1941, to the extreme disgruntlement of the Polish government and in spite of its sharp official protest.[131]

In all of this the Polish authorities might have enjoyed the small consolation that, as during the months of their sojourn in France, both Schwarzbart and the organized body of Polish Jewish emigrants in England had refrained from joining in the agitation led by British and international Jewish institutions. Schwarzbart, in fact, had expressed privately to Brodetsky and to other non-Polish Jewish leaders in London his profound reservations about the potential long-range effectiveness of such vigorous application of pressure upon the government and had protested that, as the official representative of Polish Jewry on the Polish National Council, he deserved to be consulted before non-Polish Jews approached the Polish authorities on questions of interest to the Polish Jewish community.[132] This was a situation that Zaleski and Raczyński—as well, no doubt, as others in the government—felt might be exploited to the regime's benefit. In an exchange of letters the two formulated the position that in matters concerning the rights and obligations of Polish citizens as such the government ought to insist upon dealing solely with those Jewish organizations made up exclusively of Polish nationals.[133] They also sought explicitly to enlist Schwarzbart's aid in restraining the vociferousness of other Jewish organizations with which he might carry weight. According to Raczyński, the Jewish representative readily agreed.[134]

Yet at precisely the time when the foreign minister and the ambassador in London were taking pride in their achievement of Schwarzbart's active cooperation, new influences were being felt within the communities of Polish Jewish emigrants in the West and in Palestine that were quickly to reverse their previous posture of restraint. These influences were borne by a wave of Jewish war refugees, including many of the political leaders of prewar Polish Jewry, who had succeeded in escaping Poland in the wake of the German invasion and had managed, by mid-1940, to find their way to safe havens, mainly in Tel Aviv or New York. For the most part this group of refugee leaders sought to continue the battle to secure Jewish rights in Poland from their new residences abroad, seeing in this struggle a natural continuation of their activities prior to the war. This essentially political conception of their task differed from that of the various organizations of prewar emigrants, whose activities had possessed more of a social and cultural focus. As a result, the work of the refugee leaders was generally carried on outside the existing Polish Jewish organizational framework. In New York the new arrivals gravitated toward two institutions: the American Jewish Congress, which at the outbreak of the war had created a Special Committee on Polish Jewry, and, following the transfer of its headquarters from France to the United States in June 1940, the World Jewish Congress, which created a similar committee—to the point where these two officially non-Polish Jewish organizations could actually make something of a legitimate claim to speak on behalf of the Jews of Poland.[135] In Palestine the independent Representation of Polish Jewry (Reprezentacja Żydostwa Polskiego), consisting of activists from all of the major Jewish political parties of prewar Poland save the Bund and the Revisionists, began to function in September 1940. In formally announcing its existence to the Polish government, the Reprezentacja proclaimed as its "special task the securing of equal civil, religious, and national rights for the Jewish community of the reborn Poland."[136]

None of these new centers of Polish Jewish leadership shared Schwarzbart's reticence over the application of public pressure upon the government or his apparent lack of concern in the matter of a declaration on Jewish rights. Arieh Tartakower, a noted sociologist and Labor Zionist leader in prewar Poland who had taken over the directorship of the central office of the World Jewish Congress shortly after its removal to New York and had introduced other Polish Jewish refugees into key positions within the organization, wrote to Schwarzbart on 7 August 1940 that he viewed the issue of a declaration "normalizing the status of Jews in the future Poland" as one of the most important tasks of the congress's Polish Committee.[137] He repeated this message in a second letter on 6 September, adding that the committee had determined that "an extremely firm stand" was necessary at present in dealing with the Polish government.[138] Although the Palestinian Reprezentacja had at this point not yet had the opportunity to take a formal stand on the question, it was clear that within its ranks, too, Schwarzbart's cautious approach enjoyed little credibility.[139] For Schwarzbart, of course, not only was this situation potentially embarrassing, but it actually threatened to undermine his own legitimacy as the official representative of Polish Jewry vis-à-vis the Polish government.[140] If he had been troubled before by a sense of working at cross purposes with non-Polish Jewry, he must have found his present disagreement with the new Polish Jewish leadership virtually unbearable. In any case, no doubt under pressure from New York and Tel Aviv, he changed his position on the issue of a declaration. On 8 October he addressed a lengthy memorandum to Sikorski, stressing Poland's dependence upon the goodwill of Great Britain and the United States and the strong role played by Jews in the political life of these two countries. He noted the anxiety with which both Polish and non-Polish Jews regarded the question of the Jewish future in Poland and concluded that "the present . . . is the right psychological moment for issuing a clear and sincere declaration [on Jewish rights] . . . settling the matter in principle."[141] Far from serving as a restraining influence on behalf of the government, Schwarzbart had now actually come down on the side of the forces that he had been asked to hold in check.

Evidently Schwarzbart's change of heart served as the immediate catalyst for a government reevaluation of the political equation that had hitherto led to rejection of the declaration idea. It negated once and for all the possibility of claiming that Polish Jewry had not expressed itself upon the matter.[142] With pressure from the British side continuing despite Polish efforts to repel it, and with hints that even the U.S. government might be becoming concerned with the future of the Jews in Eastern Europe,[143] the Polish authorities apparently felt that they could afford to resist no longer. It happened, too, that Schwarzbart, in cooperation with Polish Jewish organizations in Britain and with the British Section of the World Jewish Congress, had organized a one-day symposium on the status of Polish Jewry, to be held on 3 November at Woburn House in London (the seat of the Board of Deputies), to which representatives of both the Polish and the British governments had been invited. On 29 October Sikorski proposed to his cabinet that Stańczyk collaborate with him in formulating a declaration on Jewish rights in the future Poland, which the labor minister would present at the symposium on behalf of the government.[144] His motion was carried, and on 2 November Schwarz-bart was handed an advance copy of the text.[145]

Stańczyk's brief statement, read also in the presence of Zaleski, Kot, Stroński, Deputy Prime Minister Stanisław Mikołajczyk, and the secretaries-general of the president's and prime minister's offices, stressed the common war aims of the Polish and Jewish nations. It pointed out that the exordium for the current war had been provided by the "barbarous doctrine" of ethnic and racial hatred and that until the purveyors of this idea were defeated, the world would know no peace. In this regard Stańczyk confessed that in prewar Poland there had been those "who allowed themselves to be seduced by the pernicious catchwords of totalitarianism, racism, and anti-semitism," although he quickly added that these were exceptional individuals whose slogans had been rejected by the Polish community as a whole. In any case, he made it clear that the present government stood firmly opposed to all antidemocratic political ideas. But for the assembled Jewish delegates, the most significant feature of Stańczyk's remarks was the enunciation of the specific implications of his government's unalterably democratic orientation for the future of Polish Jewry:

> The Jews, as Polish citizens, shall in liberated Poland be equal with the Polish community, in duties and in rights. They will be able to develop their culture, religion, and folkways without hindrance. Not only the laws of the state, but even more the common sacrifices on the way toward Poland's liberation and the common sufferings in this most tragic time of affliction will serve to guarantee this [pledge].[146]

Such a public statement represented a major concession to Jewish pressure by the Polish government. For over a year the Polish authorities had stubbornly resisted issuing such a declaration, mainly out of fear of its possible future implications. Nor were their fears without basis. A secret letter to Kot from Janusz Radziwiłł in Warsaw, probably written in late November or early December 1940, reported that Stańczyk's speech had "made a disastrous impression in Poland even among the workmen belonging to the Polish Socialist Party" and had helped to loosen the already shaky hold that the London regime maintained over the loyalties of the Poles in the occupied homeland.[147] That the Poles in London were willing to risk this possibility with a move to assuage Jewish sensibilities in the West must have represented a radical change in their perception of Jewish power in the formation of Western public opinion and even of Allied governmental policies. Where Jewish pressure had earlier been withstood largely out of a Polish discounting of its political significance, it had now become a force with which the government felt it had to reckon. Against this background it is not at all surprising to note, for example, that Mirosław Arciszewski, Ciechanowski's successor as director-general of the Foreign Ministry, attempted in the wake of the declaration to rekindle the idea of enlisting Jewish support for Poland's eastern border claims and sounded out Jewish leaders in Palestine about its feasibility.[148] Within the Information Ministry, too, the possibility that world Jewry might be Poland's only firm ally in its war with Russia, and that the government ought therefore to coordinate its propaganda activities with those of international Jewish organizations, began to be given a serious second look.[149]

Moreover, by late 1940 Polish leaders appear to have begun to take greater interest in the potential role that the United States might play in determining the political future of Eastern Europe, and they seem to have been convinced that Jewish opinion could exert a decisive effect upon the formation of U.S. public and governmental attitudes. At a cabinet meeting on 17 October, Sikorski warned that following the upcoming elections the United States would draw progressively nearer to entering the war on the Allied side and that, as a result of the influence wielded by world Jewry in that country, the Polish government could expect U.S. pressure for full restoration of Jewish assets in Poland following the expulsion of the occupiers.[150] Similarly, in his formal instructions to Ciechanowski upon the latter's appointment as Poland's ambassador in Washington, Sikorski pointed out that "the position of the United States will have a decisive influence upon the final outcome of the war" and that the assistance of American Jewry "could have great significance" for the Polish cause. In the latter regard the prime minister observed that "it is necessary to obtain tangible assistance for Polish demands from the Jewish community, especially with regard to the return of the eastern territories."[151]

Sikorski also hinted, however, that the new ambassador should not hesitate to exert pressure in order to secure the desired Jewish support: "Such assistance will in the future facilitate the realization of the equality about which the government has issued a declaration, which otherwise [in the event that such assistance is not forthcoming] might encounter difficulties, given the well-known fashion in which the portion of Jewry under Soviet occupation has behaved."[152] This latter remark was telling, for it suggested that Stańczyk's declaration was to be regarded in government circles less as a final statement of official policy on the Jewish question than as a starting point for further discussions with Jewish representatives over the manner in which it would be implemented. Sikorski at least appears to have believed that the ability of the government to put the declaration into practice would depend in large measure upon the way in which Jews henceforth related to the Polish regime and to the Polish cause, and there seems little reason to suppose that this was not a general attitude in Polish ruling circles.

Interestingly, this approach paralleled what seems to have been the dominant Jewish view of the declaration as merely the initial offering in an envisioned extended process of negotiation. Jews, too, understood well the difference between the issuance of a statement and its actualization. The *Jewish Chronicle* delicately reflected a pervasive Jewish sentiment: "If honest professions are not to run the risk of remaining merely pious declarations . . . the Polish Government will have to recognize its imperative responsibility to tackle the [Jewish] problem in a constructive and humane manner in accordance with the policy just announced."[153]

Thus, in the wake of the declaration of 3 November, both Poles and Jews began to look carefully at the way in which the government's promise influenced the behavior of the other group, and to plan their own future actions accordingly.

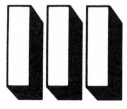

DISAPPOINTMENTS

Publicly both Poles and Jews hailed the Stańczyk declaration as the harbinger of a new era of improved relations between the two groups. A resolution by the Joint Foreign Committee of British Jewry of 12 November 1940 greeted the labor minister's speech "with great satisfaction" and termed the symposium at which it had been delivered "a demonstration of the solidarity in efforts and aims uniting Polish Jews and non-Jews in the struggle for Polish independence and freedom."[1] Similar statements were heard in subsequent weeks from the Board of Deputies of British Jews,[2] the Inter-Associate Council of Polish Jewry in Great Britain,[3] and the American Federation of Polish Jews.[4] The declaration was praised in the Jewish press in Britain, the United States, and Palestine;[5] and Schwarzbart, who until a month before its issue had remained aloof from the rising demand for a government statement on the Jewish question, now became its leading glorifier, seeking even to take credit for its achievement.[6] On the Polish side, the promise that Stańczyk's speech signified the government-in-exile's intention to "make good all wrongs" was enunciated before Jewish audiences by Raczyński in London,[7] as well as by the commanding officer of the Polish troops stationed in Palestine.[8] At a meeting of the National Council of 26 March 1941, the Peasant Party affirmed its solidarity with the declaration of 3 November,[9] as did the right-of-center Labor Party at the plenary session of 25 June.[10] *Dziennik Polski* reported on Stańczyk's statement favorably, publishing the full text in a featured location,[11] and in a following article the newspaper commented that although the guarantees of Jewish equality contained in the Polish constitution might not always have been properly upheld by previous regimes, the Sikorski government was charged with a new spirit and sincerely intended to fulfill Stańczyk's pledge.[12]

Behind this mellifluous rhetoric, however, lay an attitude of watchful waiting on both sides that did not augur well for the realization of any meaningful Polish-Jewish cooperation. The government-in-exile, for its part, seems to have been willing to take action to implement the promises of the November declaration only to the extent that it saw organized world Jewry acting in a manner likely to advance Polish interests. Such action included, to its mind, not only direct Jewish intervention on Poland's behalf in its dispute with the Soviet Union over the location of the border between the two countries, but also cessation of the public complaints about alleged Polish anti-Jewish behavior that had served over the previous half year to weaken the regime's prestige in Allied eyes. Certain Jewish spokesmen, on the other hand, felt that more was required than a simple declaration by the labor minister before they would relinquish the critical eye and clamoring voice, without which, they believed, the statement of 3 November would never have been made to begin with.[13] They expected the government to take concrete steps to eliminate the type of occurrences that had initially given rise to their complaints; if such steps were not forthcoming, they would not hesitate to expose the apparent contradiction between Polish word and deed.[14]

Here was the breeding ground for a vicious circle, in which each side waited for the other to make the next gesture toward improved relations and felt stung when the other failed fully to live up to its expectations. When, in the wake of the declaration of 3 November, the Polish government continued to evince behavior and attitudes that Jews found distressing, and when Jewish organizations gave vent to their discomfort in a fashion that Poles regarded as irresponsible and even malicious, the cycle of mutual recrimination was activated. The result was augmented friction between Jews and the Sikorski regime during the second year of the war.

Evidently Jewish leaders expected that an immediate outcome of Stańczyk's speech would be the permanent disappearance of *Jestem Polakiem* and all other Polish publications containing references to the Jewish people that Jews found offensive. Their consternation was thus considerable when they discovered not only that *Jestem Polakiem* continued to circulate but that some highly placed Polish officials had published books in English that did not seem consistent with the government's professed commitment to Jewish equality. Especially galling was the appearance in late 1940 of a 180-page propaganda piece entitled *September 1939*, whose author, writing under the pseudonym Dominik Węgierski, was believed by Jewish leaders to play an important behind-the-scenes role in government policy-making circles.[15] Węgierski devoted a full chapter to exposing "the misdeeds of the Jews" in interwar Poland, presumably, from his point of view, in order to counterbalance the negative impression of Polish behavior toward them with which the British public was ostensibly afflicted. The Jews, he wrote, "are a tactless nation [who] even in antiquity . . . shocked the Greeks and Romans with their arrogance, lack of reason, and fanaticism. These faults," he claimed further, "were responsible for the birth of antisemitism."[16] To Jews, it seemed that the only possible purpose of such remarks was to sow antisemitism among the British public.[17] In an angry letter to Kot, Schwarzbart termed the book an "unprecedented attack [*niesłychana napaść*]" against which Polish Jews felt themselves bound to offer defense.[18]

Less vituperative, perhaps, but no less disconcerting to Jewish leaders were books by Józef Retinger and by Kazimierz Głuchowski of the Polish Information Center in New York, both of which held out no hope for a solution to the Jewish question in postwar Poland in the absence of mass Jewish emigration from the country.[19] "Although these views . . . are clearly inconsistent and incompatible with the professions of democratic equality of Polish citizens, made from time to time by, or on behalf of, the present Polish Government," complained the World Jewish Congress in a memorandum to the British Foreign Office, "they have not been repudiated by that

Government or by any of its spokesmen."[20] The government did, to be sure, under strong pressure from the British press, reissue its condemnation of *Jestem Polakiem* following a cabinet meeting on 9 April 1941,[21] but this step was regarded in Jewish circles as "not impressive."[22] Jewish leaders felt that the government was in a position to block the newspaper's circulation effectively, especially in Polish military installations, where it had apparently found a noticeable following among Polish soldiers. "By doing so," wrote Schwarzbart, ". . . [the government] would clearly show that it is not only anxious to take decisions for export but it is sincerely concerned about the situation, and is determinedly striving to suppress, if not the anti-Semitic forces, then at least its [sic] manifestations." By failing to act in this direction, Schwarzbart felt, the government betrayed, "if not sympathy in disguise, at least a certain tolerance of and indifference to the activities of the Endek Party, as well as the ONR."[23]

Jewish complaints in the aftermath of the declaration of 3 November also extended to the treatment of Jewish matters by the government's official daily organ, *Dziennik Polski*. Jewish spokesmen criticized the newspaper for not taking what they regarded as sufficient steps to publicize the labor minister's statement or to educate the Polish émigré community in its spirit. This, they felt, was its obligation as the principal public voice of the regime. Schwarzbart and the World Jewish Congress even went so far as to charge (inaccurately) that the newspaper had reported Stańczyk's remarks as "the proclamation of an individual Minister, [thereby] diminishing the declaration's fundamental significance."[24] Moreover, Jewish leaders argued, *Dziennik Polski*, "while publishing full and detailed reports of the sufferings of non-Jews in Poland, . . . has paid scant attention to Nazi persecution of the Jews."[25] It angered Jews terribly to find in the newspaper's edition of 9 January 1941 a feature article highlighting the difficulties faced by Polish Catholics of Jewish ancestry who had been forced by Nazi racial laws to take up residence in the Warsaw ghetto. The piece asserted, among other things, that these "great and avid patriots, Poles for two or three generations, . . . are mistreated by the autonomous [Jewish] ghetto authorities as well as by the Jewish ghetto police, which is made up of Jewish nationalists."[26] Schwarzbart wrote an indignant reply to this report, which was published in part by the newspaper on 13 January—together, however, with an editorial comment castigating the existence of the Warsaw Judenrat and ghetto police as a form of collaboration with the Nazi occupiers.[27] This remark, to Schwarzbart's mind, contradicted entirely the spirit of the Stańczyk declaration.[28] The World Jewish Congress, too, subsequently condemned *Dziennik Polski* as "exhibiting distinctly anti-Jewish tendencies."[29]

Actually, it appears that the entire Polish Ministry of Information was perceived in Jewish circles as operating in opposition to the proclamation of 3 November. Schwarzbart, despite voting in favor of the government's budget proposal for 1941 (and thus formally expressing confidence in the Sikorski regime), felt compelled to declare before the entire National Council his dissatisfaction with "a large portion" of the ministry's activities.[30] Specifically, he complained that not only *Dziennik Polski* but also the English-language publication *Free Europe*, which was supported in part by Polish government funds, displayed a disquieting readiness to publish articles of an anti-Jewish character, and that Polish radio broadcasts to the occupied homeland, which seemed to him a crucial educational tool, made no attempt to encourage Polish-Jewish solidarity or to raise the spirits of the Jews suffering under the Nazi heel.[31] The deficiency in the operation of the Polish radio service represented to him an especially serious shortcoming, for to his mind the government's ability to implement the principles of Stańczyk's declaration depended primarily upon its success in creating among the Polish populace at large a willingness to look upon Polish Jews as equal partners in the building of the Polish state.[32] His attitude was shared by the Council of Polish Jews in Great Britain, which in July 1941 addressed to Stroński a request for "allocation of a certain number of the daily broadcasts of the Polish Radio to Jewish affairs."[33] The World Jewish Congress agreed with Schwarzbart's perception of *Free Europe* and complained to the British Foreign Office of its allegedly anti-Jewish tone.[34]

The Polish Army also came under increased Jewish scrutiny during the second year of the war. The disquiet that Jewish leaders felt over the behavior of the Information Ministry was matched by their continued anger at the persistence of discontent among Jews serving with the Polish forces in Britain. Reports of discontent grew to such proportions during the first three months of 1941 that in April Schwarzbart was moved to undertake an inspection visit to the Polish military installations in Scotland.[35] On the basis of discussions with Jewish soldiers and with their commanding officers he concluded that both a general antisemitic atmosphere and specific instances of anti-Jewish discrimination were frequently encountered in the armed forces. He subsequently told military officials that he had learned, among other things, that a group of Polish soldiers had cheered a radio broadcast of a speech in which Hitler promised to drive all Jews from Europe; that the accusation that the Jews had betrayed Poland during the September campaign was heard often in the ranks; that certain Polish officers had warned of a "day of reckoning" with the Jews once Poland was liberated; that *Jestem Polakiem*, though officially banned in army camps, was still widely read by the troops; that army chaplains had conducted anti-Jewish propaganda; that Jews had not been included among candidates for the first officers' training course; that Jewish military doctors were not promoted at the same rate as non-Jews; and that a number of individual Jews had been unjustly disciplined when they had endeavored to protest incidents of an anti-Jewish character.[36] As a result, he demanded that a program of "systematic educational work" be inaugurated in the ranks in order to make peaceful Polish-Jewish coexistence possible.[37] Other Jewish spokesmen likewise called upon the government to take vigorous action to suppress the spread of anti-Jewish propaganda among soldiers,[38] and complaints from Jews brought about a renewal of the parliamentary discussion of antisemitism in the Polish forces.[39]

Finally, Jewish leaders were upset by recurring reports that certain government officials in neutral countries and in Allied colonies discriminated in their approach to Polish Jewish refugees who had managed to find asylum from invading Nazi armies. By mid-1941, at least thirteen thousand Jewish civilian war refugees of Polish origin had made themselves known to Polish consular representatives or to Jewish organizations in unoccupied France, Portugal, North Africa, Palestine, and the Far East,[40] and according to some estimates there were twice that number in Romania, Hungary, and Yugoslavia.[41] Many of these refugees were destitute and required financial assistance; a greater percentage required legal and logistic assistance in securing their status in their places of asylum or their onward transportation to other destinations. For all of these services, Polish Jews turned automatically to the nearest official agencies of the Polish government. It appears, however, that many of the refugees were not satisfied with the response that they received from Polish officials. As early as August 1940, and perhaps even before, word of discontent among Polish Jews in Lisbon with the operation of the official Polish relief apparatus there was passed on to the Ministry of Labor and Social Welfare by Schwarzbart's Organising Committee for a Representation of Polish Jewry.[42]

Specifically, the various Polish Aid Committees that had been created to supervise the distribution of funds for relief among Polish refugees in Portugal were accused of systematically refusing requests for financial assistance made of them by Polish Jews. Kalman Stein, a Polish Jewish communal worker who had taken on a propaganda mission in Lisbon on behalf of the Polish government, testified that these committees were dominated by members of OZON or Endecja "who had discarded nothing from their antisemitic baggage of former days."[43] Moreover, according to Stein, neither the Polish Legation to Portugal nor the Polish Consulate in Lisbon could be counted upon to intervene in the Jewish interest. The latter especially, he claimed, was, according to the prevailing opinion, "not only antisemitic, but downright Jew-baiting [*nie tylko antysemita, ale wręcz żydożerca*]"; from it Jewish citizens could expect not mere unresponsiveness and lack of cooperation but active efforts to place obstacles in their way to obtaining the needed help.[44] Indeed, on 10 October 1940 a conference of representatives of Jews of Polish origin residing in Portugal charged the legation and consulate with, among other things, refusal to acknowledge the validity of Polish passports belonging to Jews, denial to Jews of letters of recommendation needed to obtain entry visas to overseas destinations (most of the refugees had entered Portugal with transit visas and were under pressure from the Portuguese government to leave), and anti-Jewish discrimination in assigning places in a scheme to evacuate several hundred Polish citizens to Brazil.[45]

During the next several months complaints from Portugal continued, and they were joined by similar allegations from Polish Jews in other countries. On 23 November 1940 Schwarzbart protested to the Polish Foreign Ministry that Polish Jews in Vichy France were being systematically excluded from the welfare activities administered by the Polish Red Cross and by the special office that the government-in-exile had established to look after the interests of Polish citizens in the unoccupied zone. He subsequently raised the issue on several occasions, both with Zaleski and with Stańczyk, but apparently did not find the situation improved.[46] Moreover, both Schwarzbart and the Palestinian Reprezentacja remonstrated sharply on several occasions over the reportedly small percentage of Jews included among Polish citizens being evacuated from Romania, Hungary, and Yugoslavia under government auspices at the end of 1940 and the beginning of 1941.[47] Even those few Jews who were evacuated, the Reprezentacja contended, were, with few exceptions, denied aid by Polish representatives in Istanbul once they reached that first transit station.[48] The Reprezentacja further charged that the Polish consul-general in Jerusalem, Witold Korsak, had refused to distribute funds that had been allocated by the government for assistance to Polish Jewish refugees in Palestine.[49] All of this, claimed Schwarzbart, vitiated the spirit of the declaration of 3 November.[50]

To many Jewish leaders, in the face of what Jews regarded as so many violations of Stańczyk's pledge, whatever basis for a policy of restraint might have existed in the wake of a declaration was significantly eroded. By April the Board of Deputies, which had for all intents remained silent on Polish Jewish affairs since the immediate aftermath of the November symposium, had come to the conclusion that verbal promises by Polish leaders were not to be taken seriously, and it took under active consideration a proposal to request the intervention of the British Home and Foreign Offices in matters in which it regarded the Polish government's behavior as unsatisfactory.[51] In the same month the World Jewish Congress actually did bring its complaints against the Polish government before the British foreign secretary.[52] The Bund, which before November had pressed the government to issue a declaration, seeing in it a political step of potentially great moment, now declared that the developments that had followed it had rendered Stańczyk's proclamation no more than "a paper promise."[53] Hence it was not surprising to find that a report on the Jewish press in the United States, prepared for the government by the Polish Consulate-General in New York on 15 April, noted with alarm that American Jewish opinion had taken a markedly unfavorable turn for Poland during the previous month.[54] It seems that by mid-1941 Jews throughout the world had lost all confidence that the government-in-exile could be dealt with any differently from Poland's prewar regime.

The upshot of this pessimistic turn was a marked change in the tone and manner in which Jewish organizations addressed the Polish government. Disappointed with the practical results of the Stańczyk declaration, they now began adamantly to demand not simply a promise regarding Jewish rights in the Poland of the future but concrete actions designed to indicate that the regime was actually working in the present to meet the specific desires of Polish Jewry. Between April and July 1941 the American Jewish Congress, the Bund, and the Reprezentacja all addressed lengthy and rather pugnacious memoranda to the government, insisting upon, among other things, the promulgation of an act repealing all anti-Jewish legislation and forbidding all discriminatory practices that had been enacted by the prewar regime or carried on with its approval; the liquidation and prohibition of all Polish-language publications containing uncomplimentary references to Jews; the repudiation of the concept that mass Jewish emigration from Poland was an essential element in the solution of the Polish Jewish problem; and the adoption of a program aimed at encouraging Polish resistance to Nazi anti-Jewish measures and at uprooting anti-Jewish prejudice among the Polish community, both in Poland and abroad.[55] These demands spelled out clearly what Jews had understood to be implicit in the Stańczyk declaration. Yet perhaps even more significant for the future of Polish-Jewish relations was the strong implication in all three documents that visible progress toward fulfillment of these demands was a precondition for active Jewish involvement in the service of Poland's political aims. In the view of the three organizations submitting the memoranda, the Jews of Poland had without question discharged their civic obligations toward their country to the fullest, both through their participation in the civil and military defense of the country during the September campaign and through their creation of a vital and active Jewish underground movement in the occupied homeland.[56] These things alone, the organizations felt, should already have induced the government-in-exile to take of its own accord the specific actions for which they now pressed. Instead, they lamented, Jewish loyalty had been rewarded with behavior reminiscent of the prewar days.[57] Further, the documents suggested, Jews throughout the world would feel motivated actively to advance the cause of renewed Polish independence largely to the extent to which they could expect postwar Poland to be governed by a regime devoted to "democracy and freedom, equality and social justice."[58] This point was most forcefully made in the memorandum of the Reprezentacja:

> The Reprezentacja stands in close, direct contact with the authoritative Jewish organizations, including the Jewish Agency for Palestine, Jewish World Congress [*sic*], World Center of Agudas Yisroel, American Jewish Congress, Board of Deputies, and others. Happily we are able to state that in the case of all of these organizations we have encountered a lively and highly sympathetic interest in Polish matters, fused with the conviction that the Polish Republic that will be recalled to life following the collective victory of those fighting for the freedom of nations over our common enemy will be a just mother to all of her sons. It will continue to be the task of the Reprezentacja to activate the above-mentioned organizations on behalf of the goals [of democracy, freedom, equality, and social justice] which it has set for itself. However, we expect from the government such comportment with regard to the Jewish question as will arouse general confidence and trust that equal rights for Jews in the future Poland will be secured in fact.[59]

This was a far cry from the intimation that some Polish officials had sensed during the early months of the war that world Jewry was inclined to stand with Poland against Russia in the dispute over the border between the two countries, and it indicated that what the Poles had hoped would be the major political benefit of the declaration of 3 November had not been, at least immediately, forthcoming. Indeed, the Reprezentacja, which had been approached directly, if unofficially, at the end of December 1940 by Mirosław Arciszewski of the Foreign Ministry with the question of the extent to which the government could count upon organized Jewish support for Poland's territorial demands in the east, steadfastly refused to commit itself on this issue.[60] It even appears that this organization tacitly rejected the proposition that support for the Polish cause ought to be regarded as one of its primary tasks.[61] A similar lack of overt concern for purely Polish interests was betrayed at this time as well by the Bund and the American Jewish Congress. The former angered its allies in the Polish Socialist Party by proposing a text for a Polish radio broadcast to Jews in the occupied homeland that omitted any expression of hope for the restoration of Poland's independence,[62] while in the latter's name Tartakower somewhat tactlessly told Sikorski that Polish Jews would prefer to fulfill their military obligations in a Jewish national army (if such existed) rather than with the Polish forces.[63]

All of this was deeply disturbing to Schwarzbart, who, apparently alone among Jewish spokesmen at the time, believed that the Stańczyk declaration, issued in response to Jewish demands, obligated Jews to reciprocate by enlisting diligently in the service of the Polish cause.[64] Indeed, even in the face of what seemed to him, no less than to other Jewish leaders, strong evidence that there was no sincere Polish intention to live up to the spirit of the labor minister's pledge, he continued to believe that Polish Jewry must cultivate a selflessly patriotic image in Polish circles. He also continued to advocate patient, behind-the-scenes negotiation within the established framework of the Polish political system as the preferred means of achieving improved conditions for Polish Jews.[65] He feared profoundly the possible backlash that the unrelenting exercise of public pressure upon the government by Jewish organizations, or even the continued private expression of dissatisfaction unmitigated by periodic public statements of sympathy for Poland and support for its aims, might arouse.[66] The Bund's "dogmatism," as he described its attitude, seemed to him "craziness" and "political stupidity";[67] the posture of the Reprezentacja, he felt, "sabotaged . . . [his] work and action."[68] He believed that the exposés of Polish antisemitic literature published periodically by the *Jewish Chronicle* indicated that the newspaper lacked "a sense of proportion in statesmanship,"[69] and he advised Stephen Wise that the "mostly hostile and protesting" character of the World Jewish Congress's contacts with the government had caused the regime to take a "very critical and cautious" attitude toward its relations with that agency.[70]

Schwarzbart's fears were not without basis. The continued flow of Jewish complaints and the apathetic attitude that many Jewish leaders seemed to demonstrate toward the Polish cause were greatly resented by the Poles. The government had taken a substantial risk in issuing a public statement favorable to Jewish interests. Stańczyk's speech of 3 November had done nothing to raise the regime's prestige in the occupied homeland and may even have done it a fair amount of harm.[71] The situation, in fact, was such that officials in the British Foreign Office expressed worry lest Sikorski "antagonize many sections of Polish opinion" by appearing too accommodating toward the demands that the American Jewish Congress had made of him.[72] The government had been willing to take this risk in the expectation of reaping certain tangible political rewards; when that expectation remained unfulfilled, an angry and bitter response was quite natural.[73] Further, the Polish authorities believed from their perspective that the Jewish charges were unfair and that in no sense could their behavior be reasonably interpreted as antisemitic. This was the message that the director of the Nationalities Department of the Ministry of Information, Olgierd Górka, brought to representatives of the Jewish press in Britain, Palestine, and the United States, at a meeting called at his request on 6 March 1941.[74] In his opening statement at this meeting, Górka claimed that "no member of the Government, and furthermore, no politically responsible person in emigration, has ever expressed, either in word or in print, anything of an antisemitic character or tone." While assuring the assembled Jewish journalists that his government had no intention of avoiding valid criticism, he argued that the recent condemnation of the regime voiced by Jewish spokesmen had been "one-sided." He thus called for "more balance in the method of conveying information."[75]

What did this balance imply from the Polish point of view? It required, first of all, in Górka's words, that Jews "show as lively an interest in the advocates of cooperation with Polish Jewry as that which all the antisemites enjoy." Such advocates of cooperation had spoken out recently and had published their views in Polish-language newspapers, yet, claimed Górka, "they pass without the least echo or reference in the Jewish press, or in the British press either."[76] This was the case, he complained, despite the fact that "friendly attitudes toward the Jewish problem in Poland" were characteristic of "important and responsible people," while the organizers of such unofficial publications as *Jestem Polakiem* were "simply a little group of irresponsible adolescents who have revealed an extreme lack of national discipline." The attention that organized Jewry paid to this admittedly antisemitic publication and the conclusions drawn from its existence regarding the attitude of the government as a whole toward the Jewish question seemed to him out of proportion to the newspaper's actual significance. Furthermore, he contended that precisely out of a sense of national discipline, those representatives of political groups which Jews often regarded as hostile, who had

been co-opted into the government or National Council in the conviction that the exile regime must reflect as broadly as possible the
ideological spectrum of Polish life, had loyally refrained from turning
the Jewish question into a major political issue. "That is a simple,
indubitable fact which nonetheless is one of basic principle," Górka
observed; "and I would be delighted if you [spokesmen for the Jewish press] took it into account."[77]

But what, asked the London correspondent for the New York Yiddish-language dailies, *Morgen Zhurnal* and *Forverts*, in the wake of
these remarks, about the harsh comments of Dominik Węgierski, or
the recent book by Retinger, which advocated mass emigration as the
only realistic solution to Poland's Jewish problem? Górka replied that
he had not found anything in Retinger's book that could reasonably
be termed antisemitic. The mere suggestion of the need for emigration, he claimed, need not be regarded by Jews with alarm, for this
was a concept that many Jews supported as well.[78] Indeed, although
on this occasion he did not raise the point,[79] he might have mentioned that many Poles who had taken this attitude also strongly
supported Jewish aspirations for an independent national home,[80]
and that even Węgierski believed that a basis existed for negotiating
a Jewish exodus "amicably and by mutual understanding."[81] In fact,
none of the writers whose current books had become the focus of
Polish-Jewish controversy had suggested that Jews who did not wish
to leave Poland should be forced to do so; they would simply cease to
be regarded as members of a distinct national minority and would
henceforth be thought of entirely as "Polish citizens of different ex-
traction or different religion."[82] With regard to Węgierski's book,
Górka admitted the existence of antisemitic passages, but categorically dissociated the government from them: "no one could defend
Węgierski's publication of comments that Jews behaved improperly
in September [1939]. . . ."[83] Had he so chosen, however, he could
have pointed out that Węgierski had not advocated that Poles take
unilateral anti-Jewish action; that he had suggested that non-Jews
were "largely responsible for that warping of the Jewish soul" which
he had described; and that he had sought "to offer a defence of the
Jews on the charge of helping the Bolsheviks and thus assisting in
the downfall of the Polish State."[84] It was in fact possible to argue
that Węgierski's comments had been meant merely to explain the
sources of past Polish-Jewish difficulties, rather than to serve as a

justification for further curtailment of Jewish rights. As it happened, this was the approach taken in the review of the book that appeared in *Free Europe*, which angered many Jewish leaders: the reviewer found Węgierski to be a "fair-minded observer who maintains a balanced view of things," and praised his "sane" approach to Jewish matters.[85]

The sensitivity that Jews displayed toward public expressions on the Jewish question by Poles thus seemed to most Polish observers highly exaggerated, and the speed with which such statements were regularly condemned by Jewish organizations was deeply resented in official Polish circles.[86] Stroński, for one, appeared more than a bit perturbed that he had read the text of the letter addressed to him by the Council of Polish Jews in Great Britain regarding the operation of the Polish radio service in Jewish newspapers four days before personally receiving the communication and two days before the date on which the actual letter had been typed.[87] This was all the more angering to the information minister because the immediate impetus for the council's protest had come from an incorrect understanding of a specific statement made during a recent broadcast. This misunderstanding, in turn, was in itself rooted, Stroński believed, in a generally mistaken impression of the manner in which his ministry viewed the Jewish question.[88] Stroński felt that the government information services handled Jewish affairs adequately and could not reasonably be faulted by organized Jewry. At one point he even attempted to prove this claim with irony, noting that Seyda had once complained to Sikorski that Polish radio broadcasts on the Jewish question appeared excessively pro-Jewish and were thus bound to do serious damage to the government's standing with the Polish community in the occupied homeland.[89]

The remark by Seyda that Stroński quoted underscored once again the very real difficulties facing the government in undertaking the sort of educational mission within the Polish community demanded of it by Jewish leaders. Polish officials regularly maintained that they were doing all that they could in this area, especially in regard to the problem of improving relations between Poles and Jews in the armed forces, but that the business of uprooting prejudice was a difficult one that required for its success, among other things, a measure of patience and forbearance from the Jewish side. When, for example, Schwarzbart raised with Sikorski the difficulties faced by Jewish soldiers in the Polish First Brigade in Scotland, the prime minister replied that he had personally investigated the situation and had taken concrete steps to remedy it—including transferring seventy officers who had contributed to the difficult atmosphere. He promised that he would eventually be able to bring matters under control to Jewish satisfaction. "But," he requested of the Jewish representative, "don't scream because of a few verbal provocations."[90] Similarly, a spokesman for the Polish General Staff, after reviewing with Schwarzbart a series of measures undertaken to improve relations in the ranks, requested that the Jewish leader encourage those members of Parliament who were wont to complain in the House of Commons about the treatment of Polish Jewish soldiers to check with the Polish military authorities before making public statements on the matter. "An entire year's worth of *Jestem Polakiem*," he remarked, "cannot do as much harm to Polish Jews as can one parliamentary interpellation by Mr. [Sidney] Silverman."[91]

A similar plea for patience was discernible in Polish reactions to Jewish charges of discrimination in the treatment of Jewish refugees. Polish officials who dealt with refugee matters regularly pointed out in response to such accusations that they were bound by serious objective constraints that often prevented them from meeting Jewish requests for assistance. Stanisław Schmitzek, the Ministry of Social Welfare's delegate for Polish refugee affairs in Portugal, indicated in several reports that he was limited in his ability to arrange for the resettlement of Jewish refugees overseas by the overtly or covertly anti-Jewish immigration policies of several potential receiving countries.[92] Other countries, he added, were not amenable to receiving any Polish refugees, Jewish or non-Jewish, except in small numbers and under stringent conditions.[93] Similar difficulties were also cited by Polish authorities in the Far East.[94] Polish officials consistently emphasized as well that the funds available to them for relief activities were limited and that scarcity brought with it the need to establish priorities for the expenditure of whatever monies were at hand. Schmitzek, Stanisław Zabiełło, who was director-general of the Polish offices in France, and Witold Korsak, Polish consul-general in Jerusalem, all solved this problem, at least in part, by eliminating from consideration requests for assistance from those who might be able to obtain aid from some other source. Evidently, since Jewish charitable organizations were active in Portugal, Palestine, and unoccupied France, the Polish officials in these countries felt justified in not concerning themselves extensively with Jewish requests for help.[95]

This attitude of the Polish authorities was reinforced in Portugal and France by the fact that only a minority of the Jewish refugees in these countries had actually fled from German-occupied Poland at the outbreak of the war. Most had emigrated well before 1939 and had taken up permanent residence in Belgium, Holland, or France. These had become refugees only in May and June 1940 with the advance of the German armies in the West.[96] Among them there was apparently a sizable number that had left Poland in early childhood, had little or no emotional attachment to it, and spoke no Polish, yet by the same token had not become citizens of any other state. Polish officials in France and Portugal were generally reluctant to regard assistance for such refugees as of equal priority with aid for those who had resided continuously in Poland up to the time of the German invasion and who intended to return after the war.

Such reluctance, moreover, possessed a definite legal foundation: according to the Polish citizenship law of 31 March 1938, a Polish citizen who had lived abroad continuously for a period of five years and "had given up all contact with the Polish state" could be deprived of citizenship.[97] In September 1938 additional legislation had been enacted requiring all Poles living outside the country to obtain endorsements in their passports affirming that their citizenship had not been revoked. Without such endorsements, according to the law, their Polish passports were not to be regarded as valid. These laws were a source of discontent among Polish Jews, for it seems that they had been employed before the war in a discriminatory fashion as a device for revoking the citizenship of Jewish emigrants.[98] Now, however, government representatives such as Schmitzek and Zabiełło felt that they had no choice but to offer assistance only to those who could produce valid documentary proof of Polish citizenship. As Zabiełło noted in a comprehensive memorandum to the Foreign Ministry purporting to elucidate the entire matter of relief for Polish Jews in unoccupied France, ignoring this requirement might well have opened the door to the filing of fictitious claims by Jews who either "never had possessed Polish citizenship or had forfeited it long ago."[99]

Thus, claimed Polish spokesmen, any fair and objective appraisal of the situation demanded the conclusion that the government's attitudes and actions with regard to Jewish affairs were proper and that Jewish accusations concerning "the prevalence of antisemitism in Polish circles close to" it were groundless.[100] In the event, as might be expected, both sides seem to have overstated their cases. It was, for example, quite unfair for Jewish spokesmen to charge *Dziennik Polski* and *Free Europe* during the period in question with a general neglect of the problems of Polish Jewry or with presenting Jewish issues in a light unfavorable to Jewish interests. The former newspaper, in the aftermath of the controversy surrounding the article on the condition of Catholics in the Warsaw ghetto, regularly printed short releases on the treatment of Jews under German and Soviet occupation and also published several longer pieces encouraging Polish-Jewish solidarity and condemning German efforts to drive a wedge between the two peoples.[101] Similarly, the latter, in its first issue, emphatically supported the right of the Jewish people to "freedom and civil liberties within a democratic framework of states," and thereafter frequently opened its columns to Jewish spokesmen promoting their cause.[102] There were also other Jewish charges that appear to have been factually untrue, such as the contention that only the Polish authorities in Lisbon were preventing the removal of Polish Jewish refugees from Portugal to Brazil. In actuality the Brazilian government had made it its policy since 1937 to restrict severely the entry of Jews into its territory, a fact that makes the Polish denial of responsibility for the absence of Jews among the evacuees to Brazil quite plausible.[103]

On the other hand, it does seem to have been the case that the attitude shown by Polish officials in Lisbon in their day-to-day contacts with Jews was generally a hostile one. Government officials in London, at least, were well convinced of this fact.[104] Moreover, there is evidence to suggest that some Polish officials abroad may have knowingly interfered with the welfare of Jewish refugees under their jurisdiction. Korsak in Jerusalem, as a result of Jewish pressure, received a special allocation of two thousand pounds sterling from the Ministry of Social Welfare for support of Polish Jewish refugees in Palestine; yet of this sum he evidently spent only seven hundred pounds.[105] Similarly, Zabiełło in France appears to have played a critical role in thwarting a proposal by the American Commission for Polish Relief to allocate 2 million French francs for relief for Polish Jews in the unoccupied zone.[106] It seems, too, that Zabiełło, while adamant about demanding valid proof of Polish citizenship from Jews applying for assistance, did not apply the same stringent standards to ethnic Poles.[107] Indeed, the fact that many Polish Jews had been deprived of their citizenship by the discriminatory policies of the previous regime appears to have been willingly exploited by Polish officials, particularly in France and Portugal, as a convenient means of reducing the numbers of those whom they were legally obliged to aid.

However, it must be kept in mind that the untoward behavior of certain Polish overseas officials toward Jewish refugees was not condoned by the Foreign and Social Welfare Ministries, to whom these representatives were responsible. Both Stańczyk and Zaleski intervened periodically on behalf of the principle of equal aid for Jews. The former was especially forceful in telling Schmitzek that "the situation described [by the Jewish refugees in Portugal] . . . is intolerable" and in demanding its immediate rectification.[108] For the most part, though, their actions were ineffective. In general, it seems that although senior officials were usually cognizant of the need to avoid scrupulously the appearance of any sort of active anti-Jewish discrimination, they were often not able to keep lower-ranking civil servants and military authorities from allowing anti-Jewish prejudices to influence their actions. This inability in turn necessarily limited their own freedom of action in Jewish matters.

The prevailing state of affairs was exemplified perhaps most graphically in a disagreement that broke out among Polish representatives in Canada in mid-1941 over the question of facilitating the entry of Jewish refugees into the Dominion. Evidently Tadeusz Romer, Poland's ambassador in Tokyo, had succeeded in arranging for the removal of several dozen Polish citizens from Japan to Canada, on the understanding that they would enlist in the Polish volunteer force then being raised in North America.[109] Since some 95 percent of the Polish refugees in Japan at the time were of Jewish origin,[110] it is not surprising that among the first twenty-three who arrived in Vancouver, there were sixteen Jews, including seven out of eight officers.[111] Apparently, however, Polish military officials in Canada were taken aback by this high proportion of Jews; they worried that it would have a negative effect upon recruitment efforts and were especially concerned lest Poles balk at accepting Jews as colleagues. The commanding officer of the Polish forces in Canada gathered statements from a group of non-Jewish officers testifying to the difficulties that would surely follow the attachment of Jewish soldiers to the Polish troops and sent them to Sikorski, evidently with a request that the commander-in-chief himself discourage the evacuation of potential Jewish soldiers from Japan. This idea, however, did not meet with the approval of the Polish legate in Ottawa, Wiktor Podoski, who promptly wrote to Sikorski urging emphatic support for the right of Polish Jews to serve in the Polish armed forces. "Let me point out," he cautioned, "that a negative decision [i.e., one that effectively prevented Jewish volunteers from Japan from joining the ranks of the Polish Army in Canada] would be understood as a rejection of these people solely on racial grounds." Moreover, he indicated, the matter would not be overlooked by the Jewish press, "which still constantly mentions your pledge in New York that Polish Jews will enjoy equal rights with Poles by virtue of their fulfillment of equal duties." Here, Podoski reminded the premier, that promise was being put to the test.[112]

It is not known how Sikorski handled this situation. It is clear, however, that from then on "the religious and racial composition of the Polish emigrant community in Canada" had to be considered by the government in deciding whether to make further efforts to permit additional Polish Jewish immigration into the country.[113] Moreover, it seems that certain civil and military officials below the top policy-making and plenipotentiary rank, by virtue of being charged with the day-to-day implementation of the government's declared principles on the Jewish question, found themselves able, deliberately or unconsciously, to thwart the government's intentions when these appeared excessively beneficent. Thus, for example, a lecture prepared for the Polish troops in Scotland as part of an official effort to improve the relations between Poles and Jews in the ranks wound up repeating the decades-old charges that Jews preferred Germany and Russia to Poland and that the Jewish-dominated press in the United States was conducting anti-Polish propaganda.[114]

Though Sikorski and his government may not have wanted such incidents to occur, it does not appear that they were overly successful in stopping them. It was not, however, they consistently maintained, for lack of trying. The British Foreign Office, for one, appears to have been convinced of their sincerity. Commenting on complaints addressed to Foreign Secretary Anthony Eden by the World Jewish Congress on 1 May 1941, for example, the acting first secretary of the Foreign Office's Central Department, Frank Kenyon Roberts, noted that "the official attitude of the Polish Government seems to be beyond reproach."[115] Jewish leaders, on the other hand, tended for the most part to insist that the Polish government was directly responsible for the behavior of all those acting in the name of the Polish state, and that as a government it possessed sufficient powers to control that behavior if it sincerely desired to do so. They were as a result generally unwilling to extend to the Polish authorities the measure of patience that the latter felt they deserved. On the contrary, though there was disagreement among them about the way in which it ought to be applied, virtually all of them, including Schwarzbart, continued to believe that regular pressure to force government action toward realizing the principles of the Stańczyk declaration in practice remained an unquestionable necessity.

Thus, by mid-1941, it was clear that the attempts of Polish spokesmen to explain their case to Jewish leaders had failed. In the meantime, nothing had happened to make the Poles any less sensitive to public criticism. On the contrary, the government's continued inability to silence Jewish complaints, let alone its lack of success in turning world Jewry into a reliable political ally, made the anti-Jewish backlash feared by Schwarzbart ever a more real possibility. Ironically, it was Schwarzbart himself who was among the first to experience its force. When, beginning in April 1941, he called upon the National Council to take two specific steps aimed at correcting past injustices toward Polish Jewry, the incipient hostile repercussions of Jewish pressure came loudly to the surface.

Schwarzbart, in keeping with his preference for exploiting established political channels in the struggle to realize Jewish demands vis-à-vis the Polish government, believed the National Council to be the body most suited to implementing the principles of the government's declaration of 3 November.[116] Hence, in the aftermath of the council's meeting of 26 March 1941, at which the Peasant Party formally announced its solidarity with Stańczyk's statement and two members of PPS offered similar indications of support,[117] the Jewish representative introduced two motions intended to induce the government to follow up its promise of Jewish equality with concrete action. The first demanded that the government repeal the provision of the citizenship law of 1938 which allowed the state to revoke the citizenship of a Polish citizen who had resided abroad continuously for five years, and which since its introduction had been applied principally against Jews. The second called upon the government to "issue as soon as possible an appropriate document stating that all executive decrees and administrative orders which tend to discriminate against any segment of the population either de jure or de facto will be repealed."[118] Both motions were included in the council's agenda and referred for consideration to its Legal-Constitutional Committee, of which Schwarzbart was a member and Herman Lieberman the chairman.

The committee's discussion of the first motion began on 28 May.[119] In presenting it, Schwarzbart indicated that over a year earlier the government had actually issued an order noting repeated past misapplications of the law by certain officials and suspending its enforcement except in cases in which a Polish emigrant had engaged in flagrant anti-Polish activity abroad. Since that time, he noted, not only had there not been a single instance of citizenship revocation under the law in question, but out of 118 requests for renewal of citizenship that had been presented to the government during its stay in France, 112 had been granted. Schwarzbart held that by not applying the law, the government had tacitly admitted its inequity; therefore its repeal would be consistent with the regime's oft-declared policy of placing the future Poland upon foundations of equal justice for all. On the other hand, he regarded rejection of his motion as tantamount to calling for the law's renewed enforcement.

His arguments, however, proved singularly unpersuasive. Only Lieberman, the PPS deputy of Jewish origin, sided firmly with Schwarzbart, stating that he viewed "the absence of a clear will for repeal [of the citizenship law] . . . as [indicative of] a form of opportunism and a lack of sufficient consistency in the fight against the evil and immoral survivals of the period before the war."[120] All other members of the committee opposed the motion. To be sure, there appears to have been a general consensus that the entire matter of the regulation of citizenship would need to be examined at some point in the future, but this conclusion was reached for reasons having little to do with the possibility that the law might lead to discrimination against a particular segment of the population. On the contrary, Seyda, representing the government in his capacity as minister of justice,[121] found Lieberman's suggestion that failure to repeal the law was to be equated with the toleration of evil to be insulting to the state.[122] Both Seyda and Labor Party representative Michał Kwiatkowski specifically denied that the law had been misapplied against Jews, the latter stating that he had observed "an immeasurable number of cases" in which the citizenship of "genuine Poles [*rdzennych Polaków*]" had been revoked under its provisions.[123] From Schwarzbart's perspective, the result of the discussion was that the committee turned a deaf ear to his plea to rectify a past wrong, in clear opposition to the government's professed intention to repudiate the errors of the prewar regime. Through a clever parliamentary maneuver, his motion was effectively laid on the table. In the end, it never came to a vote.[124]

If, in the final analysis, the discussion of Schwarzbart's first motion revealed the Legal-Constitutional Committee's unwillingness to take concrete action to remove the cause of a Jewish complaint, the debate over his second proposal, which began on 13 June, revealed outright hostility toward Polish Jewry as a whole.[125] In his presentation the Jewish representative spoke at first in general terms of the manner in which the prewar regime had enacted legislation and instituted administrative practices contrary to the guarantees of citizens' rights contained in the Polish constitution. In order to illustrate the type of legislation and administrative practices to which he referred, he recited a list of devices by which the prewar regime had played a role in subverting the civil rights of Polish Jewry. He stressed, however, that he employed these particular examples only because it was with them that he was most familiar, noting at the same time that other members of the council had on previous occasions called attention to additional instances of the phenomenon he described. The disregard that prewar governments had shown for the Polish constitution and for the principles of civic equality had, Schwarzbart warned, tainted Poland as a "semi-totalitarian, semi-fascist" state in the eyes of the nations of the West. Thus, to his mind, his motion gave the National Council a unique opportunity to strike a blow at Poland's prewar legacy, and by so doing to change the country's image for the better.

This argument turned out to be even less convincing than the one that Schwarzbart had employed in support of his first motion. Three times during his speech he was interrupted by the independent deputy Stanisław Jóźwiak, who was in attendance despite not being a member of the Legal-Constitutional Committee, with angry denials that the prewar Polish government had ever engaged in activities that could fairly be called anti-Jewish. Jóźwiak continued to develop this theme later in the meeting, when the committee granted him special permission to speak from the floor. He was supported in his contention by Endek representative Zofia Zaleska. Both Jóźwiak and Zaleska maintained, for example, that the law restricting the kosher slaughtering of meat, which Schwarzbart had cited as the prime example of antisemitic legislation enacted in the years immediately prior to the outbreak of war, had in reality been introduced for purely economic reasons and had provided for kosher slaughtering sufficient for Jewish religious needs.[126] They also justified the discriminatory hiring and admissions practices of many Polish businesses and universities on the basis of the need to eliminate the disproportionate representation of Jews in commerce and the free professions, and they saw nothing reprehensible in the common practice of segregating Jewish students in university lecture halls. Jóźwiak stated categorically that Jews had no cause to complain over their treatment at the hands of Poles through the years, and that if they continued to do so they would merely invite hatred. Michał Kwiatkowski warned that Poles would take grave offense at the suggestion hidden in Schwarzbart's motion that Poland was an antisemitic country. Zaleska, Jóźwiak, and the independent deputy Tytus Filipowicz, who was generally identified with the political left, all condemned Jewry as well for blackening Poland's name among the nations and hinted with no great subtlety that Jews throughout the world almost instinctively wished Poland ill. They chided Jews for turning their relations with Poles into a matter of international attention when instances of discrimination in other countries aroused, they argued, not nearly the same measure of protest. Filipowicz even went so far as to claim that "just as there is antisemitism among Poles, there is 'antigoyism' among Jews," and charged Jews with boycotting Christian businesses, conspiring to keep Christians out of managerial positions, and teaching their children not to buy from non-Jews.[127]

In short, the debate over Schwarzbart's second motion set loose a barrage of invective incompatible with the light in which the government wished to be viewed in the West. There was, however, little danger that this outburst would result in any serious public relations damage. Although Schwarzbart's motion was defeated in committee and not returned to the council plenum for action,[128] an alternate motion by Władysław Banaczyk of the Peasant Party, calling upon the government "to undertake at the earliest possible moment a review of the Polish legal regulations in force and to repeal such regulations as contradict the Government's declaration of 18 December 1939[129] and the welfare of a state founded upon democratic legal concepts," was adopted by the committee, with minor modifications, on 4 July 1941.[130] In this manner the Polish authorities could maintain that the committee had not only not rejected the idea of repealing existing discriminatory legislation but had even mandated the establishment of a mechanism for effecting such repeal. Indeed, Banaczyk's motion did appear on the surface significantly broader in scope than Schwarzbart's. But in light of the discussion that had preceded its passage, it was obvious that the committee's understanding of democracy, civic equality, and civil rights differed substantially from that held by Jewish leaders.

Moreover, the committee appeared to view the suggestion that Poles could take positive action to improve Polish-Jewish relations not merely as a nuisance but as a malicious provocation. The image of the Jew as an innate and inveterate enemy of Poland—an image whose influence had evidently receded during the previous nine months sufficiently to allow the government to consider seriously the possibility that world Jewry might be enlisted in support of the Polish cause—had not been laid to rest entirely, and against the background of Jewish behavior in the aftermath of the Stańczyk declaration it was perhaps only a matter of time before at least some segments of the Polish political leadership came to invoke it again actively.

Such renewed assertion of the doctrine of ineluctable Jewish malevolence toward Poland, however, coupled with the credibility that the failure of Polish overtures toward Jewry during the previous months stood to lend it, presented Polish policy makers with a serious dilemma. Although Polish hopes for the support of Jewry in the international political arena had been dealt a serious blow during the first half of 1941, most Polish leaders continued to perceive the extent of Jewish influence in that arena as great. In particular, they appear to have attached great significance to the role played by American Jewry in shaping the attitudes of the U.S. government toward the Polish question. In a letter to Interior Minister Kot, written on 16 January 1941, Sylwester Gruszka, Poland's consul-general in New York, recalled the influence that American Jews had wielded, for good and for bad, in the reconstitution of an independent Polish state, and suggested that the skill with which Polish diplomats now approached American Jewish leaders could have a decisive effect upon Poland's diplomatic future.[131] Gruszka continued to emphasize this point with Jan Ciechanowski, who replaced Potocki as Polish ambassador in Washington on 6 March. In a lengthy memorandum prepared less than two weeks after the new envoy's arrival, he outlined the organizational structure of American Jewry and discussed the necessity of altering what he termed the prevailing "anti-Polish attitudes" within it. In this survey he portrayed the major American Jewish political bodies—especially the American Jewish Committee, the American Jewish Congress, and the Jewish Labor Committee—as rich and dynamic organizations whose highly respected leadership possessed substantial connections in the most powerful circles in American life.[132]

In the circumstances in which Polish diplomacy found itself during the first half of 1941, this was a force that Polish leaders could not afford to antagonize. Britain continued to offer indications that it was interested in a rapprochement with the Soviet Union and that it might be willing to offer territorial concessions at Poland's expense in order to obtain it,[133] to the point where from the Polish perspective the cultivation of an American counterweight to this tendency became urgent.[134] Moreover, the passage of the Lend-Lease Act in March 1941 raised Polish hopes of benefiting from U.S. military aid.[135] If Polish leaders were now beginning to doubt that Jews would ever intervene on Poland's behalf in matters such as these, many of them still held out the hope of inducing Jewish neutrality. Ironically, the very reawakening of the image of Jewry as a historic Polish nemesis during this time could be seen as mandating a policy of conciliation toward Jewish organizations, which in turn required the suppression of the open anti-Jewish hostility to which that image gave rise.

What to Poles appeared to be the highly volatile attitude of at least some Jewish leaders was brought home to the government in early April, following a meeting in Washington between Ciechanowski and a combined delegation from the American and World Jewish Congresses. It had been hoped in government circles that the new ambassador would be able to develop a good working relationship with American Jewry;[136] he was himself of Jewish lineage and had during his term as director-general of the Foreign Ministry been an advocate of the cultivation of a Jewish-Polish alliance.[137] However, his first encounter with Jewish leaders proved a notable failure. Stephen Wise and Nahum Goldmann, chairman of the Administrative Committee of the World Jewish Congress, were displeased with Ciechanowski's responses to their expressed concerns; the ambassador had denied, they claimed, that antisemitic propaganda had been promulgated in the Polish Army, and he had pronounced himself opposed to the repeal of anti-Jewish legislation enacted by the prewar regime.[138] Ciechanowski, for his part, was worried when he received the Jewish leaders' written summary of their meeting. He felt that its statements "differed greatly" from what he believed he had said, and he deferred to Sikorski (who was then in the United States for top-level meetings with American officials) for instructions about how to proceed.[139]

Evidently the prime minister was also alarmed by this development. On 17 April he received Wise and Arieh Tartakower in New York in an effort to placate the Jewish spokesmen's anger.[140] According to Tartakower, Sikorski promised at this meeting that he would discuss with his government the possibility of action on the abolition of prewar anti-Jewish regulations and on the republication of the Stańczyk declaration under his own imprint.[141] This statement appears, despite its cautious wording, to have been regarded by Wise and Tartakower as satisfactory.[142] When Sikorski returned to London, he mentioned his meeting with the Jewish representatives in his report to the National Council, declaring at the same time that in his view antisemitism was inconsistent with the principles of liberalism and democracy in whose name the Allied war effort was being waged.[143] One week later the cabinet adopted a resolution condemning "the conduct of an antisemitic policy as harmful."[144]

The actual import of such proclamations, however, was nil. Sikorski and his cabinet may have expressed their disapproval of antisemitism, but from all that had transpired in the previous six months, it was clear that they understood this term quite differently than did Jewish leaders. The purpose of their statements was most probably merely to dissuade American Jewry from interfering with Polish overtures to the U.S. government while at the time committing the regime to no concrete action. Still, there were those within the government who felt that under the present circumstances, Sikorski ought to have engaged the Jewish leaders in confrontation, even at the risk of antagonizing them. Seyda, for one, sharply upbraided the prime minister for failing to deny categorically the existence of any anti-Jewish legal restrictions in prewar Poland that needed now to be nullified. "Raising such unfounded accusations against Poland," he wrote, foreshadowing the tone of the debate in the Legal-Constitutional Committee over Schwarzbart's second motion, which was to begin six days later, "causes the country heavy damage."[145] At the cabinet meeting of 11 June, at which the matter of a new declaration on the Jewish question was discussed, he continued to insist upon this point, expressing in addition serious reservations about several items in Stańczyk's earlier statement.[146] He even went so far as to reassure his party (Endecja) that no matter what Sikorski might have said to Wise and Tartakower, the government had never given actual formal approval to the Stańczyk declaration.[147]

These were sentiments that Sikorski and the government as a whole could no more afford to ignore than they could the possibility of doing damage to their cause by antagonizing Jewry. So strong were they that Sikorski actually felt compelled to offer his consent to Seyda's disclaimer of cabinet responsibility for the Stańczyk declaration.[148] As they rose in force toward mid-1941 against the background of the failed attempt to persuade organized Jewry to adopt an openly pro-Polish attitude, the prime minister and those who shared his perspective felt ever-growing frustration over a situation in which every step was seemingly mistaken. It is no wonder that when Schwarzbart met with the prime minister following the latter's return from America, he found him highly impatient and irritated with the Jewish question altogether. The Jewish representative recorded Sikorski's exasperation: "My God, how you [Jews] pester me constantly!"[149]

In these circumstances, some Polish leaders began again to consider seriously the possibility that their dilemma might be resolved through alliance with the Revisionist wing of the Zionist movement. The Revisionists were the one group among organized Jewry not likely to react in anger whenever a Polish public figure spoke of the desirability of mass Jewish emigration after the war, and they were also most desirous of developing a close working relationship with the Polish government.[150] A memo circulated in April among Polish officials in the United States by the Polish Embassy in Washington noted that "the position of the Revisionists seems to parallel our interests."[151] If then, it seemed, the Revisionists and their New Zionist Organization could win a position of influence among international Jewish bodies, the Poles would gain a congenial Jewish partner that would willingly fulfill the political mission that had been intended for Jewry as a whole.

Whether or not this strategy was a realistic one depended, of course, first of all upon whether the Revisionists could in fact become a major force in internal Jewish politics. On this question Polish opinion was divided. Consul-General Gruszka, in his survey of Jewish organizations in the United States, noted that the recent death of the Revisionist leader Jabotinsky had "set back plans for large-scale action by the New Zionist Organization in the United States and South America and created a scarcity of incoming funds which Jabotinsky was able to obtain from his many personal admirers." In any case, he claimed, "[Revisionist] neo-Zionism never had serious influence within the local community . . . , and the number of its advocates has always been small."[152] On the other hand, Stroński seems to have believed that Revisionist strength was on the rise. In a memorandum dated 24 May he noted two instances in which mainstream Zionist organizations had felt it necessary to invite Revisionist representation, and pointed to them as indicators of the growing weight carried by the Revisionists in Jewish circles.[153]

The Ministry of Information, under Stroński's direction, appears, moreover, to have been interested at this time in helping the Revisionists to augment their influence. *Free Europe* featured articles in February and March by Revisionist spokesmen Harry Schnurr and Abraham Abrahams, and it allowed the Revisionists the last word when these articles were attacked by Schwarzbart's personal secretary, Manfred Lachs.[154] Retinger, too, played a role in seeking to strengthen the Revisionist hand, promising Revisionist leaders in the United States that he would look into the possibility of obtaining a government subsidy for Revisionist publications and of furnishing political contacts for the Revisionists through the Polish Embassy in Washington.[155] In early May Retinger was approached by Interior Minister Kot with a request that he use his influence with Abrahams and with Irish Revisionist leader and Dail member Robert Briscoe toward obtaining Revisionist support for a Polish propaganda campaign in Ireland then set to begin.[156] Sikorski's secretary had long been the government's chief advocate of close association with the Revisionists, and it seems that by mid-1941 his perspective had gained broader acceptance in government circles. Indeed, the Washington embassy did play an important role in introducing Revisionist representatives to leading American journalists, clergymen, and political figures, and it appears that the Information Ministry did eventually subsidize the English-language Revisionist monthly, *Jewish Standard*.[157]

There were difficulties, however. For one thing, too close an association with the Revisionists was bound to antagonize the mainstream of organized Jewry no less than public statements by government officials favoring mass Jewish emigration from Poland after the war. This was a risk that the government does not appear to have been anxious to take.[158] For another, it was bound to antagonize the British government, for whom the Revisionist program for Palestine was anathema and who looked upon the call for mass Jewish emigration with great trepidation about its implications for British policy in the Near East.[159] For these reasons and others, the Poles refused during the period in question to accede to a request from Revisionists in Palestine to establish special Jewish units within the Polish Army. Though earlier this concept had appealed to certain Polish policy makers, its political complications now rendered it impossible to pursue.[160] Still, the government continued to view the conclusion of an alliance with the Revisionists as at least theoretically desirable. In advising the Polish Consulate-General in Jerusalem of the cabinet's negative decision regarding the creation of Jewish units, Sikorski instructed that the news be broken to Revisionist representatives "in the most gentle manner possible" and that the decision be attributed exclusively to Britain's unfriendly attitude toward the plan. He further advised that despite the government's inability to meet this particular Revisionist request, "non-obligating contact with the Revisionists is welcome."[161]

Here again, as earlier, the government's interest in the Revisionists brought little practical result. It did, however, indicate that for all of the changes that had taken place in its tactical approach to the Jewish question since its removal from France to England a year before, the government-in-exile persisted in mid-1941 in hoping that somehow the idea, favored at present only by the Revisionist faction, of mass voluntary Jewish emigration from Poland could be made acceptable both to organized world Jewry and to the Western powers as well. Indeed, in the dilemma into which the government's relations with Jewry had been thrust by the failure of the Stańczyk declaration to produce its desired effects, this seemed to at least some Polish leaders to be the only acceptable strategy.[162] In subsequent months Poles began to make overtures to the British government along these lines. Sikorski himself, upon his return from the United States in June, is reported to have sounded out a British cabinet member about the possibility of finding a suitable territory for Jewish colonization.[163] In any case, it is certain that by January 1942 he had become sufficiently bold to raise the issue informally with Foreign Secretary Eden.[164] These overtures were quickly rebuffed. Nevertheless, they demonstrated clearly that however much Jewish organizations had succeeded during the first two years of the war in sensitizing the Poles to the dangers of antagonizing Jewish opinion, they had not been able ultimately to dissuade them from their preference for an emigrationist solution to the Jewish question. On the contrary, developments in the eight months following the issuance of the Stańczyk declaration appear on reflection merely to have strengthened the Polish resolve to find a way to convince as many as possible of the justice and desirability of such an approach.

The first half of 1941, then, was a period of disappointment for both Poles and Jews. Far from witnessing an improvement in Polish-Jewish relations, this interval was characterized by a steady heightening of tension between the two groups, with each side demonstrating ever-more-obstinate attachment to the postures that had antagonized the other in the past. This deterioration in relations was to have crucial consequences for both sides, coming as it did on the eve of Germany's invasion of Russia—an event that changed the course of both Polish and Jewish history. For the Jews, the implications of the invasion as the catalyst for the inauguration of the so-called final solution to the Jewish question were not fully grasped until eighteen months later. But for the Poles, the radical alteration in the balance of forces in Polish-Allied-Soviet relations stemming from the German attack was felt immediately. Over the previous year the Polish government-in-exile had concluded that world Jewry could exercise significant influence upon that balance, if not for good, then certainly for ill. Now, with Poland's diplomatic position inestimably complicated by the alliance between its benefactor and its enemy, the problem of Polish-Jewish relations acquired an urgency for Polish policy makers greater than at any time since the close of the First World War.

RUSSIA

The German invasion of the Soviet Union on 22 June 1941—for all of the ferment it injected into Poland's relations with Britain and the United States—was viewed within the government-in-exile as on the whole a welcome development. The prospect that Soviet occupying forces would be driven from Poland's eastern territories by advancing German divisions, leaving the entire country united under the domination of a single conquering power, seemed at first to most Poles likely to help the cause of the eventual reconstruction of the Polish state within the frontiers of 1939.[1] Here the experience of the First World War seems to have exercised strong influence upon Polish thinking. If, many Polish leaders believed, Germany could manage to weaken Russia substantially before itself suffering ultimate defeat at the hands of the Western powers, Poland would be in an advantageous position to extract a favorable postwar settlement from both of its enemies.[2] At the time, this did not appear to them an unlikely possibility. The Soviet armed forces were regarded in Polish circles as unprepared to withstand the onslaught of the 160 German divisions massed along the Ribbentrop-Molotov line. Shortly before the launching of the invasion, Sikorski and Sir Stafford Cripps, the British ambassador in Moscow, had concluded that in the event of a German attack, the Russian defenses would "surely break down."[3] Raczyński even went so far as to suggest that "the USSR . . . will shortly either be completely defeated and broken up into small political units, or at any rate pushed well beyond the Soviet-Polish frontier of 1939."[4] To be sure, at least some Polish leaders were mindful of the danger in too rapid and complete a collapse of Soviet resistance. Sosnkowski, for one, warned Sikorski that "a swift and total German victory . . . could [lead to] . . . the recreation of a pro-German Lithuania to which the northern Polish territories are returned, the establishment of an independent Ukraine including the restoration of Lwów, Eastern Galicia, and Wołyń, and the creation of a reactionary, pro-German Russia with the return of Poland up to the territories annexed to the Reich." Barring this eventuality, though, Sosnkowski concurred with the prevailing Polish opinion that "the German-Soviet war represents a highly advantageous turn of events for Poland and its cause."[5]

Such an analysis of the new situation led the Polish government to perceive itself as in a position of relative diplomatic strength. The Soviets, it was supposed, would, from their position of weakness, undoubtedly seek closer cooperation from the West, thereby allowing Great Britain and the United States to extract political concessions in return, should they desire to do so. The Poles, for their part, looked forward to the application of Western pressure against the Soviets. Specifically, they expected that British and American influence would be brought to bear on their behalf in their dispute with the Russians over Poland's eastern border.[6] Moreover, the Poles appear to have believed that the presence of three hundred thousand Polish soldiers, including some nine thousand officers, in Soviet prisoner-of-war camps afforded them an important bargaining chip of their own, independent of British and American attitudes.[7] The Soviets, they felt, would not be able to do without this valuable resource and would have to approach the government-in-exile about an agreement allowing for the troops' deployment. Such an agreement would need to guarantee full Polish sovereignty within Poland's 1939 frontiers. Sikorski, in fact, had been prepared for this eventuality even before the German invasion had begun. In discussing with Cripps the possibility that Polish soldiers might take part in the effort to repulse the Nazi assault in the east, the prime minister warned that "as long . . . as Russia did not change her basic attitude to Poland and the Poles [i.e., did not accept the 1939 boundary], so long we also would not change our line of policy, which is the policy of war against Russia, imposed on us by the latter."[8] Sosnkowski, too, was adamant that although Germany had to be regarded as Poland's principal enemy, neither Polish regular nor underground forces should be permitted to support the Russian war effort actively in the absence of a Polish-Soviet agreement recognizing the continued force of the Treaty of Riga as the basis upon which relations between the two countries were to be conducted.[9]

Thus, on 24 June, two days after the launching of the German attack, Sikorski informed Gen. Frank Macfarlane, head of the British military mission to Moscow, that "collaboration with Russia [was] only possible on condition that Russia . . . fully recognises rights founded on the treaty of Riga and repudiates [the] Russo-German treaty of 23rd August 1939, [and] . . . releases all Polish citizens and soldiers from prisons or internment." He further indicated that "the forming of Polish units in Russia depends upon full attribution of sovereignty to those units, their employment solely dependable [*sic*] upon the decision of the Polish Government in London."[10] He repeated the essence of these points to Eden on 4 July and to the Soviet ambassador in London, Ivan Maisky, the next day.[11] The Soviets, however, did not prove nearly as pliable as the Poles had hoped. As Maisky told Eden on 4 July and Sikorski and Zaleski one week later, the Soviet government, though prepared to renounce its 1939 treaties with Germany, could not commit itself explicitly to the extension of Polish sovereignty beyond the limits of "ethnographical Poland."[12] It seems that the lure of Polish military cooperation did not turn out to be especially enticing to the Soviets.

Moreover, to the Poles' consternation, neither the British nor the U.S. government appeared willing to press the Russians on the territorial issue. For Britain, feeling at the time the formidable burden of carrying on the struggle against Hitler alone, battered by German aerial bombardment, and fearful of the imminent possibility of invasion, the prospect of Soviet entry into the anti-Nazi coalition was surely welcome.[13] In order to bring the Russians securely into the Allied camp, however, Polish-Soviet diplomatic relations needed to be restored. From the British point of view, it was unthinkable that two of Britain's partners should be at war with one another.[14] Thus the British government, which had in the past entertained the idea of offering political concessions to the Russians in order to draw them away from their position of salutary neutrality toward the Axis, was not about to permit Polish territorial aims to interfere with the achievement of Allied unity. The United States, for its part, though professing sympathy for the Polish position, wished for the moment to avoid all commitments related to the territorial future of Europe following the war.[15]

Hence, instead of receiving backing from the West, as they had expected, the Poles found themselves confronted with strong British pressure to accept an agreement with the Soviets that did not settle the frontier issue to their satisfaction. The pact that was ultimately concluded on 30 July 1941 lacked two of the conditions that Sikorski had stipulated as essential for the resumption of Polish-Soviet relations: it contained neither explicit affirmation of the Riga treaty nor recognition of the unconditional sovereignty of the Polish military units to be formed on Soviet territory.[16] Nevertheless, Sikorski felt that in the present circumstances he could hope for little more. His attitude, expressed in his call to the cabinet to approve the draft text of the treaty of 25 July, split his government apart and precipitated the resignation of Zaleski, Sosnkowski, and Seyda in protest.[17] This development had the effect of removing the support of Endecja and many of the former Piłsudskist elements from the government, thereby weakening its political base and contributing to a heightened sense of insecurity among its remaining supporters.[18] Adding to the government's consternation was the feeling that many of the points voiced by the agreement's opponents were in the final analysis well taken. In this context it is noteworthy that both Zaleski and Raczyński—the latter a supporter of the treaty who took over the management of foreign affairs following Zaleski's resignation[19]—separately expressed the fears that Soviet entry into the war would sharply decrease the importance to Britain of Poland's contribution to the anti-German war effort and that the Polish-Soviet agreement would have the effect of weakening support among world opinion for Poland's eastern territorial claims.[20]

In short, the interval from 22 June to 30 July 1941 witnessed the abrupt erosion of the Polish government's perceptions of its international standing and possibilities for the future. The situation was comparable in a sense to that which had prevailed after the fall of

France, when the Poles, upon transferring their base of operations to London, found themselves in less sympathetic surroundings than those to which they had been accustomed. For all of the obvious differences in the present case, it is clear that here too the Poles were forced rather indelicately to confront the fact that their sole benefactors were not as well disposed toward them as they might have wished. The events of July 1941, like those of July and August 1940, brought home to the government-in-exile the depth of its political vulnerability and forced its leaders to reexamine their possible sources of public support. Within this context the hope for an alliance with world Jewry, which but a short while before had been all but given up for dead, was quickly resurrected.

Was the possibility of concluding such an alliance any greater following the outbreak of the German-Soviet war than it had been earlier? During the second half of 1941 and the early part of 1942, government officials noted a number of seemingly encouraging signs. The interest of Jewish organizations, especially those based in London, in maintaining regular contact with government agencies appeared to several of those who dealt directly with Jewish matters to have increased markedly over this period, to the point where the government soon came to feel a strong need both for closer interagency coordination in Jewish affairs than had previously prevailed and for a more sophisticated mechanism for carrying on relations with international as well as Polish Jewish groups.[21] This development appears to have led to a growing conviction among government officials that Jews might at last be beginning to feel that they stood to gain by collaborating faithfully with the Poles. No doubt the World Jewish Congress helped to reinforce this observation when in early 1942 it requested of Sikorski (in his capacity as chairman of the Inter-Allied Conference on German Atrocities) that its representatives be allowed to participate in the conference's ongoing deliberations. The tone of this solicitation, unlike that of past contacts between the congress and the Polish premier, appeared to observers humble, almost to the point of submissiveness.[22]

In Polish circles Stańczyk seemed especially optimistic about the possibility of closer Polish-Jewish collaboration. Returning to London in March 1942 from an extended visit to the United States, during which he had, among other things, repeated the essence of his pledge of 3 November 1940 before a meeting of the Jewish Labor Committee in New York, he reported that he had found among both middle-class and socialist American Jewish groups a solid hostility toward the Soviet Union coupled with a genuine interest in the Polish cause.[23] Furthermore, there is strong evidence that during the period in question several Polish leaders believed that the political attitudes and aims of the Zionist movement would evolve of their own accord in a direction conducive to the eventual formation of a Zionist-Polish political alliance. This notion seems to have been first enunciated by Olgierd Górka in the wake of a meeting with Chaim Weizmann, president of the World Zionist Organization, on 11 September 1941. According to the description of the meeting prepared by the Polish official two weeks after the event, Weizmann told Górka that he himself had recently raised the issue of Polish-Jewish relations with his colleagues, in view of the importance he attached to the role Polish Jewry would play in building the future Jewish national home in Palestine. As the Jewish leader developed this idea further, Górka perceived a major change in Weizmann's thinking, one that brought the Zionist president, he believed, close to the Polish government's position on the Jewish question:

> I was astonished—and I ask that these observations of mine be treated in strict internal confidence—that with regard to the problem and percentage of Jews in Poland, the present position of Mr. Weizmann, who is famous for his struggle with the Revisionists, does not differ greatly from the Revisionist stance even today. Mr. Weizmann stated on his own initiative that the percentage of Jews in Poland is too high for good relations and that the departure of a significant portion of the Jewish element for Palestine is essential. This [must be accomplished] at a completely different pace and under completely different conditions than previous methods had allowed.[24]

Here, as Górka saw it, was an indication that a leading force in world Jewry had finally come to understand that organized, mass, voluntary emigration from Poland in cooperation with the Polish government was a goal seriously to be pursued. With apparent satisfaction he noted, too, Weizmann's ready acknowledgment that "the Poles now possess a certain popularity and influence in responsible English circles"[25]—where, of course, a vital key to the future of Palestine was to be found. Thus it seemed probable to him that the World Zionist Organization might now be ready to strike a deal with the government in which, at the anticipated future peace conference as well as in current propaganda activities, Polish sponsorship of Zionist aspirations in Palestine would be repaid with Jewish backing for Poland's eastern border demands.

The thought that Jews might now be ready to accept the sort of emigrationist solution to the Polish Jewish problem that Polish governments had been promoting since the mid-1930s, and the idea, moreover, that such a solution might at last be acceptable to the British custodians of Palestine, seems to have occurred to Raczyński as well, as a result of a chance discussion at the home of British Colonial Secretary Lord Moyne. At this informal gathering over the weekend of 2 October 1941, several high-ranking British officials, including Eden, spoke frankly and openly off the record about possible solutions to the Jewish question. Evidently they had noticed the same change in Weizmann's thinking as had Górka shortly before. They were, of course, unfavorably disposed toward the Zionist president's call for mass postwar Jewish resettlement in Palestine; but nevertheless, according to Raczyński, "they could not close their eyes to the gravity and urgency of the Jewish problem."[26] This recognition led to a general agreement among them that a comprehensive solution to the postwar Jewish problem would have to be found and that this solution would have to envisage some form of territorial autonomy for the Jewish people. Various territories were proposed, including Madagascar and East Prussia,[27] and the possibility that at least a part of the Zionist program in Palestine could be carried out was not rejected. Though in his written summary of the discussion Raczyński offered no evaluation, it seems reasonable to assume that he regarded the opinions expressed by the British officials as an encouraging sign. It may even be that the less-than-total negation of Zionist aspirations in Palestine that Raczyński observed encouraged Sikorski to raise the subject directly with Eden a short time later.[28] In any case, the information conveyed by Górka and Raczyński regarding Weizmann's attitudes could certainly have been taken on its face

as indicating that the mainstream of the Zionist movement was shift-
ing toward a position from which a close degree of political cooperation with the government-in-exile might appear highly desirable.

As it happened, however, this evaluation seriously misjudged the
manner in which the bulk of the Zionist leadership apprehended
their movement's political course. Weizmann had indeed come to the
conclusion by mid-1941 that a reconstituted Poland following the war
would be unwilling to absorb any more than a fraction of its former
Jewish population,[29] but this conclusion did not necessarily imply
that he was prepared then and there to join hands with the government-in-exile in formulating a postwar evacuation program. The future contours of the Jewish question in Eastern Europe were as yet
insufficiently clear to him or to other Zionist officials to permit commitment to such a course. With Russia now having joined the war
against Nazi Germany, the Zionist president understood that the Soviets would play a central role in fixing the political context in which
the movement would operate once hostilities had been concluded,
and even in determining the size of the potential reservoir of future
immigrants to Palestine.[30] In such circumstances he was hardly likely
to adopt a course of action that was certain to antagonize the Soviet
government.[31] His evaluation was widely shared throughout all segments of the Zionist camp.[32] The entry of the Soviet Union into the
war on the Allied side was perceived in Zionist circles as an opportunity for the movement to reestablish contact with the large community of Soviet Jews, which had been isolated from the major political
and ideological currents within world Jewry for almost two decades.[33] It also raised the hope that, through victory of Soviet arms,
large numbers of Jews would be saved from the Nazi terror.[34]

For their part, the Russians, just as much as the Poles, were concerned with winning the support of world Jewry for their cause.
When Maurice Perlzweig of the World Jewish Congress and Emanuel
Neumann of the Jewish Agency for Palestine paid an initial call upon
Soviet Ambassador Konstantin Oumansky in Washington in mid-
July 1941, the Russian diplomat complained bitterly of what he regarded as the unfriendly attitude of American Jewish organizations
and pointedly noted that his government would "have a word to
say" about the disposition of the Palestine issue at the anticipated
postwar peace conference.[35] There can be little doubt that Zionist

leaders valued the possibility of Soviet assistance for their Palestine program at least as much as they did that of Polish support. Within a short time following the German invasion, pro-Soviet aid committees and fronts had been formed by the Jewish communities in Palestine, Britain, and the United States, with the active involvement and co-operation of the principal leaders and institutions of the Zionist movement.[36] Although such groups generally stressed their apolitical nature in order to attract the widest possible base of support, and refused to take any official stand on Soviet government policies,[37] it was inconceivable that those who had been moved to associate themselves with these groups would become public advocates for Polish territorial demands.[38] In fact, by February 1942 the Palestinian V [for Victory] League for Soviet Russia openly acknowledged as one of its purposes "the attainment of Soviet support for the Zionist enterprise."[39]

In the meantime, Jewish organizations were encountering further points of friction with the London regime. When, in the wake of the government crisis over the signing of the Polish-Soviet agreement, the National Council had been dissolved, the Reprezentacja in Palestine had immediately demanded that in the new council that was to be summoned, Jews be represented in proportion to their percentage of the total population in prewar Poland.[40] Similarly, the Bund, the Revisionists, and Agudas Yisroel also claimed the right to representation. The Bund's request was ultimately satisfied, and in February 1942 Szmuel Zygielbojm joined Schwarzbart in the second National Council; but the other organizations were disgruntled.[41] The Bund's satisfaction, too, was tempered by the inclusion of five Endecja members in the new council, along with several ostensibly "nonparty" representatives of distinctly right-wing leanings, and by the reco-optation of a wing of Endecja into the government.[42] The Reprezentacja expressed similar misgivings.[43] In light of this apparent reemergence of the right as a force in Polish politics, Jewish leaders were unimpressed by the purportedly democratic declaration of principles presented by Sikorski at the new National Council's first meeting on 24 February 1942.[44] Both the Bund and the Reprezentacja were quick to point out the loopholes in the declaration's pledge of equality for minorities and saw these as deliberate concessions to antisemites in the council and the government. They called for unequivocal affirmations of the right of Jews to both civic equality and national autonomy in the future Poland.[45]

Against this background the first half of 1942, instead of being, as the Poles had hoped, a time of increased Jewish readiness to cooperate with the government on its terms, became a time of further deterioration in Polish-Jewish relations. On 11 February the Reprezentacja for the first time officially expressed a lack of confidence in the government's domestic policies—although it stated that it continued to support the government's conduct of foreign affairs.[46] Sikorski himself responded curtly that "beyond the declaration . . . [adopted] at the opening of the National Council," he had "nothing to add."[47] In April Bund activist Emanuel Scherer published a Polish-language pamphlet sharply attacking past Polish antisemitism and demanding full Jewish national autonomy in the future Polish state.[48] Polish officials saw this as a provocative step that could only heighten Polish anti-Jewish feelings and resolved to block its publication in English.[49] Evidence of a growing backlash soon surfaced in the National Council, where on 20 May Endecja representative Zofia Zaleska introduced a resolution expressing the council's desire for an international territorial solution to the Jewish question. The resolution was eventually carried by a large majority. Though on the surface the motion gave the impression of warm Polish support for Zionist aspirations, it was in reality motivated, as Zaleska's own remarks in introducing it made clear, by the traditional anti-Jewish bias of Endecja and the desire to see as many Jews as possible leave Poland after the war.[50] Indeed, it was as an expression of enmity, not of friendship, that the resolution was understood by most Jewish groups.[51] Shortly following its adoption, the American Jewish Congress issued a "Statement on Polish-Jewish Relations" bitterly castigating virtually every aspect of the government's handling of Jewish affairs.[52]

In an effort to calm Jewish anger, which in view of the impression he had formed of Zionist aspirations following his talk with Weizmann some months before must have come to him as a surprise, Olgierd Górka told a meeting of Revisionists in London that the eventual creation of a Jewish state would not be exploited by the Polish government as a pretext for demanding mass Jewish emigration and that the government was prepared "to support the Jewish national aims in case the Jews themselves and to the degree to which the Jews themselves ask for such . . . support."[53] The attempt met with modest success,[54] but the mainstream Zionist leadership, upset that this statement had been made before a Revisionist audience, continued to view government-Revisionist contacts as evidence that whatever it might claim to the contrary, the government was interested in fostering the Revisionist evacuation scheme.[55] Górka's speech also created friction with the British government, which looked askance upon his reference to Palestine as the future location of the Jewish state.[56]

It seems, then, that Jewish relations with the Polish government stood on essentially the same basis following the German invasion of the Soviet Union as they had before it. The hostile reactions to Zaleska's resolution and to Górka's speech showed that the change in Zionist thinking that some Poles had earlier anticipated had not materialized. Moreover, the Poles, despite their sense that the winning of Jewish favor could prove vital to their cause, were generally unwilling to take the steps demanded by Jewish leaders as indications of Polish good faith. From their perspective the Jewish complaints against them were unreasonable, and acquiescence to Jewish demands seemed to them morally unjustified.[57] Then too, even had some Polish leaders been willing to abide a moral indignity in order to placate Jewish feelings, the domestic political realities in which the government-in-exile operated precluded such a course. The opposition faction of Endecja, for example, had evidently developed plans to attack the Sikorski regime in Polish émigré circles as the lackey of Jewry and Freemasonry. In fact, the government was sufficiently concerned by this development to send an official emissary to North America for the purpose of insulating the Polish community in the United States against susceptibility to this charge.[58] Nor does it seem that many Polish leaders were likely to have believed that Jewish anger could be assuaged at all. According to a military intelligence report from mid-1942, Jews "in and around London" were gratuitously engaged in "a concerted effort to cause us [Poles] damage" in the eyes of the British public, in which far more attention was being paid to alleged past Polish anti-Jewish persecution than to present German atrocities.[59] All of this indicated that the leitmotif of Polish-Jewish relations during the two decades of Poland's independence—the image of Jewry as an implacable foe of the Polish community's claim to unencumbered sovereignty in its homeland—continued to be heard even at the close of the third year of the war. Under such conditions, the prospects for a Polish-Jewish political alliance were minimal.

The political level, though, was not the only one on which the possibility of closer Polish-Jewish cooperation was explored. Between 1939 and 1941 some 1–1.5 million Polish citizens, including perhaps as many as 400,000 Jews, had been forcibly exiled and interned in the Soviet interior.[60] The Polish-Soviet agreement of 30 July 1941 promised their release. Even before the agreement's conclusion, the Polish government had thought of organizing a relief mission to minister to the needs of the Polish deportees; indeed, concern for their welfare was probably one of the principal reasons why Sikorski consented to the terms of the agreement even though they did not satisfy the conditions he had set at the outset of negotiations.[61] The large percentage of Jews within this group gave Jewish organizations a vital interest in the government's planned relief activities. The Reprezentacja, which already in June 1941 had cabled to Sikorski its hope that, along with other Polish citizens, those Polish Jews then confined by the Soviet authorities would soon see an end to their suffering,[62] evidently heard of these plans while they were still in their formative stage, for on 22 July 1941 the organization wired Stańczyk, requesting that its representatives be included in whatever Polish delegation eventually visited the Soviet Union.[63] Later the World Jewish Congress formally associated itself with the Reprezentacja's petition.[64]

At first the Poles were somewhat cool to these suggestions. Stańczyk informed the Reprezentacja that "owing to transportation difficulties" no representatives from Palestine could be sent to Russia,[65] while the Foreign Ministry's secretary-general, Karol Kraczkiewicz, urged Ciechanowski to stress to Jewish organizations in the United States that the government would in any case distribute relief to Polish Jews on the same basis as to other Polish citizens. Kraczkiewicz also pointed out that the government had in fact already named a Jew to serve as an attaché to the newly established Polish Embassy in Moscow.[66] Quickly, though, government officials came to realize that Jews could be an important source of funds for the general Polish relief effort, and as a result they softened their opposition to the participation of delegates from the Reprezentacja.[67] By the end of October 1941, the Poles appear to have been ready to launch a joint relief campaign with Jewish organizations on behalf of all Polish citizens in Russia.[68]

By then, however, the Reprezentacja's enthusiasm for cooperation had noticeably diminished. The initial rebuff with which its request to participate had been met seems to have led the organization to doubt the beneficence of the government's intentions toward the Jews among the Polish deportees.[69] In late September the Reprezentacja Executive raised the possibility of conducting its own relief campaign for Polish Jews in the Soviet Union, independent of whatever apparatus the Polish government might eventually establish. Upon consideration, such a course was rejected, out of fear that the Polish authorities would interpret it as unfriendly behavior; but at the same time the Reprezentacja expressed its hope that the Palestinian Jewish community as a whole would take upon itself the responsibility of aiding the exiles in Russia, presumably within the framework of its contacts with the Soviet government.[70] Eventually, though, the Reprezentacja and other Jewish organizations learned that because of Soviet-imposed restrictions upon the right of the deportees to maintain contacts with foreigners, their ability to deliver aid to Polish Jews without official Polish government sponsorship would be severely circumscribed.[71] This policy obliged them to channel the funds they raised through the relief apparatus of the Polish Embassy in the USSR and necessitated ongoing coordination of the Jewish relief effort with the government-in-exile.

In the end, although no arrangement was worked out permitting them to supervise directly the distribution of the resources they raised, Jewish organizations provided a major share of the funds and materials collected for aid to Polish citizens in the Soviet Union.[72] They generally turned their collections over to the Polish authorities, however, uncomfortable over the lack of official Jewish representation in relief activities and suspicious that Jews might not receive their due share. Almost from the moment the Polish relief apparatus began to function, rumors of anti-Jewish discrimination in the allocation of aid permeated Jewish circles.[73] These rumors gained strong support from the testimonies of several Jews arriving in Palestine with the Polish forces evacuated from Russia in the spring of 1942.[74] In the middle of the year the American Jewish Congress included the charge in its "Statement on Polish-Jewish Relations."[75] This report caused at least one Jewish charitable organization to inform a Polish government official that it would be forced to reconsider its cooperation with the Polish relief effort should the news prove true.[76]

The Polish response to accusations of discrimination was uniform categorical denial. Upon hearing of the publication of unfavorable reports in the Jewish press, Kot, the government-in-exile's first ambassador to the Soviet Union, cabled the Foreign Ministry that the charge was entirely false.[77] Two weeks later the Foreign Ministry circulated a report from a Polish official in Russia stating that in several respects Jews enjoyed greater benefits from the funds distributed by the Polish relief offices than did non-Jewish Poles.[78] Polish sources also stressed that a relatively large number of Jews had been employed in the Polish relief apparatus, even though the Soviet government for a time had permitted the employment of ethnic Poles only.[79] The Foreign Ministry contended that the complaints of discrimination were voiced by individual Jews whose difficult material situation had been exploited by Soviet agents to blacken the Polish name in the West, but that these could in no way be regarded as typical.[80] In support, the Polish Embassy in the Soviet Union compiled elaborate statistics to show that it in fact "treated all Polish citizens alike, irrespective of race or creed."[81]

The figures, which were eventually published by the embassy in August 1943, were impressive indeed. They showed that over a hundred thousand Jews either received a monetary or in-kind allocation or were served by a Polish-run relief institution during the twenty-one months between August 1941 and April 1943 in which the official Polish relief apparatus functioned.[82] These represented almost 40 percent of the total number of Polish citizens who availed themselves of the embassy's relief facilities during this interval. The statistics also showed that Jews accounted for over half of the personnel employed by the relief apparatus. Since Jews made up only between one-fourth and one-third of the total number of Polish deportees, the embassy undoubtedly felt confident in asserting that there had been no pattern of anti-Jewish discrimination in its administration of relief.

Closer examination, however, reveals that the embassy's statistics were far from conclusive. For one thing, they lacked full information on the relative *amounts* of financial aid and the value of aid in kind distributed to Jewish and non-Jewish recipients. Because the beneficiaries of the embassy's assistance did not each receive a uniform allocation, there is no way to tell whether average allotments for Poles and Jews were approximately equal.[83] Secondly, the figures concerning the relative number of Jews among the Polish citizens availing themselves of the embassy's relief services related to the entire period of the embassy's operation and not merely to the months prior to June 1942, to which Jewish complaints referred. In any event there are reasonable grounds for supposing that the percentage of Jews among those served by the embassy was greater following this date than before it—not necessarily because in the wake of the publication of the Jewish charges Polish officials may have exercised greater care in allocating resources on a proportional basis,[84] but because from that time the proportion of Jews among those whom the embassy's relief apparatus was likely to serve steadily increased. A small portion of this increase was due to the relatively minuscule number of Jews included in the evacuation of Polish troops from Russia during the spring and summer of 1942. A greater portion can be attributed to restrictions imposed by the Soviet government in January 1943, according to which the embassy was permitted to maintain contact only with those who were not permanent residents of the territories seized by the Soviet Union in 1939.[85] The embassy estimated that among the Polish citizens who fell into this category, some 70 percent were Jews, since it had been "mostly Jews who fled from the Western parts of Poland, looking for escape from German persecutions."[86] These represented the relief system's potential clientele during its final three months of existence, when, according to embassy statistics, sums spent on disbursements to individuals were substantially greater than at any time before. Finally, there were several contradictions among the various figures offered by the embassy that, aside from undermining the credibility of the statistics in general, suggest that the actual percentage of Jews among those assisted by the relief apparatus may have been significantly smaller than the embassy claimed.[87]

None of this, of course, substantiates the Jewish charges of systematic discrimination. Undoubtedly there were instances of inequitable treatment of Jewish applicants for assistance by Polish relief officials, but it is impossible to ascertain how characteristic these were of the relief apparatus as a whole. Whatever inequities there were, moreover, were most likely instigated on the local level, without the knowledge or approval of the upper-echelon embassy staff.[88] All that is certain is that a large number of Jews did benefit from the services of the Polish relief network. This in itself was a major achievement, not least in light of the fact that the Soviet authorities made periodic attempts to prevent Polish Jews from availing themselves of the embassy's relief services. The Soviet government, in accordance with a decree issued by the Presidium of the Supreme Soviet on 29 November 1939, maintained that "former Polish citizens who were on the territory of the Western districts of the Ukraine and White Ruthenia [i.e., White Russia] when these became part of the USSR" had acquired Soviet citizenship and that the Polish government was not entitled to maintain any contact with them.[89] In practice, the Soviets mitigated the severity of this policy slightly, though with no benefit for Jews. On 1 December 1941 they announced that as an expression of "good will and readiness to compromise" they were prepared to treat ethnic Poles from the annexed provinces as Polish citizens. They continued to insist, however, that this exception could "in no case serve as a basis for the analogous recognition as Polish citizens, of persons of other nationalities, in particular, Ukrainians, White Russians, and Jews."[90]

In fact, immediately before the publication of this ostensible concession the Soviet authorities had in practice treated only those Jews who had been *permanent residents* of the annexed territories at the time of their incorporation as Soviet citizens (thus allowing for the release, along with the other Poles freed under the terms of the Polish-Soviet agreement, of those Jewish internees from western Poland who had fled to the Russian from the German occupation zone in 1939, and their provision with identity papers testifying to their Polish citizenship). They began in its aftermath to apply the terms of the decree to all Polish Jews, no matter what their place of origin.[91] In effect, then, because Soviet law forbade Soviet citizens to maintain contact with representatives of a foreign government without official approval, it became illegal for Polish Jews to receive—or, for that matter, even to apply for—welfare benefits from the Polish Embassy. Indeed, beginning in December 1941 a number of Jewish refugees from western Poland who earlier had been released from internment were incarcerated again, most of them on the charge of approaching

Polish officials.[92] The Soviet government persisted in this attitude for several months, during which time Jews who sought aid did so at the risk of arrest.[93]

The Soviet position on the citizenship of Polish Jews had other deleterious effects upon Jewish lives as well. Some Jewish internees, especially Zionist activists in prewar Poland, were not released as called for by the Polish-Soviet agreement, whether on the grounds that they were Soviet citizens or on other more blatantly political pretexts.[94] Moreover, Jews who wished to leave the Soviet Union and who possessed entry visas to another country were routinely denied exit permits, whereas ethnic Poles in similar circumstances were usually granted them without difficulty.[95] As a result, the overwhelming majority of Polish Jews in Russia seem to have been most anxious to obtain official classification as Polish citizens.[96] The Polish Embassy, for its part, was interested in helping them accomplish this goal. Ambassador Kot understood—indeed, the Soviet government made it quite clear[97]—that the Russians intended to use the citizenship issue as a tool to prevent the postwar reestablishment of the Riga frontier, by claiming that the disputed territories were populated in the majority by Soviet citizens.[98] Thus the Polish authorities vigorously protested both the Soviet citizenship policy in general and the specific repressive measures introduced against Jews.[99] The embassy attempted to assist Polish Jews in obtaining exit visas and made efforts to locate and secure the release of Jews who had been detained or rearrested by the Soviets.[100] It was particularly active in intervening on behalf of the two Polish Bund leaders, Henryk Ehrlich and Wiktor Alter, who after having been released from prison in September 1941 were again taken into custody on 4 December,[101] and of the Zionist activist and former Sejm deputy Emil Sommerstein.[102]

Kot, for one, appears to have believed that such actions by his embassy would be favorably received by Jews throughout the world and that because of the Soviet stance on citizenship, Jewish organizations in the West could be harnessed to the campaign to prevent international recognition of the Russian annexation of eastern Poland.[103] In general, however, this was not the Jewish response. As early as 25 September 1941, Reprezentacja leader Anshel Reiss, displaying a marked tendency to assume the worst about Polish behavior, urged the Reprezentacja Executive to protest to the Polish government "the fact that thus far we have not heard of a single Jew among the Russian exiles who has been released, while news has come to us about [the release of] various Poles."[104] In December the Reprezentacja requested to meet personally with Sikorski—who was scheduled to stop in Cairo on his way back from Moscow, where he had gone to negotiate with Stalin matters relating to the implementation of the Polish-Soviet agreement—in order to discuss ways in which the Polish authorities could help secure the release of Jews remaining in Soviet detention and obtain exit permits at least for those Jews who possessed immigration certificates to Palestine. When Sikorski snubbed this approach, the Reprezentacja's mistrust of the government was reinforced.[105] Apparently Jewish leaders believed that the Poles, despite their protestations to the contrary, could influence these matters, and they continued to express to Polish authorities their anxiety over the lack of demonstrable progress.[106]

This absence of progress was frequently interpreted as the result of Polish unwillingness to assist Jews at all. Schwarzbart complained to President Raczkiewicz in March 1942 about right-wing Polish circles that professed the hope that large numbers of Jews would be forced to remain in Russia, so that in postwar Poland the number of Jews would be greatly reduced. He pointed out—in a fashion suggesting a failure to realize that Polish officials had already understood the difficulty—that acquiescence to Soviet repressive measures against Jews was contrary to Poland's fundamental diplomatic interest, and he emphasized that "any double message in this regard must be eliminated, as it provokes justifiable suspicion of Polish intentions toward Jews."[107] A short while later the Jewish press in Palestine provided an example of this dynamic at work, as did the American Jewish Congress in its "Statement on Polish-Jewish Relations."[108] Jewish spokesmen made it clear that they regarded the pace at which Jews were released from internment and the ease with which they were able to depart Russia as tests of the sincerity of the Polish government's pledges regarding the status of Jews in postwar Poland.

All these things no doubt lent fuel to the decades-old perception of implacable Jewish enmity to the Polish cause, whose force was simultaneously being renewed in the course of Polish-Jewish interactions over political issues. Thus whatever practical cooperation was achieved between the government and Jewish organizations over funding the relief effort in Russia could not have advanced the cause of cooperation on the political level. However, what must have seemed to the Poles to be no more than yet another instance of gratu-itous Jewish hatred was in reality not so willfully malicious as they might have thought. In the event, it seems to have been rooted not only in the bitter experience of prewar times but also in contempo-rary observation of the way in which Jews were treated by another branch of the Polish administration in the Soviet Union. This was the exile Polish Army, whose creation had been mandated by the Polish-Soviet agreement. The record of this body in Jewish matters was different from that of the civilian authorities, and in the end Jews read its attitude as typical of the Polish government as a whole. In the final analysis it was the behavior of the army that negated the possibility that efforts made by the embassy on behalf of the Jews would eventually redound to Poland's gain.

Recruitment for the new Polish Army in Russia began in earnest during the second half of August 1941, following the conclusion on 14 August of a military agreement between the Soviet and Polish High Commands.[109] The latter had been created only ten days earlier with the release from prison of Lt. Gen. Władysław Anders and his appointment as commander of the Polish forces.[110] In the military agreement Anders had consented that the size of his army would "depend on manpower, equipment and supplies available"; shortly thereafter he was informed that the Soviets could initially outfit two light infantry divisions and a reserve regiment, consisting altogether of some twenty-five thousand to thirty thousand troops.[111] Evi-dently, though, he expected to be able to supply a much larger force out of Lend-Lease allocations from the United States.[112] Thus by 5 September he had already attained thirty thousand enlistments and continued to take in more every day.[113] Five days later, however, he was abruptly informed that Soviet arms would suffice for a single division alone.[114] In addition, the hope that the Western Allies would be able to pick up where the Soviets left off was dashed at the Anglo-American-Soviet military conference, which took place in Moscow between 26 September and 2 October. Here the American envoy, W. Averell Harriman, in response to pressure from his British counter-part, Lord Beaverbrook, agreed that equipment coming from the West would be placed entirely in Soviet hands, with the Russians maintaining full discretion over how much, if any, would eventually be allocated to the Poles. Obviously concerned first of all with the needs of their own forces, and seeing that the Western Allies were not about to insist upon the creation of as large a Polish army as could be mustered, the Soviet authorities now began to insist upon the recruitment of no more than thirty thousand Polish troops.[115] Efforts over the next month to soften the Soviet position, through both direct appeals and attempts to enlist American support, proved to no avail.[116]

These developments worried those Polish leaders who had placed high hopes in the new army as a safeguard against an unfavorable postwar settlement of the Polish-Soviet boundary. Some of them, most notably Kot and Anders, were particularly alarmed to discover that among those who had enlisted during the first two months of recruitment, an extremely large number—perhaps as high as 40 percent—were Jews. Kot saw this as part of a Soviet plot to flood the Polish Army with elements that the Russians hoped might prove amenable to their political position, especially with regard to the eastern Polish territories.[117] He claimed that the Soviet authorities had deliberately released Jewish before Polish internees in an attempt "to distort the national and psychological composition" of the force.[118] Anders was even more concerned: he viewed the Jews of the eastern territories as traitors who had from the beginning "ostentatiously and gleefully greeted the invading Soviet army" in 1939, and he claimed that they had harassed Polish soldiers, prisoners of war, and civilian internees and had collaborated with the Soviet secret police.[119] He made it clear that he did not want such soldiers under his command. In addition, he complained that "because the formation of the Polish Army was numerically limited by the Soviet authorities, liberated Poles . . . who reported to the Polish Army did not find a place for themselves, despite the fact that, in contrast to many Jews, they had previously served in the army and possessed appropriate qualifications."[120] Privately, he expressed the opinion that those Jews who had enlisted had turned out to be "constant malcontents and malingerers, cowards and thieves."[121] He also argued that the presence of large numbers of Jews in the ranks aroused great bitterness among the "genuine Poles."[122]

For all of these reasons, Anders began, at least from mid-October 1941, if not earlier, to seek ways of limiting the number of Jews serving with the Polish forces.[123] He personally ordered that enlistments from the ethnic minorities not exceed 5 percent of the noncommissioned officers and 10 percent of the private soldiers throughout the army; another directive from the High Command confined minority soldiers to 5 percent representation in the armored units and closed the airborne units to them entirely.[124] Anders also sought Soviet assistance in preventing Jewish enlistments.[125] Evidently his efforts were successful: according to one source, 90 percent of the Jews who reported for induction in November and December 1941 were rejected.[126] In many cases, excuses were also found to dismiss Jews who had already begun to serve.[127] Many of those Jews who remained in the ranks were deliberately assigned to base duty or to labor service.[128] An attempt was also made to segregate Jews in a special labor battalion, where, according to most accounts, conditions were well below the standard prevailing in other Polish units.[129]

It seems, however, that Kot, despite his undeniable anxiety over the high percentage of Jews in the new army, opposed such measures. Apparently he believed that although the Soviets may have hoped to turn the Jewish soldiers into a sort of Trojan horse within the Polish camp, it was not a foregone conclusion that their plan would succeed. In a letter of 11 October to his successor at the Interior Ministry, Deputy Premier Stanisław Mikołajczyk, Kot noted that "in the aftermath of the [Polish-Soviet] agreement and liberation [of the deportees], Jews are fervently accentuating their Polish citizenship." He further suggested that "in the future, when it comes to the eastern border question, this influx of Jews [into the army] will constitute a powerful political argument, especially against the background of the systematic hatred of the Ukrainians toward all things Polish."[130] Evidently, then, he felt that Jewish loyalty toward the Polish cause, in contrast to that of the Ukrainian minority, could be successfully cultivated—provided, of course, that Jewish soldiers were not antagonized in the ranks. He was also acutely aware of the negative international repercussions that would undoubtedly follow the publication in the West of news about anti-Jewish discrimination in the Polish forces.[131] Kot therefore took pains to impress upon Anders the urgent political necessity of suppressing all manifestations of antisemitism in the army. He initiated a meeting between Anders and Jewish leaders, at which the general promised to permit no anti-Jewish behavior and to make sure that Jewish soldiers were treated identically with their Polish counterparts.[132] Anders subsequently embodied this promise, no doubt at the urging of the ambassador, in an order to all troops issued on 14 November. The order, which categorically condemned all expressions of enmity toward Jews and stressed the equal rights of all Polish citizens under arms, was intended "to lay down a clear, uniform, and unambiguous line by which my subordinate commanders and all Polish soldiers shall approach the Jewish question in our army," as well as "to put an end to all of the malicious insinuations and gossip being generated behind our backs—which in all likelihood emanates from sources hostile to us—about alleged antisemitism in our forces." It also pledged no discrimination in recruitment.[133]

Anders's order was indeed clear and forceful, but in the event it was honored only in the breach. Not only did discrimination in recruitment continue apace, but the order appears to have provoked an immediate and vigorous backlash among the Polish soldiers in the ranks. They had been well nurtured upon the image of Jewish treachery in September 1939 and afterward, to the point where their attitude toward the Jews could be described by a Polish observer as "clearly unfriendly and even openly hostile."[134] It does not appear, though, that Anders was prepared for the outcry from the ranks that greeted the publication of his order.[135] In order to stem mounting criticism that he had shown Jews special consideration when their behavior did not warrant it, the general felt compelled to issue a second order on 30 November, this time to division commanders only, explaining the reasons for the earlier one and substantially undoing whatever positive effect it might have had:

In connection with my order . . . of 14 November 1941 concerning the role of Jews within the Polish Armed Forces in the USSR, I wish to explain the following . . . . : The aforementioned order sets forth categorically and officially the political credo of the commander of the Polish Armed Forces concerning the Jewish question. I hope, however, that commanding officers will not misunderstand me. I am well aware of the reasons for antisemitic outbursts within the . . . army—they are a response to the disloyal and often hostile behavior of Polish Jews from the eastern territories during the years of our ordeal 1939–40. Thus

I am not surprised that our soldiers, fervid patriots, are sharply and repeatedly bringing up this matter, since it seems to them that our government and army intend to forget about our past afflictions. Viewed from this angle, our support and defense of the Jews may appear to them incomprehensible, historically unjustified, and confusing. However, our policy—since it is at present completely and entirely connected with English policy—must be to relate positively to the Jewish question, whose influence in the Anglo-Saxon world is considerable. . . . All soldiers must understand . . . that our raison d'etat requires that we do not annoy the Jews, for at present antisemitism can bring the most disastrous and incalculable effects upon the Polish cause. Therefore I recommend that our position be explained discreetly and responsibly to the units under your command, and that the more fervid and hot-tempered be clearly warned that for now no manifestation of the struggle against the Jews is under any circumstances allowable, and that [all such manifestations] will be punished by me as . . . harmful to our cause. When we are masters in our own home after our victorious campaign, we shall dispose of the Jewish question as the greatness and sovereignty of our homeland and ordinary human justice demand.[136]

Ironically, Anders's attitude toward Jewish enlistment received indirect support only four days after the issue of his second order from the Polish official who ought to have been most sensitive to its political consequences—General Sikorski. In a casual remark made toward the close of his meeting with Stalin on 3 December (at which Kot and Anders were also present, along with Soviet Commissar for Foreign Affairs Vyacheslav Molotov), Anders observed that among the Polish citizens in the USSR there were "a great number of Jews who do not want to serve in the Army." Stalin signaled his understanding, noting, "Jews are poor warriors"; Sikorski responded that many of the Jews who had so far reported for duty had proven to be black marketeers who would "never . . . make good soldiers. These," he declared, "I don't need in the Polish Army."[137]

Under such circumstances there was little hope that Jews seeking to enroll in the Polish forces would meet with a hospitable reception or fair treatment. Nevertheless, they continued to stream toward the mobilization points. To be sure, this was in all likelihood not generally the result of Polish patriotism. For many who had been unable to find civilian employment in the physically and emotionally trying conditions of life in the Soviet interior, the army represented virtually the only opportunity to obtain regular food and shelter. Service in the Polish forces also provided at least a partial protection against being claimed as a Soviet citizen and thus against the prospect of reinternment. Moreover, it seems that by the time of Sikorski's visit rumors had begun to circulate that a portion of the Polish troops might be transferred outside the Soviet Union. The army thus offered a soldier a hope of eventually being able to leave Russia. At least some Jews undoubtedly hoped that if the army were removed to Iran, they might be able to desert and reach Palestine.[138]

These reasons for wanting to join the Polish forces were apparently well known to the Polish authorities, and they appear merely to have heightened Anders's resolve to keep Jews out of the ranks by any means possible.[139] In January 1942 the Polish commander renewed his call to the Soviet authorities to cooperate in the curtailment of Jewish enlistments.[140] Significantly, he held to this position despite the fact that during his meetings with Sikorski, Stalin had raised the number of Polish troops that he was prepared to outfit to ninety-six thousand and had consented to the mustering of an additional twenty-five thousand for immediate transfer to Polish units in Scotland and the Middle East.[141]

Coincidentally, even before Anders had repeated his request, and perhaps even before Sikorski had obtusely hinted that he was interested in seeing Jewish enlistments reduced, the Soviets had decided that they ought to take steps of their own in that direction. In conjunction with its citizenship policy, the Soviet government began as early as November 1941 to conscript Polish Jews into the Red Army.[142] Subsequently it adopted the position that only those Jews and members of other minorities who had been permanent residents of western Poland before 29 November 1939 would henceforth be eligible for induction into the Polish forces. The Poles appear to have been officially advised of this ruling—which was in fact somewhat more lenient than the general Soviet stance on citizenship at this time[143]—only toward the end of February,[144] although hints that it would be forthcoming had been transmitted much earlier.[145] By this time the Poles may have begun to sense that they had fallen into a cleverly laid trap. As with the overall citizenship regulations, Polish acquiescence to the restriction on minority recruitment would indirectly have signified agreement to the Soviet border claims. On the other hand, following the clear indications by Sikorski and Anders that Jews were not desired in the Polish Army, the Poles were in no position to mount an effective protest. In fact, in contrast to the vigorous opposition expressed by Kot to the general Soviet citizenship policy and its application in matters of release from detention and exit visas—and even to the November conscription of Polish Jews into the Red Army—no official Polish complaints appear to have been lodged over the enlistment limitations.[146] By the same token, Anders—in order, as a Polish report explained, "not to delay the organization of new units"—immediately "mandated the recruitment of Poles only, as granted . . . by the Soviet authorities."[147]

The Soviet restrictions upon Jewish enlistment did, of course, provide the Poles with a convenient means for covering up their own attitude toward Jews in their army and for sidestepping Jewish charges of discrimination. Polish military officials were advised that minority applicants for induction were to be brought before recruiting boards only if a Soviet liaison officer was present, in order to force the Soviet official to disqualify the applicant in the applicant's presence and to make it clear that it was the Russians, not the Poles, who were preventing Jews from volunteering for Polish military service.[148] To the Poles' great chagrin, however, the Soviet authorities do not appear to have been especially concerned with enforcing the rule that they had imposed, and they generally did not oblige the Poles by challenging the induction of minority recruits.[149] In fact, in a secret order to division commanders issued on 9 March 1942, Anders noted that he had recently learned of the intention of certain Soviet recruiting offices "to transfer a high percentage of Jews, who are struggling with all their might to be attached to our ranks," to the Polish forces.[150] He therefore instructed his subordinates to make certain that these Jews were disqualified on medical grounds.[151] Subsequently Polish apologists argued that medical rejections had been issued Jews in order to save them from eventual conscription into the Red Army, but few if any appear to have been taken in by this transparent pretext.[152] The facts of the matter are that the pressures that had first induced Anders to seek to decrease the number of Jews in the Polish Army continued to be felt well after the Soviets had imposed their ban on recruiting Jews from the eastern territories,[153] and that the Polish military authorities persisted on their own initiative in preventing the entry of Jews into their forces. Kot continued to note during 1942 that the army was conducting a "systematic antisemitic policy."[154]

A telling example of anti-Jewish discrimination in recruitment for the Polish Army is provided by official figures on Jewish enlistments compiled during the period 12–20 August 1942 and submitted to the Polish chief-of-staff, Maj. Gen. Zygmunt Bohusz-Szyszko, by Lt. Col. Marian Stachelski, head of the army's Administrative Bureau.[155] The figures refer to 163 individuals, 75 Poles and 88 Jews, who during the week in question sought to enlist in the Polish forces, even at this relatively late juncture, at army headquarters in Yangiyul, Uzbekistan. All of the Jews claimed to be from western Poland and thus not subject to Soviet restrictions on enlistment; and in fact, in all but 7 cases, this claim was found to be true. Yet despite the absence of Soviet interest in the outcome of the selection, only 23 out of the 88 Jews—26.1 percent—were found qualified for service, in contrast to 56 out of the 75 Poles—74.7 percent. Of the Jews 57, or 64.8 percent, were given medical disqualifications, as opposed to only 10 of the Poles, or 13.3 percent. What is more, it seems that these statistics reflect a relatively liberal attitude toward admission of Jews into the ranks. In fact, various estimates indicate that in mid-1942 Jews made up no more than 8 percent, and perhaps even less than 4 percent, of the military forces under General Anders's command.[156]

The motifs that characterized the recruitment of Jews by the Polish Army were prominently featured as well during the evacuation of Polish troops and civilians from Russia during the spring and summer of 1942.[157] Indeed, it was in the course of this episode that the fruits of the Poles' discriminatory policy, both sweet and bitter, appeared. Because evacuation was confined to soldiers and their families, it was inevitable that the percentage of Jews among the evacuees would be far smaller than their one-fourth to one-third share of the number of Polish deportees and refugees in the Soviet Union. In the event, out of almost 115,000 Polish citizens removed from the Soviet Union, at most 6,000, that is, 5.2 percent, and perhaps fewer, were Jews. Among the 77,000 military and paramilitary personnel evacuated, Jews numbered no more than 3,500, or 4.5 percent; among the 38,000 civilians, Jews accounted for at most 2,500, or 6.6 percent.

Whereas some 10.5 percent of all non-Jewish Polish citizens in the USSR were able to leave Russia with the departing Polish Army, only 1.5 percent of Jewish Polish citizens succeeded in so doing.[158]

It appears, moreover, that although the number of Jewish military evacuees was more or less fixed as a result of the previous anti-Jewish enlistment policy, the proportion of Jews among the civilian evacuees might have been greater were it not for the efforts of both the Polish and the Soviet authorities to keep their numbers to a minimum. Because the removal of Polish troops began from the Polish bases in Soviet Central Asia (mainly in Uzbekistan), most of the civilian evacuees were people already located in this vicinity. As it happened, it was precisely in this area that most of the Jewish refugees were concentrated, and Jews appear to have made up over three-quarters of the number of Polish citizens residing there.[159] Thus it seems that Jews formed a large percentage of the civilians who reported to the embarkation centers set up by the army, in the hope that their names would be included in the lists of intended evacuees. This situation, according to the Polish Embassy's liaison to the High Command, Andrzej Jenicz, created in many Poles certain "emotional difficulties": "That Jews would be evacuated solely because they happened to be in the southern regions, from which the evacuation was to proceed, while the families of many Polish soldiers were condemned to stay in the USSR because they could not make their way southward, was not popular with the army." Though Jenicz cautioned against overrating the importance of this attitude, stressing that the Soviets had placed strict limitations on the removal of ethnic minorities that the Polish authorities were bound to observe, he acknowledged that it did often interfere with the inclusion of Jews among the evacuees. "Some military personnel," he noted, "demonstrated their antisemitic attitude by applying with exaggerated rigor any official regulation that could relate to Jews." Jenicz expressed concern lest news of antisemitic behavior among Polish military officials "fall into the wrong hands" and serve as a basis for an eventual Soviet anti-Polish propaganda campaign among "international Jewish circles." At the conclusion of his report he therefore urged that those "who must know about how the evacuation proceeded" be advised that "restrictions upon the removal of Jews were applied solely and entirely because of the Soviet government's categorical ban [upon Jewish departures]."[160] Henceforth this did in fact become the government-in-exile's standard reply to all complaints directed toward it about the small percentage of Jews evacuated;[161] but Jenicz, a civilian official, made clear his belief that at least some Polish officers had taken their own initiative in limiting Jewish participation in the exodus. He stopped short, though, of intimating that such initiatives were in accord with the wishes of the top level of the military command.

Jewish leaders, on the other hand, were convinced that Anders himself was far more responsible for the small number of Jewish evacuees than was the official Soviet attitude.[162] Indeed, according to Jewish testimonies, orders to exclude Jews from transports to Iran, though usually ascribed to a Soviet-imposed ban, always came from Polish military headquarters, never from a Soviet source. Jewish spokesmen maintained, moreover, that the Soviets—although they did officially put forth strict qualifications on which members of non-Polish minorities were eligible for evacuation—were in practice not nearly as adamant about enforcing them as the Poles claimed. In one incident reported by several Jewish witnesses, the Polish command revised its evacuation lists in early August so as to eliminate all those Jews whose departure had previously been approved. Jewish representatives turned in protest to Polish Chief-of-Staff Bohusz-Szyszko, who reportedly informed them that the change had been dictated by the Soviet security apparatus and suggested that their complaints would be more properly directed at the Russians than at the Poles. However, at a meeting held in Tashkent on 19 August between the Jewish spokesmen and NKVD Gen. of State Security Yurii Zhukov, in Bohusz-Szyszko's presence, the Soviet official—according to the Jewish sources—claimed that the Poles had never requested the evacuation of any Jews and implied that if they had, the Soviets would have placed no obstacles in their way. As the Jews present recounted the course of the meeting, Zhukov stated that while the Soviet government demanded that only those members of the non-Polish minorities who had arrived in Soviet-held territory after 29 November 1939 be included in the evacuating transports, the responsibility for checking eligibility rested entirely with the Poles, and that he was prepared to approve any list submitted to him that Polish officials certified included only eligible evacuees.[163]

The Polish military leaders, of course, offered a different version of the situation. Bohusz-Szyszko stated emphatically, in a lengthy memorandum on Jewish evacuation prepared on 19 September, that before the first round of evacuations in March Anders had been officially advised by the NKVD that no Jews who were regarded as Soviet citizens could be included in the transports to Iran.[164] If a number of Jewish civilians did nonetheless manage to find a place among the evacuees, claimed the chief-of-staff, it was thanks to Anders's own action in requesting that an exception be made for the immediate families of Jews on active service with the Polish forces. Moreover, according to Bohusz-Szyszko, Anders successfully insisted upon the retention of this concession when the Soviet authorities threatened to remove it before the second round of evacuations in August. The chief-of-staff reported that on 31 July he and Anders signed an agreement with Zhukov in which the evacuation of "members of the families of Jewish soldiers serving actively in the Polish Army in the USSR" was specifically permitted.[165] When confronted several months later with the Jewish version of the meeting held on 19 August at Tashkent between the Jewish leaders and Zhukov, he claimed that he personally had initiated the conference in order to provide the Jewish spokesmen with a chance to appeal directly to the nearest official with the power to alter the situation. He also denied that the Soviet officer had stated that he would automatically confirm whatever evacuation lists were presented by the Poles.[166]

Bohusz-Szyszko's testimony, however, does not appear entirely reliable. Not only was it contradicted by a Jewish testimony that had been solicited by Polish officials to bolster the Polish case,[167] but the agreement that he and Anders signed with Zhukov on 31 July was in general not as he described it and specifically did not make direct mention of Jews.[168] Moreover, cables sent by Anders and by government emissaries attached to the army to London and to the Polish Embassy at Kuibyshev leave some doubt about whether the provision permitting the exit of the next-of-kin of minority soldiers actually represented, as Bohusz-Szyszko claimed, a concession wrung from the Soviets at Anders's insistence. To be sure, the Polish commander informed Sikorski on the day following the conclusion of the agreement that the Soviets had not intended to allow any Jewish civilians to leave but that "at my suggestion the transfer of the families of Jews serving in the army was agreed upon."[169] Four days earlier, too, Bishop Józef Gawlina, a former member of the National Council then on a pastoral mission to the Polish troops, had pre-

sented the prime minister with a similar assessment of Soviet unwillingness to permit Jewish participation in the evacuation, adding that
in his view, the Jews were behaving as if the Poles were the main
obstacle to their transfer, "which is certainly not the case."[170] However, as early as 26 July Anders had reported to Sikorski that the
Soviet government did not object to the departure of the families of
Jewish soldiers, but merely insisted that the many Jews clamoring
for evacuation who were not members of soldiers' families not be
allowed to join the withdrawing troops.[171]

It may be, of course, that the terms of the agreement signed on 31
July had been negotiated in good faith a week earlier and that the
negotiations had proceeded as Anders intimated to Sikorski. It is not
impossible that the Polish commander, despite his continuous efforts
to reduce the number of Jews in the ranks of his forces, wished to
see at least some Jews removed from Russia along with his soldiers.
In April, shortly after the beginning of the first round of evacuations,
he had traveled to London for consultations with Sikorski and British
officials. There he had first come personally into contact with Jewish
complaints over discrimination in assigning places in the departing
transports. Evidently he had determined then that "the Jewish lies
. . . could have a fatal effect upon the next evacuation."[172] Following
his return, he met with a number of rabbis and endeavored to convince them of his proper intentions, in the hope that they might be
able to restrain any future Jewish outcries against his handling of
Jewish affairs. From a number of them he obtained letters denying
the existence of anti-Jewish discrimination in the Polish Army and
praising his personal efforts on behalf of the Jewish interest.[173]
Whatever the sincerity and reliability of these testimonies,[174] it is
clear that in the interval between the two rounds of evacuations he
had developed what seems to have been a newfound regard for the
importance of cultivating Jewish public opinion.[175] It is therefore reasonable to assume that he wished to be in a position to offer proof
that he had in fact intervened with the Soviet authorities in favor of
the inclusion of Jews in the transports. Were no Jewish civilians to
leave at all, he would surely have had difficulty making the case that
he had been an ardent, even if ineffective, advocate of the Jewish
cause. Moreover, it seems that the embassy had made it known that
it was interested in the evacuation of certain individual Jews.[176]

On the other hand, Anders also had cause to want to keep the number of Jewish evacuees small, not merely because of his personal feelings and those of his subordinates. It appears that since March 1942 the government-in-exile had been subject to pressure from the British government not to allow large numbers of Jewish soldiers to be deployed with the evacuating Polish troops in Palestine, which was to be their new center of operations. Since Palestine had first been proposed as the site to which the Polish forces would be relocated, British officials had expressed concern that the presence of Jews within the Polish ranks might create difficulties in the administration of Britain's anti-Zionist mandatory policy as embodied in the White Paper of May 1939.[177] In particular, the British, noting with alarm the recent interest exhibited by the government-in-exile in promoting close relations with the Zionist movement and in exploring the possibilities for future Jewish colonization in Palestine, feared that if the evacuated Polish forces contained significant numbers of Jews, Zionist leaders might persuade the Poles to sponsor the formation of specifically Jewish units within their army, which might serve in turn as a spearhead for the creation of a unified Jewish national armed force.[178]

This fear was greatly exacerbated by a memorandum written by Sikorski and presented to Winston Churchill on 5 March 1942. This document, which was intended primarily as a survey of Soviet citizenship policy toward the ethnic minorities and an exposition of its injustice, mentioned in passing that "the number of Jews in the 5th Division [of the Polish Army in the USSR] . . . is still considerable and in some units attains 30%." It reported further that "in the 6th Division most of the Jews were detached and, in accordance with the request of the New-Zionists [i.e., the Revisionists], they formed a separate battalion."[179] These observations, undoubtedly meant simply to convince the British prime minister that the Polish Jews under Soviet occupation desired after the war to live under Polish rather than Soviet rule, were, of course, untrue;[180] but for the British, unaware that they were being misled, the purported news was a source of no small consternation. Reviewing Sikorski's memorandum, Frank Roberts of the Foreign Office noted that he was "a little surprised by the figures regarding the proportion of Jews in the 5th and 6th Polish divisions" and declared that "for political reasons we should not want a large number of Polish Jews in the Middle East."[181] Another

Foreign Office official, R. M. Mack, recommended in a separate comment on the situation that the evacuation of "the separate Jewish battalion in the 6th Division" be forestalled and that the troops sent to Palestine "be as far as possible purely Polish units."[182] His suggestions were seconded by Charles Baxter, head of the Foreign Office's Eastern Department, who emphasized "the necessity for doing the utmost to avoid the transfer of any Polish Jewish units to the Middle East" and expressed a strong preference for keeping them in Russia. "Their presence there [in Palestine] during the war," he added, "will be a continued source of trouble, and after the war the Poles, who wish to get rid of their Jews, will probably make difficulties about readmitting them to Poland."[183]

On account of these British apprehensions, Sir Cecil Dormer, Britain's ambassador to the government-in-exile, was instructed to discuss the matter with the Polish Foreign Ministry and to make clear to the Polish government that Britain would not take kindly to any policy regarding Jews in the Polish Army that did not take into consideration British interests in Palestine. He made this communication by means of a memorandum presented on 30 March to Feliks Frankowski, a senior Polish Foreign Ministry official.[184] Though the language of the memorandum was restrained, the Poles seem to have understood clearly what the British desired: Frankowski personally reassured the ambassador that the percentage of Jews among the evacuated troops would not be especially large, and Raczyński wrote a bit later that "the Polish Government are resolved to do everything in their power to prevent any political action on the part of Polish Jews which might appear to be inconsistent with the interests and views of the British Government."[185]

The desire of the British to avoid a concentration of Polish Jewish soldiers in Palestine, as well as the government's acquiescence to the British request, must have been made known to Anders, and it could certainly have given him a sound political reason for making no more than the minimum effort on behalf of increased Jewish evacuation necessary to be able to tell Jewish leaders with some conviction that he had pleaded their cause with the Soviets.[186] Moreover, it appears that shortly before the beginning of the second round of evacuations Polish officials in Russia received word that the British authorities in the Middle East might not be able to care for the entire contingent of civilian evacuees that had originally been foreseen.[187] Here was yet another incentive for Anders to try to reduce the number of civilians leaving with the troops.

In short, it seems that in dealing with the evacuation of Jewish civilians, Anders was forced to operate within a complex field of conflicting constraints and pressures that on balance led him to pursue a visible yet minimal Jewish presence in the departing transports.[188] From such a starting point, however, the Soviets were able easily to maneuver him into a position from which he would unavoidably appear as the principal obstacle to Jewish evacuation, while they could present themselves as generous benefactors of the Jewish interest. By standing at first adamantly opposed to the departure of Jews altogether, and by convincing the Polish commander that any violation on his part of the agreed-upon terms of the putative Soviet concession could bring about the suspension of the evacuation of any troops at all,[189] the Russians probably figured to induce Anders to apply a most stringent standard in interpreting the limitations upon the transfer of minorities across the border and to insist upon meticulous documentation of eligibility for evacuation, which many Jews would be unable to provide.[190] This policy in turn was bound to bring Anders into acute conflict with Jews, who would see his personal anti-Jewish feelings as the primary motivation for his stringency. At this point his only available defense would be to try to cast the blame upon the Soviet authorities. When he did so, the Russians would be free to pull the rug from beneath him by denying any interest in who was evacuated.

Anders might have avoided the Russian snare had he applied more lenient standards of documentation to the determination of Jewish eligibility for departure and then challenged the Soviet authorities to strike from the evacuation lists the names of Jews whom the Poles certified as falling within the bound of the agreement of 31 July. He seems, however, to have been unwilling to risk the possibility that the Soviets would accept the challenge, and perhaps in consequence make good their threat to curtail the entire evacuation should irregularities in the lists be uncovered. Perhaps he feared as well that if the Soviets declined the challenge, it would be harder for him in the future to reject the many Jews that he did not wish in any event to take along.[191] Whatever the case, it was the Poles, not the Soviets, who emerged from the evacuation controversy as the villains in Jewish eyes. No doubt this judgment was hastened by the Polish record of discrimination in the enlistment of Jews into the armed forces and in the treatment of those Jewish recruits who were accepted for service. In fact, the attitude toward Jews displayed by the Polish military authorities in the USSR came to dominate Jewish perceptions of the Polish government as a whole during the eighteen months following the entry of the Soviet Union into the war on the Allied side. This situation in turn made the possibility of Polish-Jewish political cooperation more remote than ever before.

Nevertheless, the leaders of the government-in-exile do not appear to have been willing, even in the face of ever-more-wrathful expressions of Jewish disgust with their behavior, to abandon the pursuit of a Jewish alliance. Since June 1941 the Poles had based their strategy vis-à-vis the Soviet Union upon two expectations: that Britain and the United States would not recognize the validity of the Soviet annexation of eastern Poland, and that the Polish Army being formed on Soviet soil would, after taking part in the liberation of the homeland from the east, be in a position to control the country's political and territorial future. By mid-1942, however, it was clear to them that neither of these expectations was about to materialize. The evacuation of the Polish Army made the possibility of Polish military involvement in the determination of the country's borders minimal, while the Anglo-Soviet treaty of 26 May 1942 underscored the precariousness of the Polish position with the Western Allies.[192] In this situation, the Poles were more in need of influential friends than ever before. In view of their belief in the crucial role played by Jewish organizations in the formation of British and American opinion, they had to continue to try to win the Jews to their side, no matter how much effort would be required to do so, and almost at any cost. Hence the latter half of 1942 was a period of intensified Polish overtures to Western and Palestinian Jewry.

These overtures differed notably from those attempted earlier by Górka and Stańczyk. Where their approaches had aimed at enticing Jewry into cooperation through the offer of positive political incentives or the exploitation of putative Jewish disgruntlement with the Soviet Union, those made during the summer and fall of 1942 were based upon the thinly veiled application of pressure. The thinking behind this change was revealed in a memorandum prepared by Karol Kraczkiewicz on 8 July 1942. In this document, the secretary-general of the Foreign Ministry acknowledged that Jews in the West had good reason to complain about the situation of their Polish core-ligionists in the Soviet Union, which was in a certain sense worse even than that of ethnic Poles. He protested, however, that the sole responsibility for this state of affairs rested with the Soviets, "who in their refusal to recognize the Polish citizenship of Jews and other non-Poles from the Soviet zone of occupation seek to create accomplished facts with regard to the [Polish-Soviet] border." Because, in his words, the Soviet government adamantly insisted that all those whom it regarded as Soviet citizens be subject exclusively to Soviet law, it had withheld amnesty from Polish Jews, refused them permission to leave the country, and malevolently interfered with the relations between them and the Polish Army and welfare apparatus. All of this, Kraczkiewicz claimed, had been explained to Jewish leaders before, for the Polish government "assumed that on the basis [of this information] Jewish representatives would not only use their influence to stop the attacks against our authorities, but also undertake action aimed at presenting the true situation before public opinion and demand that the Soviets change their position with regard to Jewish Polish citizens." He argued that the Poles could not take the lead in this regard "because of the sensitive nature of Polish-Soviet relations." Unfortunately, the government's assumption had not, to Kraczkiewicz's mind, proved a correct one. On the contrary, he noted that "international Jewry" had recently responded to an appeal from the Jewish Anti-Fascist Committee in Moscow—"which is, of course, entirely under Soviet influence"—and adopted a resolution "full of admiration for the Soviet enterprise and for Soviet Jewry and emphasizing [as well] the purported equality of rights [enjoyed by] the Jews of the USSR."[193]

Thus it seems that in mid-1942 the government-in-exile finally understood that it had earlier misapprehended not only the British and American positions in the Polish-Soviet conflict but the Jewish position as well, and that it had very little of value to offer in return for support. With regard to the Jews, however, other means of persuasion could be employed. Such apparently was the thinking of National Council member Tadeusz Kiersnowski, who visited Palestine in May and June and held unofficial talks with leaders of the Reprezentacja and the Jewish Agency. At first, according to his own account of his discussions, Kiersnowski attempted to play upon Zionist fears that the Soviet government's approach to the Jewish question would soon bring about the "denationalization" and cultural atrophy of Russian Jewry, suggesting that Polish rule over the eastern territories could prevent these things. But he struck more negative chords as well. He claimed, for example, that the difficulties in Polish-Jewish relations during the prewar years were largely the result of the failure of Polish and world Jewry to stand forthrightly behind Poland in its struggle over the eastern border during its first two years of independence. In particular, he noted, "the Polish people will never forgive the Jews" for their neutral stand in the fight over Lwów in November 1918. Similarly, he suggested, the Polish people were unlikely to forgive the enthusiasm displayed by Jews when the Red Army invaded eastern Poland in September 1939. He stated, however, that the Jews had now been given an opportunity "to rehabilitate themselves in the eyes of the Polish population by speaking out in defense of Polish interests." If Jews really deserved different treatment at the hands of the Poles from that which they had received during the prewar years—if they in fact, as they claimed, loved Poland as much as any Pole—then, declared Kiersnowski, they must prove it by coming to their country's aid in its hour of need. Only thus, he argued, might Jews legitimately demand equal rights in liberated Poland, for "the defense of a portion of [Poland's] territory against a foreign enemy . . . [is] an elementary obligation of citizenship that no Pole, no matter whether he was favored or oppressed by the pre-1939 regime, may avoid."[194]

Here was perhaps the most explicit statement offered by an exile Polish leader to date of the principle that implementation of the government's promises of equality for Jews in postwar Poland would depend upon Jewish support for the government's war aims. A similar approach was taken by Władysław Banaczyk, who had been named deputy chairman of the Second National Council, during his visit to Palestine in September 1942. Banaczyk told a delegation from the Reprezentacja that "in prewar Poland many Poles suffered at the hands of the Jews," and he expressed amazement that Poland, "on both sides of which were totalitarian states, still did not absorb these systems and did not resort to pogroms."[195] The present government, too, he stated, wished to collaborate with the Reprezentacja and to meet Jewish demands as much as possible; but, he added, "we should like to see you do something through your channels on the Russian issue." In this context he praised Schwarzbart's work in the National Council, noting that "he puts the general Polish interest in the first order of priority" and expressing the hope that the Reprezentacja would "follow the same path." At the same time, though, he warned the Jewish leaders against "spilling oil on the fire" of Polish-Jewish relations,[196] presumably by not acceding to the Polish request for support on the eastern border question.

The threat implicit in such words was clear. Other Polish leaders who attempted to induce Jewish political cooperation through the application of pressure during this period were far less subtle. Kot, for example, appears at one point, in a cable he dispatched on 30 August 1942 to Yitshak Gruenbaum and Emil Schmorak of the Executive of the Jewish Agency for Palestine, even to have attempted to link the number of Jews evacuated from Russia to world Jewry's readiness to conduct pro-Polish, anti-Soviet propaganda:

> . . . soon hope discuss matter personally however cannot hesitate even now rebuke contents your telegramme.[197] Your reaction and opinion [with regard to the Polish government's role in determining the number of Jewish evacuees] is built on totally onesided false views on [sic] real possibilities. On my part I used all means at my disposal to meet your requirements. Regret cannot say same about you. Until your worldwide action does not [sic] mobilise all factors of influence in the proper direction you will never succeed in avoiding your responsibility for your unsatisfactory evacuation results.[198]

Polish officials seem at first to have been undecided about the results of such applications of pressure.[199] Perhaps, then, it was in order to seek a more definite indication of how the new strategy was working that Kot came to Palestine for an extended stay in November 1942.[200] During his visit in the country he met with, among others, David ben Gurion, chairman of the Jewish Agency Executive, and Yitshak ben Tsvi, chairman of the Jewish National Council (Va'ad Leumi), as well as with Gruenbaum and Schmorak. He also held four separate conferences with a delegation from the Reprezentacja.

Kot must have come away from these conversations disappointed, for if anything they demonstrated just how much the Russian experience had deepened the chasm of alienation between the government-in-exile and the Jews.[201] The matter of the behavior of the Polish Embassy and Polish Army toward the Jewish refugees and deportees in the Soviet Union, for example, figured prominently even in the early stages of Kot's discussions, especially in talks with Ben Gurion on 3 December and with the Reprezentacja two days later;[202] and its mention appears visibly to have upset him. At the meeting with the Reprezentacja, in particular, the Polish diplomat evidently felt himself under heavy attack, as the Jewish spokesmen argued that the manner in which their coreligionists had been treated by the official agencies of the Polish government in Russia proved that the Sikorski regime's approach to Jewish affairs was essentially no different from that of Piłsudski's successors. The ambassador reacted to this charge with a vicious counteroffensive that included not only a repetition of the standard accusations of Jewish-Bolshevik complicity during the years between the Soviet invasion of eastern Poland and the conclusion of the Polish-Soviet agreement, but also a blanket indictment of Jews as one of the major supports of the Piłsudski regime.[203] He contended that during his tenure as ambassador he had risked his personal popularity among the Poles in Russia in order to appoint Jews to positions in the administration of the relief apparatus, and he expressed disgruntlement that he had heard no Jewish acknowledgment of his efforts. He spoke in praise of Anders, who he claimed had personally arranged for the removal of a thousand Jewish orphans to Iran, and of the government as a whole, whose official pronouncements on the Jewish question had been, to his mind, uniformly positive. That Jews could ignore such an impressive record and could continue to harbor suspicions of the government's intentions toward them was, he declared, incomprehensible; it merely reconfirmed that at bottom Polish Jews possessed no feelings of loyalty or responsibility toward their country. "It is the obligation of all citizens," he observed, "to do all that they possibly can for their homeland, but right now the Jews . . . show no sign of activity in any regard—except, perhaps, when it comes to protesting against Poland."[204]

Kot repeated similar words later that day at a press conference with the editors of the country's major Hebrew dailies, and again at a general meeting with Jewish political and religious leaders on 6 December.[205] On the latter occasion, moreover, his remarks were entirely unsolicited, as the question of the Polish Jews in Russia was not even raised by the Jewish representatives present. Again, when the Reprezentacja organized a banquet in his honor, the ambassador threatened not to attend unless the banquet chairman included in his opening remarks an expression of thanks to the government for its actions on behalf of the Jewish refugees in the Soviet Union.[206] Needless to say, Kot's vociferous persistence along these lines merely reinforced the long-accumulated negative Jewish perception of the Poles and their present government. As Moshe Kleinbaum of the Reprezentacja told Kot at a discussion devoted completely to issues whose origin was in Russia, "Your entire speech . . . proves conclusively that when it comes to the Poles' attitudes toward Jews, nothing has changed."[207]

For all of this, though, it appears that neither Kot nor the Jewish leaders had wanted their discussions to end on such a note. During the period of the ambassador's stay in the country the Jews of Palestine were brutally awakened to a dimension of their relationship with the Polish government that they had hardly considered before. On 16 November a group of Palestinian citizens who had been detained in Nazi-occupied Europe since the beginning of the war arrived at a British installation near Haifa, after having been exchanged for German nationals who had been similarly detained on Allied territory. They brought with them firsthand accounts of the systematic murder of European Jewry then being carried out on Polish soil by the German occupiers. Although news of mass killings of Jews had been reaching Palestine for some months, the thought that the Jewish population of an entire continent could be wholly annihilated with mechanical precision according to a preset plan was generally considered too fantastic for belief. The eyewitness testimonies that the group delivered to representatives of the Jewish Agency on 18 and 19 November, however, no longer left any room for doubt. From then on, the attentions of Jews in Palestine, as well as those of Jews in the West, were to be directed toward the rescue of European Jewry from the Nazi Holocaust.[208]

The Jewish leaders who met with Kot following receipt of these eyewitness reports were convinced that the Polish government could play a crucial role in determining the success of future rescue operations. It was in a stronger position than organized Jewry, they believed, to convince the Western world of the reality and the dimensions of the mass murder being conducted in Poland and to encourage the Allied and neutral nations both to take reprisals against Germany and to extend aid and asylum to those Jews who somehow managed to escape from Nazi-held territories. It could facilitate underground contacts between the Jews of the free world and their fellow Jews under German occupation. It could provide a steady flow of accurate information from underground sources about the unfolding Jewish situation. And, perhaps most important, it could mobilize the people of the occupied homeland to oppose Nazi anti-Jewish measures actively and to provide all possible assistance to their victims. In this sense, then, it was very much in the Jewish interest to pursue the best possible relations with the government-in-exile and to proffer it whatever support organized Jewry was capable of providing. Among Jewish leaders, Ben Gurion appears to have understood this fact most clearly: after pointing out to Kot the types of action Jews hoped the Polish government might now be inclined to take on their behalf, he made certain to add that although he did "not know how Jews might help Poland, . . . no people in the world is more prepared to back the struggle of the Polish people than are the Jews."[209]

Kot, of course, had definite ideas about how Jews might help to advance the Polish cause. Support for Polish territorial claims in the east was but one of them. In addition, he sought Jewish backing for the concept of a federation of Central European states to be formed after the war—an idea which formed a key element in Sikorski's diplomatic thinking and in which the prime minister was at that very moment endeavoring to interest the government of the United States.[210] He also requested that the Jewish Agency join the Polish government in demanding that the Allies take repressive measures against Germany, including in particular the bombing of German positions within Poland.[211] But most important of all, he demanded that the Jews in Palestine "conduct a single, uniform policy of maintaining [among Polish Jews] a sense of attachment to the Polish land and culture."[212] He suggested throughout his stay that it was vital for Poles to feel that their Jewish fellow citizens sincerely desired to be a part of their country and were prepared to fulfill their patriotic duty of defending at all times the good name and integrity of their homeland.

Kot appears to have been keenly aware that the news of the Holocaust of European Jewry could easily be converted into a lever for extracting from the Jewish leadership the concrete political steps that the Polish government had long sought, and he did not shirk from employing it in this fashion. At a meeting with a delegation of Jewish religious leaders from Poland on 5 December, for example, the ambassador was asked whether the Polish government could help them make contact with the Vatican and with neutral countries, especially Turkey and Iran, or locate potential places of asylum for refugees from Nazi-held territory. Kot replied that it would be extremely difficult to do so. "If," however, he suggested, "all Jewish groups would send a clever telegram to General Sikorski, who is now in Washington, this might create the desired result." Kot made clear, however, that this telegram must be one that could serve Polish propaganda purposes, insisting that it "come to the attention of American opinion." He also wondered aloud whether "certain organizations could approach the appropriate contacts in America, constantly citing the actions of the Polish government on the Jewish question."[213]

Later that day the ambassador delivered the same message, in stronger terms, to representatives of the Jewish press. Asked in no uncertain terms "what . . . the Polish government plan[s] to do about the murder of Jewish Polish citizens," and specifically whether Information Minister Stroński had broadcast instructions to the people of the occupied homeland "to resist the Nazi atrocities," Kot merely praised the government's efforts thus far to aid the endangered Jewish people and placed the responsibility for future action upon the Jews themselves:

> There is no need to influence the Polish government. There can be no unresolved matters between Poles and Jews. The fact that some Jews have come out against Poland has damaged the Polish cause. You must bring your influence to bear wherever you have access. I suggest that you send a telegram to General Sikorski with a request for further effort, declaring support and a desire to collaborate. This will make a better impression upon Roosevelt than my cable.[214]

The demand for quid pro quo, however, was enunciated most forcefully at Kot's second meeting with the leaders of the Reprezentacja. Here the Jewish delegates expressed their hope that the unsatisfactory attitude, to their minds, which the Polish government had hitherto demonstrated toward matters of Jewish concern would change in light of the horrors currently being perpetrated by the occupiers against Jews on Polish soil, and that the government would use its influence over the population of the occupied homeland to encourage action aimed at rescuing the Jewish victims of the Nazi murder campaign. The ambassador's reply was brutal:

> . . . Jews need to stop complaining and get to work. Where is the Jews' public declaration that Lwów and Wilno ought to be returned to Poland? Why have the Jews done nothing in this matter? Either the Jews express solidarity with Polish actions, or they [should] step aside, and then they will not be able to bring accusations against the Polish government.[215]

The public declaration that Kot demanded, however, was not forthcoming, nor was a cessation of Jewish complaints against the government. On the contrary, Yitshak Gruenbaum told the ambassador flatly that although the Jewish Agency did not oppose Poland's desire to expand westward at Germany's expense, it could make no commitment at this time regarding the Polish-Soviet boundary. After all, he explained, it was possible that the Soviet government might change its hitherto-negative attitude toward the Zionist movement, in which case the Jewish Agency would have to adjust its attitude toward the Soviets accordingly.[216] Anshel Reiss, too, publicly took the position that "there can be differences of opinion between us"[217] —a statement to which Kot objected strongly.[218] Thus it is not surprising that the ambassador's response to the specific requests regarding rescue presented to him by the Jewish spokesmen was on the whole far from encouraging. He did agree, to be sure, to instruct the Polish consular authorities in Jerusalem to provide the Jewish leadership on an ongoing basis with information about the situation of the Jews in Poland, and he indicated that he had asked the government to assure neutral countries that any Polish Jewish refugees to whom they granted asylum would be readmitted to Poland following the war.[219] Yet he consistently denied that the government-in-exile could do any more than it had done already either to arouse the conscience of the West or to influence Poles in the occupied homeland to shelter and protect the mortally endangered Jewish population.

Certainly the bitterness of the exchanges over the situation of Polish Jews in the USSR was not conducive to breaking this impasse. In fact, Kot seems to have felt obliged to counter Jewish accusations against the Polish government with a remark that on occasion Jews had betrayed Poles to the Nazi occupier. On two separate occasions he recounted at some length a purported incident in which the Polish inhabitants of a small town had refused a German order to shoot the town's Jews although some of the Jews had been prepared to obey a similar order to shoot the Poles.[220] Thus it appears that the dispute over official Polish treatment of Polish Jewish refugees in the Soviet Union seriously impeded the prospects for active Polish-Jewish collaboration precisely at what would seem otherwise to have been a highly propitious moment for its realization.

Nonetheless, it was clear that contacts between the two sides would have to continue, given the Jewish perception of the central role that the government-in-exile stood to play in rescue matters. Furthermore, Polish officials could hardly turn a blind eye to the unprecedented horrors being perpetrated on Polish soil against the Jewish people, especially because by the end of 1942 they had become known, at least in their general outlines, in the West. The government, whether it wished or not, would henceforth be called upon to respond to the plight of its Jewish citizens under German occupation in full public view. The character of its response would, of course, be influenced in large measure by the tenor of its previous interactions with world Jewry. But it would also be shaped in accordance with the perceptions it had formed of the precise situation of the Jews and of the nature of Polish-Jewish relations in the occupied homeland during the first three years of the war.

UNDER THE SWASTIKA

The context of Polish-Jewish relations under German occupation was, of course, fundamentally different from that which had prevailed before September 1939. Where in independent Poland those relations had been defined largely by the position of the Poles as masters in their own home against that of the Jews as troublesome and—to many—unwelcome guests, the occupation placed both groups on the level of conquered populations. Both Poles and Jews found themselves suddenly and violently shorn of the political, economic, social, and cultural frameworks about which they had organized their lives for the previous twenty years. The new frameworks that were forcibly imposed upon them instead were constructed with no regard for their own needs but exclusively for the benefit of the conquerors. Thus both groups were made objects of confiscation and plunder by their new rulers; both could be conscripted for forced labor; both could be removed from their homes at short notice and summarily deported to a new place of residence tens or even hundreds of miles away; both were denied adequate food supplies; both were deprived of the possibility of educating themselves or their children as they pleased; both were stripped of the rights of free expression, movement, and association; and both were left with no legal recourse or protection against a regime of wanton brutality and terror.[1]

Yet for all of the apparent similarities in the situation of the two peoples under the swastika, there were important differences as well. In Nazi eyes, Jews and Poles constituted two distinct populations toward whom two distinct sets of policy objectives applied. The Poles were generally regarded in Nazi ideology as people of inferior race, who were to be made into a reservoir of slave labor for the German Reich.[2] In order to facilitate their adjustment to their helot status, all vestiges of independent Polish life were to be destroyed. This goal begat, among other things, the so-called exceptional pacification procedure (*außerordentliche Befriedungsaktion* or *AB-Aktion*) of spring 1940, in addition to similar previous and subsequent operations in which educated Poles—political leaders, civil servants, clergymen, doctors, lawyers, teachers, engineers—as well as wealthy landowners and industrialists were either incarcerated in concentration camps or wantonly murdered, in order to obliterate the nation's intellectual and spiritual leadership and to stifle any possible development of resistance.[3] It also brought with it the liquidation of Polish cultural and religious institutions and the elimination of opportunities for all but vocational education beyond the primary level.[4] In a similar vein, the Germans sought to disrupt the attachment of the population to the former Polish state. On 8 October 1939 the new rulers incorporated the western provinces of Poland directly into the Reich and—to facilitate their rapid Germanization—deported at least several hundred thousand Poles, and perhaps even over a million, into the unincorporated areas under their administration, which they called the Generalgouvernement.[5]

The persecution of the Poles was ruthless. During the war 3 million of them were murdered by starvation, forced labor, or execution. Indeed, of all the peoples of occupied Europe, their suffering was the greatest—except for the Jews. For though they were destined for extinction as a nation, most of them still had a definite if ignominious function to perform as individuals in the Nazi "new order." Not so the Jews. They were looked upon in principle not as racially inferior humans but as nonhumans; they were an "anti-race [*Gegenrasse*]," driven by a biological imperative to destroy the German nation.[6] There was, in consequence, no useful function that they could perform in the Reich. Thus as early as 21 September 1939, even before the conquest of Poland had been completed, Reinhard Heydrich, chief of the German Security Police, outlined in a memorandum to the heads of the Einsatzgruppen[7] in Poland the steps to be taken toward bringing about the ultimate removal of Polish Jewry from the newly captured areas.[8] Among these were the expulsion of as many Jews as possible from the provinces to be incorporated and their resettlement in what eventually became the Generalgouvernement; the concentration of Jews in a few large cities strategically located at major railway junctions; the creation of ghettos in the concentration points, where Jews would be required to live and which they would be forbidden to leave after a certain hour in the evening; the establishment of "Jewish councils [*Judenräte*]" or "Councils of Elders [*Ältestenräte*]," upon which the full responsibility for ensuring Jewish compliance with the resettlement order would be placed; and the expropriation and "Aryanization" of Jewish factories, businesses, and real property, to the extent that this step was not likely seriously to disrupt the economy of the conquered regions. Over the next two years, these became well established as the basic lines of German policy toward Polish Jewry.[9]

Additional measures adopted in the same interval worsened conditions for Jews still further and underscored their inferiority to Poles in the Nazi occupation scheme. After 1 December 1939 all Jews in the Generalgouvernement above the age of ten were required to wear on the right arm a band with a Star of David, in order that they be immediately identifiable as Jews.[10] In January 1940 the governor-general, Hans Frank, issued an order forbidding Jews in the General-gouvernement to travel by train.[11] Where Polish elementary schools continued for the most part to function during the winter of 1940, Jewish schools were generally not permitted to open.[12] All Jewish bank accounts were blocked, with Jews permitted to hold no more than 2,000 złotych in cash per family and to draw from their accounts no more than 250 złotych per week.[13] Jewish food rations were restricted to less than one-third of those permitted Poles (which in turn were less than one-third of those allotted to Germans), while the cost of food to Jews was over twice the cost to Poles and almost twenty times the cost to Germans.[14] The living space assigned to Jews, especially following the sealing of the ghettos, was also significantly less than that available to Poles.[15] Jews, like Poles, were impressed for labor service; but whereas Poles often worked in war industry and were entitled to some small compensation for their work, Jews could be made to work without pay under the supervision of the SS.[16] Poles, though themselves subject to expropriation, were allowed to own more types of property than were Jews; and in many cases Poles actually took over goods and businesses that Jews had formerly owned.[17] It appears, in short, that whereas the conquerors displayed a modicum of interest in providing the bulk of their Polish subjects with at least the barest means of subsistence in order to permit the maximum exploitation of their labor, they exhibited no such concern with regard to Jews.

The Nazi authorities were interested in accentuating the differences in status between Poles and Jews not only for ideological but for tactical reasons as well. The occupiers feared lest the two groups develop a consciousness of common suffering or a feeling of solidarity against a mutual oppressor; their goal was to fragment potential resistance to their rule as much as possible.[18] Thus they hoped to be able to exacerbate Polish-Jewish antagonisms, which they had observed with keen interest during the prewar years.[19] Nazi propaganda regularly employed the argument that "at last the Germans are solving the Jewish Question in the Generalgouvernement, not so much for themselves as in consideration of the interest of the Polish nation," as a means of reconciling broad strata of Polish society to German rule.[20] In this connection it explained that the especially harsh regime introduced against the Jews was intended first of all to protect the Polish population's health and safety.[21] In addition, especially during the first months of the occupation, *agents provocateurs* from the Security Police organized operations designed to set Poles and Jews against one another. In Łódź, according to one account, they destroyed a Catholic church and subsequently spread rumors blaming Jews.[22] In Warsaw the authorities released two Polish madwomen from an insane asylum, who subsequently "ran through the streets, shouting that their husbands had been killed by the Jews in the Soviet [Union] and insulting and slapping on the face the Jewesses they chanced to meet on their way."[23] There are also reports that Germans encouraged Poles to "confiscate" Jewish property for their personal use: one quoted a Gestapo official informing the chief of a Polish institution that it was *"anxious to see the Polish population made aware* that any Pole may go up to any Jewish store, remove the

Jew from the premises, and according to our law take it over in trusteeship."[24]

Through such propaganda and actions the German rulers seem to have encountered little difficulty in recruiting bands of young Polish toughs to "make pogroms against the Jews."[25] During the first four months of 1940, outbreaks of violence against Jewish passers-by in the streets, in addition to pillaging of Jewish shops and buildings by Polish gangs inspired by Germans, became frequent.[26] Often German film crews would be sent (presumably by prior arrangement) to the scenes of such outbreaks, in order to record the violence for subsequent propaganda use.[27] The Nazi press also gave coverage to instances of Polish-Jewish tension in a fashion carefully designed to promote further mutual hostility.[28]

What effect did the German efforts to augment hostility between the two groups have upon the tenor of Polish-Jewish relations? The evidence is complex and contradictory, with neither Polish nor Jewish sources, taken as a whole, providing an entirely consistent picture. The Polish government was, of course, interested in presenting to the Allied public the behavior of Poles under occupation in as favorable a light as possible. Thus during the first two years of the war there appeared in the West several official and unofficial Polish publications claiming that "the reaction of the Poles [to German anti-Jewish agitation] has been exactly opposite that expected by the Germans."[29] For all of the obvious bias inherent in such statements, however, a number of *Jewish* witnesses, who might naturally be suspected of bias in the opposite direction, actually provide corroboration for this version of events. In his diary entry for 1 February 1940, for example, Haim Kaplan observed that antisemitic propaganda spread by the occupiers had made little impression upon the Polish public: "Common suffering has drawn all hearts closer, and the barbaric persecutions of the Jews have even aroused feelings of sympathy toward them. Tacitly, wordlessly, the two former rivals sense that they have a common enemy who wishes to bring destruction upon both at the same time. Such a stand on the part of the Poles in relation to the Jews has endangered the entire strategy of the conquerors. . . ."[30]

Earlier the Hebrew teacher from Warsaw had remarked that although many Jews feared "that the 'Jewish badge' would provide the local population with a source of mockery or ridicule," he, to his surprise, had encountered "no attitude of disrespect nor of making much of another's dishonor," but actual commiseration with the Jews in their humiliation.[31] The Bund activist Bernard Goldstein was likewise pleasantly struck by the efforts of many Polish intellectuals, peasants, and socialist workers to express sympathy and extend aid to Jews in distress. Even Endecja circles, he noted, though still officially committed to an anti-Jewish program once Poland was liberated, recoiled from the brutality of the Nazi version of antisemitism and openly condemned Polish cooperation with German operations against Jews.[32] A similar picture was transmitted from underground by the Labor Zionist youth organization HeHaluts in Warsaw to its movement headquarters in Geneva in 1941: "The Germans try to incite the Poles to anti-Semitism, however, without success. The intelligent Pole knows now that anti-Semitism is identical with eradication of the Polish people. Generally speaking, Poles are today in Poland far from being anti-Semitic. Conservative Poles are collaborating today with Polish Socialists and Polish Jews."[33]

Other Jewish sources, however, present a different picture. One "trustworthy Jewish personality" who had fled Poland for Romania on 12 October 1939 reported upon crossing the border that the cooperation between Poles and Jews that had characterized the period of the siege of Warsaw broke down once the Germans entered the city, and that from then on Jews had suffered much at the hands of the local population.[34] This evaluation was seconded by another Jewish witness who had left Warsaw two weeks later. He observed that "partly as a result of instigation by the Germans, the Poles have adopted a violently antisemitic attitude."[35] Still other deponents, commenting upon anti-Jewish street violence carried out by Polish gangs in March and April 1940, claimed that although educated Poles were angered by the cooperation of a Polish mob in a German-inspired pogrom, the bulk of the Polish population "stood at the Germans' disposal."[36] It even appears that in the wake of the Easter riots of 27–30 March, Kaplan may have altered somewhat his previously positive assessment of Polish attitudes. He complained that when "several hundred Poles went mad and perpetrated acts of abomination . . . no one blocked their path."[37]

The want of decisive Polish opposition to such violence also troubled the Warsaw Jewish historian and communal worker Emanuel Ringelblum:

The period from October 1939 to November 1940 . . . was a period of constant anti-Jewish violence, which steadily increased. It started with attacks on individual Jews and ended with uncontrolled pillage of Jewish wealth and recurrent pogroms in different parts of Warsaw. . . . No one will accuse the Polish nation of committing these constant pogroms. . . . The significant majority of the nation . . . undoubtedly condemned these excesses. . . . We do, however, reproach the Polish community with not having tried to dissociate itself . . . from the anti-Semitic beasts . . . and for not having actively opposed the constant excesses, for not having done anything whatsoever to weaken the impression that the whole Polish population . . . approved of the performances of the Polish anti-Semites.[38]

Can it be that most Poles were inwardly sympathetic to the Jewish plight but were afraid, in the face of the pervasive German-imposed terror, to give their sympathy any more than private, unobtrusive expression? Remarkably, most contemporary Polish testimonies presented Polish feelings in a different light. Jan Karski, in the detailed eyewitness account that he delivered personally to the Polish government in February 1940, stated categorically that the attitude of "the broad masses of the Polish populace . . . toward the Jews is overwhelmingly severe, often without pity."[39] In his estimation, an "understanding that . . . both peoples are being unjustly persecuted by the same enemy" did not exist among most Poles. The Germans, he claimed, were succeeding in their goal of creating a "schism between Jews and Poles" in their fight against the common foe.[40] Numerous other reports from Polish underground sources in subsequent months echoed Karski's conclusion. In addition, much correspondence between Poles in Poland and relatives or acquaintances abroad that came to the attention of Polish diplomatic missions was, in the words of an official of the Polish Embassy in Bucharest, "ringing with the accent of antisemitism [*brzmiące akcentem antysemityzmu*]."[41]

There were also those who spoke in somewhat less apodictic terms, but whose assessments remained in the final analysis negative. One observer wrote, "I have not encountered the opinion that the Nürnberg Laws ought to be introduced into the new [postwar] Poland, but on the other hand I have encountered relatively few indications of sympathy for Jews, even though their fate is undoubtedly very hard."[42] Another noted a class distinction similar to that mentioned by several Jewish witnesses. He stressed that whereas the "possessing classes" had generally found themselves, in contrast to the occupiers' expectations, provoked into a spirit of resistance by the German terror, "the petty bourgeoisie and the *Lumpenproletariat*, who are susceptible to Jew-baiting and for whom the Jewish policy of the occupier has opened new possibilities for income, succumb most quickly to demoralization and accommodate themselves to the present conditions."[43]

To be sure, not all Polish witnesses agreed with these evaluations. There were also reports of mounting compassion among Poles for Jews, or at least of a lack of any notable response to German attempts to fan Polish anti-Jewish hostility.[44] A letter from the underground, probably from early 1940, stated emphatically that "the oppression of the Jews by the Germans is eliciting resentment among the Polish community, and the prewar antisemitic attitudes of certain circles of the community have been significantly weakened."[45] Yet few other sources were so unqualifiedly positive. The most balanced estimate of the situation appears to have been offered in a comprehensive summary of the situation in Warsaw and the Generalgouvernement prepared by a member of the underground military organization on 31 December 1940:

> That which the occupiers have already managed to accomplish in the struggle against the Jews exceeds the wildest dreams of even the most rabid antisemites. Perhaps only the fear that following the victory of the democracies this whole fine edifice could easily come tumbling down like a house of cards disturbs their sleep. Our antisemites [even] resent the lack of consistency in some of the German measures. Many Poles are expressing satisfaction among themselves that the Jews are being removed . . . from Polish residential districts, official positions, the free professions, industry, and commerce, but they do not allow themselves to display this outwardly in any form. This is because the people are shocked by the way such measures are being carried out. Characteristically, the actions involve human suffering, and for this reason these people even express quiet sympathy for the Jews and help them where possible, or at least do not make their difficult situation any worse. (Such

things are best observable among Polish white-collar workers and merchants.) A certain percentage of the Poles clearly behave kindly toward the Jews.[46]

Any conclusions that might be reached from such disparate evaluations must be tenuous ones. It does seem, however, that although much of the prewar hostility between Poles and Jews remained in force following the German invasion, it is not fair to speak unreservedly of antisemitism as the sole spirit underlying most Poles' response to the plight of Polish Jewry under Nazi rule. It appears rather that in confronting the anti-Jewish propaganda and persecutions conducted by the German occupiers during the first two years of the war, the Polish community found itself beset by sharply conflicting emotions. The same thing can surely be said of individual Poles. Though many undoubtedly continued to believe that in the long run Polish Jewry must be weakened to the maximum extent possible, not many appear to have been enthusiastic over the prospect that this situation might come to pass as the result of wanton German cruelty similar, if not identical, to that from which the Polish population itself was suffering. There were, of course, those who were able to resolve their mixed feelings fairly easily (or, perhaps, who never had any mixed feelings at all); these were presumably the ones who, depending upon the outcome of their resolution, either expressed solidarity with their Jewish fellow citizens and took steps to alleviate Jewish suffering[47] or took part in the plunder of Jewish shops and pointed out to the German authorities Jews trying surreptitiously to pass as Poles.[48] Nevertheless, it seems reasonable to surmise that the majority of Poles were at first unsure how they ought to react outwardly to the conqueror's onslaught against the Jews, and that their ambivalence came for the most part over time to be reflected in a quiet reconciliation with the prevailing state of affairs.

Such a conclusion, though, is suggested by comparing a range of sources—Polish and Jewish; reports, letters, diaries, and memoirs—of which only some were available at the time to the government-in-exile. If, on the other hand, only the information received by the government during the first two years of the war, which consisted mainly of dispatches from the Polish underground and from Polish diplomatic missions abroad, is taken into account, a darker picture of Polish attitudes toward Jews emerges.[49] This preponderance of negative reports could well have been of central importance in the formation of the government's posture toward its Jewish citizens under German occupation, and perhaps even in the development of the attitudes of the Polish community as a whole. The basically passive attitude of most Poles toward the German anti-Jewish measures was, in effect, as Karski made clear in his report to the government, tantamount to a victory for the occupiers, for it indicated that the bulk of the Polish population had resigned itself to at least one feature of the new regime.[50] If, however, this reaction was in fact more the result of a paralysis born of an equilibrium of countervailing pushes and tugs upon Polish sensibilities than of an expression of a relentless and invariable antipathy of Poles toward Jews, then it was theoretically subject to change upon the entry of new pressures into the equation. In this respect the situation invited the intervention of the government-in-exile as a force claiming moral leadership of the Polish nation in its struggle to regain its freedom. A concerted educational effort aimed at showing how the Germans sought to exploit anti-Jewish feelings among the Polish population in order to solidify their conquest, and explaining that, in Karski's words, "everything that the Germans endeavor to do to the Polish nation is harmful to it" and had to be resisted, might conceivably have struck a responsive chord in many Poles.[51] Yet from the accounts delivered to it regarding the nature of Polish-Jewish relations under occupation, it is doubtful that the government could have sensed much genuine ambivalence among the Polish population that might have been affected by its intervention. The one report that spoke at any length about the conflicting emotions raised among the Polish community, which was dispatched at the end of December 1940, was circulated among government officials only in April 1941;[52] by that time the government must surely have concluded that, its own public pronouncements notwithstanding, Polish society had remained largely hostile to Jews even after the German conquest.[53] Thus, in a situation in which the exile government was vitally concerned with strengthening its authority over the developing Polish underground movement and among the Polish community as a whole, vigorous and persistent attempts on its part to influence Poles to oppose the anti-Jewish designs of the Nazis actively or to render assistance to Jewish victims of German persecution might well have seemed ill-advised.

Indeed, this consideration appears to have militated against any large-scale involvement by the government-in-exile with the fate of Polish Jewry under German occupation during the first years of the war. The plight of the Jewish population did not occupy a significant place in the government's communications with the homeland during this period.[54] Nor does the available evidence contain any noteworthy indication that the government endeavored to initiate serious educational activities among the Polish community regarding the tactical aspects of German policy toward Jews.[55] Furthermore, there is little to suggest that the government concerned itself with the evacuation of Jews—especially Jewish political leaders—from Poland, as it did in the case of Polish leaders,[56] or that it made any special effort during the period in question to provide needed material assistance to alleviate specifically Jewish physical suffering in the homeland.[57]

Put another way, it appears that, at least during the first two years of the war, the Polish government's involvement with Jewish affairs was restricted almost entirely to the affairs of Jews outside Poland. The immediate sufferings of the 2 million Polish Jewish citizens under the swastika do not seem to have moved it to any serious action.

Three additional considerations appear to have reinforced the government's inclination to inaction in matters concerning the situation of the Jews in the German-occupied territories. In the first place, the government-in-exile, if only by virtue of its physical location, tended on the whole to concern itself primarily with matters of foreign policy; with regard to domestic affairs its interest was naturally centered upon activities aimed ultimately at driving the foreign conquerors from the occupied homeland. Therefore the government's relationship to the Jews in Poland itself could not help but be influenced by its perceptions of the Jews' ability to assist it in achieving its aims in these two areas. In practical terms, however, there was no way that Jews subjected to the Nazi yoke could exert direct influence upon the conduct of Allied diplomacy. Thus the latter consideration was of greater consequence. Indeed, the government seems to have been most interested in knowing how Jews were responding to the German occupation. In this regard, the picture obtained from underground reports during the first two years of the war presented Jewish behavior in a highly unfavorable light. Karski claimed in February 1940, for example, that "with regard to the Germans, the Jews are docile [and] submissive . . ."; he noted "no talk of any action on their part, of *active defense* of their right to live and work." According to him, "the Jew[s] would rather commit suicide than resist the Germans . . . ; their only reaction consists of attempts to escape to Bolshevik occupation, or more often literally not to appear in the light of day."[58] Other dispatches even spoke of Jewish acts of hostility against Poles: Jews were charged, among other things, with profiteering in the sale of foodstuffs or with refusing to sell food to Poles at all.[59] At least two reports claimed further that Jews were "cooperating rather intensively with the Gestapo, . . . primarily against the Polish nation."[60] And, of course, considerable attention was paid to the existence of Communist influences among Jews, which were also said to be directed against Polish interests.[61]

In light of such intelligence, the government could hardly have concluded that the Jews in the German-occupied areas had merited its consideration and support. Moreover, much of the information obtained from the homeland during the period in question suggested that the Jews, though sorely oppressed, might in fact be objectively less in need of protection and assistance than the Polish population. This is not to say that the government did not know of the special anti-Jewish measures introduced by the conquerors; on the contrary, the information that it possessed was in general remarkably complete and accurate. Rather, it tended simply not to attach any particular importance to the existence of these special restrictions. As early as 27 October 1939 a report was dispatched from Warsaw hinting that Jewish fears of persecutions that the Nazi regime might introduce had thus far not proved justified by the behavior of the German authorities, and indicating that many of the newly imposed harsh decrees applied not only to Jews but to Poles as well.[62]

Indeed, until February 1940, most evaluations that compared the relative situations of the two peoples did not indicate that Jewish suffering was in any way exceptional.[63] After that time, the government began to receive reports clearly stating that the situation of the Jews was in general preferable to that of the Poles. Most of these reports mentioned that Jews, unlike Poles, were not sent for forced labor in Germany proper; that whereas Poles were directly subject to the German authorities, the Jews enjoyed the protection of the *Juden-räte*, which could sometimes mitigate the severity of the German decrees; and that no effort was being made systematically to eliminate the Jewish leadership comparable to the *AB-Aktion* directed against the Poles.[64] Others maintained that the German anti-Jewish measures were intended not so much to destroy the Jewish nation as to extort money and property from the Jewish communities and from wealthy individual Jews and that as a result the implementation of many decrees could be forestalled through bribery.[65] Even Karski, who made it clear that to his mind "the conditions in which . . . the Jews live in the territories annexed by the Third Reich and even in the Generalgouvernement often exceed what one can imagine of human misery," claimed that the Germans "do not particularly care *in principle* about the oppression of Polish Jews in the Generalgouvernement" and that with enough money Jews could buy their way out of most of the special restrictions.[66] In contrast, the persecution of the Poles was generally portrayed as principled and political, and the Polish community as in greater immediate danger of national extinction. Under such conditions, the government could hardly have been expected to show special concern for the affliction of the Jews.

Nor does it appear that during the first two years of the war the government was subjected to much external pressure to do so. As vocal as Jewish spokesmen were in decrying dubious utterances regarding the future of the Jewish question in Poland and hints of possible discrimination by Polish officials toward Polish Jews outside the homeland, they were virtually silent about the government's responsibility toward its Jewish citizens suffering under the Nazi yoke. Curiously, the absence of Jewish representations in this matter seems to have reflected a tendency of Jewish political organizations in the West to place the matter of Jewish legal status in the postwar world ahead of relief and rescue for Polish Jewry on their wartime agendas.[67] The eventual slaughter of over nine-tenths of Polish Jewry was at this time not anticipated; the anti-Jewish actions of the German occupiers tended rather to be viewed as little more than a pogrom of unusually large dimensions. In this context the tribulations of the Jews in Poland were understood in Western Jewish circles as a more or less inescapable by-product of the war situation, against which the best defense was as swift and decisive a defeat of the Nazi regime as possible.[68]

More important to most Jewish organizations seems to have been the creation of a postwar order in which a comprehensive solution to the Jewish question in Europe could be obtained.[69] The Zionist-oriented organizations decided as a result that whatever resources they might allocate to relief projects would be most productively directed toward helping those who had managed already to escape from Poland and who might be brought to Palestine.[70] Here the Reprezentacja in particular actively sought the cooperation and assistance of the Polish government.[71] But even those Jewish organizations and individuals that saw their primary purpose as philanthropic, such as the American Jewish Joint Distribution Committee, do not appear to have pressed the Polish government for financial or any other kind of support.[72] The reasons are unclear, but the effect was in all likelihood telling. Organized Jewish pressure was, at least from mid-1940, the only force that might conceivably have counterbalanced the various tendencies bidding the government to inaction; yet if free world Jewry did not hold the government's attitude toward the Jews of occupied Poland up to the kind of careful scrutiny that it applied to its political declarations and behavior toward Polish Jewish soldiers and refugees, then the government was understandably likely to concern itself more with the latter aspects of Polish-Jewish relations than with the former.[73]

Yet if the government possessed no compelling reason to take serious action on behalf of the Jews of German-occupied Poland, and in fact possessed several reasons not to do so, it could still make use of the plight of the Jews for its own external propaganda purposes. It seems, in fact, that the government was quite interested during the first two years of the war in publicizing in the West at least a certain amount of news of the Jewish situation, probably in the belief that such news could arouse public anger against Germany in a way that news of the persecution of Poles by itself could not. Though from the Polish point of view the German measures against the Polish population, intended as they were to destroy all possibility of independent Polish national existence, appeared more consequential than the ostensibly sporadic and inconsistent anti-Jewish actions, it was precisely in such capricious oppression that the barbarism and brutality of the German conquerors could be thrown into most vivid relief. Thus the Polish Information and Interior Ministries issued several fairly extensive and accurate descriptions of what the Nazis had been doing to Polish Jewry, although they were careful at the same time to emphasize the "lack of uniformity in the anti-semitic policy of the Germans." They described this policy as "the persecution of a people who have no means of defending themselves . . . carried out with sadistic cruelty . . . devoid of any wider purpose . . . for the sake of small profits accruing from occasional robbery."[74] "The German dignitaries," they pointed out, ". . . do not [even] observe . . . the [official] decrees, believing themselves to be entitled to act as they please; they seem to find particular pleasure in maltreating and humiliating the Jews, inflicting moral and physical tortures on them, carrying out mass executions and condemning multitudes to death by starvation."[75]

The Polish authorities also evidently felt it important to counter German propaganda that in the *Judenräte* the Jews of Poland enjoyed their own autonomous administration and that the resettlement of Jews into the Lublin region was a prelude to the eventual establishment of a Jewish state in the area. Their publications excoriated these arguments, correctly likening the "elders" of the *Judenräte* to hostages and the Lublin "reservation" to an oversized concentration camp.[76] Furthermore, by loudly expressing its abhorrence of German anti-Jewish actions, the Polish government could present itself as a defender of Jewish rights, an image that seemed advisable to cultivate. On the other hand, failure to condemn these actions, the broad outlines of which were known in the West from other sources,[77] might conceivably have weakened to an extent the government's claim to active Allied sympathy and support.

Nevertheless, the degree to which it was in the Polish government's interest to talk about the persecution of Jews in German-occupied Poland was limited by one fundamental consideration: in no way could publicity about the Jewish situation be permitted to interfere with the cultivation of public sympathy with the tribulations of the Poles. Thus, although the Polish authorities did convey to the West much information about the Nazi oppression of Polish Jewry during the first two years of the war, such information was for the most part deeply embedded in general Polish propaganda literature. In only one instance, in fact, did a separate brochure, devoted exclusively to Jewish matters, appear under official Polish sponsorship.[78]

In most other official Polish publications the amount of space allotted to the Jewish situation was relatively small. The first detailed discussion of Jewish persecution, which appeared in March 1940, occupied only 11 out of 109 pages in a report entitled *The German Attempt to Destroy the Polish Nation*. Similarly, in 1941 the Information Ministry published a 571-page description entitled *The German New Order in Poland*, in which the section on Jews was 36 pages long.[79] The *Polish Fortnightly Review*, a primary vehicle through which the government released information to the Western press, virtually ignored the Jewish plight until mid-1941. Even then, in its issue of 1 June 1941, entitled "The German Rule in Poland," an article titled "The Terror against the Jews" took up only slightly more than one of its sixteen columns.[80] And a twenty-eight-page mimeographed circular headed "Notes on the Situation of Poland under German Occupation," probably dating from late 1940, contained only scattered references to Jews, never more than one or two sentences long.[81] It seems that only the government's official Polish-language newspaper, *Dziennik Polski*, paid more than passing attention to Jewish suffering, at least from the beginning of 1941, although the extent of its coverage was perhaps attributable in part to the controversy surrounding its treatment of Jewish matters, which had at that time just broken into the open. The only other official Polish-language publication to deal in any noteworthy measure with the Jewish situation during the period in question, a mimeographed report prepared by the Interior Ministry on the activities of the occupation authorities over the fourteen-month interval following the outbreak of war, conformed to the more general pattern, devoting to the subject a scant four pages.[82] This report stressed that although the Jews' physical conditions were worse than those of the Poles, their overall situation was considerably less precarious, to the point where "the Jewish population itself senses the advantage in its position relative to that of the Poles."[83]

It seems, then, that the government's attitude toward publicizing the Jewish situation in German-occupied Poland was largely a reflection of a fundamental principle of policy that took shape during the first two years of the war—namely, that the needs and interests of the Jewish citizens of the subjugated homeland paralleled those of the Polish community only to a limited extent.[84] In this principle there was no small measure of irony, for in a sense the government's attitude signaled at least some measure of success for the Nazi drive to set Pole and Jew against one another. The conquerors' tactic of distinguishing between the status of the two groups in order to break apart whatever feelings of solidarity might develop between them bore fruit in what must have been a highly unexpected fashion when the Polish government determined that it ought to concern itself with the welfare of the conquered Polish community alone. In this fashion, a force that might have played a central role in arousing Allied sympathy for the Jewish plight, in facilitating the extension of effective succor to the suffering Jewish masses, and in educating the Polish community in Poland to the necessity of resisting Nazi measures aimed not only at it directly but at the Jewish population as well was effectively neutralized—and this of its own volition. To be sure, the government professed its awareness of the German desire to divide Poles from Jews and condemned it; but this act merely heightened the irony in its behavior. The government itself was prepared to mobilize only minimal resistance to the German onslaught against the Jews.

It was against this background that the government received the first news of the mass murder of Polish Jewry. Systematic mass killings of Polish Jews as part of a program aimed at the total biological annihilation of the Jews of all of Europe began almost immediately upon the German invasion of the Soviet Union on 22 June 1941.[85] The killings had first been envisioned several months earlier, as the invasion was being prepared, and in May four Einsatzgruppen were organized "to carry out executive measures against the civilian population" of the territories expected to fall under German control.[86] Once the German forces had crossed the Ribbentrop-Molotov line, the Einsatzgruppen went quickly to work. Within three weeks, by conservative estimate, almost 40,000 Jews had been slaughtered in the former Polish territories alone, not to mention thousands more gunned down in the Baltic states, Bukovina, Bessarabia, and the pre-1939 Soviet regions. By the end of October the number of Polish Jewish dead had risen to 150,000, out of a total of upwards of half a million Jewish victims of the Nazi mobile killing squads.[87]

Even while this slaughter was proceeding, the groundwork was being laid for the extension of the murder campaign to western Poland. In these territories, the mobile death units were to be replaced by specially constructed killing centers, to which Jews from the Polish ghettos, and eventually from the rest of Europe as well, could be easily transported. Beginning in December 1941, Jews in the Warthegau were brought to an abandoned mill near the woods at Chełmno; there they were loaded into sealed vans whose exhaust fumes were redirected into the cargo area, asphyxiating their passengers within fifteen minutes. In late February 1942 a second center was completed at Bełżec, a former labor and internment camp on the rail line between Lublin and Lwów. Here for the first time permanent gas chambers were constructed, capable of killing up to fifteen thousand victims a day. Once these installations had been tested, daily transports began to arrive from Lublin and the surrounding towns. The Jews who filled the transport trains had been told that they were to be "resettled" in the East; in fact they were smothered in the gas chambers shortly after arrival.[88] In the spring two more gassing centers began to operate: one at Sobibor, on the eastern border of the Generalgouvernement; the other at Birkenau, next to the concentration camp at Auschwitz (Oświęcim) in Upper Silesia. An additional killing installation was constructed at Treblinka, east of Warsaw, in June, and gas chambers were erected at the Majdanek concentration camp on the outskirts of Lublin a short time thereafter. In all, some 1.8 million Polish Jews—not to mention a similar number of Jews from other European countries—met their deaths in these centers for murder by the end of the war.[89]

The Polish government did not know of these new developments immediately. For many reasons, the German conquerors sought to keep their systematic murder of European Jewry a secret. They took pains to shroud their actions in a web of euphemisms: shootings by the Einsatzgruppen were referred to as "special treatment [*Sonderbehandlung*]," transportation to the gas chambers as "resettlement [*Umsiedlung*]," the murder program as a whole as the "final solution [*Endlösung*]" of the Jewish question. At one point an express order was even issued in Hitler's name forbidding public reference to the actual fate of the Jews.[90] Such efforts to camouflage and suppress the truth made it difficult at first for the Polish underground—and, by extension, the government-in-exile—to obtain an accurate picture of the new Jewish situation. The difficulty was compounded by the fact that the killings took place at remote locations; the work of the

Einsatzgruppen in particular was carried on for the most part close to the front lines, in areas subject to tight military security. Thus even once underground members close to a particular killing site learned of murders being committed nearby, delays in the transmission of intelligence to Warsaw, whence it could be forwarded to the government in London, were inevitable. It was only in October 1941, at the earliest, that news of mass shootings in the eastern territories could have been relayed from the occupied homeland to the West.[91] Reports of the events in western Poland, on the other hand, reached Warsaw with less delay: the first information about gassings at Chełmno was dispatched in early 1942, while in the spring the deportations from Lublin to Bełżec were noted in the capital.[92]

At least some of the news assembled in Warsaw, though, seems to have taken a long time to reach the government. For example, one report prepared on 15 December 1941, which noted that "Jews in the east . . . are being systematically murdered," arrived in London only on 19 October 1942.[93] Nevertheless, there is evidence that as early as November 1941 certain Polish officials in the West were aware that large numbers of Jews had "simply disappeared" from the eastern territories.[94] Mass shootings of Jews in Lithuania and White Russia were mentioned, albeit briefly, in official Polish publications in April and May 1942, so that it is certain that some reports of this new aspect of the Nazi war against the Jews had been received, at latest, by early spring.[95]

However, a comprehensive report, which described not only the killings in the east but the operation of the gas chambers in western Poland, and which unequivocally related these developments to a systematic German plan to murder all of Polish Jewry, does not appear to have reached the government-in-exile until the end of May. This report came not from a Polish source but from the underground leadership of the Bund in Warsaw, and it was directed to the Bund representative on the National Council, Szmuel Zygielbojm. In its opening sentence it starkly declared that "from the day the Russo-German war broke out, the Germans embarked on the physical extermination of the Jewish population on Polish soil." It then went on to list the numbers who had been killed in Lithuania, White Russia, and the Ukraine—including fifty thousand in Wilno, thirty thousand in Lwów, and fifteen thousand in Stanisławów—and set forth the process by which Jews in town after town were marched into the woods, forced to dig their own graves, and shot. It described the operation of the gas vans at Chełmno, in which, it observed, forty thousand Jews, "plus an indefinite number of Gypsies," had met their deaths by March, and told of the deportation of the Jews from Lublin "to an unknown destination." In the course of this deportation, the report stated, all trace of the Jews had been lost, and in the town of Lublin itself there remained not a single Jew. In all, it claimed, seven hundred thousand Jews throughout Poland had been murdered by the Germans. According to the Bund leaders, these developments proved conclusively "that the criminal German government has begun to carry out Hitler's prophecy that five minutes before the end of the war, whatever its outcome, he will have murdered all of the Jews of Europe."[96]

Did the government believe the Bund report? Raczyński, among others, was later to claim that he "had difficulty accepting it as the total truth": "It seemed to me so devilish, it seemed to me so horrible, that at first I thought it was exaggerated."[97] This could well have been the case with many Poles. Systematic mass murder on the scale described was, after all, unprecedented, and reasonable minds can be forgiven for recoiling from the prospect that such horrors might in fact be possible. Indeed, this was a common reaction in Allied and Jewish circles as well.[98] Yet on the other hand, as early as December 1941 Jan Wszelaki, head of the Polish Foreign Ministry's Anglo-American desk, had discussed with Frank Savery an underground report which claimed that the Gestapo had formulated a plan to massacre "as much of the native population in the occupied countries as will be technically feasible" in the event that the tide of battle should turn against Germany. At this time Wszelaki had argued strongly that the Germans were indeed capable, both materially and psychologically, of carrying out "a disaster unparalleled in modern history," and he insisted that "some mental preparation to [*sic*] such a possibility seems to be necessary."[99] Even though the murder of Jews was not mentioned specifically in this conversation, it appears that, at least in Raczyński's own Foreign Ministry, the prospect of the deliberate total annihilation of whole groups of innocent people by the German occupiers was not dismissed out of hand.

Whatever the case, the news that Jews were being slaughtered en masse on Polish territory did not on the whole occupy a significant position in official Polish propaganda or press releases during most of 1942. Before the receipt of the Bund report, Polish information organs offered little to suggest that anything different was happening to Jews in the newly conquered eastern territories than had occurred following the German conquest of western Poland two years before. A few short notices appeared in *Dziennik Polski* about the establishment of ghettos in Wilno and Lwów, but for the most part the newspaper concentrated in its reportage of Jewish matters upon the squalid living conditions and high mortality in the western ghettos, especially Warsaw.[100] Much attention was paid also to the deportation of German Jews to Poland. The same pattern was followed in the weekly Yiddish-language press bulletins issued by the Polish Information Center in New York for the benefit of Jewish newspapers in the United States, while the government's English-language publications ignored developments related to Jews in the east altogether.[101] It was not until April 1942 that a comprehensive Interior Ministry report on the situation in Poland mentioned mass shootings of Jews in Lithuania.[102] *Dziennik Polski* followed on 5 May with a short paragraph (buried in a longer survey of the general state of affairs in the eastern territories) noting that "the Jewish population has 'disappeared' completely from most of the cities and towns in White Russia."[103] Until June, this appears to have been all concerning the mass slaughter of Polish Jewry that the Polish government officially made known.

Such relative silence may have been merely a reflection of a skeptical attitude toward the veracity of the news of mass killings emanating from the homeland or may have indicated the understandable inability of Polish officials to deduce a plan of total annihilation from the limited, fragmentary intelligence that was available to the government-in-exile before the Bund report was received. Nevertheless, it contrasted sharply with the government's general willingness, within limits, to publicize the sufferings of the Jews in the ghettos of western Poland. In the event, it appears that whatever other factors entered into their treatment of the situation in the east, the Poles also had a strong political reason for wanting to keep public discussion of this horrible new aspect of the German war against the Jews to a minimum. Widespread publicity concerning mass murders of Jews in Poland could reasonably have been expected to make the Poles' own suffering seem less acute by comparison, and in consequence less worthy of attention and sympathy. It was, of course, not in the Polish community's interest for this to happen. Thus even the materials that the government offered for publication in the Jewish press tended to magnify the Polish plight as much as possible, at the expense of that of the Jews. Jewish misery was portrayed mainly as the result of difficult physical conditions, whereas the Poles were depicted as the primary victims of German terror.[104] The same thing can be said of other official Polish organs as well.

In another area of its activity, too, the government seems deliberately to have endeavored to prevent notice being drawn to the Jews' dire straits. On 13 January 1942 Sikorski chaired an Inter-Allied Conference on German Atrocities. Spokesmen for nine occupied countries attended the meeting at the Palace of St. James, and British and American representatives were present as observers. Despite much that was said in the course of the meeting about German bestiality toward conquered populations, the plight of the Jews was not discussed at all. Raczyński in particular vigorously denounced crimes committed by the Germans against Polish citizens, but he passed over the Jewish situation altogether. The declaration of the conference, too, though promising postwar retribution for the German "regime of terror characterised in particular by imprisonments, mass expulsions, executions of hostages, and massacres," made no mention of crimes committed specifically against Jews.[105] This omission greatly angered Jewish leaders. The British Section of the World Jewish Congress complained about it to Sikorski, who replied on 9 May that since "the character, the race or religion of the victim ought not in any case to constitute an element susceptible of modifying the criminal nature of an act or the degree of its illegality, there was no reason specifically to recall the sufferings endured by the Jews, all the more so as such a reference might be equivalent to an implicit recognition of the racial theories which we all reject."[106] To a similar objection from the Board of Deputies, Sikorski replied on 16 May that the conference's declaration could automatically be understood to have included within its scope atrocities perpetrated against Jews.[107] These were feeble excuses. It appears rather that the Polish government simply wished to avoid calling special attention to the German massacre of the Jewish population of Poland. Even as late as July 1942 the government still rejected a request from Jewish organizations for observer status at future conference sessions.[108]

Moreover, aside from its failure to move the Polish government to alert the West to the new situation, the first news of the immediate mortal danger in which Polish Jewry now found itself does not seem to have had any significant impact upon the government's readiness to attempt to aid that threatened community more directly. An indifference to problems of relief and rescue similar to that which the Polish authorities had displayed during the first two years of the war seems to have prevailed, with some exceptions, in mid-1942 as well.[109] So too, evidently, did the government's hesitancy about urging the Polish population to resist Nazi anti-Jewish actions. To be sure, on the day following the German invasion of the Soviet Union the government advised its delegate in the homeland of "the necessity of warning the nation not to give in to German baiters and not to adopt an active anti-Jewish attitude in the territories freed from Soviet occupation," but this was far from a positive instruction to show solidarity with persecuted Jews.[110] Nor does it appear to have been followed by any additional exhortations, even of so restrained a scope, after the news of the mass killings in the east surfaced in London.

On the contrary, the government seems as a matter of policy to have refrained from including so much as a mention of the systematic murder of Polish Jewry in its regular radio broadcasts to Poland. Such a policy was evidently crystallized in April 1942, when the government, in cooperation with the Political Intelligence Department of the British Foreign Office, established a secret radio station near London, known as ŚWIT, whose broadcasts were to be camouflaged so as to create the illusion that they emanated from within the occupied homeland. According to a general directive that set forth the station's basic functions and guidelines for broadcasts, "atrocity propaganda" was to be kept to a minimum. Tales of German inhumanity and terror were held to be "more appropriate to countries which have not experienced the German occupation." "Do not weaken verisimilitude," the document continued, "by informing the Poles of things they see daily."[111] With regard to Jewish matters, it was recommended that the station "limit itself to expression of sympathy for the persecutions which they [the Jews] experience at the hands of the Germans" and that it "avoid controversial matters," such as the question of the Jewish role in postwar Poland.[112] It is true that the discouragement of "atrocity propaganda" had the effect of curtailing reportage of anti-Polish terror as well.[113] But the Polish population, as the ŚWIT directive rightly pointed out, did not need London's assistance to become aware of what was happening to it. The secret radio station could, on the other hand, have served as a powerful tool for encouraging Poles to assist their Jewish fellow citizens actively, but its use as such was abjured from the start.[114]

The receipt of the Bund report appears to have affected the government's behavior only slightly. To be sure, Sikorski, in a broadcast to the homeland over the European Service of the BBC on 9 June, made mention for the first time of mass executions of Jews in Wilno, Lwów, Stanisławów, and elsewhere, and commented that the Germans intended to "slit the throats of all Jews, no matter what the outcome of the war."[115] His remarks clearly echoed passages from the Bund letter. But most of the information contained in the report, including the description of the gas vans at Chełmno, did not find its way into the prime minister's speech. In fact, only a single paragraph of the broadcast—a bit over 5 percent of the total—was devoted to Jewish matters of any kind.[116] The rest, not surprisingly, concerned German terror against Poles; and even the few sentences about the Jews left the impression that they had more to fear from hunger than from German machine guns. Where the Bund report stated categorically that "the Germans have thus far murdered 700,000 Polish Jews," the prime minister spoke of only "tens of thousands" who had been slaughtered. Once again it appears that the dimensions of the Jewish catastrophe were deliberately reduced, so as not to overshadow the sufferings of the Poles.

In fact, it was probably fortuitous that the Jewish situation entered into the Sikorski broadcast at all. Evidently, at approximately the time that the Bund report arrived in London, the government received word that a new wave of anti-Polish "lawlessness and atrocities" had broken out following Himmler's visit to Poland in early spring, and that in conjunction with this repression Poles were being impressed into the German army. Sikorski opened his speech with reference to these new developments in a fashion which suggested that they had prompted the broadcast. The purpose of his remarks, the prime minister made clear, was to impress upon the Allied governments that "the perpetrators of these crimes must be brought to account, and this principle must become a fundamental guideline of Allied war policy." Indeed, while the Poles had played a leading role in bringing about the St. James's Palace declaration of the nine occupied countries the previous January, the British and American governments had refrained from formally associating themselves with the call for postwar punishment of war criminals and had thereby weakened the declaration's impact.[117] The Polish government, however, continued to insist, in Sikorski's words, that "only the specter of punishment and retaliation . . . can stop the German thugs' frenzy in its tracks"; and with the arrival of reports of stepped-up German persecution of Poles, it seemed to it more urgent than ever that England and the United States issue an unequivocal declaration of policy in this direction. The National Council, too, on the day following the prime minister's speech, issued its own "appeal to the parliaments of free nations" for a promise that those who carried out war crimes would be suitably punished.[118] In this context it is not surprising that Sikorski would mention something of what he had learned in the Bund report, in order to underscore his contention that enormous numbers of lives were at stake—as long, of course, as the suffering of the Polish population was not thereby overshadowed. Such disclosure, however, was evidently not deemed essential, for the National Council resolution of 10 June did not refer to Jews at all.[119]

In the wake of the Sikorski broadcast, but probably more as a result of the Nazi massacre at Lidice on the same day, the British government began a comprehensive review of its policy concerning punishment of war criminals.[120] The Poles, however, do not seem to have been aware that this review was under way, or if they were, they were not overly sanguine about the outcome; for in subsequent weeks their propaganda organs continued to hammer away at the theme of German atrocities against the Polish people. In this stepped-up campaign the Jewish situation occupied a more prominent place than the government had been willing to afford it previously. On 1 July the *Polish Fortnightly Review* devoted a portion of its issue on "German Attempts to Murder a Nation"—the Polish nation, of course—to the "Destruction of the Jewish Population." This section described, among other things, the liquidation of the Lublin ghetto, reporting that most of the ghetto's inhabitants had been "murdered with gas, machine-guns and even by being bayoneted," and naming the villages of Sobibor and Majdan Tatarski as the sites at which the killings had been carried out.[121] On 8 July the National Council adopted a second resolution, adding to the proclamation of 10 June a reference to "the newly-revealed facts of the systematic destruction of the vital strength of the Polish Nation and the planned slaughter of practically the whole Jewish population."[122] The next day Mikołajczyk, Stroński, Zygielbojm, Schwarzbart, and two other members of the National Council participated in a press conference at the British Ministry of Information under the chairmanship of the British Information Minister Brendan Bracken, at which the two Jewish representatives passed on information obtained from the Bund report and other sources and Mikołajczyk stated explicitly that the situation of the Jews was "still worse" than that of the Poles.[123]

For all of this, however, discussion of the Jewish situation was still not permitted to exceed the bounds of a device for amplifying the Polish community's plight. The mention of Jews in the National Council resolution of 8 July took up only half of one sentence in a proclamation of six paragraphs; the speeches of Zygielbojm and Schwarzbart at the following day's press conference, together with the paragraph about the catastrophe of the Jews in Mikołajczyk's statement, occupied only about one-fifth of the meeting's total time. This, to be sure, was far more attention than the Poles had previously officially devoted to the Jewish population's systematic annihilation, but it still was not sufficient to give the impression that the life of every Jewish man, woman, and child was in imminent danger.

That the murder of Polish Jewry was not to be permitted to assume the spotlight in Polish propaganda was graphically demonstrated at the National Council meeting of 7 July, after Mikołajczyk had presented a detailed report on German atrocities in the homeland and issued the call for a new resolution, which was formally adopted the next day. Before taking up the interior minister's charge, the council heard a report from the Legal-Constitutional Committee on a motion that had been referred to it by the chairman on 12 May, before receipt of the Bund report. The motion, of which Zygielbojm was the principal author, criticized the government's homeland-relief activities as insufficient in light of the fact that the Germans aimed at the cultural and moral destruction of the Polish nation and "the complete physical extermination" of the country's Jews; the motion called upon the council to "express the opinion that the Polish population, and especially the Jewish population in the ghettos, ought to be treated by the outside world on the same basis as prisoners of war," so that food parcels and medical supplies could be distributed to them under the aegis of the Red Cross. At the plenary session on 7 July, the committee recommended that the motion be amended so as henceforth to read: "The National Council, taking note of the efforts that the government has made until now in the area of relief for the homeland, calls upon the government not to cease its exertions in the direction of obtaining from the Allied governments conditions for the distribution of shipments of medicines, clothing, coffee, and tea." Zygielbojm's original motion, the committee declared, was "subsumed by the amendment." Thus the National Council passed over the opportunity to adopt a resolution in which the danger of deliberate total annihilation faced by Polish Jewry was featured.[124]

Yet if the Polish leaders were reluctant to call special public attention to the immediate peril in which the Jews of Poland stood, why did they augment the role of the Jewish situation in their propaganda at all? Most likely they believed that Jewish suffering stood to arouse more sympathy in the West than the suffering of the Poles and thought that the time had come, in view of the lack of an immediate response by the British and U.S. governments to their earlier call for a declaration on postwar retribution, to attempt to mobilize this potential sympathy in support of the Polish demand. Thus Raczyński, who at the beginning of the year had failed to take notice of the Jewish situation in his speech before the St. James's Palace Conference, now associated his government with the efforts of the Council of Polish Jews in Great Britain to draw the attention of key British government officials to what was happening to Jews in the occupied homeland.[125] In the event, there were grounds for the belief that the public might display a special interest in news of Polish Jewry's mass murder. On 24 June the management of the BBC issued an internal directive summarizing information that it had received concerning shootings of Jews in the Wilno, Lublin, and Łódź regions and instructed its newswriters to "give full prominence" to the story.[126] The next day the London *Daily Telegraph* printed a major article prepared by Zygielbojm based upon the Bund report. The BBC determined to give the contents of the article "the fullest possible publicity in all languages." In accordance with this policy, Zygielbojm himself broadcast its principal facts over the network's Foreign Service on 26 June.[127] On 29 June Schwarzbart and the British Section of the World Jewish Congress read from the Bund report at a press conference, and three major British newspapers featured the story in their following day's editions.[128] Reports on German terror against Poles had generally not aroused such attention.

Apparently Polish leaders believed as well that information of Jewish origin might be afforded greater credibility in British and American eyes than that which the Poles presented themselves. One of the Interior Ministry's publications from the period in question pointedly observed that "if the Polish reports from the homeland do not find credence with the Anglo-Saxon nation and are considered to be unreliable, they surely must believe the reports from Jewish sources."[129] It thus seemed to be in the interest of the Polish community to make every effort to enlist the news of the murders of Polish Jews in the service of its cause.

The Poles' activities in this direction, which culminated in Mikołajczyk's press conference on 9 July, seem in the event to have been highly successful. An article in the London *Times* of 10 July made the danger to the Poles appear greater than that to the Jews,[130] and the account of the conference broadcast over the BBC Home Service so closely intertwined information about the plight of the two peoples that it was impossible to infer any difference between them.[131] Even the *Daily Telegraph* now made Polish suffering at least as prominent as Jewish.[132] What is more, Brendan Bracken, in his introduction to the press conference, actually made a firm and unequivocal statement on behalf of the British government pledging that "the people responsible for these murders and outrages in Poland will be brought to justice."[133] The principal aim of Polish information policy with regard to Jewish matters over the previous month was thus almost entirely realized.

It remained to be seen, however, whether the Polish government, having achieved its primary purpose in increasing the extent to which it disseminated information about the mass murder of Polish Jewry during late June and early July, would continue to distribute new information on at least the same scale, or whether it would revert to its earlier practice of endeavoring to minimize public attention to the German war against the Jews. As it happened, it was but a short while until the government's intentions were put to the test.

Less than two weeks after the press conference at the British Ministry of Information, the Germans turned their attack directly upon Europe's largest Jewish community. Between 22 July and 12 September 1942, over 265,000 Jews were removed from the Warsaw ghetto and transported to the death camp at Treblinka. This mass deportation, which culminated in the murder of over three-fourths of the remaining Jewish population of the Polish capital, marked the apogee of the Nazi onslaught against the Jews of the occupied homeland.[134]

The removal of Jews from the Polish capital at the average rate of almost five thousand per day was carried out in full view of the local Polish population, including the central leadership of the underground. The underground command also learned of the fate of the deportees more quickly than it had in the case of any previous Nazi anti-Jewish murder action. Franciszek Zabecki, a soldier in the underground Home Army (Armia Krajowa) who worked under cover as traffic superintendent at the Treblinka railway station, witnessed the arrival of the first transports from Warsaw on 23 July under heavy armed guard—a condition that, as he later told a British journalist, made him discount the official announcement that the deportees were being "resettled." His curiosity aroused, he made a note of the figures that had been chalked on the side of each railroad car to signify the number of occupants, then set out on a reconnaisance of the camp. "I heard machine-guns, and I heard people screaming. . . ," he subsequently recalled; "I cycled back and wrote a message to my [Home Army] section chief . . . that some disaster was happening in my district."[135] That message was evidently quickly relayed to Warsaw. According to the Home Army's deputy commander, Gen. Tadeusz Bór-Komorowski, "as early as July 29th we had learned from the reports of railroad workers that the transports were being sent to the concentration camp at Treblinka and that there the Jews disappeared without a trace." "There could be no further doubt this time," Bór-Komorowski concluded, "that the deportations were but a prelude to extermination."[136]

Yet even before the destination of the transports had become known in Warsaw, underground leaders had already begun to relay information about the deportations to the government in London. Stefan Korboński, chief of the underground's Directorate of Civilian Resistance (Kierownictwo Walki Cywilnej), indicated in his memoirs that he had personally reported to the government on the German action shortly following its onset.[137] Moreover, on 25 July a detailed account of the beginning of the deportations was included in the underground's periodic survey of the situation in the homeland. The report presented a frightening picture:

> In the past few days the liquidation of the Warsaw ghetto has begun. . . . On 22 July, notices were posted on the walls of the ghetto, according to which 6,000 Jews from Warsaw were to be resettled daily in the East. This undoubtedly signifies shipment to a place of execution. The "resettlees" have the right to take with them 15 kg. of baggage and any jewelry. The resettlement does not include employees of the community or hospitals, doctors, order police, holders of work cards, and persons certified by the medical commission as fit for work (no such commission was established). After the resettlement has been carried out, those Jews remaining in the ghetto will be quartered in barracks and put to work. That same day machine guns were stationed at the ghetto gates, and in the streets "thugs [*junacy*]"—Lithuanians, Latvians, Ukrainians—appeared. Shooting began at passers-by. The deportation action is carried out in the following manner: A closed apartment building is picked at random, and the Jewish police pull everyone out of it, without regard to age or state of health. After the elimination of those not subject to deportation, the remaining are transported by truck or streetcar to a waiting train. Several trains (of open cars enclosed with barbed wire) have already left. Blocking off of apartment buildings is going on at several points in the city. Independently of this, acts of hooliganism—so far sporadic— have begun. The thugs force their way into apartments and shoot all present. . . . The victims of the first day of the "resettlement" action were mainly old and sick people, invalids, children, infants, women, and a large percentage of foreign

Jews. The young people attempted to hide. The terrified population runs into the streets or wanders from apartment to apartment. Complete depression. Many suicides. The chairman of the *Judenrat*, Czerniaków, hanged himself.[138]

The report also told of the shooting to death of the Polish doctor Franciszek Raszeja, a former professor at the University of Poznan, who on the evening of 21 July had been summoned to the ghetto by a Jewish doctor for consultation. Caught in a police raid, he had been summarily executed, together with the Jewish doctor who had called him and the patient whose life they had both tried to save.

In London the first news of the liquidation of the ghetto evidently reached the government on 27 July. On that day Schwarzbart cabled the World Jewish Congress in New York that he had been "officially informed" that the "Germans have begun mass murder in [the] Warsaw ghetto."[139] The source of this information was evidently Mikołajczyk. What happened afterward, however, is shrouded in obscurity, and its reconstruction poses a historical puzzle of the first order of difficulty. Slightly over two years later, on 24 October 1944, Schwarzbart noted in his diary that he would "never forgive Mikołajczyk for having remained silent about the reports concerning the extermination of the Jews between July 1942 and September 1942."[140] In light of the communication between the two on 27 July 1942, this comment is certainly a curious one. Can it be that Schwarzbart simply forgot that the Polish interior minister had shared with him a report concerning precisely that matter as soon as it had been received? Can it be that Mikołajczyk told the Jewish representative only part of what he knew, suppressing details that might have brought home to Schwarzbart the urgency of the situation?[141] Or might it be that Schwarzbart's complaint referred only to the weeks following Mikołajczyk's original revelation? Unfortunately, on the basis of the available documentary evidence it is impossible to ascertain exactly what the interior minister knew of the liquidation of the ghetto on 27 July, or exactly what he revealed to the Jewish leader.[142] Nevertheless, certain features of the government's behavior in the wake of the receipt of the first news of the mass deportations of Jews from Warsaw give cause for wonder and call for detailed investigation.

What is known is that on 27 July, evidently the day on which the first news of the deportations reached London, a brief report on the German action was carried over Reuter's wire service. It was printed, in nonfeature locations, in the *Palestine Post* and three Hebrew-language Palestinian dailies on 28 July, and its essence appeared as part of a more general article in the *Manchester Guardian* on the same day.[143] The language of the report, as of the others that were to follow from different sources, is significant:

> The Germans have started the mass expulsion of Jews from the Warsaw ghetto with the view to their extermination, according to news reaching the Polish Government in London. Posters have appeared in the streets ordering the deportation of 6,800 Jews for an unspecified destination in the east. Already two trainloads have left Warsaw. It is feared that when they reach their destination, they will be executed, as Jews deported from other Polish towns have been.[144]

The Jewish Telegraphic Agency also received news of the deportation on 27 July. The next day a release appeared in its daily press bulletin. This report was somewhat more detailed than the Reuter's dispatch:

> The Nazis have started mass deportations of Jews from the Warsaw Ghetto, according to information reaching official Polish circles here. An order has been issued by the Governor of the Warsaw Ghetto providing for the deportation of 6,800 Jews as a first step in the wholesale evacuation of the Ghetto. Two trainloads of Jews have already left for an unknown destination in the East. The Jews were allowed to take with them 15 kg. of hand luggage. The deportations are accompanied by mass killings of Jews considered unfit for manual work. Shootings are taking place in the streets, and Gestapo detachments are searching the houses for people to be executed. The number of suicides among Jews is on the increase.[145]

Two other wire services, the Palestine Telegraphic Agency and United Press International, carried reports of the onset of the deportations on 28 July. Each of these contained notable variations from the previous day's releases. The former was printed on 29 July in the Tel Aviv daily *HaMashkif*, the organ of the Palestinian Revisionists:

The Gestapo has started a pogrom in the Warsaw ghetto—this is information received in official Polish circles. During the past week announcements were posted in the streets of Warsaw "heralding" the expulsion and transfer of the residents of the ghetto to the East. The first transport of deportees, numbering 6,000, will be leaving during the next few days. In fact, two crowded trains packed with Jewish men have already left Warsaw. Further investigation reveals that after the Gestapo announcement [was posted] and the order for all ghetto residents to remain inside their houses [was issued], the Gestapo one night broke into the apartments, picked out the healthy men fit for work from among the residents, and following this action slaughtered the older men.[146]

The United Press dispatch appeared on 29 July on page 7 of the *New York Times*, as part of a more general discussion of events in Eastern Europe:

Nazi authorities in Poland are planning to "exterminate" the entire Warsaw ghetto whose population is estimated at 600,000 Jews, a Polish spokesman asserted tonight on the basis of reliable reports from the Continent. Preliminary notices have been posted ordering the deportation of 6,000 Jews from the Warsaw ghetto to the East, the spokesman said, and "up to now two trainloads of Jews have departed toward their doom without anything further being heard from them." The spokesman said that a wave of despair and suicides had swept the Warsaw ghetto at news of the latest persecutions, which came after the disclosure that Heinrich Himmler . . . had made a surprise visit to Poland for conversations with occupation officials. The spokesman asserted that Gestapo agents killed all members of the National Medical Council and other doctors and patients, all Jews, in a raid on a council meeting in the Warsaw ghetto. It was believed that the Germans would deport all Polish Jew [sic] officials from the ghetto first, taking 6,000 officials of the Jewish administration in Warsaw and 2,000 policemen.[147]

The discrepancies among the four basic versions invite speculation about, among other things, whether they point to the existence of more than one informant who knew of the deportations and made contact with the press or whether they reflect merely differences in understanding, emphasis, and interpretation of news supplied to all four news agencies by a single source. It also seems curious that in none of the four versions was the story attributed unequivocally to an official spokesman for the Polish government. Reuter's based its dispatch upon "news reaching the Polish Government," but it did not indicate that the government itself had in fact released the news officially.[148] The other services were even more vague, citing "information reaching official Polish circles" or "a Polish spokesman." These hedges appear significant in light of the report on the deportations that appeared in *Dziennik Polski* on 29 July:

> News has reached London of a new case of persecution of Jews in Poland. An order has gone out concerning the resettlement of 6,000 Jews from the Warsaw ghetto to the East. According to this order those resettled may take 15 kg. of baggage per person, plus jewelry. No doubt this order is intended to draw jewelry out into the open where it is taken by the Germans as loot. Thus far two trains have already been sent away without any news to their death.[149] News of this has aroused despair in the ghetto and has led to numerous suicides. The Polish auxiliary police force was withdrawn and replaced by imported Lithuanian Nazi sympathizers, Latvians, and Ukrainians. Uninterrupted shooting is heard in the streets and houses of the ghetto. During a medical consultation, Prof[essor] Raszeja of Poznan University was shot, together with another doctor and a patient—both Jews.[150]

This report, the only one of those appearing at the end of July that can with complete certainty be immediately ascribed to an official Polish government source, differed from the others in at least two important respects. Alone among them it failed to offer even the slightest hint that the initial deportation of 6,000 (or 6,800) Jews—the actual number sent to Treblinka on 22 July was 6,250[151]—was but a prelude to the "wholesale evacuation" of the Jewish population from the ghetto. It gave the impression instead that the Germans had ordered the removal of 6,000 Jews only and that this was to be a one-time occurrence. The deportation was, it suggested, merely "a new case of persecution" whose primary purpose was robbery. Moreover, it devoted a significant proportion of space to information of relatively peripheral import—that the Polish police in the ghetto had been replaced by police of other nationalities and that Professor Raszeja had been killed. Thus the article had the threefold effect of minimizing the danger faced by Warsaw's Jews, maximizing the sensation of Polish suffering as a result of the German action, and absolving Poles of responsibility for complicity in the deportation. In this regard it accorded with long-standing objectives of the government's information policy with regard to Jewish matters. In contrast, the accounts appearing in the other newspapers, by stressing (to a greater or—in the case of the Palestine Telegraphic Agency dispatch—lesser degree) that virtually all of the Jews of the ghetto had now been slated for removal (and, in all likelihood, execution) and by ignoring altogether the story's purely Polish aspect, ran counter to what the government conceived as its interest in propaganda concerning the situation of Polish Jewry.

That the government might not have wished to publicize the full extent of Warsaw Jewry's peril is suggested as well by two further official statements concerning the deportations, both of which were printed in the Yiddish-language *News Bulletin on Eastern European Affairs.* The first appeared on 4 August 1942:

News has arrived from an authoritative source concerning a new wave of anti-Jewish persecutions in occupied Poland. It is reported that the Germans wish to "liquidate" the Warsaw ghetto. An announcement has appeared on the walls of the ghetto regarding 6,000 Jews who have been sent away from Warsaw in an unknown direction. The deportees had the right to take with them only 15 kg. of baggage. In connection with the new decree, an understandable panic has broken out in the ghetto, and numerous suicides have been noted. The Polish auxiliary police force has been removed from the Warsaw ghetto and has been replaced with Lithuanian, Latvian, and Ukrainian divisions. In the streets and houses of the ghetto one hears constantly the sharp sound of gunfire. Professor Raszeja of Poznan University, who had been called for consultation to a sick woman in the ghetto, was shot during a police raid together with the Jewish patient and the Jewish doctor who had summoned him.[152]

Here, in contrast to the *Dziennik Polski* article, the "liquidation" of the ghetto was specifically mentioned, although it was cast more as a hope for the future than as a definite program whose implementation had already begun.[153] On the other hand, the article continued to imply that only 6,000 had been deported on only a single day. What is more, any mention that the deportees had likely been sent to their death was pointedly missing. The release stated merely that the Jews had been sent off "in an unknown direction"; the only Jewish deaths mentioned were suicides brought on by panic and the deaths of the doctor and patient caught in a police raid. Thus the story of the deportations from the Warsaw ghetto was made to appear even less urgent than it had been made to seem a week earlier in the government's official Polish-language daily. And as if to underscore its relative unimportance, the release was placed at the bottom of page 3 of the four-page press bulletin.

The second statement exhibited an even more pronounced tendency to downgrade the importance of the news. This notice, which appeared on 14 August, took up only three lines as an appendix to an item at the bottom of page 2 dealing with the forced return to Poland of Polish Jews who had emigrated before the war to Belgium. No headline or other highlighting device drew attention to its content. There was, for that matter, little to which attention could be drawn; the report stated merely that "persistent rumors are . . . circulating that the Nazis plan to 'liquidate' the Warsaw ghetto, after having imprisoned within it hundreds of thousands of Jews from various cities and towns."[154] Here again, although the Nazi goal of liquidation was noted, it was presented as something "planned" for the future instead of as an actual campaign that had already, by the date of publication of the report, claimed 120,000 Jewish victims. And the veracity of the news itself was denigrated by relegation to the status of "rumor," when only ten days earlier the first information about the deportation given in the *News Bulletin* had been attributed to "an authoritative source."

It is meet also to point out in this context that the principal vehicles for disseminating Polish propaganda in the English language, *Polish Fortnightly Review* and *Free Europe*, said nothing about the deportations from Warsaw during the entire seven-week period in which they were under way. At best, then, it can be said that the

Polish government did not look upon the systematic emptying of the ghetto and the presumed murder of the evacuees as an especially newsworthy item. Moreover, even when it did publish news of the event in its own official press organs, it appears to have been interested in deemphasizing the immediacy of the danger to the ghetto population and in highlighting both the lack of Polish involvement in the action and the supreme sacrifice of a prominent Pole who had undertaken to assist a sick Jewish woman. Because the reports carried over the Western and Jewish wire services did not present the story in this fashion, there seem to be substantial grounds to suspect that the lack of unequivocal attribution in any of them directly to an official Polish government spokesman or communiqué may indeed indicate that the news agencies in question actually received their information from someone other than an authorized representative speaking explicitly on the government's behalf.

If this was in fact the case, who might the source of the information have been? One possibility, of course, is Schwarzbart; he had, after all, been made privy to at least some details of the German action on 27 July and had evidently been sufficiently alarmed by the news to notify his colleagues at the World Jewish Congress in New York. Another possibility is Zygielbojm. It is certain, in fact, that he offered a statement on the deportations to the Jewish Telegraphic Agency on 28 July, one day after the service had carried its first version of the story. In this statement the Bund representative made it clear that he had seen a report received by the government the day before; on its basis he "expressed the conviction that the Nazis have decided to apply the policy of mass extermination of Jews, which has already been carried out in many provincial centres, also to the Warsaw Ghetto, and that they are obviously aiming at the complete extermination of the Jews in Poland."[155] However, it is impossible to ascertain whether Zygielbojm had been in a position to deliver information on 27 July. In any case, either of the two, though not an official representative of the Polish government, could conceivably have qualified as the "Polish spokesman" referred to in the United Press dispatch. It may even be that both served as informants. Indeed, the fact that the two releases issued on 27 July cited a figure of 6,800 Jews deported and the two of 28 July a figure of 6,000 suggests that the two sets of reports may have emanated from two separate sources. Unfortunately, on the basis of the available documentary evidence, such a reconstruction of events, however plausible, cannot be regarded as more than surmise.

But even if the four wire services had received their information not from a Jewish representative but from an official spokesman of the Polish government, there are still other features of the government's handling of the news of the deportation that prompt questions. None of the published reports, for example—neither those carried by foreign news agencies nor those appearing in official Polish organs—indicated that the deportations had actually been going on for several days or that the figure of 6,000 (or 6,800) deportees represented a *daily* quota rather than the total number whose removal to the east had been definitely arranged. All of them rather gave the impression that beyond the evacuation of the initial contingent, a definite program regarding the extent and timing of future deportations had not yet been formulated. In contrast, the dispatch from the underground of 25 July stated quite explicitly that 6,000 Jews were being deported every day, while according to both Korboński and Bór-Komorowski daily reports concerning the situation in the ghetto were dispatched from Warsaw to London. There was thus a clear discrepancy between the information sent to the government by the underground and the information that the government and other sources reported in the West. Even if the picture that the newspaper reports offered constituted an accurate reflection of the information held by the government at the end of July, it is certain that during August and September the government received further news that ought to have made the danger appear more immediate than had been indicated in the press. Specifically, after 29 July the daily signals from Warsaw described by Korboński and Bór-Komorowski ought to have included some mention of Treblinka as the deportees' destination and of the murder being carried out there. There is, in fact, definite documentary proof that such notice was received in London at the latest by 25 August.[156] Yet the Polish government passed on no information to this effect until the end of November, long after the deportations had ceased and 265,000 Jews from the Polish capital had been sent to their deaths.

In the event, the three successive official Polish statements published on 29 July, 4 August, and 14 August not only failed to convey a sense of increasing urgency but actually made the situation appear progressively less serious. Following the appearance of the third of these notices, only one additional event related to the deportations was reported in a government organ. This was a notice about the death of Adam Czerniaków, the head of the Warsaw *Judenrat*, who had committed suicide on 23 July, the day following the onset of the deportation, rather than assume responsibility for carrying out the German evacuation order.[157] On 19 August *Dziennik Polski* published a short article stating that the Jewish leader had learned that at least 100,000 Jews were to be sent from the ghetto to "an unknown destination in the east" and that he had been commanded by the German authorities "personally to organize a list of the Jews, who were to be deported in groups of 7,000 per day."[158] Essentially the same item appeared in Yiddish in the *News Bulletin on Eastern European Affairs* the following day.[159] These reports, however, as the *Dziennik Polski* article explicitly acknowledged, did not represent a revelation of hitherto-unknown information by the government but were rather almost literal translations of a Reuter's dispatch of 15 August that had appeared two days later in the London *Times*.[160] This dispatch, in turn, had originated in Zürich, a dateline that made it unlikely that it emanated from an official Polish government source.[161] It is important to recall in this connection as well that mention of Czerniaków's death had been made in the underground report from Warsaw of 25 July (although there it had been incorrectly stated that the *Judenrat* chairman had hanged himself). Moreover, the suicide had not only sent shock waves through the ghetto but had been reported in the secret newspaper of the Home Army, *Biuletyn Informacyjny*, on 30 July.[162] It is thus plausible to assume that additional news about Czerniaków had been sent to London shortly after the event and that the government knew of his death and of the circumstances surrounding it before it was noted in Western newspapers. In fact, it appears that following the arrival of the news from Zürich in London the government was prepared to confirm its authenticity. However, it added no details to what Reuter's had already reported.[163]

It seems, too, that Polish officials gave careful thought to how the government ought to react to the publication of the report of Czerniaków's suicide before deciding that the best course was simply to repeat the Reuter's dispatch in its own press organs. On 18 August, the day following the appearance of the news in the *Times*, Tadeusz Ullman, director of the Political Department of the Polish Interior

Ministry, prepared a memorandum in which he suggested that "in connection with the information reaching London about the death by suicide of . . . Czerniaków," the government sponsor a public memorial observance for him. "An occasion for the Polish government to take the initiative before the various Jewish groups and subgroups start fighting with each other to be the first to honor Czerniaków's memory," he wrote, "must be exploited by our propaganda in the Jewish sphere." He further commented that "it will make a very good general impression in the English-speaking communities . . . that the Polish government places equal value upon the heroic efforts of all its citizens on the battlefront and at home."[164] Evidently, though, Ullman's recommendation was not accepted, for no Polish-sponsored memorial service for Czerniaków appears to have been held.

The deportations from the Warsaw ghetto were to continue apace for three more weeks following the publication of the news about Czerniaków, during which time over 80,000 more Jews were sent from the Polish capital to Treblinka.[165] The government, however, said no more about them, although there were several occasions that might have lent themselves to the revelation of additional information. On 1 September 1942 the Reprezentacja sponsored a "Day for Polish Jewry" in Palestine in protest of Nazi terror in Poland. Sikorski sent a brief telegram for the event but spoke only in the most general terms of the "unprecedented German atrocities . . . which to such a great extent are also directed against Polish citizens of Jewish origin."[166] Ten days later the secret radio station ŚWIT deviated from its earlier reluctance to speak of German persecution and broadcast a report devoted to the Nazi destruction of the homeland and the occupiers' large-scale murders of Poles. There was, however, not only no mention of the overall Jewish situation in this broadcast, but no hint of what was happening to the 5,199 Jews of Warsaw who were carried off to their deaths on that same day.[167] On 29 October, long after the mass deportations had ceased, Sikorski appeared in person at a mass protest meeting at Royal Albert Hall in London sponsored by the Board of Deputies. Here again his remarks were brief, and although he noted that the Jews in Poland were being "persecuted and ruthlessly exterminated," he offered no specific news, either of the liquidation of the Warsaw ghetto or of any other Nazi anti-Jewish action. He did, on the other hand, promise that Polish Jewry would "benefit fully from the blessings of the victory of the United Nations, in common with all Polish citizens"—a rather ironic statement, considering that according to the information already in his government's possession at least one-third of the country's prewar Jewish population would not be alive to enjoy any benefits of victory at all.[168]

Such considered silence bordered on at least one occasion upon deliberate prevarication. On 6 November the Reprezentacja wrote to Rosmarin in Tel Aviv requesting official government confirmation of reports in the Palestine press that the population of the Warsaw ghetto had dwindled from half a million to 100,000.[169] Rosmarin forwarded the request to the Foreign Ministry on 10 November; his cable was received two days later.[170] The next day a cable arrived from the Polish Legation in Stockholm stating that local Jewish sources had heard similar news and likewise sought confirmation from the government.[171] Raczyński, however, in a decision evidently coordinated with the Interior Ministry, replied on 23 November that the news could not as yet be confirmed, although efforts were under way to obtain reliable intelligence.[172]

The denial was disingenuous. Although the government may not have received any precise estimate of the numbers remaining in the ghetto, it certainly had sufficient information to permit it to respond affirmatively to the two requests. On 2 October the Bund had transmitted news to London that 300,000 Jews in Warsaw had been killed.[173] Two weeks later the Foreign Ministry itself had distributed to the Polish president, premier, and interior minister a cable received from the Polish Consulate-General in Istanbul, to the effect that Jewish representatives in that city had received "from completely reliable sources" news of the stepped-up physical liquidation of the ghetto in Warsaw and other Jewish population centers.[174] On 18 November Schwarzbart wired the World Jewish Congress in New York that "according [to] official reports . . . which arrived here some days ago," 140,000 Jews had remained in the Warsaw ghetto at the beginning of September, "with rations allowed for [one] hundred thousand only."[175] Moreover, at the time Raczyński's cable was dispatched, Jan Karski, the courier who in February 1940 had delivered the first comprehensive description of the situation of the Jews in the homeland to the government in Angers, had arrived in London on his second successful mission from Poland.[176] This time he carried with him even more horrible information about the Jewish fate. According to his testimony, Karski had met with two Jewish underground leaders—probably Leon Feiner (Berezowski) of the Bund and the Zionist Menahem Kirschenbaum—who had accompanied him through the ghetto following the conclusion of the mass expulsion. They had also arranged for him to visit a camp where, he stated, he had actually witnessed an execution taking place.[177] Such a firsthand account gave the government as much confirmation as it could possibly require.

It happened, too, that in the interval between the receipt in London of the telegrams from Tel Aviv and Stockholm and Raczyński's negative reply to the Reprezentacja, the group of Jewish exchangees from Poland had arrived in Palestine and offered their eyewitness testimony concerning what the Germans were doing to Jews on Polish soil. The essence of their tale was released to the press by the Jewish Agency on 23 November—the day that Raczyński indicated his inability to confirm reports of the Warsaw ghetto's liquidation.[178] Once this news was published, the government could no longer continue to draw the curtain over its own knowledge. Accordingly, Karski's report, which described the full course of the Warsaw deportations and offered details about the methods of murder employed in Bełżec and Treblinka, was passed on to Alexander Eastermann of the British Section of the World Jewish Congress on the evening of 25 November.[179] On 27 November the National Council, under heavy prodding from Schwarzbart, adopted a resolution protesting "the German crimes directed against the Polish nation, and with particular bestiality against the Jewish population of Poland."[180] Only after all this, on 30 November, did Raczyński acknowledge in a second cable to Rosmarin that the information to which the Reprezentacja had referred over three weeks earlier was in fact substantiated by reports from the underground, "and as such must be regarded as reliable."[181] Over four months after the deportations from Warsaw had begun, and over eleven weeks after they had come to an end, the Polish government finally broke its official silence.

With the release of the testimony of the Palestinian exchangees and of the Karski report, the government found itself confronted for the first time with substantial organized Jewish pressure for action to aid and rescue what remained of Polish Jewry. On 22 November the Reprezentacja sent a second cable via Rosmarin to Raczyński, noting that witnesses (undoubtedly the new arrivals from Poland) had testified that "in some localities the behavior of the Polish population toward the Germans during these bloody [anti-Jewish] actions was not beyond reproach" and calling upon the government, "in the face of the Polish Jews' most horrible situation, immediately to begin an action exhorting the Polish people in the homeland not to give in to the influence of the occupiers' antisemitic action and to resist." The cable complained as well that official Polish broadcasts to the homeland had never contained "one word about the necessity . . . for mutual assistance between Poles and Jews."[182] Five days later Eastermann and his colleague at the World Jewish Congress, Noah Barou, approached the foreign minister with a request that the government initiate among the Allies both a declaration that "Germans, citizens of other Axis countries, and Nazi sympathizers would be held responsible for all deeds leading to the mass murder of Jews or to their deportation with a mind to their extermination" and an appeal to the people of the occupied countries to help save the threatened Jewish population from death.[183] On 30 November and 1 December the Jews of Palestine held mass protest demonstrations and work stoppages, in the wake of which the leadership of the Jewish community in that country relayed to the Polish government through Kot a series of far-reaching demands for rescue action.[184] Quickly it appeared that the entire focus of world Jewry's relations with the government-in-exile had moved from political concerns to the immediate extension of succor to the Jews of the homeland.[185]

The government was sensitive to Jewish pressure and reacted to it quickly. Since the story of the deportations from the Warsaw ghetto had now broken in the West, and Jewish circles had begun finally to absorb the notion that Polish Jewry was being subjected not merely to a continuous pogrom but to a deliberate program of total biological annihilation, the government had to take some official cognizance of the events. In consequence it now began to publish lengthy accounts of what had been happening to Jews in the homeland over the past six months. The *News Bulletin on Eastern European Affairs* devoted its issue of 28 November to a description of the Nazi murder of Polish Jewry centered on the Warsaw deportations, as did the *Polish Fortnightly Review* issue of 1 December.[186] Likewise, the final

Interior Ministry report on events in Poland for 1942 devoted twenty-eight pages to "the liquidation of the Jews in Poland."[187]

Raczyński also "drew attention" to the Nazi murder of Jews in a letter to Eden of 1 December, and on 10 December he presented a lengthy memorandum to the Allied governments, making it "clear that the German plans for the extermination of the Jews of Europe were being fulfilled by wholesale massacres of Jews in the Polish ghetto area." This document—the first public statement since mid-1940 that the Polish government devoted exclusively to the sufferings of the Jews—told of the development of the "present policy of extermination" from the time of the establishment of the ghetto in Warsaw in late 1940, adding that following the outbreak of the German-Soviet war "the mass murders of Jews reached such dimensions that at first people refused to give credence to the reports." It insisted, however, somewhat ironically in light of Raczyński's reply to the Reprezentacja on 23 November, that "the reports . . . were confirmed again and again by reliable witnesses." After describing the liquidation of the Warsaw ghetto and the operations of the death factories at Chełmno, Bełżec, Treblinka, and Sobibor, it estimated that over 1 million Jews had "perished during the last three years,"[188] and concluded with a call to find a way "of offering hope that Germany might be effectively restrained from continuing to apply her methods of mass execution."[189]

Raczyński's note was of extreme importance, for it represented the first time that any Allied government had undertaken to act as a spokesman for the Jews under Nazi rule. It led directly to the issue on 17 December of a joint declaration by the three principal Allies and the exile governments of nine occupied countries strongly condemning the Germans' "bestial policy of cold-blooded extermination."[190] Although this declaration was to have little immediate practical effect upon the prospects for saving Jewish lives, it did mark the official acknowledgment by all of the Allies that the Jews of Europe faced a special immediate danger. This development was without question the direct result of Polish actions in late November and early December. No matter how dubious the regime's behavior in handling the news of the deportations from Warsaw, the Poles in London were still the first to convey effectively to the governments of the West even some appreciation of the Jewish situation.

But the approaches made by Jewish organizations to Polish representatives during the same period indicated that the Jews expected the government to do even more. Here they were to be disappointed. Despite the undoubted impact of the Karski report, Polish leaders proved loath to instruct their citizens in the homeland to render active assistance to the threatened Jewish population. This position was most clearly enunciated by Stroński, to whom Raczyński had referred the Reprezentacja's cable of 22 November on this matter.[191] Stroński's reply was unequivocal: after recalling the government's statements on the Jewish situation in June, Sikorski's speech at Albert Hall, and the National Council's recent declaration, he concluded that it would be "superfluous to exhort the [Polish] community, for it is precisely the homeland which passes on the information and protests against the oppression of the Jews, and an exhortation would be grist for the Germans' mill."[192] The second part of the information minister's explanation appears to have been merely a camouflaged assertion that any intervention from London of the sort demanded by Jewish leaders would most likely antagonize the people of the homeland and alienate them from the government, and should therefore not be undertaken. In this respect, at least, the realization of the special character of the Jewish peril does not seem to have had much immediate effect upon the government's policy toward its Jewish citizens under the swastika.[193]

Indeed, it seems questionable whether the end of 1942 represented a real turning point for any aspect of Polish thinking about the Jewish question. To be sure, the government had broken its silence about the deportations from Warsaw, but only when it was obvious that the essence of the story would soon become known from other sources. It happened, though, that at precisely this time the government received word of a new feature of the Nazi war against the Jews that was as yet unknown in the West. On 15 November a situational report from the underground noted that "tens of thousands of people," mostly Jews and Soviet prisoners, had been transported to the concentration camp at Auschwitz "for the sole purpose of their immediate extermination in gas chambers."[194] Information to this effect was received by the Poles in London no later than 27 November.[195] Here was important news that the camp which the Poles regarded as the most awful of all, where tens of thousands of Polish prisoners had been sentenced to hard labor and where mortality owing to horrible physical conditions had reached frightening proportions,[196] had now been enlisted in the campaign to annihilate the Jews of Europe. Yet—perhaps precisely because the Poles wished Auschwitz to continue to serve as a symbol of their own suffering, and feared that their distresses might be overshadowed were it to become widely known that Jews were being gassed to death there— the name of this location was not included in the list of death camps given by Raczyński in his memorandum of 10 December. Nor did the government make any special effort subsequently to publicize the fact. The existence of gas chambers at Auschwitz was noted in the Interior Ministry's long mimeographed report of 23 December as one of a series of methods employed for murdering the camp inmates, but only in an appended parenthesis was it mentioned that "Bolsheviks and lately Jews," along with those too sick to work, were killed in this fashion.[197] The news may thus not have been altogether suppressed, but it was certainly so deeply buried and so downplayed that only the most careful and thorough of readers would have noticed it at all, and hardly anyone would have attached to it any particular importance.

If knowledge of the systematic destruction of the Jews of Poland was to inaugurate a new stage in the attitude of the Polish government toward the future of Polish-Jewish relations, this was a most inauspicious beginning.

CONCLUSION

The Polish government's actions and inactions with regard to the promulgation of information on the fate of Polish Jewry reflected the fact that the government-in-exile, like its prewar counterparts, tended to view its obligations toward the Jewish citizens of the Polish Republic as of a lesser order than its obligations toward ethnic Poles. As had all Polish governments since the reestablishment of Polish independence in 1918, the exile regime in London took as its primary responsibility the satisfaction of the needs and interests of the Polish community. Only secondarily did it concern itself with the welfare of those Polish citizens who belonged to other ethnic groups, and then only to the extent that such concern stood to contribute to the satisfaction of the Polish community's requirements and desires. Humanitarian considerations, on the other hand, or even a sense of responsibility for the welfare of *all* Polish citizens, no matter what their ethnic origin, played but a minor role in the government-in-exile's approach to Jewish matters. Thus news received from the underground about conditions for Jews in German-occupied Poland, and particularly news about the implementation of the final solution, was generally passed along to the West only when such transmittal was deemed likely to arouse public anger against the Nazi regime in general,[1] and then only when it was unlikely to make Polish suffering seem insignificant by comparison.

The operation of this principle, unquestionably an inheritance from prewar years, was observable in other aspects of the government-in-exile's relations with Jews as well. The attitudes of Polish military officials in the Soviet Union toward the enlistment of Jews in the Polish exile army and their inclusion among the evacuees to the Middle East in 1942, for instance, seem to have embodied, at least in part, a feeling that Jews ought not to be permitted to displace ethnic Poles in a situation in which only a limited number of Polish citizens could benefit from the Polish government's protection. A similar belief appears to have influenced the behavior of Polish officials in Palestine, Portugal, and unoccupied France with regard to the distribution of relief to Jewish refugees claiming Polish citizenship. And no doubt a certain part of the anger of at least some government officials over repeated Jewish complaints of discrimination in the treatment of Jewish Polish citizens was at bottom an expression of incredulity at the suggestion that the needs of Polish Jews ought to be as dear to a Polish government as those of ethnic Poles.

Yet there were other encounters between the government-in-exile and the Jews in which this principle does not appear to have been rigorously applied. Raczyński's note to the Allied governments of 10 December 1942, to take one instance, clearly placed the peril to Jews in the international spotlight, without any simultaneous reference to the Poles' own plight. Jewish refugees in the Soviet Union, too, whatever the discrepancies and lacunae in the official statistics, do appear to have benefited substantially from the services of the civilian relief apparatus maintained by the Polish Embassy, and a substantial number of Jews were actually employed in the administration of the system. Moreover, those Polish relief agencies which did periodically or systematically withhold assistance from Jewish applicants were upbraided for such behavior by the responsible government ministers. In fact, the government seems on the whole to have disapproved of actions taken by civilian and military officials aimed ostensibly at promoting the welfare of Poles through anti-Jewish discrimination, and though it generally felt compelled to defend such officials publicly, in private it was not loath to make its displeasure known.

Obviously, then, there were other factors operating in Polish-Jewish relations that at times served to offset the severity of the Jews' a priori exclusion from the government-in-exile's universe of obligation. Of these, by far the most consequential was the significance the government attached to the role purportedly played by world Jewry in the formation of public opinion, especially in Great Britain and the United States. The Poles had been rudely awakened to the scrutiny with which the British press and Parliament examined the treatment of Jewish soldiers in the Polish Army and of Jewish subjects in Polish newspapers soon after the government's removal to London following the fall of France, and they were perplexed by the extent to which attitudes toward their government seemed to be affected by the disposition of matters primarily of concern to Jews. Breaking with the assessment of the political insignificance of world Jewry—upon which Beck had built his approach to the Jewish question during the 1930s—and returning to the conception of Jewry as an international power capable of vitally influencing Poland's future—which had prevailed in the aftermath of World War I—the government-in-exile came to be wary of antagonizing Jewish circles in the West.

Thus from late 1940 on the government embarked upon a strategy of periodically affirming publicly its commitment to equal civil and national rights for all Jews in liberated Poland, even as behind the scenes it continued to see the optimal solution of the Jewish question in the voluntary emigration of as many Jews from the country as possible in the shortest possible time. It was not averse on occasion, in response to Jewish complaints, to instructing military officials and civil servants to desist from anti-Jewish discriminatory practices, despite the undoubted understanding with which at least some of its members regarded the motives for those officials' actions. It anticipated and attempted to forestall Jewish dissatisfaction over treatment of the refugees in the Soviet Union by appointing Jews to administrative positions in the civilian relief apparatus, despite the dubious propriety in principle of such action. And when news of the deportations from the Warsaw ghetto finally became widely known in the West toward the end of 1942, the government responded to Jewish pressure with Raczyński's forthright, powerful diplomatic note of 10 December. In short, the government clearly saw the need for maintaining good relations with world Jewry, and from time to time it took specific actions toward that end.

World Jewry, though, proved difficult to satisfy. The legacy of mistrust and suspicion of successive Polish governments that the interwar years had engendered among Jews appears to have influenced strongly the skepticism with which Jewish leaders tended to greet the government-in-exile's ostensible concessions toward them. This hesitancy was no doubt reinforced by the tenor of the contacts between the two sides during the first year of the war, when the government, not yet convinced of the Jews' political importance, refused to accede to Jewish petitions for a declaration on Jewish rights in postwar Poland. Thus the Stańczyk declaration of November 1940— the government's first substantial overture toward Jewish opinion— was on the whole discounted by Jews as insufficient, and suspicion was expressed of the sincerity behind virtually every subsequent government statement or action meant to assuage Jewish dissatisfaction.

Suspicion of the government's sincerity was, to be sure, not out of place, in view of the exile regime's conception of itself as first and foremost the international advocate for the Polish community and its hope that the Jewish population of postwar Poland would be sharply reduced through mass emigration. But on the other hand, the tests of its intentions that Jewish leaders frequently placed before it were often of such a demanding and uncompromising nature that, even had the government been a forthright and energetic promoter of the cause of Jewish civil and national equality in Poland, it is doubtful that it could have stood them successfully. On occasion Jewish complaints concerning the behavior of Polish officials were inaccurate or exaggerated, yet Jewish leaders tended for the most part to dismiss the government's refutations of them as contrived and self-serving. There were also certain Jewish demands to which the government, for political reasons, could not accede. It was impossible, for example, to exclude Endecja from the governing coalition solely because of its antisemitic orientation, or to employ a man's attitude toward the Jewish question as a primary measuring stick for judging his fitness to hold an official post. Moreover, the government felt its ability to satisfy the Jews limited by what it took to be the prevalence of anti-Jewish sentiments among broad sections of the Polish populace and Polish officialdom. Its task of retaining the confidence of the population it purported to represent from its position in exile was difficult enough in any case; it feared that to allow itself to be perceived as especially solicitous of Jewish interests might critically impair its success. Only those who sat in London or who maintained regular contact with the principal Western allies were really aware of the possible adverse international political repercussions likely to ensue from antagonizing Jewry; lower-level officials, not to mention the Poles of the occupied homeland, did not always understand the need for keeping the Jews satisfied. On the whole, however, Jewish leaders demonstrated little sensitivity toward the government's predicament and little tolerance for its attempts to balance conflicting principles and pressures.

All of this tended to frustrate government leaders, and their exasperation over the lack of Jewish willingness to compromise with them created the basis for a strong anti-Jewish backlash. The political tradition inherited from the interwar years held Jews to be implacable enemies of the Polish state, and by mid-1941 many Poles could find putative proof for this view in Jewish behavior in the wake of the Stańczyk declaration. It seems that at this point sentiment was mounting within government circles in favor of ending the strategy of seeking good relations with world Jewry through piecemeal accession to Jewish demands and returning to the virtual war footing on which Polish-Jewish political interactions had taken place during the period of the Second Republic. Indeed, within the international political context in which the government-in-exile operated before the German invasion of the Soviet Union, it was fairly easy to argue that the risks in such a change of direction were outweighed by the damage to the government's standing in the eyes of the Polish people that continued pursuance of the policy of conciliation was likely to cause. The frustrating negotiations over the Polish-Soviet agreement and the diplomatic whirlpool into which the Poles were thrust in its wake, however, made this position appear less tenable. Now strong voices within the government suggested that it had become essential not only to avoid angering the Jews but to make every effort to enlist them as active allies in support of Poland's eastern border claims.

For a while, the government appears to have believed that this reconciliation could in fact be accomplished. The publication, beginning in mid-1942, of strong Jewish complaints about discrimination in the administration of relief to Jewish Polish refugees in the Soviet Union, in their recruitment into the Polish exile army, and in their inclusion in the evacuation transports damaged this hope severely. Now the internal tensions that had pulled the government's Jewish policy in conflicting directions since the end of 1940 began to seem virtually incapable of resolution. The government could not afford simply to write off world Jewry as an implacable foe, even though empirically it appeared more and more that such was in fact the case. For a while many Polish policy makers had hoped that the Revisionist movement, which appeared to be willing to cooperate with the Polish government on its terms, would be able to gain the upper hand in the Jewish political arena; but that possible escape vanished even as the need for such a way out became much more acute. Eventually it became clear to the government that only by exerting powerful pressures upon the major Jewish organizations of the free world could the sought-after Polish-Jewish political partnership be effected.

The difficulty was that the government had little leverage that it could bring to bear upon Jewry, for collectively the Jewish people were not likely to be seriously hurt by government rejection of most of the demands that they had voiced during the first three years of the war. This situation changed, however, when, toward the end of 1942, the Jews of the free world finally began to sense what was actually happening to their fellows throughout German-occupied Europe. Suddenly the Polish government-in-exile became the primary link between the intended victims of the Nazi Holocaust and those with even the slightest possibility of rescuing them, and its response to the news of the final solution appeared to be a matter of life and death for large numbers of human beings. It was now conceivably in a position, should it so desire, to parlay Western Jewish anxiety over the fate of the Jews of Europe into a bargaining chip with which to cajole Jewry into public support for Poland's basic war aims.

Kot seems to have probed this possibility extensively during his meetings with Palestinian Jewish leaders at the end of 1942: confronted by impassioned Jewish entreaties for government action to assist threatened Polish Jewry, he made it clear that the government had far-reaching demands upon the Jews as well. To some of the Jewish requests he responded encouragingly; with others he was evasive; but in all cases he left the unmistakable impression that in the future the manner in which Jews related to the Polish cause would strongly influence the government's approach to the question of rescuing Jews.

The leaders of the Palestinian Jewish community with whom Kot spoke were prepared to respond in kind to a limited extent only. They agreed to join with the Polish government in demanding Allied bombing reprisals against Germany and to explore further the concept of a Central European federation to be established after the war; but they balked at committing themselves on the vital matter of Poland's eastern border. Furthermore, they declined to heed Kot's implicit but unambiguous admonition to refrain from further public outcry regarding Polish treatment of Jewish refugees in the Soviet Union. As a result, Kot left Palestine disappointed; he had been unable to find the key that might release the government-in-exile from its perplexity concerning its relations with world Jewry.

From its perch on the horns of this nagging dilemma the government was to make decisions that might, for what was known at the time, have vitally affected millions of lives. An early indication of the direction in which such decisions were likely to fall so long as the government's internal tension was not conclusively resolved was provided by the failure to give prominence to the news of the murder of Jews in gas chambers at Auschwitz. There was a force militating against widespread publication—the fear that such an announcement might so distract public attention from the plight of the Poles that it would be difficult to regain that attention. Yet there was another force pulling, as it were, in the opposite direction. As early as January 1941 the Polish government, undoubtedly in response to reports from the underground concerning the establishment of a concentration camp for Poles at Auschwitz, had requested of British military authorities that the camp be bombed by the Royal Air Force.[2] The request had been refused, but there is no reason to suppose that the Poles subsequently abandoned their hope that through Western military action the camp's operations could be crippled. In this context, a serious Polish campaign to publicize the especially egregious fate of Auschwitz's Jewish prisoners might conceivably have aroused sufficient anger within Western public opinion to force the British government to reconsider its attitude.

On earlier occasions, specifically during the interval between Sikorski's radio broadcast of 9 June 1942 and the press conference at the British Ministry of Information one month later, Polish officials had been willing to risk the eventuality that despite all precautions, Polish suffering would be overshadowed by news of the systematic mass murder of Jews, because they believed that transmittal of such information might help to elicit a specific desired response from the British and American regimes—in this case, an unequivocal declaration concerning the punishment of war criminals following the conclusion of hostilities. The situation that faced the government with receipt of the news about Jews in Auschwitz was similar to this earlier one, except that in the interval new factors had entered into the government's thinking that made similar risks appear less worth taking. In June most Polish leaders still appear to have been fairly sanguine about the prospects of bringing Jews willingly into a political alliance with the government, although the chain of incidents which was to explode that belief had already begun; in November and December they had come to believe that an alliance could be brought about only with the application of pressure. To give away such vital information, of which Jewish circles at the time had no inkling, must have appeared to the Polish authorities as tantamount to releasing a valuable commodity to a potential trading partner without any quid pro quo. If the government was to use its favorable position as a link between threatened Jews and potential rescuers as a lever for extracting political commitments from Jewish organizations, then it could not afford to provide such a commodity, as it were, free of charge.

Had Jews been more forthcoming in their response to Kot's overtures—had they, for instance, firmly promised to desist from further complaints about the treatment of Jewish refugees at the hands of Polish officials or that of Jewish soldiers in the Polish army, and had they issued a statement calling for a return to the territorial status quo ante in Eastern Europe following the conclusion of hostilities—might the Polish government have behaved otherwise? Polish leaders seem to have valued world Jewish support much more than any sensible appraisal of Jewish influence in the West would have allowed, and many were evidently prepared to go to great lengths to obtain it. Perhaps in this situation the Jewish leadership could actually have turned the tables on the Poles, converting the Polish belief in the power of world Jewry into a lever for inducing the government to take meaningful rescue action. Indeed, it is arguable that had the Jews in late 1942 presented their future behavior on the Polish question as conditional upon active Polish assistance to Polish Jewry, the government might have found itself under enormous pressure to respond positively. But this must remain a matter for conjecture. What is certain, however, is that without a more forthcoming response from the Jewish side, there was, at the end of 1942, virtually no possibility of inducing the Polish government to receive the Jews' entreaties concerning rescue with a sympathetic ear.

This impasse should not have come as a surprise to the Jewish leadership; as early as December 1940 the government had indicated that it was vitally interested in Jewish attitudes toward the Polish-Soviet dispute, and in the interval it had explicitly stated what it desired from Jewry on a number of occasions. Why, then, were Jews on the whole not willing to go farther to meet Polish demands? Part of the answer undoubtedly has to do with Jewish attitudes and strategy vis-à-vis the Soviet Union. After 22 June 1941 the Russians appeared to many Jews, as also to many Britons and Americans, as the best hope for the swift defeat of Hitler. Moreover, it was clear to

Jewish leaders that once this came about, the Soviets would be in a powerful position to influence the political configuration of the postwar world as a whole, as well as of the specific place of the Jewish people in it. Finally, the Soviet government controlled the destiny of the largest Jewish community in Europe and the second largest in the world. For all of these reasons, this factor merited careful consideration in Jewish councils before any response to the Polish side could be offered.

But there appears to have been another factor at work as well, one that may in the end have exerted an even more powerful influence upon Jewish thinking. Just as the Poles were heirs to a legacy of attitudes toward the Jewish question left from the interwar years, so too Jews carried with them memories of their relations with Poles during the same period. Among these was the recollection that Polish Jewry had initially put its faith in politics as the most effective means of attaining its particular group goals. Polish Jewish political parties had stood for election and returned deputies to the Polish parliament; they had joined coalitions, both governing and oppositional, and had forged political alliances of various types in various directions; in short, they had tried out a host of strategies that they had believed would ultimately guarantee the prosperity—spiritual as well as material, collective as well as individual—of some 3 million Jewish Polish citizens. These beliefs had been shattered in the second decade of Polish independence, and Polish Jews had looked to new strategies, that is, self-help, public protest, and pressure from international Jewish organizations, as more promising means of securing their future. This lack of confidence in the efficacy of political give-and-take was carried over by most of the leaders of Polish Jewry who escaped to the free world in the early stages of the war. Thus when the call came from the Polish side to make what was in essence a political deal with the government-in-exile, it appears to have been greeted with deep distaste.[3] It was clear that Jewish leaders by and large did not trust the Polish authorities, and they were not about to relinquish their prerogative to resort to tactics that in the past had proved more effective than political bargaining.

It thus seems of paramount significance that Jewish leaders first began to demand Polish action to rescue Jews caught up in the Holocaust precisely at the moment when the relations between the government-in-exile and the organized Jews of the free world were at an all-time low. The anger and bitterness expressed on both sides during Kot's conversations in Palestine over the allegations of anti-Jewish discrimination by Polish officials in the Soviet Union were hardly conducive to the formation of a political partnership; from the exchange Jewish leaders learned that the present government-in-exile was essentially not different from the prewar regime and that Jews' attempts to realize their goals through the political process would prove just as futile now as they had in the past. At the time when Jews needed the Polish government the most, circumstances presented themselves which, given the political-cultural baggage that Jews had carried out from the prewar world, made it extremely difficult for them to take the conciliatory steps that might have induced the Poles to take risks on their behalf. As it happened, the Jews offered the Poles no substantial reason why they ought to accede to their demands for rescue action, other than to insist upon the Polish government's duty to come to the aid of all threatened Polish citizens. Sadly, they addressed this argument to a government that had long since decided that Jews were not a part of their universe of obligation.

By the end of 1942, then, the Polish government-in-exile had developed a fully formed set of guidelines according to which it could respond to the ongoing news of the Nazi Holocaust. With these guidelines in mind, can it be said that "the manner in which Poland treated Polish Jews between the two world wars contributed to making the immense tragedy which was to befall them under the Hitlerite yoke possible?"[4] To the extent that the experiences of these years helped to create a political culture that excluded Jews from the body of those whose needs and interests a Polish government undertook to serve, on the one hand, and caused the Jewish leadership to despair of the possibility of successfully defending the needs and interests of Polish Jewry through the political process, on the other, the statement appears to be an accurate one, at least for the period under discussion here. There were also more specific manifestations of attitudinal continuity, which were revealed primarily in the facility with which Poles adduced proof of ineluctable Jewish hostility toward Poland, as well as in the frequent readiness of Jews to interpret Polish behavior in the most unfavorable light possible.

But was the prewar legacy a sufficient determinant of the guidelines that the government-in-exile developed during the first three years of the war? This is a far less tenable proposition. The government appears to have based its attitudes toward matters involving Jews far more upon an assessment of its interests than upon an assessment of its obligations. That former assessment, in turn, though heavily influenced by prewar perceptions, appears to have been based even more upon empirical observation of a wide variety of variables, including the character of Polish-Jewish relations under German and Soviet occupation, the exigencies of wartime Polish diplomacy, and the actual results of the interactions between the government and the Jewish organizations of the free world. It is fairer to conclude, it seems, then, that the Polish government-in-exile's approach to Jewish matters was forged out of the complex interaction of an entire range of factors, both of principle and of self-interest, both hereditary, as it were, and conjunctural, in a fashion that cannot be schematized, but merely narrated and described.

Yet though the government-in-exile's guidelines were fully formed by the end of 1942, their product was not unalterable. The conjunctural factors that had contributed to their formation might at any time exert influence in a different direction. The course of the war was unpredictable, and any change might produce a corresponding change in the diplomacy of the great powers regarding the future of Eastern Europe. Jewish organizations, too, were free to change their approach to the government, and there was reason to anticipate that the unprecedented systematic mass murder of the Jews of Nazi-occupied Europe might bring about such a change. The unprecedented character of the Holocaust might also have affected the Poles, both in exile and in the occupied homeland, whether by bringing the humanitarian sentiments in them to the fore or by instilling in them the fear that once the Nazis finished with the Jews, the Poles would be next. The unfolding international situation, then, would now be joined by the impact of the Holocaust upon Jews and Poles alike as the most significant influences upon the relations between the Polish government-in-exile and the Jews.

NOTES

ABBREVIATIONS USED IN THE NOTES

AH	Histadrut Archives
AILM	Archives of the Israel Labour Movement
AIP	Archiwum Instytutu Polskiego
AKD	*Armia Krajowa w Dokumentach*
CZA	Central Zionist Archives
DH	*Documents on the Holocaust*
DPSR	*Documents on Polish-Soviet Relations*
DRI	Diaspora Research Institute
FRUS	*Foreign Relations of the United States*
HIA	Hoover Institution Archives
-MSW	Ministerstwo Spraw Wewnętrznych
-PG	Polish Government*
-RN	Poland. Rada Narodowa
-US	Poland. Ambasada US
JI	Jabotinsky Institute
JTA	Jewish Telegraphic Agency
NPCA	National Polish Committee of America
PRO	Public Record Office
SPP	Studium Polski Podziemnej
WL	Wiener Library
YVA	Yad Vashem Archives

INTRODUCTION

1. Korzec, *Juifs en Pologne*, p. 282.
2. Fein, *Accounting for Genocide*, p. 33.

*As this book goes to press (August 1986), the Hoover Institution Archives is in the process of reorganizing the collection known as Polish Government. The present collection will eventually be divided into four separate collections: Poland. Ministerstwo Spraw Zagranicznych; Poland. Ministerstwo Informacji i Dokumentacji; Poland. Ambasada Great Britain; and Poland. Ambasada France. Unfortunately, no key has been kept that will allow translation from the old system to the new one. It will therefore be necessary to enlist the assistance of the archive staff in locating the documents from the Polish Government collection cited here.

3. See Iranek-Osmecki, *He Who Saves One Life.*

4. See Bartoszewski and Lewin, *Righteous among Nations.*

5. Davies, *God's Playground,* 2:260–65.

6. Fein, *Accounting for Genocide,* pp. 50–92.

7. An example of the fruitlessness of this manner of argument with regard to the behavior of the government-in-exile during the war can be found in the exchange between Avital, "The Polish Government in Exile and the Jewish Question," pp. 43–51, and Iranek-Osmecki, Lichten, and Raczyński, "The Polish Government-in-Exile and the Jewish Tragedy," pp. 62–67.

8. A recent sociological study of Poles who assisted Jews during the Holocaust has found that most of them displayed a "high level of marginality." Tec, "Righteous Christians," pp. 167–72, especially p. 170; idem, *When Light Pierced the Darkness,* pp. 152ff.

9. There is also a more practical reason: at the time of this writing a detailed study by Yisrael Gutman and Shmuel Krakowski of Polish-Jewish relations in occupied Poland is in press. Although there is some overlap with their study, the present volume deals with a substantially different set of incidents.

10. Republic of Poland, Ministry of Foreign Affairs, *The Mass Extermination of Jews in German Occupied Poland.*

CHAPTER I

1. Kruszyński, *Dążenia żydów,* p. 9. Translations are the author's unless otherwise indicated.

2. Polish foreign minister to Polish ambassador, London, 12 May 1939 (Nr. E. I. 287-1/46), HIA-US, Box 66, File 8. Cf. Polish Foreign Ministry, Consular Department, Emigration Policy Bureau (W. T. Drymmer?), to Polish ambassador, United States, 10 June 1939 (Nr. E. I. 287-1), ibid. See also Melzer, *Ma'avak Medini beMalkodet,* pp. 339–56.

3. Bujak, *Jewish Question,* pp. 3–4.

4. Mahler, *Yehudei Polin,* p. 18.

5. Ziemiński, *Problem emigracji żydowskiej,* p. 20.

6. According to the 1931 census, 76.4 percent of Polish Jews resided in cities, compared with 22 percent of non-Jews. In that year Jews, who made up 9.8 percent of the total population, accounted for 27.2 percent of the city dwellers. Moreover, 78.8 percent of the Jews were engaged in commercial or industrial pursuits, as opposed to 25.4 percent of the population as a whole. Mahler, *Yehudei Polin,* pp. 25, 31, 38.

7. In the former Congress Poland in 1897, Jews accounted for 28.0 percent of those engaged in manufacturing and 75.4 percent of those engaged in commerce. By 1921 the percentage of artisans had risen slightly, to 29.6, but that of merchants had fallen sharply, to 66.8. A similar trend is observable in Galicia: in 1910, 25.8 percent of those involved in manufacturing and 83.4 percent of those involved in commerce were Jews, whereas in 1921 the corre-

sponding figures had dropped to 20.3 percent and 74.1 percent, respectively. Bronsztejn, *Ludność żydowska*, pp. 50, 57.

8. The 1921 census revealed that 64.7 percent of all Polish agricultural holdings, populated by over 10 million individuals, were under five hectares in size. Such holdings could not support their households. Kagan, "Agrarian Regime," pp. 241ff.

9. Ziemiński, *Problem emigracji żydowskiej*, p. 20.

10. Golczewski, *Polnisch-jüdische Beziehungen*, pp. 106–20.

11. See "Report of Conversations with Mr. Dmowski on October 6, 1918 . . . ," in *Memorials Submitted to President Wilson*, p. 18.

12. See Bujak, *Jewish Question*, p. 45: "The eternal Jewish monopoly for [sic] trade was bound . . . to come into conflict with the national tendency of the Christian population towards trade. . . . The Polish people could not for ever [sic] continue to quietly look at others taking their place in certain functions, as this would cost them too dear. . . ."

13. In 1914, 25.6 percent of Jewish artisans in the territories later to be incorporated into the Polish state worked in establishments that employed twenty or more workers. By 1921 the figure had dropped to 16.2 percent. In contrast, the 1921 census revealed that 79.5 percent of non-Jewish artisans were employed in the large factories. Bronsztejn, *Ludność żydowska*, p. 70; Mendelsohn, *Class Struggle*, pp. 19–23.

14. Mahler, *Yehudei Polin*, pp. 127–32.

15. Waldman, *Conditions Up to Date in Poland*, p. 9.

16. Glicksman, *L'aspect économique de la question juive*, p. 169.

17. Mahler, *Yehudei Polin*, pp. 193–94.

18. Bujak, *Jewish Question*, p. 45.

19. The Polish nationalist movement consisted of three broad ideological streams: a bourgeois-capitalist, a populist, and a socialist. See Wandycz, *The Lands of Partitioned Poland*, pp. 288–303. During the interwar period these streams manifested themselves in a broad spectrum of political parties. Holzer, *Mozaika polityczna*, passim.

20. Kieniewicz, *Historyk a świadomość narodowa*, pp. 34–58 passim.

21. Heller, *Edge of Destruction*, pp. 62–71. The phrase "Polish community" is used here throughout as the equivalent of the Polish term *polskie społeczeństwo*. This term, often misrendered in English as "Polish society," defines a group linked by a sense of a shared past and a common historic destiny. For a fuller discussion, see Rothschild, *East Central Europe*, p. 28.

22. See *Materiały w sprawie żydowskiej*, 2:23–28; Tenenbaum, *La question juive en Pologne*, pp. 58–63.

23. Poland in 1921 was inhabited by 3,988,000 Ukrainians (14.3 percent of the total population), 1,060,000 White Russians (3.9 percent), and 1,059,000 Germans (3.9 percent), in addition to more than 2,855,000 Jews. On the derivation of these statistics, see Polonsky, *Politics in Independent Poland*, pp. 35–42.

24. Chojnowski, *Koncepcje polityki narodowościowej*, pp. 18–26.

25. The Polish Socialist Party (Polska Partia Socjalistyczna—PPS) periodi-

cally affirmed its support for the principle of communal autonomy for minorities "inhabiting a defined territory." This formulation ipso facto excluded the Jews, who were distributed throughout the whole of Poland. Holzer, *PPS*, p. 109. On the other hand, some socialists were prepared to permit a nationally organized Jewish corporation to administer schools and cultural and charitable agencies, provided that in all activities conducted under its auspices only the Polish language was employed. See Hołówko, *Kwestia narodowościowa*, pp. 46, 63. For a survey of the attitudes of other Polish parties to the Jewish question, see Cang, "Opposition Parties," pp. 241–56; Golczewski, *Polnisch-jüdische Beziehungen*, pp. 311–21.

26. NPCA, *The Jews in Poland*, p. 60; cf. Bujak, *Jewish Question*, p. 41.

27. *Sprawozdanie stenograficzne z posiedzenia Sejmu Ustawodawczego*, 25 February 1919, cols. 209–12.

28. Kruszyński, *Dążenia żydów*, pp. 7–8.

29. Bujak, *Jewish Question*, pp. 41–42.

30. The appellation came from *Litwa*, the Polish name for Lithuania, whence many of the immigrants came.

31. See, among others, Wasilewski, *Die Judenfrage in Kongreß-Polen*, pp. 20–24; Laudyn-Chrzanowka, *Sprawa światowa*, pp. 23–30. It is worth noting that these two writers came from opposite points on the Polish political spectrum: Wasilewski was a socialist and a close confidant of Piłsudski; Laudyn was an extreme right-wing Catholic émigré and a rabid antisemite. A hostile attitude toward the *Litwaki* was also taken by some assimilationist Polish Jews; see Feldstein, *Polen und Juden*. A critical evaluation of this attitude was offered by Kleinman, *Miezhdu Molotom i Nakovalnei*, pp. 34–43, 65–66. See also Levin, *In Milkhome Tsaytn*, pp. 80–85. On the origins of the identification of Jews with Russifying tendencies, see Mishkinski, "HaSotsializm haPolani," in press; Golczewski, *Polnisch-jüdische Beziehungen*, pp. 96–101.

32. Wasilewski, *Die Judenfrage in Kongreß-Polen*, pp. 20–22, 23. The apparent contradiction between these two alleged *Litwak* tendencies was dismissed by Wasilewski as illusory: "Was verschlug es, daß ein bedeutender Teil dieser Juden sich zum jüdischen Nationalismus bekannte und der russischen Regierung sogar feindlich gesinnt war, wenn in ihrem sonstigen Alltagsleben diese Juden Russen waren, die das russische Element im Lande stärkten und dessen Widerstandskraft gegen die russifikatorischen Umtriebe der Regierung bedeutend schwächten? Rußland hatte sie vertrieben, aber sie kamen nach Polen, hier ein neues Rußland zu bauen!"

33. This argument was analyzed by Kleinman, *Miezhdu Molotom i Nakovalnei*, pp. 43–49.

34. See Zechlin, *Die deutsche Politik und die Juden*, pp. 116–54.

35. Golczewski, *Polnisch-jüdische Beziehungen*, pp. 140–52, 171–75.

36. Dmowski, *Polityka Polska i odbudowanie państwa*, 1:229–32.

37. The charge of Jewish-Ukrainian complicity was a factor in several pogroms in eastern Galicia. See Bendow, *Der Lemberger Judenpogrom*; Chasanowitsch, *Die polnischen Judenpogrome*, pp. 21–23; Cohen, *Report on the Pogroms*,

pp. 9–10. On the identification of Jews with Bolsheviks, see Golczewski, *Polnisch-jüdische Beziehungen,* pp. 233–40; Korzec, *Juifs en Pologne,* pp. 110–12. Polish newspapers frequently reported that during the Polish-Ukrainian and Polish-Soviet conflicts, Jews had fired upon Polish troops. A collection of these reports is located in WL—W6b/S2a: Polish Jewry, Press Cuttings, 1919. In one widely publicized incident, a Polish military court sentenced to death and executed the rabbi of Płock, Haim Shapiro, for allegedly directing the fire of Soviet troops at the Polish armies from his balcony overlooking the scene of the confrontation. See Heller, *Edge of Destruction,* pp. 52–53.

38. Chasanowitsch, *Die polnischen Judenpogrome,* pp. 27–31, and Cohen, *Report on the Pogroms,* pp. 11–20, counted over 100 towns and villages in which anti-Jewish violence occurred, ranging from petty plunder of Jewish shops to the burning of Jewish homes and synagogues and—in 19 locations—to the killing of Jews. Some of the riots were marked as well by active complicity with the rioters on the part of the local police and militia, and in several instances pogroms were carried out by Polish troops under the pretext of self-defense. In November 1918, 72 Jews were killed and some 300 injured in connection with actions by Polish soldiers in the Jewish quarter of Lwów. During succeeding months, similar incidents involving regular Polish forces took place in Pińsk, Lida, Wilno, and Minsk. In these riots some 170 Jews lost their lives. Bendow, *Der Lemberger Judenpogrom,* passim; Golczewski, *Polnisch-jüdische Beziehungen,* pp. 182–208, 219–33; Korzec, *Juifs en Pologne,* pp. 75–81, 297–98; Shohat, "Parashat haPogrom beFinsk," pp. 135–73.

39. Chasanowitsch, *Die polnischen Judenpogrome,* pp. 116–40; Korzec, *Juifs en Pologne,* pp. 81–83.

40. It should be pointed out that Polish Prime Minister Paderewski requested the dispatch of the American mission, so that he could prove to Western observers that no excesses had taken place. See Goodhart, *Poland and the Minority Races,* p. 7 and passim; Lifschütz, "HaPogromim beFolin baShanim 1918–1919," pp. 66–97, 194–218. The reports of the chairmen of the American and British missions and the alternate reports submitted by other members, together with analysis and commentary by a Polish émigré nationalist group, were published in NPCA, *The Jews in Poland.* On the French mission, see Korzec, *Juifs en Pologne,* pp. 84–85.

41. Feinberg, *La question des minorités,* pp. 32–44, 76–94; Robinson et al., *Were the Minorities Treaties a Failure?* pp. 17–26; Viefhaus, *Minderheitenfrage,* pp. 74–100, 138–51; Lundgreen-Nielsen, *Polish Problem,* pp. 302–7, 341–48.

42. Text of the treaty in Viefhaus, *Minderheitenfrage,* pp. 231–34.

43. See Paderewski's memorandum to the Allied powers at Versailles, 16 June 1919, quoted in Robinson et al., *Were the Minorities Treaties a Failure?* p. 159. See also Viefhaus, *Minderheitenfrage,* pp. 198–207; Korzec, "Polen und der Minderheitenschutzvertrag," pp. 515–55.

44. *Sprawozdanie stenograficzne z posiedzenia Sejmu Ustawodawczego,* 31 July 1919, col. 96.

45. See *Prawda Robotnicza,* 25 July 1919, quoting Paderewski: "Jewish

groups abroad have been prepared already for two years with a treaty of this sort worked out in all its details. . . . This treaty, which met with a most favorable reception in American and English circles, envisaged quite simply *a second equal Jewish nationality and a second official Yiddish language in Poland"* (emphasis in original).

46. NPCA, *The Jews in Poland*, p. 2.

47. Kruszyński, *Dążenia żydów*, p. 9.

48. On the development of this perspective, see Netzer, *Ma'avak Yehudei Polin*, pp. 13–35. It should be pointed out that the particularistic orientation united Jewish political parties of widely divergent ideological tendencies: the Marxist Bund, which, though steadfastly maintaining that the solution to the Jewish question lay in the overcoming of capitalism by the revolutionary proletariat of all nations, nevertheless acknowledged the legitimacy of national distinctions based upon cultural differences and sought to represent the cultural interests of Jewish workers within the international workers' movement; the traditionalist Agudas Yisroel, which demanded that the state show due regard for the sensibilities of religious Jews and that Jewish communities be regarded as essentially religious corporations; the Zionist bloc, in its bourgeois, socialist, and religious variants, for which the Jewish question could not be solved without the establishment of a national home for the Jewish people in Palestine and large-scale Jewish settlement there, but which sought in the meantime to strengthen the ethnic consciousness of Jews throughout the world; and the so-called Folkist Party (Folkspartay), which held that the Polish Jewish question could be solved in Poland, without social revolution and without the creation of a national home in Palestine, by granting Jewry autonomous corporate status and proportional representation in the state's governing institutions. For a general survey of these parties, see Haftka, "Żydowskie stronnictwa polityczne," pp. 249–85; Marcus, *Social and Political History*, pp. 261–91. For an indication of the appeal of these parties to Jewish voters in comparison to general Polish parties or Jewish groups promoting an assimilationist solution to the Jewish question, see the analysis of the Jewish vote in the elections to the Constituent Sejm in Netzer, *Ma'avak Yehudei Polin*, pp. 81–82.

49. See *Pol'iaki i Yevrei*, pp. 3–7. For a discussion of the proposals regarding the establishment of urban self-government in Congress Poland and the restriction of Jewish representation in connection with it, see Chmielewski, *Polish Question*, pp. 138–60.

50. Foremost among them was Ze'ev Jabotinsky; see *Pol'iaki i Yevrei*, pp. 9–18.

51. "Yevreiskiye obshchestvennie deyateli goroda Minska . . . ," CZA—A127/56.

52. Gruenbaum, *Milhamot Yehudei Polin, 1906–1912*, pp. 102–6. According to Gruenbaum, what Poles feared most was that were the urban self-government bill to contain no anti-Jewish restrictions, Jews from the Russian interior would find political conditions in Poland more attractive than in their

places of residence and would thus be induced to move. If the Poles were fully sovereign, though, he argued, they would be able to control immigration into their territories and would thus have no compelling reason to attempt to restrict Jewish voting rights.

53. Netzer, *Ma'avak Yehudei Polin*, pp. 25–27.

54. It is important to emphasize that this was not exclusively a Zionist position. For a statement of the same conclusion from an anti-Zionist socialist perspective, see *Tsukunft*, January 1915 (P. Liebman, "Der tsarizm, di Poliaken, un di Yidn").

55. See, for example, the bitter appraisal in Rosenfeld, *Polen und Juden*, pp. 6–10.

56. According to the 1910 Austrian imperial census, there were in Galicia 3,731,861 Poles, 3,379,616 Ruthenians (Ukrainians), and 871,906 Jews. The Ukrainians were concentrated almost entirely in the area east of the rivers San and Stryj, where they formed the majority of the population.

57. It does appear, though, that Ukrainian support may have played a role in the 1907 electoral success of two of the four members of the Jewish caucus in the imperial Reichsrat. See Gelber, *Toledot haTenu'ah haTsiyonit beGalitsiyah*, p. 540.

58. See Rosenfeld, *Die polnische Judenfrage*, p. 157: "In den Versammlungen muß man sich noch heute nach rechts und links verbeugen und erklären, man sei weder den Polen noch den Ruthenen gegenüber feindlich oder aggressiv gesinnt." See also Mendelsohn, *Zionism in Poland*, pp. 97–101.

59. For statements of a Zionist position, see, among others, "Die Zionistische Organisation in Königreich Polen zur Frage der politischen und nationalen Rechte der Juden," n.d. [April 1918], CZA—Z3/148; Rosenfeld, *Die polnische Judenfrage*, pp. 53–54. The Folkist attitude was stated by the founder of the Folkspartay, Noah Pryłucki, in 1917: "Our affiliation is with a Polish state; we wish to take part in every general collective action aimed at . . . winning the greatest freedom for . . . the entire population [of Poland]." Pryłucki, *Mowy*, p. 123. On the position of the Bund, see Johnpoll, *Politics of Futility*, pp. 44–45, 73; Bunzl, *Klassenkampf in der Diaspora*, p. 93. On Agudas Yisroel, see Mendelsohn, "Agudas Yisroel," pp. 47–60. See also Zechlin, *Die deutsche Politik und die Juden*, p. 182.

60. The words of the Russian Zionist publicist Moshe Glickson expressed the fear shared by Jews throughout the world: "Whoever possesses sufficient courage to look straight into the face of cruel reality must admit . . . the imminent danger of total economic and political ruin for the Jews of Poland." *HaShilo'ah* 32 (1915–17): 104. See also Golczewski, *Polnisch-jüdische Beziehungen*, pp. 171–72; Mendelsohn, *Zionism in Poland*, p. 41.

61. Gruenbaum, *Milhamot Yehudei Polaniah, 1913–1940*, p. 55.

62. It is worth noting in this context that the declarations of the various Jewish parties greeting the prospect of Polish independence also contained statements of basic Jewish political demands. See above, n. 59.

63. Pryłucki, *Redes oif Varshever Shtot-Rat*, p. 10.

64. See, for example, Rosenfeld, *Die polnische Judenfrage*, pp. 40–41; Gruenbaum, *Milhamot Yehudei Polaniah, 1913–1940*, pp. 70–72.

65. *HaOlam*, 19 October 1939 (Yitshak Gruenbaum, "Vilna").

66. Johnpoll, *Politics of Futility*, pp. 81, 97–99; Nowogrodzki, "HaBund," p. 75. It should be pointed out that the Bund's ideological orientation was on the whole anti-Bolshevik; see *Lebensfragen*, October 1918 (Vladimir Medem, "S'iz unzer Khoyv"). The Bund did not wish to see a Soviet takeover of Poland, but called instead for a negotiated peace between the two belligerents. Nonsocialist Jewish organizations, including the Jewish caucus in the Constituent Sejm, did not dissociate themselves officially from the war, and in July 1920, with the Red Army approaching Warsaw, they called upon Jews to enlist in the defense of the Polish state. See *Inwazja bolszewicka a Żydzi*, 1:107–8.

67. Tenenbaum, *La question juive en Pologne*, pp. 29, 36–39. In the end, however, Tenenbaum did not explicitly oppose Polish territorial demands in eastern Galicia; he spoke instead of a federation of autonomous nationalities under the overall mantle of a reconstituted Poland.

68. Golczewski, *Polnisch-jüdische Beziehungen*, pp. 213–17.

69. See Tenenbaum, *La question juive en Pologne*, p. 38: "Les terribles souffrances que des milliers de Juifs ont eu à endurer n'ont d'autre cause que la non-reconnaissance de leur nationalité, et si le sang juif a coulé à flot, c'est qu'on considère que les Juifs n'ont pas les droit disposer d'eux-mêmes, mais que leur rôle doit se borner à tirer les marrons du feu pour les Polonais."

70. Gruenbaum, *Milhamot Yehudei Polin, 1906–1912*, p. I.

71. *Myśl Niepodległa*, 12 June 1919 (Andrzej Niemojewski, "Komisja Prowokacyjna").

72. For a more detailed discussion of these measures, see Netzer, *Ma'avak Yehudei Polin*, pp. 75–76, 86–88, 168–77.

73. Ibid., pp. 141–42, 183–87. The stereotype of the Jews as Bolsheviks, epitomized by the coinage *Żydokomuna* (Jew-Commune), seems to have colored many Poles' perceptions of the Jewish question during the interwar period. To be sure, the Polish Communist Party (KPP) was heavily Jewish, with Jews making up about one-third of the countrywide membership in the 1930s and perhaps as much as two-thirds of the membership in Warsaw. However, the KPP was always an extremely small group; its greatest membership probably did not much exceed 10,000. Thus, although it is true that many Communists were Jews, very few Jews were Communists. See Marcus, *Social and Political History*, pp. 290–91.

74. Heller, *Edge of Destruction*, p. 101.

75. Ibid., p. 304.

76. Segal, *The New Poland and the Jews*, p. 178; Marcus, *Social and Political History*, p. 331.

77. Segal, *The New Poland and the Jews*, pp. 192–93.

78. Haftka, "Ustawodawstwo Polski Odrodzonej," pp. 234–35. On various aspects of the ongoing debate over the removal of these restrictions, see

Netzer, *Ma'avak Yehudei Polin*, pp. 178–83; Chojnowski, *Koncepcje polityki narodowościowej*, p. 137; Korzec, *Juifs en Pologne*, p. 205; Marcus, *Social and Political History*, p. 327.

79. See Melzer, *Ma'avak Medini beMalkodet*, pp. 97–101.

80. Golczewski, *Polnisch-jüdische Beziehungen*, pp. 275–80; Netzer, *Ma'avak Yehudei Polin*, pp. 191–98.

81. Glicksman, *L'aspect économique*, p. 169.

82. Korzec, *Juifs en Pologne*, p. 191; Chojnowski, *Koncepcje polityki narodowościowej*, p. 139.

83. Segal, *The New Poland and the Jews*, pp. 145–46; Melzer, *Ma'avak Medini beMalkodet*, pp. 17–18.

84. Korzec, *Juifs en Pologne*, p. 191; Heller, *Edge of Destruction*, pp. 104–5.

85. Melzer, *Ma'avak Medini beMalkodet*, p. 55.

86. Heller, *Edge of Destruction*, p. 104.

87. Korzec, *Juifs en Pologne*, p. 249.

88. Mahler, *Yehudei Polin*, p. 172.

89. In 1921 the government successfully opposed an attempt by the University of Lwów to introduce quotas in its medical and law faculties. From 1924 on, however, successive Polish governments took an attitude of noninterference in internal university affairs. See Heller, *Edge of Destruction*, pp. 120–21.

90. Segal, *The New Poland and the Jews*, p. 196.

91. Ibid., p. 199.

92. Melzer, *Ma'avak Medini beMalkodet*, pp. 111–17, 230–42.

93. The most complete analysis of the pogroms is offered by ibid., pp. 78–96, 216–19. Additional information is contained in Korzec, *Juifs en Pologne*, pp. 244–48; Heller, *Edge of Destruction*, pp. 115–18. Among contemporary accounts, see Cohen, *Jews in Poland*; Kahn, *Condition of the Jews*.

94. Wynot, "A Necessary Cruelty," pp. 1035–58.

95. See above, n. 93.

96. Netzer, *Ma'avak Yehudei Polin*, p. 82; Próchnik, *Pierwsze piętnastolecie*, pp. 46–49. The eleven deputies representing the Jewish ethnic parties, of whom ten organized themselves into a formal Jewish caucus, were not the only Jews in the Sejm. Three Jews were elected on the PPS list, and two represented the Jewish-Polish Civil Equality Party (Partia Równości Obywatelskiej Żydów-Polaków), a Jewish list that denied the existence of particularistic Jewish ethnic concerns. Five Jews were also among the delegates coopted from East Galicia, where elections had not been held owing to the uncertain legal status of the territory.

97. Netzer, *Ma'avak Yehudei Polin*, pp. 88–90; Korzec, *Juifs en Pologne*, p. 98.

98. Netzer, *Ma'avak Yehudei Polin*, pp. 88–90; Korzec, *Juifs en Pologne*, p. 98.

99. Mendelsohn, "The Dilemma of Jewish Politics," pp. 203–19.

100. Nossig, *Polen und Juden*, passim. The strategy of seeking a Polish-Jewish accord had actually first been suggested from the Polish side by Roman Dmowski, who on one occasion reportedly declared himself willing to

lead a campaign to end all manifestations of antisemitism in Poland if Polish Jewry would appoint a delegation to speak in favor of Poland's territorial claims before the Versailles conference. However, it appears that such a proposal was never made public, and no negotiations were begun along these lines; Micewski, *Z geografii politycznej*, pp. 21–22. For an extended discussion of the attempts to reach a formal understanding for parliamentary cooperation between the government and the Jewish caucus, see Netzer, *Ma'avak Yehudei Polin*, pp. 217–52.

101. Haftka, "Działalność parlamentarna," pp. 316–20.

102. Korzec, "Block der Nationalen Minderheiten," pp. 193–219; Landa, "Gush haMi'utim," pp. 365–96.

103. Golczewski, *Polnisch-jüdische Beziehungen*, pp. 341–55; Korzec, *Juifs en Pologne*, pp. 130–35.

104. Korzec, "Der Zweite Block der Nationalen Minderheiten," pp. 77–81.

105. Text of the agreement (as published on 6 May 1926 by the Jewish caucus) in Korzec, "Heskem Memshelet W. Grabski," pp. 203–7. Specifically, the government pledged to work toward modifications in the Sunday Rest Law so as to prevent religious Jews from being placed at a competitive disadvantage, to admit more Jews to the civil service and officer corps, to recognize Hebrew and Yiddish as official languages for the conduct of internal Jewish affairs and for instruction in state-supported Jewish schools, and to end the numerus clausus in higher education. See also Landa, "Mekomah shel ha'Ugoda,'" passim.

106. Quoted in Korzec, "Heskem Memshelet W. Grabski," p. 187.

107. Displays of bad faith by the government were manifold. On 16 July 1925, only nine days following the signing of the agreement, the official Polish Telegraphic Agency published a truncated version of the text containing only twelve of its forty-two points and ignoring the most important provisions, regarding the abolition of economic and political discrimination. Stanisław Grabski (the premier's younger brother), who as minister of education and religious affairs had played a major role in the negotiations with the Jewish caucus, stated publicly that he knew nothing of the remaining thirty provisions. During the following months the younger Grabski expressly refused to take action against the imposition of a numerus clausus by the Law Faculty of the University of Lwów and affirmed in principle the right of all Polish institutions of higher learning, as autonomous corporations, to determine their own enrollment practices without state interference. In all likelihood such perfidy was animated by the attacks of Endecja, which predictably accused the Grabski government of delivering Polish sovereignty into the hands of the Jews. Korzec, "Heskem Memshelet W. Grabski," pp. 194–96.

108. Landa, "Hafichat Mai 1926," pp. 237–86; Marcus, *Social and Political History*, pp. 313–19.

109. Korzec, *Juifs en Pologne*, pp. 181–87; Marcus, *Social and Political History*, pp. 319–20.

110. Quoted in Heller, *Edge of Destruction*, p. 277.

111. See Jabotinsky in *Pol'iaki i Yevrei,* p. 16; *HaShiloah* 32 (1915–17): 107; *Tsukunft,* September 1918 (A. Liesin, "Amerika un dos Poylish-Rusishe Identum").

112. Reich, "La situation des Juifs," p. 48; Tenenbaum, *La question juive en Pologne,* pp. 27–29; memorandum from Julian W. Mack, Louis Marshall, and Stephen S. Wise to President Woodrow Wilson, 2 March 1919, in *Memorials Submitted to President Wilson,* pp. 3–4. It should be pointed out that unofficial statements appearing in the Jewish press of various countries were not always quite so cautious. The weekly *Jüdische Rundschau,* organ of the Zionistische Vereinigung für Deutschland, even went so far as to demand that the de jure independence of Poland be regarded by the Allies as conditional upon Polish Jewry's satisfaction with the behavior of Poles toward it; cf. *Jüdische Rundschau,* 27 November 1918 ("Polnischer Judenpogrom") and 3 December 1918 ("Lemberg").

113. See "Clauses for the Treaty of Peace concerning Protection of Minorities in Poland," 29 April 1919, CZA—A243/118; memorandum of Comité des Délégations Juives, 10 May 1919, in Viefhaus, *Minderheitenfrage,* pp. 228–29.

114. Korzec, "Polen und der Minderheitenschutzvertrag," pp. 517, 523–24.

115. Korzec, *Juifs en Pologne,* pp. 191–99, 215–17.

116. See, for example, "Raport polityczny No. 16/29: w sprawie zajść antysemickich we Lwowie i Poznaniu," 17 June 1929, HIA-PG, Box 712, File: "Raporty polityczne."

117. Korzec, "Polen und der Minderheitenschutzvertrag," pp. 537–42; Melzer, "Relations between Poland and Germany," pp. 193–94.

118. See, for example, St. Patek, Polish ambassador, Washington, to Beck, 26 September 1934 (No. 851/SZ-tjn./8), HIA-US, Box 66, File 3.

119. See, for example, Polish Foreign Ministry to Polish ambassador, Washington, 26 October 1936 (Nr. P. I. Mnj/264/20/36), HIA-US, Box 66, File 4.

120. Melzer, "Relations between Poland and Germany," p. 205. Some contemporary observers denied German influences upon Polish attitudes toward Jews; see Wynot, "A Necessary Cruelty," p. 1037.

121. See Wildecki, *Niebezpieczeństwo żydowskie;* Halicki, *Chrześcijaństwo, Komunizm, a Żydostwo;* Krasnowski, *Światowa polityka żydowska;* Snopek, *Zmienianie nazwisk;* Kowalski, *Żydzi chrzczeni;* Papajski, *Rola Żydów w dziejach Polski;* Zaderecki, *Tajemnice alfabetu hebrajskiego.* Another important source for the dissemination of antisemitic ideas was the Poznań-based organization Samoobrona Narodu, which published a weekly newspaper by the same name, as well as a series of propaganda calendars decorated with antisemitic slogans and cartoons.

122. Melzer, "Relations between Poland and Germany," pp. 198–99.

123. Rybarski, *Program gospodarczy,* pp. 117–27.

124. One antisemitic writer took the Polish publicist Wojciech Stpiczyński to task for claiming that a mass Jewish exodus from Poland would cause Polish commerce to disintegrate altogether; Wildecki, *Niebezpieczeństwo żydowskie,* p. 37. Rybarski also worried over the pervasiveness of this attitude:

"The tremendous predominance of Jews in many sectors of the Polish economy . . . has generated a certain suggestion that the Jews are indissolubly bound to our economy, and at the same time we convince ourselves that we owe to the Jews quite a few of our material achievements." Rybarski, *Program gospodarczy*, p. 117.

125. An outstanding example of such hesitancy was offered by Tadeusz Hołówko, a PPS expert on the minorities question prior to the Piłsudski coup and director of the National Institute for Minority Affairs under the marshal. Hołówko saw Jews (with the possible exception of those Jewish socialists who regarded themselves primarily as Poles) as "people . . . who will do business even with the Devil at Poland's expense, if they believe it will benefit their people," and hoped that most of them would willingly emigrate to Russia. "Every government in Poland, especially a socialist one," he wrote, "will support the emigration of those merchants, middlemen, and speculators who upset the economic atmosphere in Poland as energetically and effectively as possible." However, he was not prepared to countenance any state action to force such an exodus or, for that matter, any ill-treatment or discrimination against them. In his words, "It is not their fault that 600 years ago [King] Kazimierz the Great allowed their ancestors to settle in Poland—they have the same rights as any other citizen. . . ." Hołówko, *Kwestja narodowościowa*, pp. 47–54.

126. Quoted in Cang, "Opposition Parties," p. 249.

127. See Borski, *Sprawa żydowska a socjalizm*. See also Melzer, *Ma'avak Medini beMalkodet*, pp. 143, 158; Korzec, *Juifs en Pologne*, p. 269.

128. Two smaller groups, the liberal Democratic Party and the Communists, did take a stand against the popular anti-Jewish wave. See Heller, *Edge of Destruction*, p. 129; Korzec, *Juifs en Pologne*, p. 270; Melzer, *Ma'avak Medini beMalkodet*, p. 192.

129. See, among others, Pobóg-Malinowski, *Najnowsza historia*, 2:806–21; Melzer, "HaDiplomatiyah haPolanit," pp. 211–49; Melzer, *Ma'avak Medini beMalkodet*, pp. 140–63, 313–38; Korzec, *Juifs en Pologne*, pp. 249–55; Chojnowski, *Koncepcje polityki narodowościowej*, pp. 219–26.

130. "Memorandum Submitted by the Polish League of Nations Federation on the Jewish Question," January 1938, WL—X3f INT.

131. Ibid. This argument gave further expression to the irony inherent in Poland's adoption of the emigration concept; during the debates over the Minorities Treaty at Versailles, it had been used to advise the Allies that Poland was capable of solving its Jewish question without any tutelage or assistance from the West. See Kutrzeba, *La question juive*, p. 2; Bujak, *Jewish Question*, pp. 6–8.

132. "Memorandum Submitted by the Polish League of Nations Federation" (see above, n. 130).

133. "Notatka z rozmowy Pana Ministra Becka z ambasadorem amerykańskim p. Biddlem . . . ," 25 August 1938, HIA-US, Box 64, File 4. Cf. Ziemiński, *Problem emigracji żydowskiej*, p. 30: "While we may regret the means employed in this fight [of the urban population, the peasantry, and the

young intelligentsia against the Jews], we must keep in mind their symptomatic importance."

134. Beck to Polish ambassador, London, 12 May 1939 (No. E. I. 287-1/46), HIA-US, Box 66, File 8. The British had long perceived the government's position on Jewish emigration to be moderate compared to that of Endecja: where the government sought "to persuade the Jews in their own interests to leave voluntarily in sufficient numbers," the right-wing opposition held "that an economic boycott of Jewish shops and enterprises should be organised in the hope that the Jews will prefer even uncomfortable surroundings elsewhere to remaining in this country without a livelihood." Sir Howard W. Kennard, British ambassador to Poland, to Anthony Eden, British foreign secretary, 11 May 1937, PRO—FO 371/20763.C3699.

135. Quoted in Melzer, "HaDiplomatiyah haPolanit," p. 245. The words represent Strang's summary of his conversation with Raczyński on 12 December 1938.

136. See above, n. 130.

137. Yahil, "Madagascar," pp. 316–18.

138. *Opinion*, 15 February 1932 (I. Gruenbaum, "The Power of World Jewry").

139. See Reiss, *BeSa'arot haTekufah*, pp. 138–45.

140. *HaOlam*, 7 July 1938 ("Al haPerek—Evian"). On the other hand, Simon Segal, one of the leaders of the American Federation of Polish Jews, could conclude his 1938 study of Polish-Jewish relations with the hope that "public opinion of the democratic countries of the world . . . could well make clear to the Polish rulers that they cannot with impunity . . . attempt to emulate Nazi Germany." Segal, *The New Poland and the Jews*, p. 212.

141. Tartakower, *Nedudei haYehudim*, pp. 36–37.

142. Johnpoll, *Politics of Futility*, pp. 216–18; cf. "Manifest fun Algemaynem Yidishn Arbeter-Bund . . . ," 13 November 1937, in [Ehrlich and Alter], *Henryk Ehrlich un Wiktor Alter*, pp. 272–82.

143. Melzer, *Ma'avak Medini beMalkodet*, p. 145.

144. Ibid., pp. 145–63, 319–38. Cf. above, n. 119.

145. Quoted in Melzer, *Ma'avak Medini beMalkodet*, p. 148.

146. Ibid., pp. 150–51; Benari, *Tochnit haEvaku'atsiyah*, passim; Schechtman, *Fighter and Prophet*, pp. 334–40.

147. Engel, "HaBerit haNichzevet," in press.

148. Melzer, "HaDiplomatiyah haPolanit," p. 216.

149. Melzer, *Ma'avak Medini beMalkodet*, pp. 328–32; Reiss, *BeSa'arot haTekufah*, pp. 179–92. On the other hand, Gruenbaum—now speaking as a member of the Jewish Agency Executive in Palestine, having left Poland in 1932—urged Polish Jews to prepare for large-scale emigration, even though he claimed to oppose the Revisionist "evacuation" program. Gruenbaum, *Milhamot Yehudei Polaniah, 1913–1940*, pp. 407–25.

150. Schechtman and Benari, *History of the Revisionist Movement*, pp. 395–401.

151. Johnpoll, *Politics of Futility*, pp. 220–24.

152. Melzer, *Ma'avak Medini beMalkodet*, pp. 69–73.

153. Three particularly noteworthy instances of mass Jewish protest were the half-day strike of Jewish workers on 17 March 1936, called in response to the pogrom at Przytyk; the two-hour work stoppage in Jewish businesses on 24 May 1937, called as the initial reaction to the pogrom at Brześć; and the demonstration in Warsaw on 19 October 1937, featuring a march by Jewish school youth, called to combat the institution of ghetto benches in Polish universities. Melzer, *Ma'avak Medini beMalkodet*, pp. 86–88, 220–21, 234–36.

154. Heller, *Edge of Destruction*, pp. 287–91.

155. Korzec, *Juifs en Pologne*, p. 272.

156. "Address by Dr. Henry Shoshkes [*sic*] . . . ," 19 June 1939, HIA-US, Box 66, File 7.

157. Sylwester Gruszka, Polish consul-general, New York, to Polish Embassy, Washington (Nr. R851e: "w sprawie zjazdu Rocznego Fed. Żyd. Pol."), 23 June 1939, HIA-US, Box 66, File 7.

158. Ibid.

159. Melzer, "HaDiplomatiyah haPolanit," pp. 236–37.

160. Text in ibid., pp. 248–49.

161. See Beck to Polish ambassador, London, 29 July 1938 (Nr. E. I. 287-1/42), HIA-US, Box 65, File 4; "Notatka . . . w sprawie zapatrywaniu Rządu Polskiego na przebieg i wyniki konferencji w Evian," 14 September 1938, ibid.

162. Wynot, "A Necessary Cruelty," pp. 1056–57; Melzer, "Mifleget ha-Shilton OZON," pp. 412–13.

163. Korzec, *Juifs en Pologne*, p. 274.

CHAPTER II

1. Melzer, *Ma'avak Medini beMalkodet*, p. 354.

2. Ibid.

3. *Jewish Chronicle*, 8 September 1939 ("Polish Jews Play Their Part").

4. Ibid.

5. During the campaign 31,216 Jewish soldiers were killed; over 60,000 more were taken prisoner by the Germans. Canin, "HaYehudim baTsava ha-Polani," pp. 509–18; Krakowski, "Fate of Jewish Prisoners," p. 299.

6. Ringelblum, *Polish-Jewish Relations*, pp. 24–32; Gutman, *Yehudei Varshah*, p. 21.

7. *Jewish Chronicle*, 15 September 1939 ("Polish Jews' Heroism"); see also ibid., 8 September 1939 ("Gallant Little Poland").

8. *Zionist Review*, 21 September 1939.

9. *Der Tog*, 9 September 1939 (R. Mahler, "Poylen's Frayhayt iz durkh die letste 150 Yohr eng tsunoyfgebunden mit'n Forshrit fun demokratishn Gayst"); ibid., 10 September 1939 ("Nokh iz Poylen nit farloyren").

10. *Davar*, 10 September 1939.

11. *HaBoker*, 10 September 1939 ("LiShe'elot haSha'ah").

12. Potocki to Wise, 13 September 1939; Montor to Wise, 15 September 1939; "Mobilizing Public Opinion in Sympathy with the Polish Republic," CZA—A243/119. It seems that in this case the Poles were less than anxious to avail themselves of the Jewish offer; Wise had to press Potocki for a follow-up meeting. See Wise to Potocki, 18 September, 6 October 1939, ibid.

13. Centre de la Collaboration Polono-Juive en France, "Memoriał złożony na ręce Pana Ministra Strońskiego," 30 May 1940, YVA—O55/1. Cf. *Przyszłość*, 25 March 1940 (R. Rajchman, "Żydzi Polscy na wychodźtwie").

14. [Kaplan], *Scroll of Agony*, p. 2.

15. *HaOlam*, 22 September 1939 (Y. Gruenbaum, "Varshah").

16. *HaPo'el haTsa'ir*, 27 September 1939 (Y. Lufbahn, "LiMe'ora'ot ha-Yamim"). The words "Poland is not yet lost" form the opening line of the Polish national anthem.

17. Montor to Wise, 15 September 1939, CZA—A243/119.

18. [Kaplan], *Scroll of Agony*, p. 5 (3 September 1939). Similarly, in his entry for 5 September (p. 7), Kaplan wondered: "The Poles complain against Germany, and justifiably. . . . But . . . why did not the Poles join in our sorrow when Hitler ordered the burning of our synagogues, which were consumed in smoke together with scrolls of the Torah? We didn't hear a word of consolation. On the contrary, they enjoyed it; they were happy at our misfortune."

19. See above, n. 16. Cf. *Jewish Chronicle*, 8 September 1939 ("Gallant Little Poland"): "The Polish people can now estimate how much of so-called Polish anti-Semitism was 'Fifth Column' work of Nazi Germany. . . . It has been largely a case of ignorance and malice duped [*sic*] by Berlin."

20. *HaPo'el haTsa'ir*, 13 October 1939 (Tuviyahu, "Polin").

21. See above, n. 17. Polish Zionist leader Moshe Kleinbaum, who took part in the September campaign, fell prisoner to the Soviets, and escaped to the West via Wilno in early 1940, noted the various feelings among Jews toward Poland in an extensive memorandum prepared for Nahum Goldmann, chairman of the Executive Committee of the World Jewish Congress, and Stephen Wise, on 12 March 1940: "Among all Polish Jews of all classes and ideological persuasions you will find a strong patriotic feeling toward Poland, which finds much more definite expression now . . . than before the war, when the practice of antisemitism repressed this feeling among the Jews. In the larger Jewish world there remains a kind of psychological resistance to Poland in certain circles, resulting from the strong antisemitic movement in independent Poland and from a number of antisemitic incidents even today." Kleinbaum himself, however, displayed no such ambivalence: "The entire Jewish world must know that there can be no rescue for Polish Jewry without the rescue of Poland. . . . True, the Poland of Chjeno [the right-wing political alliance that received more than twice as many votes as any other list in the parliamentary elections of 1922] and the Poland of OZON committed many sins against the Jews; but the minute that Poland became the first to take arms against Hitlerism, many of its sins were forgiven. . . . We have had and shall continue to have many clashes with the

Polish government, but this should not deflect us from the main lines of the direction of our policy. In the present historic movement, the entire Jewish people (and not merely Polish Jewry) is on *purely objective* grounds the ally of the Polish people. . . ." Kleinbaum, "El Dr. N. Goldmann," p. 574 (emphasis in original).

22. *Jewish Chronicle*, 29 September 1939 ("Polish Jews' Bravery: Tribute by Sejm Leader").

23. *Der Tog*, 4 September 1939 ("News and Views").

24. *JTA Bulletin*, 27 September, 2 October 1939. See also Z. Tygel to Polish ambassador, United States, 3 October 1939, HIA-US, Box 66, File 7; Reiss, *BeSa'arot haTekufah*, pp. 194–96.

25. See "La situation des Juifs en Pologne occupée par les Allemands," n.d., HIA-PG, Box 469, File: "Sprawy uchodźce, PCK i inne"; "Bericht aus Warschau," 7 November 1939, HIA-Mikołajczyk, Box 12, File: "Jews in Occupied Poland, 1939–1944."

26. It must be borne in mind that at this time no one—most likely not even the Nazi conquerors themselves—foresaw the systematic murder of some 3 million of the 3,330,000 Jews living in Poland in 1939. Both Poles and Jews expected at the outset of the war that the Germans would be defeated in due course and the Polish Republic reestablished, with Jews, despite having sustained severe losses under the occupation, continuing to constitute a significant percentage of the state's population. The Jewish question as projected for postwar Poland was thus conceived by Poles and Jews alike during the early stages of the war in essentially the same terms as it had been during the prewar years.

27. The concept of a "government-in-exile" was evidently a Polish invention that sought to respond to two unexpected events: the sudden collapse of the country's defenses in the wake of the German and Soviet invasions, and the internment of Polish President Ignacy Mościcki and the members of his cabinet who fled from Poland to Romania on 18 September 1939. In this situation, in which the legally constituted Polish government could not function, the idea was raised—evidently by several sources, among them Polish diplomatic officials, who since 18 September had lacked formal authority for their acts, and opposition elements to the Sanacja regime—of establishing an extraterritorial government under the protection of the Western Allies. As the 1935 Polish constitution permitted the president of the Republic to choose his successor, a legal basis for such a maneuver could easily be adduced. The president of the exile government, Władysław Raczkiewicz, was in fact appointed by Mościcki. On the internment of the prewar government and the origin of the idea of creating a government-in-exile in France, see Zabiełło, *O rząd i granice*, pp. 11–22. For details on the process of naming a new president, see also Raczyński, *In Allied London*, pp. 39–44. On the concept of a government-in-exile as a legal device for perpetuating the sovereignty of a conquered nation, see Bell and Dennen, "The System of Governments-in-Exile," pp. 134–47.

28. Of the former, the most prominent were Sikorski and Information

Minister Stanisław Stroński. Sikorski, who had held the Polish premiership for six months following the assassination of Narutowicz in December 1922, had been an outspoken opponent of the Piłsudski regime and from 1928 to 1933 had lived in self-imposed exile in France and Switzerland. In 1936 he, together with Paderewski, another voluntary refugee from Sanacja hegemony, had organized the so-called Front Morges, a loose coalition of leaders of the anti-Piłsudski right and center seeking to strengthen the effectiveness of political opposition in the country. He was a francophile, and one of the principal points of contention between him and the prewar regime had been Beck's growing denigration of the importance of close Polish-French ties. Stroński, a nominal Endek who had helped lead the right-wing opposition to Sikorski during the latter's earlier tenure as premier, had become a close collaborator of the general during the 1930s in the course of efforts to organize interparty cooperation on the right against Sanacja. He too had been active in the creation of Front Morges, despite his party's refusal to affiliate with it formally. Actually, he had been asked by Raczkiewicz before Sikorski to form a government, but sensing that he lacked sufficient support, he had yielded the task to the general.

Other prewar opposition leaders who soon were co-opted into the government were Deputy Premier Stanisław Mikołajczyk and Interior Minister Stanisław Kot of the Peasant Party, Labor Minister Jan Stańczyk of PPS, and Ministers without Portfolio Marian Seyda of Endecja and Gen. Józef Haller of Front Morges. Among former Sanacja associates were Raczkiewicz, a past president of the Senat and chairman of the Organization of Poles Abroad, and Foreign Minister August Zaleski, who had occupied the same post from 1926 to 1932 before being shunted aside by Beck. Gen. Kazimierz Sosnkowski, a one-time confidant of Piłsudski and Poland's ranking military officer, joined the government as Raczkiewicz's designated successor upon his arrival in Paris in November. The only apparent holdover from the post-Piłsudski years was Adam Koc, who served as finance minister. Koc had been the principal organizer of OZON, the political front of Sanacja. He was, however, demoted after two months to the level of deputy minister. See Kwiatkowski, *Rząd i Rada Narodowa*, pp. 11–13; Kacewicz, *Great Britain*, pp. 38–40; Micewski, *Z geografii politycznej*, pp. 306–8.

29. Kacewicz, *Great Britain*, pp. 40–43.

30. See Sikorski's statements of 6 October and 18 December 1939, quoted in Kwiatkowski, *Rząd i Rada Narodowa*, pp. 14, 19; his statement of 3 January 1940, quoted in *Keesing's Contemporary Archives*, 13 January 1940, no. 3870C; Raczkiewicz's statement of 30 November 1939, quoted in Polonsky, *Politics in Independent Poland*, p. 505.

31. Kwiatkowski, *Rząd i Rada Narodowa*, pp. 37–41.

32. Duraczyński, *Kontrowersje i konflikty*, pp. 58–66; Duraczyński, *Stosunki w kierownictwie podziemia*, pp. 13–14; Gross, *Polish Society*, pp. 264–65, 273–74.

33. The French government made this necessity clear from the outset when it announced that it would not recognize the continued sovereignty of a Polish state headed by Mościcki's original choice for president, General

Bolesław Wieniawa-Długoszowski. Wieniawa, who had been Poland's ambassador to Italy, was regarded as too much of a protégé of Beck to suit French tastes. Zabiełło, *O rząd i granice*, pp. 17–20; Micewski, *Z geografii politycznej*, p. 307.

34. Sikorski had opposed the formation of the left-center opposition bloc to Piłsudski (Centrolew) in 1929 out of an ideological objection to the participation of the left in the exercise of political power. See Korpalska, *Sikorski*, p. 162; Wapiński, *Sikorski*, p. 185.

35. See Sikorski's radio address to Poland, 19 December 1939, quoted in Kwiatkowski, *Rząd i Rada Narodowa*, p. 19 ("Poland will be a state standing, as in the past, upon a foundation of Christian culture and principles"); Paderewski's statement at the opening session of the Polish National Council (Rada Narodowa), 23 January 1940, quoted in ibid., p. 112 ("We are not fighting for a Poland of nobles, peasants, or workers, . . . [but] for Mother Poland, a mother to her faithful children, . . . for the Poland of the Chrobry and Jagiełło dynasties . . ."); Sikorski's speech on the same occasion, quoted in ibid., pp. 114–15 ("The Government which I lead . . . insists upon [popular] controls, with, of course, the reservation that these not hinder us in our constructive efforts"). See also Duraczyński, *Kontrowersje i konflikty*, pp. 34–36. Cf. the platform of Front Morges, quoted in Korpalska, *Sikorski*, p. 182.

36. "Dekret Prezydenta Rzeczypospolitej . . . o powołaniu Rady Narodowej RP," 9 December 1939, YVA—M2/1. See also Kacewicz, *Great Britain*, pp. 43–44.

37. Korboński, *The Polish Underground State*, pp. 22–39; Duraczyński, *Stosunki w kierownictwie podziemia*, pp. 24–46.

38. Duraczyński, *Kontrowersje i konflikty*, p. 11; Micewski, *Z geografii politycznej*, p. 291. None of this, however, is meant to suggest that the government-in-exile did not enjoy the support of the majority of the Polish people. Whether the same government would have survived the test of a popular election, had one been held early in the war, is a moot but not terribly important question. What is more significant, given the context in which Polish political life had to be carried on during the war, is the fact that the majority of underground forces looked upon Raczkiewicz as the legitimate head of the still-sovereign Polish state and upon the government he appointed as an authoritative one. The many conflicts between the underground parties in Poland and the exile government (as well as those among the parties themselves) can as easily be understood as maneuvering for postwar political hegemony as an indication of public nonacceptance of the exile regime. See Gross, *Polish Society*, pp. 274–79, 287–91; Zabiełło, *O rząd i granice*, pp. 22–23.

39. Hence the government-in-exile's sharp reaction to Jewish complaints regarding alleged anti-Jewish discrimination in the Polish Army and in the distribution of relief, and regarding purported antisemitic expressions in the official and semiofficial Polish exile press. On this matter, see below; see also Bertish, "Pezurat Yehudei Polin," p. 281.

40. Kwiatkowski, *Rząd i Rada Narodowa*, p. 14.

41. Ibid., p. 19.

42. Korzec, *Juifs en Pologne*, pp. 139–40. Sikorski had further aroused Jewish anger during his brief term later by expelling from Poland more than 12,000 Jewish refugees who had fled the onslaught of the White armies during the Russian Civil War. On the other hand, it must be borne in mind that Sikorski's primary task on this occasion had been to pacify the right following the election and assassination of Narutowicz; any concessions to Jewish interests would perforce have defeated this purpose.

43. See his comment following the election of Narutowicz: "This election is astoundingly senseless, provocative, inflammatory; it creates a state of affairs against which the Polish majority must fight." Quoted in Tomaszewski, *Rzeczpospolita wielu narodów*, p. 7. Yet for all of this, Stroński was actually, within the context of the antisemitism of the prewar Polish right, something of a moderate, in that he opposed the pogrom as a tactic in the anti-Jewish struggle. See Melzer, *Ma'avak Medini beMalkodet*, pp. 60–61.

44. Melzer, "Mifleget haShilton OZON," pp. 406–7; Wynot, "A Necessary Cruelty," pp. 1048–51; Marcus, *Social and Political History*, p. 379. To be sure, these theses had been adopted following Koc's replacement as head of OZON, but his association in the public eye with the prewar government front remained.

45. See Raczyński, *In Allied London*, p. 2: "The idea of shaking off the invidious obligations of the treaty was a brainchild of mine, fostered from infancy and preserved by various devices from collapsing . . . until it sprang into maturity under Beck's vigorous care at Geneva." In fairness to Raczyński, it should be pointed out that his objections to the Minorities Treaty seem to have sprung mainly from the fact that it provided a weapon with which Germany had been able to harass Poland in the diplomatic arena, and only secondarily from his association of the treaty with Jewish influence. Still, however, he regarded the Sanacja regime's handling of Jewish matters as proper and in no sense unfair to Polish Jewry; see Raczyński interview.

46. Retinger, *All about Poland*, pp. 65–66. Elsewhere in the same book (p. 67), Retinger wrote: "The faulty occupational structure of the Polish Jew is by no means exceptional in the world. It is a permanent feature of the Jewish nation and has consistently appeared in all its centres. . . . In this way the natural expansion of the Gentile population has been inhibited and stopped. The Polish peasant who wishes to migrate from his village to the towns encounters insuperable difficulty in establishing himself. . . . In such conditions, the only solution for this burning question is that offered by emigration." See also [Retinger], *Memoirs*, p. 35.

47. *Jewish Chronicle*, 13 October 1939 ("Who's Who in New Polish Government?").

48. See ibid., in which Sikorski was praised for consulting "a number of Jewish friends" during his tenure as war minister (February 1924–November 1925), Stroński was reported to have lately criticized his party's anti-Jewish platform, and Koc was credited with a possible change of heart; see also *HaTsofeh*, 3 October 1939 ("Mi Hem Havrei haMemshalah haPolanit haHada-

shah?"), in which Stroński was portrayed as a moderating force among antisemites, and no adverse comments were made about Koc. Somewhat stronger was an article by British Labour MP Rhys Davies in the American Labor Zionist journal *Jewish Frontier*, April 1940 ("The Jews and the Polish Government"). Davies complained about the appointment of Stroński, Koc, and Haller to the government, but lauded Sikorski as a democrat. The only Jewish expression of dissatisfaction with Sikorski appears to have been an article published by the Polish Jewish sociologist Ya'akov Leszczyński shortly after his escape from occupied Poland and arrival in Palestine in October 1939. This article's wholesale condemnation of the Sikorski government for its right-of-center character, however, was not representative of prevailing Jewish opinion at the time. *HaPo'el haTsa'ir*, 26 January 1940 (Ya'akov Leszczyński, "HaMemshalah haPolanit beFariz").

49. These concerns can best be followed in the pages of the *Jewish Chronicle*, especially 8 December 1939 ("Pogrom for Polish-Jewish Legionnaires?"), 22 December 1939 ("Jew for Polish National Council . . . and Two Anti-Semites"), 29 December 1939 ("Offensive Article in Official Polish Organ"), 12 January 1940 ("Polish Government Honour Jew-Baiter: Official Inconsistency"), 2 February 1940 ("Polish Government's Broken Pledge: Official Organ Still Jew-Baiting"). All of these issues were raised also by Rhys Davies in his article in *Jewish Frontier*; see preceding note.

50. On this law and its effect upon Polish Jews outside Poland, see below, chapter III.

51. See *Jewish Chronicle*, 20 October 1939 ("Premier Visits Paris Synagogue"), 3 November 1939 ("Citizenship Restored to Polish Jews"), 22 December 1939 ("Jew for Polish National Council . . . and Two Anti-Semites"), 23 February 1940 ("Former Anti-Semite's Apology: Polish General's Past Mistakes," "One Polish Anti-Semite Recants").

52. Ibid., 23 February 1940 ("Executive Committee's First Report"). Stein also served as president of the Anglo-Jewish Association.

53. See Raczyński's record of his conversation with the newly installed president of the Board of Deputies, Selig Brodetsky, 14 February 1940, published (in German translation) in Korzec, "General Sikorski und seine Exilregierung," pp. 241–43. For the government's initial statements on the character of the regime to be created in postwar Poland, see above, n. 30.

54. *Jewish Chronicle*, 24 November 1939 ("Jews in the Future Poland"). See the editorial, "New Polish Government and the Jews," in the same number.

55. Korzec, "General Sikorski und seine Exilregierung," passim.

56. Ciechanowski to Polish ambassador, London, 2 March 1940, ibid., pp. 243–44. This letter was sent by Ciechanowski, director-general of the Polish Foreign Ministry, at Zaleski's behest, as an official instruction to Raczyński, who on 14 February had been presented with the suggestion regarding a declaration by the incoming president of the Board of Deputies, Selig Brodetsky. At the time Raczyński had promised to respond to Brodetsky's proposal at a later date. Shortly after receiving Ciechanowski's instruction, Raczyński

met with Brodetsky again and conveyed to him the approved government position. See Raczyński's summaries of his conversations with Brodetsky, 14 February, 7 March 1940, ibid., pp. 241–45.

57. Raczyński's conversation with Brodetsky, 14 February 1940, ibid., pp. 241–43; Raczyński to Retinger, 14 March 1940, ibid., p. 247.

58. Zabiełło, *O rząd i granice*, pp. 30–32; Kacewicz, *Great Britain*, p. 73.

59. Kacewicz, *Great Britain*, pp. 75–77.

60. Rosmarin had been a Zionist activist in prewar Poland and had himself participated in the organizing conference of the World Jewish Congress in 1936. Because of his background and his diplomatic post, he was frequently to act as an intermediary between Jewish organizations and the Polish government.

61. Rosmarin to Polish Foreign Ministry, 29 March 1940, in Korzec, "General Sikorski und seine Exilregierung," pp. 254–55. Interestingly, this memorandum coincided with the arrival of Polish Zionist leader Moshe Kleinbaum in Palestine. Two weeks earlier Kleinbaum had recommended to Nahum Goldmann and Stephen Wise of the World Jewish Congress that "the time has now come to include the struggle against Stalinism as part of Jewish policy, for the sake of the liberation of the five million Russo-Polish Jews and of the Jewish community in the Baltic States and Bessarabia. . . ." The timing suggests that Kleinbaum may have been the catalyst for Rosmarin's suggestions. Kleinbaum, "El Dr. N. Goldmann," p. 572.

62. *Contemporary Jewish Record*, November–December 1939, pp. 35–42 ("The Jewish Press on the Partition of Poland and Its Consequences"). Cf., among others, *HaBoker*, 18 September 1939 ("LiShe'elot haSha'ah"); *HaPo'el haTsa'ir*, 24 October 1939 (B. V., "Parashat haHeskem haRusi-Germani"); *Tsukunft*, October 1939 (Y. Vilyatsker, "Der Hitler-Stalin Bund un di Poylish-Idishe Tragedie"); *Jewish Chronicle*, 22 September 1939 ("Russians in Poland"). For a discussion of the effect of Russian actions after 23 August 1939 upon the attitudes of socialist Jews in Palestine toward the Soviet regime, see Shapira, *Berl*, pp. 610–17. Cf. *HaPo'el haTsa'ir*, 25 December 1939 (A. G., "LeHa'arachat haMishtar haSovieti"); 24 May 1940 (Ben Shelomo, "HeHaluts baMahteret").

63. Memorandum from Ciechanowski, 9 April 1940, in Korzec, "General Sikorski und seine Exilregierung," pp. 254–55.

64. "Uwagi w sprawie ukraińskiej," 13 March 1940, AIP—KOL. 30/I/2; Ciołkosz to prime minister's office, 25 April 1940, AIP—PRM. 36/4/5. Ciołkosz believed that the Bund, whose position had suffered under the Soviet regime, would form the vanguard of worldwide Jewish anti-Soviet activity. Rosmarin, on the other hand, looked to Zionist groups to take the leading role.

65. Ciołkosz's comment was made in response to a memorandum demanding such a declaration addressed to the government by the Bund Central Committee in April 1940: "Memorial fun Ts. K. fun 'Bund' tsu der Poylisher Regirung," YVA—M2/269.

66. Raczyński to Polish foreign minister, 22 January 1940 (Nr. 851/e/2: "w sprawie stosunków Żydów angielskich do Polski"), HIA-PG, Box 758, File: "Mniejszości w Polsce i sprawy z nimi związane poza Polską," Subfile: "Propaganda żydowska przeciw Polsce." Raczyński's comments about the attitude of the *Jewish Chronicle* toward Poland were not entirely fair. The newspaper had indeed strongly condemned behavior of Polish government representatives and of official Polish agencies that seemed to it inconsistent with the notion of Jewish civil equality (see above, n. 49), but it had also roundly praised what it considered examples of proper behavior toward Jews (see above, n. 51). In fact, from the outbreak of war to the date of Raczyński's complaint, articles, editorials, and letters to the editor reflecting an essentially sympathetic disposition toward Poland exceeded essentially hostile expressions by some 50 percent.

67. Later on the government's attitude on this matter changed radically. See below.

68. This does not mean that the Polish authorities did not adopt the idea of criticizing Soviet treatment of Jews in their own propaganda. See, for example, the document entitled "The Situation in Soviet-Occupied Poland," HIA-US, Box 33, File 2.

69. An exception was the Bund memorandum of April 1940; see above, n. 65.

70. M. Dowgalewski to Polish foreign minister, 31 March 1940, in Korzec, "General Sikorski und seine Exilregierung," pp. 252–53.

71. Raczyński to Polish foreign minister, 22 January 1940, ibid., pp. 239–40. Raczyński's suspicion was not without basis. On 29 December 1939 a strongly worded letter to the editor, demanding not only that the Polish government issue a declaration on Jewish rights but that the declaration be countersigned by the Allies, had been published and favorably commented upon by the *Jewish Chronicle*. Neville Laski, outgoing president of the Board of Deputies, had raised the possibility at a public meeting in January 1940, a fact noted by the Polish ambassador in his other communication with Zaleski of the same day (see above, n. 66). In April the concept was endorsed by Labour MP Rhys Davies, who further advocated setting up a special international body that would guarantee the rights of Polish Jewry; see above, n. 48.

72. See the anonymous, undated report beginning with the words "Wyjechałem ze Lwowa dnia 18 b. m.," transmitted through the Polish Legation in Budapest and distributed by the Polish Embassy in Paris on 11 November 1939, HIA-Mikołajczyk, Box 9, File: "Committee on Occupied Poland, Paris, Correspondence, November–December 1939."

73. See "Wiadomości o położeniu Żydów w Polsce," 7 February 1940 (Nr. 2235/32), YVA—O25/73; "Raport z Kraju z marca 1940: Żydzi," HIA-PG, Box 921, File N55; "Obraz sytuacji w Kraju w początku czerwca [1940]," HIA-Mikołajczyk, Box 9, File: "Committee on Occupied Poland, Paris, Correspondence, June–August 1940."

74. "Zagadnienie żydowskie w Kraju," HIA-PG, Box 921, File N55. On the

history, date, and authorship of this crucial document, see Engel, "Early Account of Polish Jewry," pp. 1–4. Unless otherwise indicated, subsequent quotations from Karski are from this document. Jan Karski was later to play an important role in establishing the credibility of the reports concerning the existence and operation of mass killing centers in Poland that began to reach the West during 1942; see below, chapter V.

75. Karski, *Story of a Secret State*, pp. 77–106.

76. The attitudes of the Jewish population of the predominantly White Russian areas of the Polish Republic have been reconstructed on the basis of numerous postwar testimonies and analyzed in Cholawski, *Al Neharot ha-Nieman vehaDnieper*, pp. 30–34. The eyewitness testimony by Moshe Kleinbaum conveyed some of the complexities of the Jewish response to the invading armies: "[In Łuck, the major city of the province of Wołyń], throngs of people lined the main road, along which marched the Soviet tanks, artillery, and mechanized infantry. Most watched the show out of curiosity. Ukrainian peasants . . . and young Jewish Communists, especially women, received them with applause and friendly cries. The number of Jewish admirers was not particularly large. However, their behavior on that day was notable for its vociferousness. . . . Hence it was possible to get the mistaken impression that the Jews were the most festive guests at this celebration. . . . Among the Jews of Łuck, the following joke was circulating already on 18 September: 'We were condemned to death, but now we have been granted a reprieve—life imprisonment.' . . . Life under Soviet rule is perceived as a sentence of life imprisonment—[the Jews are] alive, but . . . they have ceased to be free men. . . . At least 80 percent of the Jews . . . accepted Soviet rule with a sigh of relief after many weeks of fear over the danger of the Nazi invasion, but on the other hand with a moan of concern: what will tomorrow bring?" Kleinbaum, "El Dr. N. Goldmann," pp. 561–62. It should be pointed out that the Soviet invasion at first also aroused much confusion among the Polish population about just how it ought to respond. In some places Poles too greeted the Soviets as allies, in the mistaken conviction that the Red Army was heading west to fight Hitler. See Grudzińska-Gross and Gross, *War through Children's Eyes*, pp. 5–6.

77. On the position of the Jews in the Polish territories under Soviet occupation, see, among others, Cholawski, *Al Neharot haNieman vehaDnieper*, pp. 39–45; Schwarz, *Yidn in Sovetn-Farband*, pp. 14–22; Pinchuk, *Yehudei Berit-haMo'atsot*, pp. 28–36; Bertish, "Pezurat Yehudei Polin," pp. 267–72; Shlomi, "Yehudei Polin biVerit haMo'atsot," pp. 105–8.

78. On this movement, see Schwarz, *Yidn in Sovetn-Farband*, pp. 22–23; Litwak, "She'elat haEzrahut," pp. 85–86; Levin, "Berit haMo'atsot veHatsalat haYehudim," pp. 185–86. On the other hand, when, in late 1939, these refugees were given the choice of accepting Soviet citizenship or returning to their former homes in German-occupied territory, most refused Soviet citizenship. The better part of them were evidently not returned to the German zone but deported eastward. Nevertheless, Moshe Kleinbaum reported a

significant movement of Jewish refugees back into the German zone; Klein-baum, "El Dr. N. Goldmann," p. 563. Historical investigation has yet to confirm this report, however.

79. On the contrary, the reports seem to have been accepted in government circles as a matter of course. Thus Retinger, who in a conversation with Brodetsky on the matter of a declaration on Jewish rights attempted to cast doubt upon the Jewish leader's protestations of world Jewry's loyalty to the Polish cause, announced that he possessed sufficient evidence of Jewish disloyalty "even if we overlook the pro-Russian attitude of the Jewish proletariat in the Soviet-occupied territories" (which presumably was so self-evident as to be devoid of any special significance). Retinger to Raczyński, 19 March 1940, in Korzec, "General Sikorski und seine Exilregierung," pp. 247–51. Karski, too, noted with regard to the alleged enthusiasm of Jews for the Soviet regime, "Their attitude seems to me quite understandable."

80. See "Wyciąg z listu z Kraju z lutego 1940: Żydzi," HIA-PG, Box 921, File N55; "Wyciąg z listów z Kraju: Żydzi," 15 March 1940, ibid.; "Raport Ambasady RP w Bukareście: Żydzi," 19 April 1940, ibid. These reports quoted from correspondence among Poles and included such comments as "Będzin does not smell of Jews as it once did"; "Our Jews have finally lived to get what they deserved and what we were never able to do to them"; and "I am glad that when the snows melt they [the Jews] will move on to Australia or the Coral Islands, because things cannot be as they are any longer." For more on the attitudes of Poles under German occupation toward Jews during the early months of the war, see below, chapter V.

81. In fact, Karski even seems at the time to have suggested that the government explore the possibility of reaching a temporary agreement with the Soviet Union in order to enlist its aid in the struggle to oust the Germans. His wording of this proposal bears quotation in full: "I do not know how to do this, or even how to begin, or even who could do it, or on what scale in the long run (if it is possible at all)—but might it not be possible to a certain extent, in the face of the existence of three enemies (if, of course, one should currently regard the Jews as enemies), to endeavor to create something along the lines of a common front with the two weaker partners against the third more powerful and deadly enemy, leaving accounts to be settled with the other two later?"

82. It is a telling indication of the depth of anti-Jewish feeling among at least some segments of the Polish population that in the German as well as the Soviet zone, Jews evidently continued to be looked upon by many Poles as their enemies. A number of reports reaching the government-in-exile during the first year of the war concerning the situation of the Jews under German occupation stressed not only Communist agitation being led by Jews in cities of the Generalgouvernement but also the presence of Jews among Gestapo informers. Cf. "Komunikat ogólno-informacyjny Nr. 14, załącznik Nr. 4," 14 January 1940, HIA-Mikołajczyk, Box 9, File: "Committee on Occupied Poland, Correspondence, February–May 1940"; "Raport polityczno-gospo-

darczy z okupacji niemieckiej za okres od 7–14 stycznia 1940," 15 January 1940, ibid.; "Zeznanie p. Druchowskiego," 24–25 May 1940, HIA-PG, Box 921, File N55. For all of this, however, it must be stressed that Polish-Jewish relations under the Nazi occupation possessed additional ramifications, and their character was more complex than these documents reveal. See below, chapter V.

83. For a comparison of the two versions, see Engel, "Early Account of Polish Jewry," pp. 9–14.

84. See, among others, Raczyński to Polish Foreign Ministry, 14 February 1940, in Korzec, "General Sikorski und seine Exilregierung," pp. 241–43; *The Monthly Future: A Polish-American Forum,* June 1940 ("The Persecution of the Jews").

85. See, for example, Sikorski to Justin Godart, 31 May 1940 (Nr. 630/PC/16/40), AIP—PRM. 15a/8. This letter was written in response to a memorandum "relatif aux minorités israélites oprimées" presented to Sikorski by the French senator and former minister of labor. After assuring his correspondent that he regarded all Polish citizens as equal, and after repudiating the racial distinctions that informed German persecution of Jews, Sikorski commented: "Il est de même tout à fait évident qu'il ne se pose de problème juif que pour tous ceux d'entre eux qui demandent ou exigent un traitement ou des privilèges spéciaux. Posé de cette façon ce problème dépasse d'ailleurs nettement le cadre d'une seule nation et demande une solution sinon internationale—du moins européenne." The argument that the Jewish question resulted from a Jewish demand for "special privileges" had served frequently as a rationale for anti-Jewish statements and actions during the prewar years. By the same token, the phrase "international [or European] solution" was a codeword for emigration.

86. "Memoriał R. Knolla, Warszawa," March 1940, AIP—PRM. 15a/6 (emphasis in original). This program was obviously connected to Polish plans for breaking apart the Soviet empire after the war; on this matter see Kacewicz, *Great Britain,* p. 73.

87. Lewis Namier, the distinguished historian and Zionist activist, held Kot in high regard, noting that he had been deprived of his chair in history at the University of Kraków "because he had organised a protest against the ill-treatment of political prisoners." Coutouvidis, "Lewis Namier," pp. 421–22.

88. See Zygmunt Vetulani, Polish consul-general, Bagdad, to Polish Foreign Ministry, 23 December 1939, HIA-PG, Box 758, File: "Mniejszości w Polsce . . . ," Subfile: "Propaganda żydowska. . . ."

89. The two Jewish leaders repeated this message to Retinger upon their return to London. Retinger to Kot, 19 April 1940, in Korzec, "General Sikorski und seine Exilregierung," pp. 257–61.

90. Zygmunt Graliński, Polish Research Centre, London, to Raczyński, 18 April 1940, ibid., p. 256.

91. Raczyński to Stefan Danycz, 30 January 1940, ibid., pp. 240–41; Karol

Dubicz, Polish Legation, Lisbon, to Polish Foreign Ministry, 30 July 1940, HIA-PG, Box 499, File: "Żydzi"; Zaleski to Polish Legation, Lisbon, 29 August 1940, ibid.

92. Retinger to Kot, 19 April 1940, in Korzec, "General Sikorski und seine Exilregierung," pp. 257–61; Abrahams to Retinger, 17 June 1940, JI—G4/5/14.

93. Jabotinsky, *HaMediniyut haTsiyonit*, pp. 170–72.

94. See above, n. 92; see also Potocki to Polish Foreign Ministry, 1 June 1940 (Nr. 851-e/SZ/tjn-67: "w sprawie akcji Wł. Żabotyńskiego"), HIA-PG, Box 499, File: "Żydzi." For more on contacts between the Revisionists and the Polish government during the first year of the war, see Engel, "HaBerit haNichzevet," in press.

95. "Memoriał R. Knolla" (see above, n. 86).

96. Retinger to Kot, 19 April 1940, in Korzec, "General Sikorski und seine Exilregierung," pp. 257–61. A gloss in the margin pointed out, however, that the Federation of Polish Jews was an organization not of Jewish Polish citizens but of Jews of Polish origin.

97. See Schwarzbart's speech to the National Council, 2 April 1940, YVA—M2/17; see also *Dziennik Polski*, 8 August 1940 ("Stanowisko Żydów Polskich"). Schwarzbart's position was that the government should launch a systematic educational program aimed at bringing about a fundamental change in the Polish population's attitude toward Jews; see *Przyszłość*, 25 March 1940 ("Pierwsze zadania").

98. Dowgalewski to Polish foreign minister, 31 March 1940, in Korzec, "General Sikorski und seine Exilregierung," pp. 252–53.

99. In addition, the Poles possessed yet another layer of insulation, as it were—the alleged betrayal by Jews of the Polish cause during and in the wake of the Soviet invasion. Thus in April 1940, when representatives of the British Embassy to Poland and the British War Office sought to investigate the allegations of antisemitism among Polish troops in France, they were told that Polish soldiers could be expected to be hostile to those whose coreligionists had contributed to the defeat of their country. Both offices later reported to the Foreign Office that they found this explanation satisfactory. See Wasserstein, *Britain and the Jews of Europe*, p. 121.

100. "Streszczenie rozmowy pomiędzy P. Savery a P. Romerem," 28 July 1940, AIP—PRM. 20/6. The suggestion regarding the replacement of Sikorski with Zaleski as prime minister was not an idle one. Ten days prior to this conversation, Raczkiewicz had attempted precisely such a maneuver, only to retreat when Zaleski, under threat of force of arms, had declined the premiership. Savery remarked to Romer that the intervention of Polish Army officers in this episode had made a "fatal impression" and that official British circles had had "to take all possible steps [to ensure] that the matter did not become public knowledge." On this incident see Babiński, *Przyczynki historyczne*, pp. 33–38; Mitkiewicz, *Z Generałem Sikorskim*, pp. 79–80. In light of the Savery-Romer conversation, the version of the episode presented in Kukiel, *Generał Sikorski*, pp. 134–35, which denies any military intervention, seems doubtful. Savery's comments also seem to contradict Zabiełło's asser-

tion that the British were favorably inclined toward Sikorski; *O rząd i granice*, p. 45. In the event, it appears that British attitudes toward the Sikorski government were at this time in a state of flux. Prior to the crisis, British opinion was clearly negative, to the point where as early as March 1940 the Foreign Office had been reticent to become involved with the Poles in joint propaganda ventures in the United States; see the correspondence and minutes in PRO—FO 371/24469.C4098. Once Sikorski had defeated the attempt to unseat him, however, Foreign Office officials began to express the opinion that "the Poles cannot easily do without him." By mid-1941, Sikorski was widely viewed in British government circles as a positive influence. See Terry, *Poland's Place in Europe*, pp. 195–96.

101. Raczyński, *In Allied London*, pp. 37–38. Lloyd George was not alone; Churchill evidently also regarded the Soviet invasion as essentially defensive in nature, as did other senior British cabinet ministers. Zabiełło, *O rząd i granice*, pp. 28–29; Churchill, *Second World War*, 1:448–49.

102. "Anglicy o sprawie odbudowy Polski," n.d., AIP—PRM. 20/13.

103. Ciechanowski to Polish ambassador, Washington, 31 October 1940, AIP—A.12. 49/WB-Sow/1.

104. See Lord Halifax, British secretary of state for foreign affairs, to Zaleski, 27 November 1940, in *DPSR*, 1:97. See also Polonsky, *The Great Powers and the Polish Question*, pp. 16–17, 73–79.

105. See Schwarzbart's descriptions of his first encounter with such soldiers, in his diary entry for 6 July 1940, and of his discussion of the matter with Brodetsky, David ben Gurion, Berl Locker, Lewis Namier, and others at a meeting of the Zionist Executive, in his entry for 9 July, YVA—M2/745.

106. *Jewish Chronicle*, 26 July 1940 ("Anti-Semitism at Polish Camp in Britain: Authorities' Strange Inaction").

107. Ibid., 16 August 1940 ("Misbehaving Guests").

108. *Evening Standard*, 20 August 1940 ("Jewish Influence"). See also *Daily Herald*, 21 August 1940 ("Poles Publish Anti-Semitic Paper"). Calling *Jestem Polakiem* an antisemitic publication is problematic; the newspaper did not deal with Jewish issues directly until its issue of 25 August 1940, after criticism of it had surfaced. Before this date, its only reference to Jews was an obituary of Jabotinsky (11 August 1940); in it, the Revisionist leader was praised as "a straightforward politician" because he understood that "the real national interest of the Jewish community demands . . . a massive effort directed toward the exit of this mass to its national territory." The newspaper did, on the other hand, clearly identify itself with Dmowski and the heritage of Endecja and claimed that the Western powers had been weakened by an excess of liberalism, democracy, and parliamentarism. See the inaugural issue, 4 August 1940 ("Gdyby politycy czytali Dmowskiego"; "Potrzeba przemian istotnych"). In the issue of 18 August, an article appeared calling for the installation of a Catholic religious regime in Poland and stating that the secular tendencies of the interwar period must be fought (Ks. Xawery Omikron [pseud.], "Naród Katolicki: Za pozwoleniem władzy duchowej").

After the appearance of the first attacks in the British press, *Jestem Polakiem* counterattacked. It branded the *Jewish Chronicle* as "an . . . organ known for its hostile attitude toward the Polish nation" and suggested that the purpose of the press campaign against it was to interfere with Poland's independence in a fashion reminiscent of the First World War. See the issue of 25 August ("Napaści na nasze pismo").

109. Jędrzejewicz, *Poland in the British Parliament*, 1:435–42.

110. "Sprawozdanie o debacie w Izbie Gmin nad ustawą o armjach sojuszniczych," 23 August 1940, AIP—PRM. 20/14.

111. Untitled, anonymous document, beginning "Działalność czasopisma 'Jestem Polakiem . . . ,' " apparently dating from September 1940, AIP—PRM. 37b/61.

112. Strasburger to Sikorski, 23 August 1940, ibid. See also Strasburger's remarks at the cabinet meeting of 28 August 1940, "Protokół posiedzenia Rady Ministrów," AIP—PRMK. 102/28d.

113. PEN Club Polski w Londynie to Sikorski, 3 October 1940, AIP—PRM. 37b/61.

114. Quoted by Sir E. Grigg in the House of Commons, 21 August 1940, Jędrzejewicz, *Poland in the British Parliament*, 1:442.

115. "Przyczynek do [naświetlenia] zagadnienia żydowskiego w Armii Polskiej," 6 August 1940, AIP—PRM. 36/4. The memorandum cited the following in support of its contention: On 7 July 1940, all Polish citizens of draft age arriving in England from France were ordered to report for induction into the Polish Army. Two draft boards were set up to process the inductions—one at the Fulham transit camp, the other at the refugee hostel at Norwood. Of those ordered to report to Fulham, 60 failed to do so; of these, 58 were Jews. Another 32, of whom 27 were Jews, failed to report to Norwood. The Jewish draft evaders told Polish consular officials in the presence of British military representatives that the Polish forces were rife with antisemitism and that they were therefore not prepared to serve. Almost all claimed further that their Polish citizenship had been previously revoked and that they were thus not liable for service with Polish units. On the other hand, almost all had arrived in England with Polish military transports and had identified themselves as Polish citizens at their port of entry. All these things indicated to the author of the memorandum that a large percentage of Jews were openly hostile to the Polish state and that many regarded Polish citizenship as no more than an article of convenience, to be worn, as it were, when advantageous, but to be removed whenever demands were made on its account.

116. Schwarzbart Diary, 25 August 1940, YVA—M2/745 (Polish), 760 (English). See also Schwarzbart's further comments: "In all Polish circles my motion was gauged as being hostile to Poland and discrediting Poland's name. In consequence of a clear opposition hailing from General Sikorski's office even those favoring my motion turned against it. . . . Even those friendly Poles are getting adverse to the Jewish cause, claiming that my action is challenging and hurting Poland. . . ."

117. "Protokół posiedzenia Rady Ministrów," 28 August 1940, AIP—PRMK. 102/28d.

118. Ibid.; see also Sikorski to Mikołajczyk, 21 August 1940 (L. dz. 2002/XVI/40), AIP—PRM. 37b/61.

119. "Protokół posiedzenia Rady Ministrów," 28 August 1940, AIP—PRMK. 102/28d.

120. Ibid.

121. "Przekład wywiadu współpracownika 'Daily Herald' z redaktorem 'Jestem Polakiem,'" 28 August 1940, AIP—PRM. 37b/61.

122. *Dziennik Polski*, 27 August 1940 ("Polska i antysemityzm").

123. See Wasserstein, *Britain and the Jews of Europe*, p. 122; Jędrzejewicz, *Poland in the British Parliament*, 1:459–64.

124. Schwarzbart Diary, 26, 28, 30 August 1940, YVA—M2/745; *Jewish Chronicle*, 30 August 1940 ("Polish Anti-Semites in Britain"). According to the *Jewish Chronicle*, the renewal of pressure was a direct result of the appearance of *Jestem Polakiem*.

125. "Protokół z posiedzenia Komitetu Politycznego [Rady] Ministrów," 24 August 1940, AIP—PRMK. 102/28c.

126. "Notatka w sprawie stosunków polsko-żydowskich," AIP—PRM. 36/6.

127. *New Review*, 29 August 1940 ("The Polish Julius Streicher"); *Cavalcade*, 7 September 1940 ("Warsaw Group Start 'Streicher' Journal in London"). Julius Streicher was the Nazi Gauleiter of Franconia and publisher of *Der Stürmer*, a newspaper that combined racial antisemitism with pornography in purveying the vicious calumnies that formed the ideological basis of the Holocaust. The comparison between him and Seyda was entirely out of place and could lead to a fair evaluation of neither.

128. Jędrzejewicz, *Poland in the British Parliament*, 1:445–46; Wasserstein, *Britain and the Jews of Europe*, p. 122.

129. *Jewish Chronicle*, 27 September 1940 ("Conscription of Poles in Britain"). See also Schwarzbart Diary, 6, 28 August 1940, YVA—M2/745.

130. Jędrzejewicz, *Poland in the British Parliament*, 1:447; *New Statesman and Nation*, 7 September 1940 ("Poles and Jews").

131. See Captain S. W. T. Adams, MP, to secretary of state, 13 September 1941, and minute by J. G. Ward, 25 September 1941, PRO—FO 371/26440.C10475; R. R. Stokes, MP, to secretary of state, 7 November 1941, and minute by J. G. Ward, 15 November 1941, PRO—FO 371/26440.C12454; minute by J. G. Ward, 24 November 1941, PRO—FO 371/26640.C12784; Raczyński to Eden, 3 December 1941, PRO—FO 371/26640.C13448.

132. Schwarzbart to Zionist Executive, London, 24 July 1940, CZA—Z4/15625; Schwarzbart Diary, 9, 12 July, 25, 28 August 1940, YVA—M2/745. Schwarzbart had in the past, within the confines of the National Council, criticized certain aspects of government handling of Jewish affairs, but he had avoided making his criticism public and had never called upon the regime to issue a declaration on Jewish rights. Shortly after his arrival in En-

gland, he had given an interview to the *Jewish Chronicle* in which he had presented a favorable picture of Polish-Jewish relations and had stressed that Polish Jews felt themselves inextricably bound to Poland. This interview had earned him praise in the Polish press; see *Dziennik Polski*, 8 August 1940 ("Stanowisko Żydów Polskich"). For Schwarzbart's position on Polish-Jewish relations as expressed in the National Council, see "Protokół z posiedzenia Rady Narodowej," 8 March, 2 April 1940, AIP—A.5.

133. Raczyński to Polish Foreign Ministry, 26 August 1940 (Nr. 851-e/37), HIA-PG, Box 449, File 851-e; Zaleski to Raczyński, 13 September 1940 (Nr. 851/e/40), ibid.

134. Raczyński to Polish foreign minister, 23 September 1940, ibid.

135. Tartakower, "HaPe'ilut haMedinit," pp. 169–71.

136. Reprezentacja, *Sprawozdanie*, p. 7.

137. Tartakower to Schwarzbart, 7 August 1940, YVA—M2/530. Tartakower hoped first to reach an understanding with the Polish American community and to issue a joint call for a declaration. He believed that this step might exert a decisive influence upon the government.

138. Tartakower to Schwarzbart, 6 September 1940, ibid.

139. See the dubious attitude expressed by Yitshak Gruenbaum, Anshel Reiss, Apolinary Hartglas, and Eliyahu Dobkin toward Schwarzbart's earlier optimistic report on conditions for Jews in the Polish Army and his claim of success for his method of dealing with the government: "Sikkum miYeshivat haVa'adah leInyanei Polin," 13 May 1940, CZA—J25/15.

140. The legitimacy of his position had been a matter of concern for Schwarzbart virtually since he first took his seat on the National Council. Neither in Sikorski's initial invitation to him to join the council, issued on 15 December 1939, nor in the official act of appointment signed by Raczkiewicz on 21 December, was any mention made that Schwarzbart was to be regarded as the official representative of Polish Jewry; YVA—M2/1. If Schwarzbart nevertheless spoke in the name of all Polish Jews, he did so at first without any formal mandate. During the time of the government's sojourn in Angers, he had made an initial effort at establishing about him an advisory body of Polish Jewish emigrants and refugees in France reflecting the various ideological divisions within the Polish Jewish community, which would in turn name him as its official representative before the Polish regime. He had also attempted to induce five Polish Jewish leaders from Palestine to come to Angers and join this group. These efforts, to his disgruntlement, were rebuffed. In London he had continued his efforts under the banner of an Organising Committee for the Representation of Polish Jewry (not to be confused with the Reprezentacja in Palestine). In fact, the Reprezentacja in Palestine posed something of a challenge to Schwarzbart by its very existence, not only because it had come into being independently of his own efforts, but also because it possessed direct access to the government through Rosmarin's office in Tel Aviv. Although Schwarzbart was eventually made a nominal member of the Reprezentacja and acknowledged as its delegate in London, an attitude of mistrust and lack of confidence between the

two sides was to prevail throughout the war. See, among others, "Sikkum," 13 May 1940 (see above, n. 139); Schwarzbart and Marceli Dogilewski to Executive, Jewish World Congress [sic], 10 July 1940, YVA—M2/461; Komitet Organizacyjny Reprezentacji Żydostwa Polskiego to Polish Foreign Ministry, 13 August 1940, HIA-PG, Box 449, File 851-e; "Sprawozdanie z pracy w Londynie Nr. 1," 16 August 1940, CZA—J25/1/I; Gruenbaum to Schwarzbart, 4 September 1940, YVA—M2/599; Reprezentacja to Schwarzbart, 22 September 1940, ibid.; Schwarzbart to Reiss, 25 November 1940, ibid.; Schwarzbart to N. Barou, 24 December 1940, YVA—M2/461.

141. Schwarzbart to Sikorski, 8 October 1940, AIP—A.9. V/2.

142. Several weeks earlier Polish Jewish refugee leaders in the United States, together with two Polish emigrants said to be acting on behalf of the American Polish community, had drafted a proposed text for a declaration, which proclaimed, among other things, that Polish Jewry must be regarded as "a distinct national-cultural group identifying itself with Polish statehood" against which no discrimination or agitation could be tolerated, and as "a permanent element," not to be made the object of "any plan about emigration or evacuation." These were more explicit and far-reaching demands than had hitherto been voiced by non-Polish Jewish organizations or in the Jewish press. "Draft of a Joint Polish-Jewish Declaration," 19 September 1940, HIA-US, Box 64, File 3.

143. Potocki to Polish foreign minister, 14 September 1940 (Nr. 3/SZ-tjn-27: "w sprawie rozmów z Podsekretarzem Stanu p. Berle"), HIA-PG, Box 449, File 851-e.

144. "Protokół posiedzenia Rady Ministrów," 29 October 1940, AIP—PRMK. 102/30c. It is essential to note this cabinet decision in view of the subsequent mistaken claim by Jewish leaders that Stańczyk had spoken in his own name alone. See below, chapter III.

145. Schwarzbart to Executive, Jewish World Congress [sic], 7 November 1940, YVA—M2/530.

146. The full text of Stańczyk's declaration is reproduced in Reprezentacja, *Sprawozdanie*, pp. 8–10.

147. "List z Kraju," n.d., HIA-Mikołajczyk, Box 9, File: "Committee on Occupied Poland, Correspondence, September–October 1940." Since it refers to Stańczyk's speech of 3 November, it is obviously misfiled. A copy of the letter was obtained by the British Foreign Office on 9 January 1941, and an English translation was prepared. A handwritten note at the head of the English document reads: "Communicated by Mr. Savery, who made this translation of a recent letter from Prince Radziwill in Warsaw. Shown him under seal of secrecy by Professor Kot. The fact that we have seen this letter should *not* be revealed to anyone *including the Poles*." "A Letter from Poland," PRO—FO 371/26723 (emphasis in source).

148. See memorandum by Anshel Reiss, "Pegishati im H. M. Arciszewski . . . ," 29 December 1940, CZA—J25/3.

149. See the report by Olgierd Górka, director of the Nationalities Division of the Ministry of Information, "Uwagi o taktyce sowiecko-polsko-ukraiń-

skiej ostatnich czterech miesięcy," 14 November 1940, AIP—KOL. 30/I/2; "Uwagi Ministra Strońskiego dodane do sprawozdania Profesora Górki," 18 November 1940, ibid. Górka postulated that because of its overriding interest in breaking apart the Hitler-Stalin pact, world Jewry represented Poland's "most sincere ally in today's world." In his reply, Stroński indicated that in his view this convergence of interests was only temporary and would vanish once Hitler broke with the Bolsheviks or once the character of the regime in Germany changed. Nevertheless, he advised exploiting this temporary constellation to the maximum extent possible, although he did not say precisely how.

150. "Protokół posiedzenia Rady Ministrów," 17 October 1940, AIP—PRMK. 102/30b.

151. "Instrukcje dla Ambasadora R.P. w Waszyngtonie," n.d. (filed 15 January 1941), AIP—PRM. 21/4.

152. Ibid.

153. *Jewish Chronicle*, 8 November 1940 ("The New Poland").

CHAPTER III

1. "Joint Foreign Committee Report," 12 November 1940, YVA—M2/486.

2. "Poland and Its Jewish Citizens," 17 November 1940, YVA—M2/479.

3. "Resolution Passed by the Inter-Associate Council of Polish Jewry in Great Britain on the Declaration of the Polish Government," 8 November 1940, CZA—J25/1/I.

4. Henryk Szoszkies and Benjamin Winter to Schwarzbart, 8 January 1941, YVA—M2/565.

5. See "Sprawozdanie z przeglądanej prasy żydowskiej za okres od 10 grudnia 1940 r. do 10 stycznia 1941 r.," YVA—O55/1; see also, among others, *Jewish Chronicle*, 8 November 1940 ("The New Poland"); *HaPo'el haTsa'ir*, 15 November 1940 (H. L. Kroi, "Hats'harat haMemshalah haPolanit").

6. Schwarzbart to Executive, Jewish World Congress [*sic*], 7 November 1940, YVA—M2/530. See also "Ważki Krok—O Deklaracji Polskiego Rządu," YVA—M2/654; *Przysłość*, 1 February 1941 (I. Schwarzbart, "Ku nowej Polsce").

7. *Jewish Chronicle*, 24 January 1941 ("Democracy in the New Poland: Count Raczynski at Relief Fund Luncheon").

8. Ibid., 17 January 1941 ("'We Will Make Good All Wrongs': A Polish Promise in Palestine").

9. "Deklaracja Stronnictwa Ludowego . . . ," 26 March 1941, YVA—M2/149.

10. "Oświadczenie Stronnictwa Pracy . . . ," 25 June 1941, YVA—M2/151.

11. *Dziennik Polski*, 5 November 1940 ("Akademia Żydostwa Polskiego"; "Żydzi w wolnej Polsce: Przemówienie min. Stańczyka").

12. Ibid., 15 November 1940 ("Echa Akademii").

13. See *HaPo'el haTsa'ir*, 15 November 1940 (H. L. Kroi, "Hats'harat ha-Memshalah haPolanit"). The author of this article wondered why, from among all members of the government, it had been precisely the minister of labor and social welfare who had been chosen to speak on Jewish matters. Perhaps, he suggested, this choice implied that the government regarded the Jewish question as purely a social problem. Or, he asked, could it be that Stańczyk had been selected because, alone among his colleagues, he could promise Jews full equality without any semblance of affectation or violation of personal anti-Jewish feelings? As welcome as the declaration was for this author, he was not prepared on its strength alone to relinquish his doubts about the government's intentions.

An even stronger reservation was voiced by Arieh Tartakower of the World Jewish Congress. He believed that any pronouncement on the Jewish question, in order for it to be regarded as an official statement of policy by the Polish government, ought to have been made by the prime minister personally, or at least by the minister of the interior. "With all due respect to Stańczyk, who is a most fair and straightforward person," he explained to Schwarzbart, ". . . my personal but unfortunately well-founded impression is that [the government] simply wanted to wriggle out of a solemnly made declaration, and thus chose such a means [of presentation] and such a representative." Tartakower to Schwarzbart, 13 November 1940, YVA—M2/530. In the event, Tartakower's "well-founded impression" was not so well-founded at all; on this matter, see above, chapter II, n. 144. Nevertheless, the World Jewish Congress, in contrast to most other Jewish organizations, consistently denigrated the significance of the Stańczyk declaration, seeing in it little more than an attempt to assuage Jewish indignation over the appearance of *Jestem Polakiem*. See "Memorandum on Polish-Jewish Relations Submitted by the World Jewish Congress to the Rt. Hon. Anthony Eden, MP . . . ," n.d. (transmitted by Sidney Silverman to Eden, 1 May 1941), PRO—FO 371/26769.C4878.

14. See Wise and Nahum Goldmann to Ciechanowski, 2 April 1941, HIA-US, Box 67, File 3; *Congress Weekly*, 11 April 1941 (Jacob Lestchinsky [*sic*], "Attention General Sikorski!"); Wise to Sikorski, 17 April 1941, AIP—PRM. 57/3.

15. "Memorandum on Polish-Jewish Relations" (see above, n. 13).

16. Węgierski, *September 1939*, p. 148.

17. "Memorandum on Polish-Jewish Relations" (see above, n. 13); *Jewish Chronicle*, 17 January 1941 ("A Polish Anti-Semite's Book: Encouraging Jew-Hatred in this Country?").

18. Schwarzbart to Kot, 7 January 1941, YVA—M2/72.

19. Retinger, *All about Poland*; Głuchowski, *Na marginesie Polski jutra*.

20. "Memorandum on Polish-Jewish Relations" (see above, n. 13).

21. "Protokół posiedzenia Rady Ministrów," 9 April 1941, AIP—PRMK. 102/35b; see also *Daily Herald*, 4 April 1941.

22. Schwarzbart Diary, 10 April 1941, YVA—M2/761.

23. Ibid. ONR is the abbreviation for Obóz Narodowo-Radykalny (National-Radical Camp), an extreme right-wing and avowedly antisemitic party founded in 1934.

24. "Memorandum on Polish-Jewish Relations" (see above, n. 13); "Rezolucja do budżetu Ministerstwa Informacji i Dokumentacji," 8 March 1941, YVA—M2/24. There was no basis to this charge. In the edition of *Dziennik Polski* of 5 November 1940, two articles were devoted to the symposium of 3 November (see above, n. 11). The first contained a general description of the symposium; the second reproduced the text of Stańczyk's speech. The first article contained the following sentence: "Minister Stańczyk, whose speech we offer on page 3, spoke in the name of the government of the Republic of Poland." The second article highlighted Stańczyk's own assertion, "I speak in the name of the Polish government," by printing it as a separate paragraph. Moreover, the follow-up article of 15 November (see above, n. 12) explicitly referred to "the declaration presented in the name of the government by Minister Stańczyk" and in another place identified the minister's speech as "the government declaration."

25. "Memorandum on Polish-Jewish Relations" (see above, n. 13).

26. *Dziennik Polski*, 9 January 1941 ("Ci co cierpią najbardziej").

27. Ibid., 13 January 1941 ("W sprawie Polaków w 'ghetto' warszawskim"); cf. ibid., 3 January 1941 ("Żydowska policja w 'ghettach' ").

28. Schwarzbart to Polish information minister, 17 January 1941, YVA—M2/56.

29. "Memorandum on Polish-Jewish Relations" (see above, n. 13).

30. "Declaration by Dr. I. Schwarzbart at the full meeting of the Polish National Council," 5 April 1941, YVA—M2/91.

31. Schwarzbart to Polish information minister, 17 January 1941, YVA—M2/56; "Rezolucja do budżetu" (see above, n. 24). See also Schwarzbart to Sikorski, 21 March 1941, YVA—M2/78.

32. Cf. Schwarzbart to Paderewski, 16 March 1941, YVA—M2/144.

33. Rada Żydów Polskich w Wielkiej Brytanii to Polish information minister, 17 July 1941, AIP—A.21/5/3.

34. "Memorandum on Polish-Jewish Relations" (see above, n. 13).

35. See, among others, *Jewish Chronicle*, 10 January 1941 ("Polish Jewish Soldiers in Britain: Reported Arrests"); ibid., 17 January 1941 ("Detained Doctors Released"); ibid., 21 February 1941 ("Polish Jews at British Universities: A 'Numerus Clausus'?"); ibid., 14 March 1941 ("Conscription of Allied Nationals").

36. "Provisional Report Nr. 17," April 1941, YVA—M2/91; Schwarzbart Diary, 7, 10 May 1941, YVA—M2/762; "Sprawy wojskowe," 13 May 1941, YVA—M2/93; Tokarz, Oddział II Sztabu Naczelnego Wodza, to Kot, 15 May 1941, AIP—A.9. V/2; "Notatka o audencji u Gen. Klimeckiego . . . ," 6 June 1941, YVA—M2/93; "Rozmowa z maj. Laskowskim," 13 June 1941, ibid.

37. "Provisional Report Nr. 17" (see preceding note).

38. Wise and Goldmann to Ciechanowski, 2 April 1941, HIA-US, Box 67, File 3; Wise to Sikorski, 17 April 1941, AIP—PRM. 57/3.

39. Jędrzejewicz, *Poland in the British Parliament*, 1:452–54.

40. The estimates are as follows: unoccupied France—7,000; Portugal—2,000; North Africa—600; Palestine—1,750; Far East—1,750. Except for the last, these figures are from Jewish sources: for France, Schwarzbart and M. Lachs to Polish Foreign Ministry, 23 November 1940, HIA-PG, Box 587, File 738/Z; for Portugal, "Rapport sur la situation des refugiés Polonais," 13 December 1940, YVA—M2/387; for North Africa, Kalman Stein to Schwarzbart, 20 October 1940, ibid.; for Palestine, Schwarzbart to Polish Ministry of Social Welfare, 11 February 1941, YVA—M2/599. The figures in Polish documents for France and Portugal are lower, but they include only those receiving specific services from Polish relief organizations: for France, Stanisław Zabiełło to Polish Foreign Ministry, 22 March 1941 (Nr. 951/II), HIA-PG, Box 449, File: "Uchodźcy Żydzi"; for Portugal, "Sprawozdanie Delegata do Spraw Uchodźców Polskich w Portugalii," 26 August 1940, YVA—M2/63, and Stańczyk to Stanisław Schmitzek, 6 March 1941, YVA—M2/387. The figure for the Far East is from a document entitled "Uchodźcy Polscy w Portugalii i na Dalekim Wschodzie," 8 April 1941, AIP—PRMK. 102/35b. One must assume as well that there were some Polish Jews in each of these countries who did not wish to be identified as Jews or as Polish citizens and who thus did not make themselves known to Polish or Jewish representatives. In addition, there was an undetermined number of Polish Jewish refugees in Turkey and Switzerland, and probably in Spain and Sweden as well.

41. See "Movement of Jewish Population in Europe since the Outbreak of Hostilities up to March 1942," WL—Doc. 548/8.

42. Ludwik Grosfeld, Polish Ministry of Social Welfare, to Komitet Organizacyjny Reprezentacji Żydostwa Polskiego, 5 September 1940 (L. dz. 250/40), enclosing reports by Stanisław Schmitzek, 23 July, 26 August 1940, YVA—M2/63.

43. "List z Ministerstwa [Pracy i Opieki Społecznej] do Delegata w Portugalii," n.d., YVA—M2/387; Stein to Schwarzbart, 20 October 1940, ibid.

44. Stein to Schwarzbart, ibid.

45. Untitled document dated 14 October 1940, beginning, "Dnia 10. października 1940 odbyła się konferencja przedstawicieli żydów z Polski na emigracji w Lizbonie," attached to letter from Polish Ministry of Information to Polish Foreign Ministry, 25 October 1940, HIA-PG, Box 499, File 851-e.

46. Engel, "The Polish Government-in-Exile and the Deportations of Polish Jews from France," pp. 93–94.

47. Stańczyk to Komitet Organizacyjny Reprezentacji Żydostwa Polskiego, 23 October 1940, YVA—M2/63; Reiss and Abraham Stupp to Rosmarin, 12 December 1940, CZA—J25/3; Schwarzbart to Polish Foreign Ministry, 2 January 1941, HIA-PG, Box 587, File 738/Z; "Protokol miYeshivah Plenarit," 27 January 1941, CZA—J25/15; Schwarzbart to Polish Ministry of Social Welfare, 22 February 1941, YVA—M2/63.

48. Cable, Reprezentacja to Schwarzbart, 17 December 1940, YVA—M2/599; see also Schwarzbart to Polish Foreign Ministry, 2 January 1941, HIA-PG, Box 587, File 738/Z.

49. See cable, Schwarzbart to Reprezentacja, 16 January 1941, YVA—M2/599; cable, Schwarzbart to Reiss, 21 March 1941, ibid.

50. Schwarzbart to Polish Foreign Minister, 19 May 1941, YVA—M2/61.

51. *JTA Bulletin*, 5 April 1941 ("Board of Deputies and 'Jestem Polakiem' . . .").

52. "Memorandum on Polish-Jewish Relations" (see above, n. 13).

53. *Unzer Tsayt*, April–May 1941 (H. Lezgin, "London un Varshe").

54. "Sprawozdanie z przeglądanej prasy żydowskiej za okres od 10-go marca do 15-go kwietnia 1941 r.," AIP—A.9. V/2.

55. Wise to Sikorski, 17 April 1941, AIP—PRM. 57/3; S. Mendelsohn, E. Scherer, and S. Zygielbojm (Bund) to Polish government (via Mikołajczyk), May 1941, YVA—M2/269; M. Kleinbaum, B. Minc, and A. Stupp (Reprezentacja) to Polish government, 24 July 1941, in Reprezentacja, *Sprawozdanie*, pp. 13–21. In addition to these demands, which were common to all three documents, there were others that were voiced by only one or two organizations. Among these were calls for equality in refugee assistance (Reprezentacja), for a guarantee that Jewish property would be restored after the war to its former owners on the same basis as Polish property (Bund), and for a formal ratification of the principles of the Stańczyk declaration by the Polish prime minister personally (American Jewish Congress).

56. The American Jewish Congress seems to have been somewhat less specific than either the Bund or the Reprezentacja on this point. Comments upon the loyal behavior of Polish Jews were not included in the written memorandum presented to Sikorski but rather were offered orally by Tartakower at the meeting with the prime minister in New York on 17 April at which the memorandum was delivered. The only indication of what Tartakower actually said on this matter is his own rather sketchy summary: Tartakower to Schwarzbart, 25 April 1941, as intercepted and transmitted by British Postal and Telegraph Censorship, 14 May 1941, PRO—FO 371/26769. C5410.

57. This feeling was explicitly enunciated in the Bund memorandum (see above, n. 56). After recounting how Jews had kept faith with Poland under attack and occupation, the document declared: "Unfortunately . . . neither the cruel persecution nor the heroic struggle for freedom of the Jewish masses in Poland has as yet elicited an appropriate reciprocation from the Polish government."

58. Reprezentacja, *Sprawozdanie*, p. 15.

59. Ibid., p. 16.

60. Arciszewski's approach to the Reprezentacja had been made through one of the Jewish group's leading members, Anshel Reiss, at a private meeting that Reiss had initiated on 29 December 1940 (see above, chapter II, n. 148). Reiss apparently wished to impress upon Arciszewski that the government did not stand to gain from close association with the Revisionists; it was in this context that Arciszewski raised the question of what the government stood to gain from association with the parties that made up the Reprezentacja. Reiss answered that with regard to the border issue, the

Reprezentacja was prepared to endorse Polish territorial acquisitions in the West at the expense of Germany, but it was as yet too early for it to formulate a position on the eastern frontier. When Reiss reported on his conversation to the Reprezentacja Executive Committee, no one raised the eastern border question for discussion; "Yeshivat haVa'ad haPo'el," 6 January 1941, CZA—J25/15. Reiss himself did not even mention this issue in his report on the meeting with Arciszewski at the Reprezentacja plenum; "Protokol miYeshivah Plenarit," 27 January 1941, ibid. It seems that in general during this period the Reprezentacja was unwilling to discuss matters pertaining to the postwar political order, on the grounds that it was as yet too early to foresee all of the possibilities that might ultimately emerge for a postwar settlement. Significant in this regard are the comments by Yitshak Lew at the plenary session of 27 January 1941 (ibid.), those by Lew, Moshe Kleinbaum, Apolinary Hartglas, and Maurycy Richter at the plenary session of 14 May 1941 ("Protokol miYeshivah Plenarit," 14 May 1941, ibid.), and those by Kleinbaum and Shim'on Feldblum at the plenary session of 22 May 1941 ("Protokol miYeshivah Plenarit," 22 May 1941, ibid.). It is also noteworthy that when the Executive Committee took the decision that ultimately resulted in the dispatch of the memorandum of 24 July, it was stipulated that the proposed communication with the government would not indicate the stand of the Reprezentacja on the border question; "Protokol Yeshivat haVa'ad haPo'el," 27 June 1941, ibid.

61. At the meeting of the Executive Committee of 4 May 1941, Abraham Stupp observed: "We must discuss the activities . . . that we wish to undertake on behalf of Poland. We cannot simply approach [the government] with complaints regarding Jewish affairs. We must cooperate in general Polish concerns. . . ." Reiss dismissed his suggestion out of hand with the abrupt remark, "At this time this would be merely an academic discussion." No more was said on the matter at this or any subsequent meeting, either of the Executive Committee or of the plenum, prior to the dispatch of the memorandum of 24 July to the government. "Protokol miYeshivat haVa'ad haPo'el," 4 May 1941, CZA—J25/15.

62. Schwarzbart Diary, 26 May 1941, YVA—M2/762.

63. See above, n. 56. Next to this statement a British Foreign Office official made the handwritten comment: "And yet these people expect to be treated as 100% Polish citizens!"

64. *Przyszłość*, 1 February 1941 (I. Schwarzbart, "Ku nowej Polsce").

65. *Jewish Chronicle*, 17 January 1941 ("Dr. Schwarzbart's Watchful Eye: Polish Government's Attitude").

66. See Schwarzbart Diary, 2 May 1941, YVA—M2/761, and 12 May 1941, YVA—M2/762. Schwarzbart was in general wary of provoking a backlash with criticism of the government's behavior toward Jews, although this caution did not necessarily deter him from censuring particular practices when such censure seemed to him warranted. See his diary entry for 17 March 1941, YVA—M2/761: "I took the floor [in the National Council] and delivered a speech of almost one hour's duration. . . . I continued to tell the story of

the increasing antisemitism in the Polish Army. . . . It is a difficult situation. The Polish Army has its own difficulties; the Jewish question figures as only one of them. And then there gets up a Jew and constantly warns the General Staff and Supreme Command about antisemitic practices. One cannot but develop into a nuisance in their eyes."

67. Ibid., 26 May 1941, YVA—M2/762.

68. Ibid., 9 April 1941, YVA—M2/761.

69. Ibid., 9 May 1941, YVA—M2/762.

70. Schwarzbart to Wise, 14 December 1940, YVA—M2/530; see also Schwarzbart Diary, 2 May 1941, YVA—M2/762.

71. See above, chapter II, n. 147.

72. Minute by F. K. Roberts, 26 May 1941, PRO—FO 371/26769.C5410; see also minute by F. K. Roberts, 13 May 1941, PRO—FO 371/26769.C4878.

73. See Sikorski's alleged comment to Schwarzbart upon the former's return from his visit to the United States in the spring of 1941: "For God's sake let the Jews not be oversensitive, because I might lose my temper too and become an antisemite." Schwarzbart Diary, 6 June 1941, YVA—M2/762.

74. "Sprawozdanie z konferencji prasowej odbytej w Ministerstwie Informacji i Dokumentacji z prasą żydowską," 6 March 1941, HIA-PG, Box 455, File 851/e, Subfile: "Żydzi w Wielkiej Brytanii, 1941." Górka was a respected historian who was known among Jews for his critical excoriation of common anti-Jewish arguments during the prewar years; see Górka, *Naród a Państwo*, esp. pp. 249–60, 301–10.

75. "Opening Remarks," attached to letter from Stroński to Polish prime minister and others, 11 March 1941, HIA-PG, Box 455, File 851/e, Subfile: "Żydzi w Wielkiej Brytanii, 1941."

76. Ibid. Górka appears to have had in mind specifically the appearance of an article by the prominent Polish journalist Ksawery Pruszyński in Schwarzbart's journal, *Przyszłość*, on 1 February 1941. The same issue of the newspaper also featured an article by Górka, which argued that antisemitism in interwar Poland had been mainly the result of German influence and that because that influence had now been replaced by an orientation toward Britain and France, Jews had no reason for anxiety over the future of their relations with the Poles.

77. See above, n. 75.

78. "Sprawozdanie z konferencji" (see above, n. 74). Górka's deputy, Stanisław Paprocki, apparently used the same argument in a conversation with Schwarzbart. See the latter's diary entry for 9 April 1941, YVA—M2/761: "[Paprocki] said to me in the interests of the Jews of Poland it would be best if at least 1,000,000 Jews were to emigrate from Poland over a period of 30–40 years after the war, unless, of course, Poland would be so enlarged as to reach to the River Dnieper. . . . I frankly told Mr. Paprocki, 'No.' But Mr. Paprocki referred to Yitzhak Gruenbaum, who himself recognized that 1,000,000 Jews have to leave Poland. Unfortunately I could not deny that Mr. Gruenbaum had said this." For Gruenbaum's actual attitude toward the emi-

gration idea, see Gruenbaum, *Milhamot Yehudei Polaniah, 1913–1940*, pp. 407–25.

79. He did, however, in August 1941, in a speech to a meeting of Revisionists in London. HIA-PG, Box 459, File 851/e, Subfile: "Emigracja Żydów, Państwo żydowskie."

80. See Głuchowski, *Na marginesie Polski jutra*, p. 5; Bielski, *Głos z Kraju*, p. 70.

81. Węgierski, *September 1939*, p. 150.

82. Głuchowski, *Na marginesie Polski jutra*, p. 5. It is noteworthy, too, that even as Głuchowski took this position, he also strongly urged that the organized Polish emigrant community in the United States reach an understanding with American Jewry on the position of Jews in postwar Poland (p. 14). Such an understanding had long been sought by the World Jewish Congress office in New York and resisted by Polish American organizations. See Karol Ripa, Polish consul-general, Chicago, to Polish Consulate-General, New York, 11 September 1940 (Nr. Tjn. 263-SZ-17; "w sprawie współpracy polsko-żydowskiej w Ameryce"), HIA-PG, Box 499, File 851-e; see also *Congress Weekly*, 24 January 1941 (Jacob Apenszlak, "A Polish-Jewish Agreement").

83. "Sprawozdanie z konferencji" (see above, n. 74).

84. Węgierski, *September 1939*, pp. 152–54.

85. *Free Europe*, 10 January 1941 (E. H., "On Poland").

86. See Górka's more candid comments from a private letter: "The Jewish press . . . in London occupies itself excessively with making mountains out of molehills and with blowing out of all proportion the expressions of irresponsible snot-faces [*smarkaczy*]. . . ." Górka to [S. L.] Schneiderman, 19 March 1941, YVA—O55/1.

87. Stroński to Rada Żydów Polskich w Wielkiej Brytanii, 21 July 1941, AIP—A.21/5/3.

88. The council had charged that in reporting Sikorski's remarks to the National Council on 4 June on the need to establish a liberal democratic order in postwar Poland—which had been made in response to demands submitted to the prime minister by Wise and Tartakower during their meeting in New York on 17 April—the radio announcer had added on his own initiative the comment, "Let us remember that the democracies of England and America will not understand any other position." The council maintained that in this way the broadcast had tried to apologize for Sikorski's statement on the grounds that it had been necessitated by momentary tactical considerations; Rada Żydów Polskich w Wielkiej Brytanii to Polish Information Ministry, 17 July 1941, AIP—A.21/5/3. In actuality, Sikorski himself had included in his statement the sentence, "Please be aware that any other conception of this difficult problem [of the character of the regime in the future Poland] would never be understood by the people either of America or of Britain, who together with us are carrying on the difficult and inexorable struggle against the ideology of Hitlerism." Stroński felt that the ministry should be commended for broadcasting this part of Sikorski's speech with-

out any editorial curtailment, because his entire speech to the National Council was quite long and could not be included in its entirety in a brief radio summary. The full text of Sikorski's speech was printed in *Dziennik Polski*, 6 June 1941 ("Cele i Wyniki: Przemówienie gen. Sikorskiego na posiedzeniu Rady Narodowej R. P. d. 4 czerwca 1941 r.").

89. Stroński to Rada Ministrów, 21 July 1941 (L. dz. 4088/41/Rd/Mnj.), AIP—A.21/5/3.

90. "Notatka o przebiegu audjencji u Gen. Sikorskiego . . . ," 6 June 1941, YVA—M2/93.

91. "Rozmowa z maj. Laskowskim," 13 June 1941, ibid.

92. See the two reports dated 23 July 1940 and 26 August 1940, attached to Grosfeld to Schwarzbart, 5 September 1940, YVA—M2/63.

93. Schmitzek to Polish minister of social welfare, 4 October 1940, HIA-PG, Box 455, File 851/e, Subfile: "Różne." Cf. Zaleski to Schwarzbart, 17 March 1941 (No. 738/Z/41), YVA—M2/387; Raczyński, *In Allied London*, p. 85.

94. See cable, Tadeusz Romer, Polish ambassador, Tokyo, to Polish Foreign Ministry (no. 15), 7 February 1941, AIP—KOL. 5/2, Japan, File 16 (microfilm reel 3); "Uchodźcy wojenne z Polski w Szanghaju," 18 March 1942, AIP—KOL. 5/2, Shanghai Consulate-General, File 2 (microfilm reel 3). Officials in London shared these perceptions; see "Uchodźcy Polscy w Portugalii i na Dalekim Wschodzie," 8 April 1941, AIP—PRMK. 102/35b; Schwarzbart Diary, 16 May 1941, YVA—M2/762.

95. See Schmitzek to Polish minister of social welfare, 2 January 1941 (Nr. 185/40), YVA—M2/387; Schwarzbart to Polish Ministry for [*sic*] Social Welfare, 11 February 1941, YVA—M2/599; Zabiełło to Polish Foreign Ministry, 22 March 1941 (Nr. 951/II), HIA-PG, Box 449, File: "Uchodźcy Żydzi." The Polish offices in France (Biura Polskie we Francji) took the place of a Polish diplomatic representation, which the Vichy government had been prepared to admit but which Germany had vetoed. See Zabiełło, *O rząd i granice*, p. 42.

96. Schmitzek reported that 80–90 percent of the Jewish refugees in Portugal at the beginning of 1941 fell into this category; see preceding note. According to Schwarzbart, only about 1,100 of the 6,000–7,000 Polish Jews in unoccupied France had left Poland during the war or immediately before; the rest had previously resided in the West. Schwarzbart and M. Lachs to Polish Foreign Ministry, 23 November 1940, HIA-PG, Box 587, File 738/Z.

97. *Dziennik Ustaw Rzeczypospolitej Polskiej*, Nr. 22, poz. 191. The introduction of this law had the effect, among others, of prompting the Nazi German government to expel the approximately 70,000 Polish Jews living in the greater Reich. When the initial transports arrived at the Polish frontier on 28 October 1938, Poland at first refused to admit the deportees. Eventually a settlement was reached between the two countries, but not before the son of one of the deported families, who was at the time studying in Paris, shot and killed an official of the German Embassy to France. This incident touched off the infamous Kristallnacht pogrom of 10 November 1938. See Melzer, *Ma'avak Medini beMalkodet*, pp. 294–302; Schleunes, *The Twisted Road to Auschwitz*, pp. 236–39.

98. A possible indication of this discriminatory application can be found in the files of the Polish Legation to Portugal. Of 261 Polish residents in Portugal whose citizenship was revoked under the terms of this law between 24 May and 21 August 1939, 223 bore identifiably Jewish first names. HIA-Poland, Poselstwo (Portugal), Box 14, File 719. On the other hand, it appears that the majority of the Polish colony in Portugal at that time was of Jewish origin; see Związek Obywateli Polskich w Portugalii to Polish foreign minister, 8 May 1939, ibid.

99. Zabiełło to Polish Foreign Ministry, 22 March 1941 (Nr. 951/II), HIA-PG, Box 449, File: "Uchodźcy Żydzi."

100. Wise to Sikorski, 17 April 1941, AIP—PRM. 57/3.

101. In *Dziennik Polski* see, among other articles, 18 January 1941 ("Żydzi wierzą w Polsce"), 13 February 1941 ("Ghetto warszawskie"), 14 February 1941 ("'Mała Polska' w Palestynie"), 18 February 1941 ("Żydzi i Polacy w Palestynie"), 22 February 1941 ("Nowy Kurjer Warszawski—[Wycinki]"), 26 March 1941 ("Żydzi, wszy, tyfus"), 4 April 1941 ("W Radzie Narodowej RP"), 22 April 1941 ("Przemówienie Min: Stańczyka w Klubie Anglo-Palestynskim . . ."), 30 April 1941 ("Żydzi w Armii Polskiej"), 9 May 1941 ("Życzenia Żydów Polskich na 3 maja"), 5 July 1941 ("Na ziemi gdzie Paderewski był pierwszym siewcą i oraczem").

102. In *Free Europe* see, among other articles, 17 November 1939 ("The Meaning of the Present War"), 29 December 1939 ("The Tragedy of the Jewish People"), 12 January 1940 (J. Cang, "Jewish War Aims"), 26 January 1940 (J. Cang, "Jewish Peace Aims"), 5 April 1940 (Szymon Wolf, "The Jewish Problem in Eastern Europe"), 15 November 1940 ("Free Jews in Free Europe: Polish Government's Pledge"; Gabriel Haus, "For a United Jewish Peace Aim Program"), 2 May 1941 ("Future of Polish Jewry; Polish Minister's Address"). In fact, it appears that the only piece appearing in the newspaper that could reasonably have aroused Jewish anger was the favorable review of Węgierski's book (see above, n. 85); and space was allotted for a Jewish reply to this review on 7 February 1941.

103. On the policy of the Brazilian government with regard to Jewish immigration, see Lipiner, "A Nova Imigracão Judaica," p. 145; Shatzky, *Yidishe Yishuvim*, pp. 96–97. The head of the Jewish refugee organization HICEM in Lisbon, James Bernstein, also confirmed that the difficulty lay on the Brazilian and not on the Polish side; "Rapport sur la situation des refugiés polonais," 13 December 1940, YVA—M2/387. Nonetheless, sixteen Polish Jews are reported to have entered Brazil from Japan prior to January 1941; cable, Polish Embassy, Tokyo, to Polish Foreign Ministry, 2 February 1941 (no. 12), AIP—KOL. 5/2, Japan, File 16 (microfilm reel 3).

104. "List z Ministerstwa do Delegata" (see above, n. 43). Bernstein reported that his office was constantly requested by Polish Jews to intervene on their behalf with the Polish Legation and that in doing so he had become aware of the ill will shown by the local Polish authorities toward their Jewish citizens. At one point he commented: "Nous ne pouvons pas croire qu'il y aura un temps où les autorités polonaises traiteront leur nationaux tout de la

même manière sans distinction de réligion. . . ." "Rapport sur la situation" (see preceding note).

105. See cable, Schwarzbart to Reiss, 21 March 1941, YVA—M2/599; Schwarzbart Diary, 16 May 1941, YVA—M2/762; Schwarzbart to Zaleski, 19 May 1941, YVA—M2/61.

106. Engel, "The Polish Government-in-Exile and the Deportations of Polish Jews from France," pp. 96–97.

107. Ibid., p. 96. The necessity for special strictness with regard to Jews was also emphasized in Zabiełło's letter to the Foreign Ministry of 22 March 1941 (see above, n. 95): "Since according to the statute approved by the French authorities the Polish Red Cross is entitled to aid Polish citizens exclusively, the question of establishing the citizenship of Jews applying for relief takes on a grave significance."

108. See cable, Zaleski to Zabiełło (via Polish Legation, Madrid), 29 November 1940, HIA-PG, Box 587, File 738/Z; Zaleski's handwritten comments on the letter to him from Schwarzbart, 2 January 1941, ibid.; "List z Ministerstwa do Delegata" (see above, n. 104).

109. Efforts had been made since the first months of the war to recruit ethnic Poles living in North and South America for the Polish Army. During the First World War some 30,000 Poles from the United States alone had fought with the Polish Legions in France. Sikorski's trip to the United States and Canada in the spring of 1941 was in part intended to promote enlistment, and a center for recruits was set up in Canada. However, the number of recruits from the Western Hemisphere was small. See Kukiel, *Six Years of Struggle*, pp. 17–18.

110. Cable, Polish Embassy, Tokyo, to Polish Foreign Ministry, 2 February 1941 (no. 12), AIP—KOL. 5/2, Japan, File 16 (microfilm reel 3).

111. Wiktor Podoski, Polish legate, Ottawa, to Polish prime minister and commander-in-chief, 17 June 1941, AIP—PRM. 57/9.

112. Ibid. The reference to Sikorski's "pledge in New York" is to a statement made to Wise and Tartakower on 17 April regarding the government's commitment to Jewish equality. On this matter, see below.

113. Director, Aid Department, Polish Ministry of Social Welfare, to Polish Foreign Ministry, 14 July 1941 (L. dz. 3729/41), YVA—M2/387. Of course, the negative attitude of the Canadian government toward the admission of Jewish refugees may also be reflected in this statement; see Abella and Troper, *None Is Too Many*, passim.

114. Lisiewicz, First Polish Army Corps Command, to cultural officers, 19 April 1941 (Nr. 2504/Prop. i Osw./41), YVA—M2/90. The essential theme of this lecture was that Poles no longer had any need to fight Jews, because as a result of the war the Nazi and Communist empires would be destroyed and the new Russian and German states that would be established on their ruins would attract an influx of over 1.5 million Polish Jews. Thus anti-Jewish statements by Poles during the war were counterproductive, as they were exploited by Nazi and Communist propaganda to incite the U.S. press (which was "90 percent in the hands of Jewish financiers") against Poland.

115. Minute by F. K. Roberts, 13 May 1941, PRO—FO 371/26769.C4878. See also additional minutes to ibid.; also draft reply by secretary of state for foreign affairs to R. R. Stokes, MP, n.d. [November 1941], PRO—FO 371/26440.C12454.

116. See Schwarzbart to Executive, Jewish World Congress [*sic*], 7 November 1940, YVA—M2/530.

117. "Protokół z posiedzenia Rady Narodowej," 26 March 1941, AIP—A.5. The same meeting also featured a statement by General Lucjan Żeligowski calling for the creation of a Jewish state to be followed by mass Jewish emigration from Poland. To this proposal Schwarzbart replied that 99 percent of Polish Jewry rejected the notion that the existence of a Jewish state precluded continued Jewish residence in Poland.

118. "Wniosek p. Dra. Schwarzbarta i Kolegów," 13 June 1941, HIA-Polish Research Centre, microfilm reel 7. This document gives the text of both motions as they were transmitted from the council plenum to the Legal-Constitutional Committee. In inaugurating the discussion of the latter motion before the Legal-Constitutional Committee, Schwarzbart inserted the words "legal acts" before "executive decrees" and changed the phrase "will be repealed" to "are repealed." See "Posiedzenie Komisji Prawno-Konstytucyjnej," 13 June 1941, HIA-RN, Box 1, File 3. It should be kept in mind that the National Council was an advisory body with no legislative authority; thus motions were generally phrased in the form of a "sense of the council" resolution that "expressed an opinion" concerning what the government ought to do about a particular issue.

119. "Protokół z posiedzenia Komisji Prawno-Konstytucyjnej Rady Narodowej R. P.," 28 May 1941, HIA-RN, Box 1, File 3.

120. Ibid. Lieberman appears to have favored the motion not so much because the Citizenship Law had been directed primarily against Jews as because he saw it as a device for preventing the return to Poland of political exiles, such as he himself had been between 1931 and 1939.

121. Seyda had assumed the justice portfolio following the government's reestablishment in Britain.

122. Three speakers (Seyda, Michał Kwiatkowski, and Bishop Józef Gawlina) wished to see the Citizenship Law reformulated in a way that would give the state a freer hand in dealing with the German and Ukrainian minorities.

123. See above, n. 119.

124. Discussion of the motion was continued on 30 May, at which time it was joined to discussion of a parallel motion by Władysław Banaczyk to study the entire problem of discriminatory legislation before recommending repeal of specific laws (see below). At the conclusion of the meeting it was decided that no vote should be taken on Schwarzbart's motion but that both of his proposals should be considered together with Banaczyk's motion as alternatives one to another. "Protokół z posiedzenia Komisji Prawno-Konstytucyjnej . . . ," 30 May 1941, HIA-RN, Box 1, File 3. In his diary Schwarzbart wrote that the committee approved his motion on 16 June.

There is no support for this claim in the committee's minutes; in fact, the committee did not meet on 16 June. See Schwarzbart Diary, 16 June 1941, YVA—M2/762.

125. "Posiedzenie Komisji Prawno-Konstytucyjnej" (see above, n. 118).

126. For a discussion of the actual history and motivation of this law, see Melzer, *Ma'avak Medini beMalkodet*, pp. 97–100.

127. For Filipowicz's remarks, see "Protokół z posiedzenia Komisji Prawno-Konstytucyjnej," 17 June 1941, HIA-RN, Box 1, File 3.

128. During the plenary debate on Banaczyk's motion that took place on 4 July (see below), Adam Ciołkosz introduced an amendment that restored much of the sense of Schwarzbart's proposal. As a result, both the amendment and the main motion were returned to committee for deliberation. On 10 July the committee voted to reject Ciołkosz's amendment and not to report on it before the plenum. Schwarzbart objected and threatened to introduce the amendment in the form of a minority report, but his right to do so was challenged by the committee. The matter was referred to the chairman of the council for decision, but decision was evidently not rendered prior to the council's dissolution in the aftermath of the Polish-Soviet agreement. "Sprawozdanie z posiedzenia Komisji Prawno-Konstytucyjnej . . . ," 10 July 1941, HIA-RN, Box 1, File 3.

129. See above, chapter II, n. 30.

130. The final approved text read as follows: "The National Council expresses the opinion that it is necessary to study the legal regulations in force from the perspective of their agreement with the principles of democracy, especially with the principles of civic equality, respect for civil rights, and the independence of the judicature, and to change or repeal those regulations which are inconsistent with these principles. To this end the government must appoint a commission, whose task will be to formulate appropriate legal regulations in as short a time as possible." A commission was in fact appointed, and the repeal of the Citizenship Law recommended. This was accomplished by a presidential decree of 28 November 1941 (*Dziennik Ustaw Rzeczypospolitej Polskiej*, Nr. 8, 1941, poz. 22). The decree was not retroactive, however, so that Schwarzbart's original goal remained unsatisfied. When a second National Council was called in 1942, Schwarzbart moved that the decree be applied retroactively. His motion was carried on 11 March 1942; "Protokół z posiedzenia Rady Narodowej . . . ," 11 March 1942, HIA-RN, Box 2, File 10.

131. Gruszka to Kot, 16 January 1941, AIP—A.9. V/2.

132. Gruszka to Polish ambassador, Washington, 17 March 1941, HIA-PG, Box 455, File 851/e, Subfile: "Żydzi w St. Zjednoczonych." Schwarzbart, from his side, also did his best to create this impression of American Jewry among Polish governing circles; see the memorandum that he presented to Sikorski and the foreign minister prior to the premier's departure for North America, "Uwagi o społeczeństwie żydowskim w Kanadzie i w St. Zjedn. A. P. z wyszczególnieniem żydostwa polskiego," 15 March 1941, ibid. See also the

anonymous article entitled "Tell American Jewry," which appeared in his occasional newspaper, *Przyszłość*, 1 February 1941.

133. Raczyński, *In Allied London*, pp. 73–74, 89, 351–53. The Poles had good reason to be apprehensive about British intentions, as is indicated by the words of the outgoing British ambassador to the Polish government, Sir Howard Kennard, in a note of 2 May 1941 to Assistant Under-Secretary of State for Foreign Affairs William Strang: "It may be said that the present composition of the Polish Government is of little importance as it is certain that, if Poland regains her liberty, the present Government would be purely one of transition; but in view of the fact that, no matter whether we win a decisive victory or not, Poland will undoubtedly have to accept major sacrifices, especially on her Eastern frontiers, it seems unfortunate that the existing Government should be so weak. . . ." Kennard to Strang, 2 May 1941, PRO—FO 371/26768.C4598. Kennard was, however, known for his antipathy to Sikorski and was about to be replaced by the more sympathetic Sir Cecil Dormer; see Terry, *Poland's Place in Europe*, pp. 195–96. See also Kacewicz, *Great Britain*, p. 88.

134. See "Instrukcje dla Ambasadora R.P. w Waszyngtonie," n.d. (filed 15 January 1941), AIP—PRM. 21/4. As it happened, the United States also believed that Britain sought a rapprochement with the USSR and was, for reasons of its own, interested in preventing such a step. Izek, "Roosevelt and the Polish Question," pp. 11–12.

135. See Under-Secretary of State ([Sumner] Welles) to President Roosevelt, 7 April 1941, *FRUS*, 1941, 1:232–33; Ciechanowski, *Defeat in Victory*, pp. 18–22; Raczyński, *In Allied London*, p. 84.

136. See "Instrukcje dla Ambasadora" (see above, n. 134); "Protokół posiedzenia Rady Ministrów," 7 January 1941, AIP—PRMK. 102/32a; Gruszka to Kot, 16 January 1941, AIP—A.9. V/2.

137. On Ciechanowski's Jewish ancestry, see Schwarzbart Diary, 14 May 1941, YVA—M2/762; see also Karski interview.

138. Goldmann and Wise to Ciechanowski, 2 April 1941, HIA-US, Box 67, File 3. According to Schwarzbart, Wise stated in the aftermath of this conversation that Ciechanowski was "a dangerous man." Schwarzbart regarded this statement as silly but nevertheless informed Zaleski that the Jewish leaders had not been satisfied with their encounter. He emphasized to the foreign minister the great political weight carried by the World Jewish Congress, pointing out "the detriment which can possibly be done to Polish-Jewish relations in the States" by angering this powerful body. Schwarzbart Diary, 14, 16 May 1941, YVA—M2/762.

139. Handwritten annotation by Ciechanowski, 3 April 1941, to letter from Goldmann and Wise (see preceding note).

140. It was at this meeting that the memorandum of the American Jewish Congress to the Polish government was presented. See above, n. 55.

141. Tartakower to Schwarzbart, 25 April 1941, PRO—FO 371/26769.C5410.

142. *Congress Weekly*, 25 April 1941 ("Timely Topics—General Sikorski's As-

surance"). See also Tartakower, "HaPe'ilut haMedinit," p. 173.

143. "Protokół z posiedzenia Rady Narodowej," 4 June 1941, AIP—A.5. See also "Wyimek z mowy Gen. Sikorskiego wygłoszonej na publicznym posiedzeniu Rady Narodowej R. P. w Londynie," 4 June 1941, YVA—M2/78; *Dziennik Polski*, 6 June 1941 ("Cele i Wyniki"; see above, n. 88).

144. "Wniosek Prezesa Rady Ministrów na Radę Ministrów w sprawie polityki wobec Żydów," 11 June 1941, AIP—PRMK. 102/36Ia.

145. Seyda to Sikorski, 7 June 1941, AIP—A.21/5/3.

146. "Protokół posiedzenia Rady Ministrów," 11 June 1941, AIP—PRMK. 102/36Ia.

147. Seyda to Władysław Folkierski, president, National Party, 4 June 1941, AIP—PRM. 57/7. Seyda was technically correct; the cabinet had never formally approved the actual *text* of Stańczyk's declaration before it was issued. It had, however, delegated the labor minister to speak in its name and had in effect given him carte blanche to compose, with Sikorski's approval, such remarks as he saw fit. Seyda claimed further that Stańczyk had been instructed only to deliver greetings and that in issuing his declaration he had exceeded his mandate. The minutes of the cabinet meeting of 29 October 1940, however, do not bear out this claim. In the event, although the Jewish organizers of the symposium on 3 November had requested only a greeting from the government, it appears that the Poles themselves voluntarily took the extra step. See Schwarzbart's "Report No. 3," 18 November 1940, CZA—J25/1/I.

148. Seyda to Sikorski, 4 June 1941, AIP—PRM. 57/7. Seyda had apparently discussed the content of his letter to Folkierski (see preceding note) with Sikorski before composing it, and the two had agreed that the Jewish press should be blamed for misconstruing what Sikorski had told Wise and Tartakower.

149. See above, n. 90.

150. See the concern expressed in the Presidium of the New Zionist Organization in January 1941 that the organization's standing with the Polish government might be impaired because, among other things, organized Polish Jewry in the United States had begun to "fight bitterly against our evacuation idea." "Minutes of the Meeting of the Nessiut," 31 January 1941, JI—G5/1/3. See also Engel, "HaBerit haNichzevet," in press.

151. "Notatka w sprawie żydowskiej," 11 April 1941, HIA-US, Box 64, File 1.

152. Gruszka to Polish ambassador, Washington, 17 March 1941, HIA-PG, Box 455, File 851/e, Subfile: "Żydzi w St. Zjednoczonych."

153. "Notatka w sprawie wiadomości uzyskanych przez Nową Organizację Sjonistyczną o niepokojach arabskich w Palestynie," 24 May 1941 (L. dz. 2901/41/wiad/Mnj.), AIP—A.9. V/2.

154. *Free Europe*, 7 February 1941 (Harry Schnurr, "Peace and the Jews"), 7 March 1941 (Abraham Abrahams, "Towards the Solution of the Jewish Problem"), 4 April 1941 (letter to the editor from M. Lachs), 2 May 1941 (letter to the editor from Schnurr and Abrahams). Evidently the initial proponent of

the Revisionists within the Information Ministry was Paprocki. Stroński desired personal contact with Revisionist circles, but owing to a protracted illness he was unable to establish contact at this time. "Minutes of the Meeting of the Administrative Committee," 3 April 1941, JI—G4/27/1; "Sprawozdanie do użytku Dra. Retingera," 11 May 1941, AIP—PRM. 57/5.

155. "Minutes of the Meeting of the Nessiut," 12 April 1941, JI—G5/1/3.

156. "Sprawozdanie do użytku Dra. Retingera" (see above, n. 154).

157. Engel, "HaBerit haNichzevet," in press; see also Schwarzbart Diary, 15 June 1941, YVA—M2/762.

158. See the note by Stanisław Westfal of the Interior Ministry, 3 March 1941, AIP—A.9. V/2. See also Engel, "HaBerit haNichzevet," in press.

159. See minute by F. K. Roberts, 13 May 1941, PRO—FO 371/26769.C4878: "Since there are some 3,000,000 Jews in Poland (10% of the population of prewar Poland) and many of these are not very well assimilated, any Polish Government must inevitably aim at finding some solution of this problem by emigration. Since, however, no other country is willing to accept Polish Jews, and the absorptive capacity of Palestine is strictly limited, it is not in the interest of HM Government to encourage such a policy on the part of the Poles. All we can do is express the pious hope that the Poles will in fact do their best to assimilate the Jews."

160. "Protokół posiedzenia Rady Ministrów," 6 May 1941, AIP—PRMK. 102/36a; cable, Sikorski to Polish Consulate-General, Jerusalem, n.d. (filed at Interior Ministry, 20 June 1941), AIP—A.9. V/2. The opinion was also expressed that the government would be better advised to work toward the creation of a separate Jewish army not under Polish command. In this way, it was argued, it would be possible to stipulate that Polish Jews who volunteered for service in the Jewish army would forfeit their Polish citizenship and would thus be prevented from returning to Poland after the war. See "Notatka," 6 May 1941, YVA—O25/87.

161. Cable, Sikorski to Polish Consulate-General, Jerusalem, n.d., AIP—A.9. V/2. See also Engel, "HaBerit haNichzevet," in press.

162. See Seyda's comments to the cabinet, "Protokół posiedzenia Rady Ministrów," 6 May 1941, AIP—PRMK. 102/36a.

163. See above, n. 90.

164. "Note on conversation between the Secretary of State and General Sikorski," 19 January 1942, PRO—FO 954/19b/400.

CHAPTER IV

1. Sir Stafford Cripps, Britain's ambassador to the Soviet Union, also professed this view to Sikorski four days before the German attack; see "Note made by General Sikorski on his conversation with Sir Stafford Cripps on the imminent outbreak of war between Germany and the USSR . . . ," 18 June 1941, in *DPSR*, 1:106. See also Terry, *Poland's Place in Europe*, p. 57.

2. Raczyński interview. It is interesting to note that even more than forty years after the event, Raczyński continued to express regret that the Germans had not succeeded in capturing Moscow or in holding the line at Stalingrad. Had the Russian counterattack at the end of 1942 been repulsed, he argued, Poland might eventually have been liberated from the West and the Soviets obliged to restore relations with the Polish government on terms far more favorable to the latter than those which finally obtained. See also Zabiełło, *O rząd i granice*, p. 58.

3. "Note made by General Sikorski" (see above, n. 1).

4. "Memorandum on the proposed negotiations with the Soviet Government," 1 July 1941, in Raczyński, *In Allied London*, p. 96.

5. Sosnkowski to Sikorski, 22 June 1941, in Babiński, *Przyczynki historyczne*, p. 583.

6. Babiński, *Przyczynki historyczne*, pp. 43–44; Ciechanowski, *Defeat in Victory*, pp. 29–32.

7. Already on 18 June Cripps had told Sikorski that "Poland's assistance [to Russia] could be more effective [than Britain's] because of the great number of Polish officers and soldiers in Russia, and the Polish gift for organisation." When Sikorski mentioned the number of Polish troops available, Cripps remarked that "Polish assistance would be priceless. . . ." "Note made by General Sikorski" (see above, n. 1). See also Zabiełło, *O rząd i granice*, p. 58.

8. "Note made by General Sikorski" (see above, n. 1).

9. Babiński, *Przyczynki historyczne*, pp. 52–55. The Treaty of Riga, signed on 18 March 1921, established the Polish-Soviet border; it was renounced by the Soviets when they invaded Poland on 17 September 1939. On 1 and 2 November 1939, the Soviet government formally annexed the conquered Polish territories to the Ukrainian and Byelorussian Soviet Republics, on the basis of plebiscites that had been held in them shortly before. These plebiscites hardly represented an uncoerced expression of opinion. On the manner in which they were conducted, see Grudzińska-Gross and Gross, *War through Children's Eyes*, pp. 21–26. Sosnkowski's view was shared by Zaleski and Seyda; Zabiełło, *O rząd i granice*, p. 58.

10. "Letter from General Sikorski to General Macfarlane on conditions of military collaboration between Poland and Russia . . . ," 24 June 1941, in *DPSR*, 1:113.

11. "Record of a conversation between General Sikorski and Mr. Eden on re-establishment of Polish-Soviet relations," 4 July 1941, in *DPSR*, 1:114–16; "Record of a conversation between General Sikorski and Ambassador Maisky on the conditions of resumption of Polish-Soviet relations," 5 July 1941, in *DPSR*, 1:117–19. It should be noted that the record of the conversation with Eden shows Sikorski demanding merely that the Soviets acknowledge "as null the German-Soviet agreements of August and September 1939," without insisting specifically upon Russian acceptance of the Treaty of Riga. However, as the record of the conversation with Maisky demonstrates, the prime minister assumed that the former action was tantamount to the latter;

see "Broadcast by General Sikorski to the Polish Nation on: 'Poland and the German-Soviet war,' " 23 June 1941, in *DPSR*, 1:109. It should also be mentioned that Sikorski personally appears to have been prepared to consider a compromise with Russia over the eastern border provided the Soviets did not insist that Poland surrender its claim to the Riga frontiers in advance; see "Conversation between Ernest Bevin, Secretary of State for Labour, and General Sikorski (Extracts)," 3 July 1941, in Polonsky, *The Great Powers and the Polish Question*, pp. 80–81. His government, however, was for the most part not prepared to support him in this course. See Polonsky, *The Great Powers and the Polish Question*, p. 18; Terry, *Poland's Place in Europe*, pp. 126–27.

12. "English Protocol" to Sikorski-Eden conversation, 4 July 1941 (see above, n. 11); "Record of a conversation between General Sikorski and Minister Zaleski and Ambassador Maisky, held in the presence of Mr. Eden, concerning the resumption of Polish-Soviet relations," 11 July 1941, in *DPSR*, 1:128–32.

13. On the eve of the German invasion Churchill is reported to have remarked, "If Hitler invaded Hell, I would at least make a favourable reference to the Devil in the House of Commons." [Cadogan], *Diaries*, p. 389.

14. Kacewicz, *Great Britain*, p. 92; Zabiełło, *O rząd i granice*, pp. 57–58.

15. Izek, "Roosevelt and the Polish Question," pp. 20–21.

16. "Polish-Soviet agreement . . . ," 30 July 1941, in *DPSR*, 1:141–42. With regard to the former condition, the agreement stated merely that "the Government of the Union of Soviet Socialist Republics recognises the Soviet-German Treaties of 1939 as to territorial changes in Poland as having lost their validity." Neither the Soviet nor the British government viewed this statement as implying any guarantee of the 1939 frontier; see "Statement made in the House of Commons by Mr. Eden concerning the Polish-Soviet Agreement," 30 July 1941, in *DPSR*, 1:143–44; see also Polonsky, *The Great Powers and the Polish Question*, p. 83 n. 1. With regard to the latter condition, the agreement provided for "the formation on the territory of the Union of Soviet Socialist Republics of a Polish army under a commander appointed by the Polish Government in agreement with the Soviet Government, the Polish army on the territory of the Union of Soviet Socialist Republics being subordinate in an operational sense to the supreme command of the Union of Soviet Socialist Republics, upon which the Polish army will be represented."

17. *DPSR*, 1:578–79; Babiński, *Przyczynki historyczne*, pp. 67–68.

18. Babiński, *Przyczynki historyczne*, pp. 78–84; Zabiełło, *O rząd i granice*, p. 66. Contributing to this sense of insecurity was the existence of opposition to the Polish-Soviet agreement even within the parties that remained associated with the government, as well as the hostile attitude of, among others, President Raczkiewicz and Ambassador Ciechanowski. Sikorski appears to have been especially concerned that Ciechanowski was attempting to encourage the U.S. government to oppose the agreement; see Polonsky, *The Great Powers and the Polish Question*, pp. 19, 84 n. 1.

19. Raczyński served as director of the Foreign Ministry (Kierownik Ministerstwa Spraw Zagranicznych) from August 1941 to July 1943. In this ca-

pacity he was de facto the foreign minister of Poland, and he will be referred to as such henceforth. According to Raczyński, the designation was his own choice; he did not take the official title of foreign minister because he remained at the same time ambassador to Britain, and it was not deemed proper that an ambassador should be simultaneously a government minister. Raczyński interview.

20. On Raczyński's attitude, see Eden to Sir Cecil Dormer, British ambassador to the Polish government-in-exile, 18 August 1941, in Polonsky, *The Great Powers and the Polish Question*, pp. 88–89. On Zaleski's attitude, see Babiński, *Przyczynki historyczne*, pp. 85–86.

21. See "Protokół posiedzenia porozumiewawczego w sprawach żydowskich," 9 January 1942, HIA-PG, Box 459, File 851/e; "Zarys programu pracy w zakresie zagadnienia żydowskiego," 7 ᴵ .bruary 1942, AIP—[EP], "Sprawy żydowskie."

22. Cable, Wise and Goldmann to Sikorski, 29 January 1942, HIA-US, Box 64, File 4; "Audiencja u Gen. Sikorskiego," 4 March 1942, YVA—M2/78. Schwarzbart characterized the congress's presentation to Sikorski on the latter occasion in this way: "If I had spoken the way he [Sidney Silverman] did, I would have been accused of obsequiousness."

23. "Notatka ze sprawozdania p. min. Stańczyka o spostrzezeniach na odcinku żydowskim w czasie pobytu w Ameryce," 21 March 1942, HIA-PG, Box 459, File 851/e, Subfile: "Żydzi w Stanów Zjednoczonych." For the repetition of the pledge, see Olszer, *For Your Freedom and Ours*, pp. 267–69.

24. "Rozmowa z Panem Weitzmanem," 25 September 1941 (Nr. 2454/VIII/410), YVA—O25/79.

25. Ibid.

26. Confidential memorandum by Raczyński (untitled), 6 October 1941 (Nr. 49/WB/152), HIA-PG, Box 455, File: "Mniejszości Żydzi," Subfile: "Żydzi w W. Brytanii."

27. Raczyński was asked how the Polish government felt about East Prussia as a territory for a Jewish homeland. He replied that Poland required East Prussia for its own purposes.

28. "Note on conversation between the Secretary of State and General Sikorski," 19 January 1942, PRO—FO 954/19b/400. It is not clear to what extent the Polish government was actually prepared at this time to support, in accordance with Zionist wishes, a specifically *Palestinian* territorial solution to the Jewish question. In his conversation with Eden, Sikorski spoke of Palestine as *the* solution and did not raise any other possibility. On the other hand, there is evidence to suggest that the government may have viewed Palestine much as did the British officials to whose conversation Raczyński had been privy, as at best only a partial answer to the problem. It appears, for example, that the government was prepared to look favorably upon an Iraqi plan to promote the designation of some colonial territory as the focus for Jewish postwar emigration, with Palestine remaining merely "the symbolic center of Zionism." See A. Poniński, Polish minister plenipotentiary, Istanbul, to Polish foreign minister, 31 March 1942 (No. O/A.P/17/42: "w

sprawie Poselstwa Iraku do Stanów Zjednoczonych i zagadnień arabsko-
żydowskich"), HIA-PG, Box 459, File: "Mniejszości żydzi."

29. See Weizmann to Jan Smuts, 15 August 1941, in [Weizmann], *Letters
and Papers*, Series A, 20:184.

30. See Weizmann to Anthony de Rothschild, 22 January 1942, ibid., p.
258: "My own conversations, and also the conversations which the British
authorities have had with representatives of the Czechs and Poles in this
country [England], drive me to the conclusion that at least one-third of the
Jewish population of these states cannot be reintegrated when the states are
restored. . . . Of course . . . much will depend on the attitude of Soviet
Russia. I am prepared to assume that within Soviet Russia no problem will
arise, but the size of the emigration problem will also depend on the frontiers of the new Poland. . . ."

31. On Weizmann's attitude toward the Soviet Union during the war, see
Kedem, *Haim Weizmann beMilhemet haOlam haSheniyah*, pp. 150–54.

32. Even the Revisionists noted "the importance for Zionism of the return
of Russian Jewry to the forefront of Jewish affairs. . . ." "Minutes of the
Consultation of the Presidency in New York," 11 August 1941, JI—G5/1/3.

33. See *HaPo'el haTsa'ir*, 3 October 1941 (H. H., "Teshuvot haYishuv le-
Yahadut Rusiah"). See also Redlich, *Propaganda and Nationalism*, pp. 125–38.

34. See "Likrat Magbit haEzra liVerit haMo'atsot," April 1941, AILM—519
IV (Printed Materials); *HaBoker*, 23 June 1941 ("HaIsh shebeKoho lehamtin");
HaTsofeh, 23 June 1941 ("Beged Bogedim").

35. "Exchange of Letters between M. L. Perlzweig and Lord Halifax," 23
July 1941, and "Comments by M. L. Perlzweig," in Hirszkowicz, "The Soviet
Union and the Jews," pp. 75–78. The Polish government was aware that such
pressure was being applied. In January 1942 Rosmarin cabled Raczyński regarding the importance of counteracting Soviet propaganda among American Jews with pro-Polish propaganda in Palestine. He told the foreign minister that, thanks to his influence, the local Jewish press had frequently and
unanimously pointed out that the Polish-Soviet agreement contained explicit
Soviet recognition of the Riga treaty. In the event, the press had not done so
(see below, n. 38). Rosmarin was probably trying to augment Polish regard
for Palestinian Jewry as a potential political ally, as well as to enhance his
own prestige in the eyes of his superiors. Cable, Rosmarin to Polish Foreign
Ministry, 14 January 1942, HIA-PG, Box 459, File 851/e.

36. Redlich, *Propaganda and Nationalism*, pp. 100–104, 138–40. See also
"Yeshivat haVa'ad haPo'el," 17 July 1941, AH—Minute Books, Executive;
Goldmann, *Staatsmann ohne Staat*, p. 281. In October the Histadrut (General
Federation of Jewish Workers in Palestine) launched a "Campaign of Soli-
darity and Aid for the Fighters of the USSR," under the chairmanship of
Golda Myerson. Within one month the campaign took in 6,000 Palestine
pounds ($24,000) in cash and pledges. "Yeshivat haVa'ad haPo'el," 6 Novem-
ber 1941, AH—Minute Books, Executive.

37. See the undated, handwritten record of a statement attributed to the
Palestinian pro-Soviet activist Shlomo Tsirulnikov (filed with papers dating

from mid-1942), beginning with the words (in Hebrew): "The direction and tendencies of the Movement to Aid the Soviet Union need not and cannot be determined by sympathy or lack of sympathy with the political and social regime in the Soviet state or with its national policy." AILM—519 IV/1A.

38. On the contrary, what few Jewish public expressions on the border issue were made at the time tended implicitly to reject the Polish position. See, for example, *Palestine Post*, 1 August 1941 ("Russia and Poland"): "Though the text of the [Polish-Soviet] agreement . . . contains no direct reference to the vexing dispute over the Ukrainian and White Russian territories won by Poland in 1920 and lost again in 1939, the fact that the territorial division effected by Russia . . . is now explicitly declared void opens the way for a reconsideration of the question as soon as the war emergency is over. . . . The question will presumably have to be decided in the end by plebiscite. . . ."

39. "Liga V lema'an Rusiah haMo'atsatit: Yediot haMazkirut haArtsit," February 1943, AILM—519 IV (Printed Materials).

40. Reprezentacja, *Sprawozdanie*, pp. 22–23.

41. See cable, [Sylwin] Strakacz, Polish Consulate-General, New York, to Polish Foreign Ministry, 24 October 1941 (no. 50), HIA-PG, Box 449, File 738/Z, Subfile: "Żydzi w Sowietach"; cable, Central Committee, New Zionist Organisation of Poland in Palestine, to Raczyński, 7 November 1941, HIA-PG, Box 455, File 851/e; Jacob Rosenheim, Agudas Yisroel, New York, to Ciechanowski, 6 February 1942, HIA-US, Box 64, File 4; Reprezentacja, *Sprawozdanie*, p. 24. The second representative was selected from the Bund because this was believed to have been the largest Jewish party in Poland immediately before the war and because many Polish leaders were convinced that it exercised strong influence among American Jews. The official Polish explanation of the selection stressed that it was "independent of any sympathy which the government might feel for particular Jewish movements and their programs." See cable, Raczyński to Korsak, 11 November 1941 (no. 363), HIA-PG, Box 455, File 851/e.

42. See *Unzer Tsayt*, January 1942 (E. Scherer, "Der Ongrif fun der poylisher Reaktsie"); ibid., March 1942 (Sh. Mendelson, "A Nayer Kurs?"). Endecja had divided during the months following the signing of the Polish-Soviet treaty. The so-called Poznań faction, led by Seyda, reconciled itself with the government, while a second group, led by Tadeusz Bilecki, remained in opposition. Zabiełło, *O rząd i granice*, p. 66.

43. Reprezentacja, *Sprawozdanie*, p. 26; see also "Protokol Yeshivat haPlenum," 11 February 1942, CZA—J25/15.

44. The declaration promised, among other things, that the future Poland would be a "democratic and republican state, with a national assembly elected by general, equal, direct, and secret vote," and that it would guarantee "the rights and liberties of all loyal citizens, regardless of national, religious, and racial differences." *Keesing's Contemporary Archives*, 28 February 1942, no. 5061.

45. See *Unzer Tsayt*, April 1942 (E. Scherer, "A Brik tsum Morgen oder a

Shrit tsurik?"); "Przemowienie Dra. I. Schwarzbarta," 17 March 1942, YVA—M2/17.

46. "Uchwały powzięte na plenarnym posiedzeniu Reprezentacji Żydostwa Polskiego," 11 February 1942, in Reprezentacja, *Sprawozdanie*, pp. 27–28.

47. Cable, Sikorski to Reprezentacja, 12 March 1942, ibid., p. 28. A longer but equally harsh denial of the Reprezentacja's complaints was sent by the Foreign Ministry on 28 March. Ibid., pp. 28–29. For the text of the latter reply, see below, n. 57.

48. Scherer, *Polska a Żydzi*.

49. Ciechanowski to Stefan Ropp, Polish Information Center, New York, 5 May 1942, HIA-PG, Box 459, File 851/e. The pamphlet was in fact never released in English.

50. "Stenogram z XVII posiedzenia Rady Narodowej," HIA-RN, Box 2, File 10. See also *Biuletyn Klubu Narodowego*, July 1942 ("Odprawa ataków z przemówienia Zofii Zaleskiej na plenum Rady Narodowej").

51. See Polish Consulate-General [Tel Aviv, to Polish Foreign Ministry], n.d. (Nr. 851e/Pl/30: "Państwo żyd. w Polskiej Radzie Nar."), YVA—O55/2.

52. "Statement on Polish-Jewish Relations," n.d., HIA-US, Box 64, File 4. See attached documents for evidence on source and approximate date.

53. The text of the speech, made on 16 August 1942, is in HIA-PG, Box 459, File 851/e, Subfile: "Emigracja Żydów, Państwo żydowskie."

54. See *Jewish Chronicle*, 21 August 1942 ("Poland and Her Jews").

55. See cable, Korsak to Polish Foreign Ministry, 4 September 1942 (no. 365), HIA-PG, Box 459, File 851/e; cable, Stroński to Polish Consulate-General, Jerusalem, 22 September 1942 (no. 377), ibid. Antoni Serafiński of the Interior Ministry had earlier advised against sending a representative to the Revisionists' conference, fearing adverse political repercussions on several fronts. "Notatka," 12 August 1942, AIP—A.48.10/C1.

56. See Dormer to Raczyński, 7 September 1942 (Nr. 48/20/42), HIA-PG, Box 459, File 851/e, Subfile: "Emigracja Żydów, Państwo żydowskie."

57. The clearest indication of this stance was contained in the Foreign Ministry's reply to the Reprezentacja memorandum of 11 February 1942 (see above, n. 47). According to this document: "1. The objections concerning the purported antidemocratic and antisemitic attitude of several members of the government are groundless in light of the unanimous acceptance by all government members of a declaration giving clear expression to a government policy based upon the principles of democracy and equal rights for minorities. 2. The government is putting these principles into practice, as is shown by, among other things, the equal and just treatment of all citizens [and] the repeal of the laws concerning revocation of citizenship. 3. The complaint about the failure to assign Jews proportional representation in the National Council cannot be regarded as well taken, because the principle of proportional representation was not taken into account in [any of] the nominations. . . . Besides, Jewish representation was increased to two members. . . . The clear stance and policy of the government . . . permits the government to demand full support from the Reprezentacja, not only in matters of

foreign policy." Government spokesmen further stressed that the government-in-exile was of necessity a government of national unity, which could no more exclude the right wing of the political spectrum than it could the left, and that therefore the demand to keep Endecja off the new National Council was unfair.

58. "Raport z pobytu na terenie Konsulatu Generalnego w New Yorku ks. prałata Zygmunta Kaczyńskiego," 20 May 1942, HIA-Poland, Konsulat Generalny New York, Box 1. Evidently the government feared that the Polish American community might be susceptible, as its organizations had in the past rebuffed government suggestions to cooperate with Polish Jewish circles in the United States in fund-raising and public relations activities. See Polish Foreign Ministry to Ciechanowski, 21 October, 10 November 1941, HIA-PG, Box 455, File 851/e, Subfile: "Żydzi w St. Zjednoczonych." On political currents within the American Polish community at this time, see Lukas, *The Strange Allies*, pp. 107–10.

59. F. Szelag, Polish Prime Minister's Office, to Stroński, 29 June 1942 (L. dz. 1538/42), YVA—O55/2.

60. Following the Russian occupation of eastern Poland in September 1939, the Soviet regime inaugurated a policy of deporting certain of the inhabitants of the conquered territories to the Soviet interior. These included mostly local leaders, political activists, civil servants, police officers, and professional people, as well as small farmers and agricultural workers. Many who had fled east from the German-occupied territories (mainly Jews) were also removed. By robbing the occupied regions of their political and intellectual leadership, the Russians hoped to facilitate their eventual Sovietization. On this policy, see "Deportations of Polish Citizens from Soviet-Occupied Poland to the Interior of the USSR, 1940–1941," n.d., HIA-US, Box 30, File 8. This document was later included in a publication entitled *Final Report of the Polish Embassy in the USSR, Compiled in Teheran in August 1943* . . . ; a copy is located in HIA-PG, Box 129, File: "Ewakuacja obywateli polskich z ZSRR." This brochure was in turn extracted from a 169-page report entitled "Udzielona Pomoc i Opieka nad Ludnością Żydowską w ZSRR," prepared by Zygmunt Sroczyński, HIA-Poland, Ambasada USSR, Box 16. For the number of deportees, as well as descriptions of their experience, see Grudzińska-Gross and Gross, *War through Children's Eyes*, pp. xxii–xxiv, 239–41, and passim. On the number of Jews among the deportees, see Kot to Mikołajczyk, 11 October 1941, in Kot, *Listy z Rosji*, p. 136; see also Grudzińska-Gross and Gross, *War through Children's Eyes*, p. xxiii. For a discussion of the deportations of Jews, see Pinchuk, *Yehudei Berit-haMo'atsot*, pp. 18–22, 48–60.

61. Terry, *Poland's Place in Europe*, pp. 64–65.

62. Reprezentacja, *Sprawozdanie*, p. 22; see cable, Reprezentacja to Schwarzbart, 1 July 1941, YVA—M2/600.

63. Cable, Reprezentacja to Stańczyk, 22 July 1941, CZA—J25/2; Stańczyk's reply, 28 July 1941, ibid. On 5 August the Reprezentacja, following Stańczyk's request, nominated former Sejm deputy Apolinary Hartglas and

Rabbi Zalmen Soroczkin from Łuck as its candidates for inclusion in the delegation. Cable, Reprezentacja to Stańczyk, 5 August 1941, ibid.

64. Tartakower to Ciechanowski, 30 August 1941, HIA-US, Box 64, File 3; Sidney Silverman to Raczyński, 10 October 1941, HIA-PG, Box 449, File 738/Z, Subfile: "Żydzi w Sowietach."

65. Rosmarin to Reprezentacja, 25 August 1941, CZA—J25/2.

66. Kraczkiewicz to Polish ambassador, Washington, 26 September 1941 (Nr. 738/Sow/41), HIA-US, Box 64, File 3. The Jew was Ludwik Seidenmann, who had been active in the Zionist movement in Poland before the war.

67. Cable, Raczyński to Polish Embassy, Moscow, 9 October 1941 (no. 75), HIA-PG, Box 449, File 738/Z, Subfile: "Żydzi w Sowietach"; Sikorski to Raczyński, 29 October 1941 (L. dz. 2530/VIIa/41), ibid. Schwarzbart appears to have played a role in bringing the Polish authorities to this conclusion; see Schwarzbart to Sikorski, 11 October 1941, ibid.

68. Cable, Raczyński to Polish Embassy, USSR, 31 October 1941 (no. 117), ibid.; cable, Raczyński to Polish Diplomatic Offices, Buenos Aires, Ottawa, Jerusalem, 10 November 1941 (v.n.), ibid.; cable, Raczyński to Polish Embassy, Washington, 10 November 1941 (no. 413), ibid.

69. Reprezentacja, *Sprawozdanie*, p. 22.

70. "Protokol miYeshivat Va'ad [*sic*] haPo'el," 25 September 1941, CZA—J25/15.

71. Cable, Korsak to Polish Foreign Ministry, 18 December 1941 (no. 448), HIA-PG, Box 449, File 738/Z, Subfile: "Żydzi w Sowietach."

72. According to one report, Jewish groups contributed 42 percent of the amount raised in the Western Hemisphere in 1942. "Jak przedstawia się pomoc organizacyj społecznych z terenów Stanów Zjednoczonych . . . w r. 1942 dla uchodźców polskich w ZSRR," YVA—M2/331. See also Nussbaum, *VeHafach lahem leRo'ets*, pp. 49–50.

73. Reprezentacja, *Sprawozdanie*, p. 26.

74. See Komisja do Spraw Żydów Polskich przy Agencji Żydowskiej, "Prawda o ewakuacji z Rosji Żydów polskich, uchodźców," CZA—J25/34. One of the testimonies attached to this report (załącznik 3) relates the following incident: In Tashkent a relief official ordered all Jews to leave a breadline, claiming that no bread was available. The deponent, however, who presumably was able to conceal his Jewish identity, did not leave the line and received two kilograms of bread—"the bread that supposedly did not exist"—with no difficulty. Shortly after this testimony was taken in Jerusalem on 10 May 1942, it was conveyed to local Polish authorities; Hartglas to delegate, Polish Ministry of Social Welfare, 19 May 1942, AIP—KOL. 25/24.

75. See above, n. 52.

76. Canadian United Jewish Refugees and War Relief Agency to Wiktor Podoski, 21 June 1942, YVA—M2/328.

77. Cable, Kot to Polish Foreign Ministry, 17 June 1942 (no. 495), AIP—PRM. 88/2.

78. Untitled, undated document with handwritten marginal annotation,

"Pismo to otrzymał Lachs 4/7 z r. Kraczkiewicza w MSZ," YVA—M2/326. The author argued that since Jewish refugees tended to concentrate in cities, they were able to purchase a greater variety of goods and services in exchange for the relief funds they received than were non-Jewish Poles, who were scattered throughout the countryside on *kolkhozy*. He further claimed that since he had arrived in Russia in September 1941, he had not heard a single Jewish complaint about discrimination.

79. Untitled memorandum by Kraczkiewicz, 8 July 1942, YVA—O55/2.

80. Ibid.; also cable, Polish Embassy, Kuibyshev, to Polish Foreign Ministry, distributed 24 November 1942 (no. 218), HIA-Lt. Colonel Borkowski, Box 1.

81. *Final Report of the Polish Embassy* (see above, n. 60).

82. Ibid. The term "relief institution" refers to orphanages, homes for the disabled, hospitals, schools, adult education centers, first aid posts, feeding centers, and the like, which were established and maintained by the Polish Embassy.

83. It should be pointed out that Jewish complaints about discrimination in relief appear generally to have alleged complete denial of assistance to Jews by some Polish officials, rather than the awarding of systematically smaller allocations to Jews than to Poles.

84. This is a possibility that cannot be ruled out, although the available evidence tends neither to confirm nor to deny it.

85. The Soviet government claimed all those who were permanent residents of these territories as Soviet citizens and thus officially denied them access to all agencies of the Polish government. On the citizenship question, see below, n. 91.

86. *Final Report of the Polish Embassy* (see above, n. 60).

87. Ibid. One set of figures, for example, showed that 39.3 percent of those who had received assistance through the Polish relief apparatus—106,602 out of 271,325—were Jews. Another set stated that the total expenditures of the relief apparatus during its twenty-one months of operation had amounted to 111,700,492 rubles, or "an average of 263 rubles per Polish citizen included in the relief." If this latter statistic is accurate, then a total of 424,717 Polish citizens must have received assistance, rather than the 271,325 reported in the first set of figures. If 106,602 of these were Jews, then the percentage of Jews among those served was 25.1 rather than 39.3. This figure is somewhat lower than most estimates of the percentage of Jews among the Polish citizens displaced east of the Riga line. With regard to the number of Jews employed by the relief apparatus, too, the published statistics conflict with other documentary evidence showing a much lower percentage. See Nussbaum, *VeHafach lahem leRo'ets*, p. 64.

88. At least one Jewish deponent stated that the local officials who were directly responsible for the distribution of relief were "riffraff [*hołota*]" and that their superiors, who maintained no contact with applicants for relief themselves, were unaware that the local officials deliberately concealed the

names of many Jewish applicants. See Engel, "HaSichsuch haPolani-Sovieti," in press.

89. "Decree of the Presidium of the Supreme Council of the USSR concerning the acquisition of citizenship of the USSR by the inhabitants of the Western districts of the Ukraine and Byelorussia," 29 November 1939, in *DPSR*, 1:92.

90. "Note from the People's Commissariat for Foreign Affairs . . . ," 1 December 1941, in *DPSR*, 1:217–18.

91. The citizenship issue is extremely complicated and requires detailed explanation. For the sake of analysis, the former citizens of Poland who had been interned in the Soviet interior before the signing of the Polish-Soviet agreement can be divided into three categories. First were those who had been permanent residents of the eastern Polish provinces annexed to the Soviet Union in November 1939, whom the Soviet authorities had deported as part of their drive to Sovietize the new territories and eliminate traces of their former Polish identity. On this matter, see above, n. 60. Second were refugees from the German zone of occupation who had been offered Soviet citizenship early in the war but had refused to accept it and had been sent to the interior in consequence. In the final group were some 180,000 prisoners of war. Reliable statistics on the percentage of Jews in each category are lacking, but most estimates hold Jews to have constituted some 20 percent of the first group and a majority (perhaps 70 percent) of the second class. In addition, there were Polish citizens located in the Soviet interior who had not been sent there forcibly by the Soviet authorities. These included refugees from the German advance in June 1941, as well as those who had migrated eastward voluntarily in order to find work and some 150,000 conscriptees into the Red Army. According to a strict interpretation of the Soviet citizenship decree of 29 November 1939, all of these, with the exception of the prisoners of war, were to be considered Soviet citizens.

However, following the conclusion of the Polish-Soviet agreement and the signing of an order granting "amnesty to Polish citizens deprived of their freedom" on 12 August 1941, former Polish citizens from all categories began to be released from internment. There were many, though, who were not released. Ambassador Kot reported to Sikorski on 10 September 1941 that the Soviet authorities placed the total number of deportees eligible for release at a bit less than 400,000, and he guessed that the authorities continued to regard the remainder as Soviet citizens; Kot *Listy z Rosji*, p. 87. Similarly, the British ambassador to the Soviet Union, Sir Stafford Cripps, protested to Soviet Deputy Commissar for Foreign Affairs Andrei Vyshinsky on 3 November that "large numbers of Poles remained in the camps"; "Note from Ambassador Cripps on his interview with Deputy Commissar Vyshinsky," 3 November 1941, in *DPSR*, 1:191. Vyshinsky told Cripps on this occasion that "there was a difficulty which might account for some individuals not being released in regard to the people evacuated from the Ukraine and White Russia, as these had been declared to be Soviet citizens." Furthermore, even among those who were released, not all were provided with papers attesting to their Polish citizenship.

Thus it seems that between August and November, especially with the first category of deportees, the Soviet authorities behaved inconsistently. They tended to make fewer problems with deportees of the second category and virtually none with the third (although they had evidently already murdered over 8,000 officers at Katyn). They also do not appear during this period to have made any distinctions between ethnic Poles and members of the various ethnic minorities. With their statement of 1 December 1941 the Soviets apparently sought to clarify their position: they said in effect that they regarded their decree of 29 November 1939 as still in force but that they were prepared, of their own free will and not because of any legal obligation to do so, to permit ethnic Poles only to enjoy the benefits of Polish citizens in accordance with the Polish-Soviet agreement. This statement possessed several far-reaching implications, of which two are of immediate importance for the discussion here. First, the statement applied not only to deportees but to refugees and voluntary migrants as well. Second, it reserved for the Soviet authorities the exclusive right to regulate the relations between Polish Jews and the Polish Embassy and armed forces. In the event, the Soviet government did act in this area, sometimes tacitly, sometimes explicitly, in a fashion that made it difficult to determine at any given moment what sort of contacts were permitted or forbidden. This confusion was especially consequential with regard to the enlistment of Jews in the Polish Army; on this matter, see below. On various aspects of the citizenship problem, see Litwak, "She'elat haEzrahut," passim; Shlomi, "Yehudei Polin biVerit haMo'atsot," pp. 109–10; Redlich, "The Jews under Soviet Rule," p. 76. The numerical estimates are from Grudzińska-Gross and Gross, *War through Children's Eyes*, p. xxii; Nussbaum, *VeHafach lahem leRo'ets*, pp. 25–26.

92. Redlich, "The Jews under Soviet Rule," p. 79.

93. Anonymous document (see above, n. 78).

94. Shlomi, "Yehudei Polin biVerit haMo'atsot," pp. 110–12. Many Poles also were not released; see above, n. 91.

95. See unsigned letter to Schwarzbart, 21 December 1941, YVA—M2/327; Schwarzbart to Weizmann, 24 December 1941, CZA—Z4/15265; "Sytuacja obywateli polskich narodowości żydowskiej lub wyznania mojzeszowego," 23 March 1942, HIA-Mikołajczyk, Box 12, File: "Jews in Occupied Poland"; "Deportations of Polish Citizens" (see above, n. 60).

96. Kot to Polish foreign minister, 5 January 1942, in Kot, *Listy z Rosji*, pp. 249–53.

97. "Note from the People's Commissariat for Foreign Affairs to the Polish Embassy in the USSR on the subject of Polish citizenship," 5 January 1942, in *DPSR*, 1:259.

98. See Kot, *Rozmowy z Kremlem*, pp. 70–71.

99. Protests were made not only to the Soviet government but to the British government as well; see Sikorski's memorandum to Churchill, "The atti-

tude of the Soviet Government towards the Polish national minorities," 5 March 1942, in Hirszkowicz, "The Soviet Union and the Jews," pp. 79–82.

100. See, among other documents, cable, Raczyński to Polish Embassy, USSR, 31 October 1941 (no. 117), HIA-PG, Box 449, File 738/Z, Subfile: "Żydzi w Sowietach"; "Wiadomości nadesłane przez Ambasadora Kota . . . ," 13 November 1941, ibid.; Ludwik Seidenmann, Polish Embassy, Kuibyshev, to Sikorski, 10 December 1941, CZA—J25/2; Kot to Polish foreign minister, 5 January 1942 (see above, n. 96); Polish Embassy, Moscow [sic], to People's Commissariat for Foreign Affairs, 21 March 1942 (Nr. D-697/42), YVA—M2/61; cable, Polish Embassy, Kuibyshev, to Polish Consulate General, Jerusalem, 18 September 1942 (no. 8), YVA-O55/2. See also Schwarzbart's correspondence with Polish Embassy, USSR, 1941–42, YVA—M2/322. The embassy later summarized its activities on behalf of Polish Jews in the USSR in a fifteen-page report entitled "Sprawa Żydów obywateli polskich w świetle oficjalnych dokumentów oraz praktyki władz radzieckich," 11 August 1942, HIA-US, Box 64, File 1.

101. See the documents compiled under the heading "Sprawa Altera i Ehrlicha," 4 December 1941–2 June 1942, HIA-Poland. Konsulat Generalny New York, Box 1; see also the correspondence in HIA-PG, Box 585, File 738/Z, Subfiles: "Alter i Ehrlich" and "Noty." Ehrlich and Alter were executed shortly following their arrest, but the Soviet government did not acknowledge the executions until February 1943. In the meantime, the case attracted international attention.

102. Shlomi, "Yehudei Polin biVerit haMo'atsot," pp. 111–12.

103. See Kot to Polish Foreign Minister, 12 June 1942, in Kot, Listy z Rosji, pp. 331–33.

104. See above, n. 70. The implication that Poles had been given preference in being released before Jews and that protest should be directed toward the Polish government was grossly unfair. The Polish authorities had virtually no control over who was released.

105. Reprezentacja, Sprawozdanie, pp. 24–25.

106. See cable, Gruenbaum to Brodetsky and Schwarzbart, 15 March 1942, CZA—Z4/15265; cable, Reprezentacja to Stańczyk, n.d. [22 March 1942], YVA—M2/63.

107. "Audiencja u Prezydenta Raczkiewicza," 6 March 1942, YVA—M2/77.

108. See above, n. 52; see also Polish Consulate General [Tel Aviv, to Polish Foreign Ministry], n.d., (Nr. 851e/Pl/49: "Żydzi polscy w Rosji"), YVA—O55/2.

109. "Polish-Soviet Military Agreement," 14 August 1942, in DPSR, 1:147–48.

110. Anders, Bez ostatniego rozdziału, pp. 63–65.

111. Terry, Poland's Place in Europe, pp. 200–201.

112. The use of Lend-Lease equipment was called for in the military agreement, even though Poland had not yet officially been made eligible to receive Lend-Lease assistance. Official approval did not come until 4 Septem-

ber; see Ciechanowski, *Defeat in Victory*, p. 55. According to Kot, Anders spoke during the first week in September of a Polish force of 100,000; Kot to Sikorski, 5 September 1941, in Kot, *Listy z Rosji*, p. 82.

113. Kot to Sikorski (see preceding note).

114. Kot to Sikorski, 10 September 1941, in Kot, *Listy z Rosji*, p. 91.

115. Terry, *Poland's Place in Europe*, pp. 203–9; Kacewicz, *Great Britain*, p. 152.

116. Ciechanowski, *Defeat in Victory*, pp. 59–64.

117. Kot to Mikołajczyk, 11 October 1941, in Kot, *Listy z Rosji*, p. 136.

118. Kot to Polish foreign minister, 8 November 1941, ibid., p. 154.

119. "Sprawozdanie z rozmowy Generała Andersa z przedstawicielami żydowstwa [*sic*] polskiego na terenie ZSRR," 24 October 1941, HIA-Mikołajczyk, Box 16, File: "Polish Army in USSR. Jewish Question"; Anders, *Bez ostatniego rozdziału*, pp. 31, 99.

120. "Sprawozdanie z rozmowy" (see preceding note).

121. See "Sprawa żydowska," 1 September 1939–1 August 1942, AIP—KOL. 11/24. This document appears to be a set of notes made by Anders for his own recollection and perhaps for eventual use in preparing a full written account of Jewish affairs in the Polish Army. It also contains complaints about "the Judaization of the Embassy [*zażydzenie Ambasady*]" and "the impudence of Alter and Ehrlich, to whom I showed the door." Significantly, the record of his one meeting with Ehrlich and Alter does not bear out his description; "Sprawozdanie z rozmowy" (see above, n. 119).

122. Anders, *Bez ostatniego rozdziału*, p. 99.

123. On 11 October Kot reported that the military leaders were interested in imposing a numerus clausus upon Jewish enlistments; see above, n. 117. It may be, however, that Anders had considered the idea even when it appeared possible that he would be able to raise a force of 100,000. According to Kot, the question of recruiting Jews was discussed at their very first meeting, on 5 September. Kot evidently dissuaded Anders from taking anti-Jewish measures at this time because of possible adverse political reactions abroad; Kot to Sikorski, 5 September 1941 (see above, n. 112).

124. Nussbaum, *VeHafach lahem leRo'ets*, pp. 54–55.

125. Ibid., p. 54; Gutman, "Jews in General Anders' Army," pp. 243–44.

126. Reprezentacja, *Sprawozdanie*, p. 33. The rejections were generally made on the grounds that the Jewish applicants were not physically fit for service. There is, however, strong evidence not only that a much more stringent physical standard was applied to Jews than to Poles but that recruiters were instructed in advance to reject Jews on this basis. See Gutman, "Jews in General Anders' Army," pp. 239–42; Nussbaum, *VeHafach lahem leRo'ets*, p. 55.

127. Gutman, "Jews in General Anders' Army," pp. 239–42; Nussbaum, *VeHafach lahem leRo'ets*, p. 55. Some Jewish soldiers were subjected to repeat physical examinations, as a result of which they were found unfit for service and discharged. Others were expelled from the ranks for absence without

leave—an offense that for Polish soldiers was usually recorded as a minor disciplinary infraction.

128. Nussbaum, *VeHafach lahem leRo'ets*, pp. 55–56.

129. Gutman, "Jews in General Anders' Army," pp. 264–71; Redlich, "Jews in General Anders' Army," p. 95. The segregation in a labor battalion was evidently the outgrowth of a proposal submitted to the Polish authorities in the USSR by Revisionist activists Marek Kahan and Miron Szeszkin: shortly following their release from internment, they suggested creating a separate Jewish national unit within the Polish Army; the proposal unwittingly gave the Polish authorities an excuse to take this discriminatory measure. See Nussbaum, "'Legyon Yehudi,'" pp. 47–54; Litwak, "HaYehudim biTseva'o shel haGeneral Anders," pp. 51–55.

130. See above, n. 117.

131. Kot to Sikorski, 5 September 1941 (see above, n. 112).

132. "Sprawozdanie z rozmowy" (see above, n. 119). At this meeting Anders also sought, however, to justify giving preference to Poles over Jews in recruitment. He cast strong aspersions on Jewish motives for seeking to join the army, stating that "there can be no further doubt that there has frequently turned up among the Jews an element that is not terribly committed [to the army], for whom, under current war conditions, the army is a sort of refuge—as long, of course, as it does not go to the front." He also repeated accusations of Jewish disloyalty during the September campaign and charged that Jewish internees had behaved improperly toward their Polish comrades in the camps. It thus appears that he did not share Kot's more optimistic assessment of the role Jewish soldiers might play in the armed forces, and his promise to prohibit antisemitism (which, he stated, would require Jewish assistance to implement) was made mainly for show.

133. Dowództwo Polskich Sił Zbrojnych w ZSRR, "Udział żydów w PSZbr. w ZSRR," 14 November 1941 (L. dz. 1730 Kanc. Sztab.), HIA-Mikołajczyk, Box 16, File: "Polish Army in USSR. Jewish Question."

134. H. Szumski, "Żydzi," 27 November 1941, ibid. For descriptions by Jews of the atmosphere in the ranks, see Gutman, "Jews in General Anders' Army," p. 276.

135. On the outcry, see Nussbaum, *VeHafach lahem leRo'ets*, pp. 71–72.

136. Dowództwo Polskich Sił Zbrojnych w ZSRR—Sztab, "Do rąk własnych Dowódcy," 30 November 1941 (L. dz. 607/tjn. Kanc. Sztab. 41), HIA-Mikołajczyk, Box 16, File: "Polish Army in the USSR. Jewish Question." Anders later claimed that the order, which was intended to be kept secret but was eventually, in June 1943, published in a Palestinian Hebrew weekly, was a forgery, but ample evidence has been adduced (in addition to the existence of the copy cited) to prove its genuineness. See Gutman, "Jews in General Anders' Army," pp. 271–77; Nussbaum, *VeHafach lahem leRo'ets*, pp. 71–72.

137. "Minute of the conversation held in Kremlin between General Sikorski and M. Stalin on the outstanding problems of Polish-Soviet relations," in

DPSR, 1:241. In his recording of the conversation, Kot (*Rozmowy z Kremlem*, pp. 167–68) attributed Sikorski's comment to Anders, but he was certainly not accurate in doing so; see Gutman, "Jews in General Anders' Army," p. 245.

138. Redlich, "Jews in General Anders' Army," p. 93. Anders's suspicions of the motivations of Jews for wanting to join the army thus appear in at least some cases to have been well-founded. See above, n. 132.

139. See Kot to Polish foreign minister, 8 November 1941, in Kot, *Listy z Rosji*, p. 164.

140. Gutman, "Jews in General Anders' Army," pp. 243–44.

141. "Memorandum on Problems Relating to Poles in Russia," n.d. (handwritten marginal date: "end of May 1942"), AIP—KOL. 39/4. See also Terry, *Poland's Place in Europe*, pp. 219–22. This increase, of course, put the lie to Anders's statement to Jewish leaders the previous October to the effect that the small allowable size of the fighting force was what necessitated restrictions on enlistment of Jews. Jewish spokesmen confronted him (via the embassy) with this inconsistency in March, and the charge was regarded in the embassy as a serious one. See "Żaly ze strony Żydów (poważnych)," 8 March 1942, HIA-Mikołajczyk, Box 16, File: "Polish Army in USSR. Jewish Question."

142. See Polish Embassy, Kuibyshev, to People's Commissariat for Foreign Affairs, 10 November 1941, in *DPSR*, 1:200–201.

143. This is one of the instances in which the Soviets sought to exploit their claim to jurisdiction over Polish refugees and former deportees in the Soviet Union in order to regulate the relations between Jews and the Polish authorities (see above, n. 91). Technically, the Soviets could have forbidden all Jewish enlistment in the Polish Army on the grounds that all Jews who had been "in the territories" annexed to the Soviet Union at the time of their annexation were Soviet citizens. By confining the scope of their ban on Jewish enlistment to *permanent residents* of the annexed territories, however, they in effect gave approval to the enlistment of Jewish refugees from western Poland.

144. See cable, Anders to commander-in-chief [Sikorski], 21 February 1942 (no. 275), AIP—KOL. 11/24; cable, Kot to Anders, 25 February 1942 (no. 596), ibid.; cable, Anders to Polish ambassador, Kuibyshev, 2 March 1942 (no. 294), ibid.

145. See cable, [Tadeusz] Rudnicki to chief of staff, 26 January 1942 (no. 200), ibid.; cable, Rudnicki to Anders, 30 January 1942 (no. 227), ibid. According to a report by the chief of staff, Maj. Gen. Zygmunt Bohusz-Szyszko, in September 1942, the Soviets had decided on 26 December 1941 to forbid all enlistment of Jews in the Polish forces and to require the expulsion of all Jews who had already been inducted. Anders was said to have learned of this decision from NKVD General of State Security Yurii Zhukov some time in January 1942. According to Bohusz-Szyszko, who was present during Anders's conversation with Zhukov, Anders protested vehemently, and it was because of his protest that the Soviets agreed to the more lenient

policy that ultimately went into effect. "Memoriał w sprawie żydowskiej podczas ewakuacji W. P. z Sowietów na teren Iranu," 19 September 1942 (L. dz. 121/42), AIP—KOL. 25/24. This, however, appears to be a fanciful justification after the fact by one who, along with Anders, stood accused of interfering with the inclusion of Jews in the later evacuation of Polish troops from the Soviet Union. It is inconsistent with Anders's own cable to Sikorski of 30 December 1941, in which the general reported that he had heard unofficially that the Soviets had decided to curtail recruitment of Jews from the eastern territories; see Gutman, "Jews in General Anders' Army," p. 247. In any case, in light of subsequent behavior on both the Polish and the Soviet sides, it seems highly improbable.

146. Gutman, "Jews in General Anders' Army," p. 250. A Polish survey of the minority recruitment situation claimed that the imposition of the restrictions "immediately became the object of intervention by those appointed to do so" and that the Soviet agreement to allow the enlistment of minorities from western Poland was the result of Polish-Soviet negotiations; "Pobór mniejszości narodowych do polskich sił zbr.," n.d., AIP—KOL. 25/24. However, no documentary evidence has as yet been uncovered to substantiate this claim. On the contrary, the incessant attempts of Polish officials to ascertain precisely what the Soviet policy was point to a unilateral Soviet decision in the matter; see above, n. 144. The Commission on Polish Jewish Affairs of the Jewish Agency for Palestine also reported that it had approached the Polish government with a suggestion that Jewish organizations intervene against the Soviet position, but that this suggestion was rebuffed; Komisja do Spraw Żydów Polskich przy Agencji Żydowskiej, "Prawda o ewakuacji" (see above, n. 74). It should be kept in mind that the reference here is to Soviet restrictions on enlistment of Jews in the Polish Army only. The Polish Embassy did protest the general Soviet citizenship policy; see above, n. 99.

147. "Pobór mniejszości narodowych" (see preceding note).

148. Ibid.

149. Gutman, "Jews in General Anders' Army," pp. 250–52.

150. Quoted in Nussbaum, *VeHafach lahem leRo'ets*, p. 61.

151. Ibid. See also ibid., pp. 54–55; Gutman, "Jews in General Anders' Army," pp. 239–44; Reprezentacja, *Sprawozdanie*, p. 33.

152. See unsigned, unaddressed letter beginning with the words: "w dn. 19 b. m. wysłałem depeszę . . . ," 21 March 1942, HIA-Mikołajczyk, Box 16, File: "Polish Army in USSR. Jewish Question"; see also unsigned cable to Rosmarin, n.d. (handwritten marginal date: 19 May 1942), YVA—M2/61.

153. See "Memorandum on Problems" (see above, n. 141).

154. Quoted in Nussbaum, *VeHafach lahem leRo'ets*, p. 62.

155. "Sprawozdanie," 20 August 1942, AIP—KOL. 11/24.

156. Nussbaum, *VeHafach lahem leRo'ets*, pp. 62–63. See also Eliezer Rudnicki to Jewish Agency for Palestine, 8 September 1942, HIA-US, Box 66, File 6; Reprezentacja, *Sprawozdanie*, p. 35.

157. On the evacuation, see Terry, *Poland's Place in Europe*, pp. 212–44.

158. On the number of Polish soldiers and civilians evacuated, see Nuss-

baum, *VeHafach lahem leRo'ets*, p. 65. His figures are in substantial agreement with those of Pobóg-Malinowski, *Najnowsza historia*, 3:241. Reprezentacja, *Sprawozdanie*, p. 38, claims 134,000 evacuees, including 96,000 military personnel—a figure far greater than the overall actual strength of the Polish armed forces at the time. The figures for Jews are from Komisja do Spraw Żydów Polskich przy Agencji Żydowskiej, "Prawda o ewakuacji" (see above, n. 74). Nussbaum holds that only 1,900 Jewish soldiers and 1,688 civilians were evacuated. This figure is undoubtedly too low, although a Polish source lists a number almost as low—4,226 total Jewish evacuees; Łunkiewicz, Polish Defense Ministry, Political Department, to Polish Foreign Ministry, 6 September 1943 (L. dz. 735/WPol/43), AIP—A.12/755/2. Anders also reports that "over 4,000 Jews left the Soviet Union together with the Polish Army." Elsewhere, however, he implies that he arrived in Palestine with 4,000 Jewish *soldiers*; Anders, *Bez ostatniego rozdziału*, pp. 158, 201. It thus may be that his first figure and that of the Polish archival document cited refer to military evacuees only, although their language suggests the opposite.

159. The only figures available regarding the relative geographical distribution of Polish Jews and non-Jews in the USSR come from the embassy's statistics on those availing themselves of the relief apparatus. These show that of all Jews served by the relief system, approximately two-thirds were located in the Uzbek, Tadzik, Turkmen, and Kirghiz Republics and in southern Kazakhstan, whereas only 13 percent of the non-Jewish Poles seeking assistance resided there. The main centers of the non-Jewish population, on the other hand, were northern Kazakhstan (where 30.7 percent of all non-Jews seeking assistance lived) and Siberia (36.8 percent). It seems reasonable to assume that these figures are representative of the overall population. *Final Report of the Polish Embassy* (see above, n. 60); see also Nussbaum, *VeHafach lahem leRo'ets*, pp. 28–35.

160. "Sprawozdanie ewakuacyjne Delegata Ambasady R. P. przy D-ctwie P. S. Zbr. w Z. S. R. R. w Jangi-Jul," n.d. (September 1942), AIP—KOL. 25/24.

161. See, for example, Frank Savery to F. K. Roberts, 24 August 1942, PRO—FO 371/31086.C8265. It seems that the embassy had come to the conclusion that the sole responsibility lay on the Soviet side several months earlier; see cable, Polish Embassy, Kuibyshev, to Polish Foreign Ministry, 27 June 1941 (no. 537), AIP—A.48.10/C1.

162. See Komisja do Spraw Żydów Polskich przy Agencji Żydowskiej, "Prawda o ewakuacji" (see above, n. 74); see also Gutman, "Jews in General Anders' Army," pp. 286–89.

163. See "Edut miPi haRav Hager . . . ," 10 September 1942, YVA—M2/328; Rudnicki to Jewish Agency (see above, n. 156); Jehiel Szlachter, "Odpowiedz na sprawozdanie przedstawiciela Agencji Żydowskiej o ewakuacji Żydów . . . ," 12 November 1942, AIP—KOL. 25/24. It is important to note that Szlachter's testimony was solicited by Polish officials in order to refute the anti-Polish conclusions expressed by Rudnicki in his report to the Jewish Agency; nevertheless, although differing in several minor details, it con-

firmed the essential outlines of the meetings with Zhukov contained in the other two sources. Rudnicki's report, which was a composite of testimonies of a number of Jewish evacuees gathered in Teheran, recounted also a similar incident, in which another NKVD officer confirmed Zhukov's statement and added, "For every Jew [excluded] I shall throw one Pole off the transport." When told by Jewish leaders that Anders had asked them not to go to the NKVD, the officer replied, "General Anders ought not to play the fool [*Pust' General Anders duraká nye valyaet*]!"

164. "Memoriał w sprawie żydowskiej" (see above, n. 145). Since at the time virtually all Polish Jews, both from the eastern territories and from western Poland, except those few who had entered Soviet-held territory illegally after 29 November 1939, fell into this category, this position was tantamount to an almost total ban on Jewish participation in the evacuation.

165. According to the text quoted in ibid. On the genuineness of this text, see below. "Members of family" were defined here as including "only parents, spouses, minor children, or infirm siblings cared for by a soldier."

166. Bohusz-Szyszko to Polish ambassador (Kuibyshev), n.d. (handwritten marginal notation: "read 2.XII.42"), AIP—KOL. 25/24.

167. That of Jechiel Szlachter (see above, n. 163).

168. The agreement in fact stated that "exit permits will be given to family members of soldiers in the Polish Army who are residents of the Western Ukraine and Western Byelorussia and are of non-Polish nationality only if documentary proof is provided that the applicants are next-of-kin of soldiers in the Polish Army in the USSR." Quoted in Nussbaum, *VeHafach lahem leRo'ets*, p. 65. See also Gutman, "Jews in General Anders' Army," pp. 287–88. According to Rabbi Hager's testimony, Zhukov rebuked Bohusz-Szyszko for insisting to the Jewish representatives that the agreement was the basis for the imposition of restrictions on Jewish evacuees; see above, n. 163.

169. Cable, Anders to Polish commander-in-chief, 1 August 1942 (no. 1035), AIP—KOL. 11/24.

170. Cable, Gawlina to Polish commander-in-chief, 28 July 1942 (no. 1008), ibid.

171. Cable, Anders to Polish commander-in-chief, 26 July 1942 (no. 997), ibid.

172. "Sprawa żydowska" (see above, n. 121).

173. Such letters are located in AIP—KOL. 11/24, and in HIA-Mikołajczyk, Box 16, File: "Polish Army in USSR. Jewish Question."

174. Rabbi Hager later testified that Anders had forced him to write such a letter, threatening that if he did not, no Jews would be allowed to participate in the evacuation; see above, n. 163.

175. His cable to Sikorski of 26 July 1942 (see above, n. 171) demonstrated his concern: "I foresee many difficulties, as a mass of several tens of thousands of Jews is gathering here . . . which has nothing in common with the army, but which will want to leave. I shall not be able to take them along, as the Soviet authorities clearly indicate that [evacuees] must be family members of soldiers. I have just received notice from the rabbis that if they are

not taken out [of the country] they will cable Roosevelt. I am informing you of this because in my opinion it is already necessary now to conduct propaganda action in America explaining these [Soviet] conditions."

176. See above, n. 169.

177. On the White Paper, see, among others, Bauer, *From Diplomacy to Resistance*, pp. 16–51; Wasserstein, *Britain and the Jews of Europe*, pp. 17–26.

178. See cable, Sir Harold MacMichael, high commissioner for Palestine, to British minister of state, Cairo, 31 January 1942 (no. 36), PRO—FO 371/31099.C1274. Such a prospect, of course, was anathema to the British; see Wasserstein, *Britain and the Jews of Europe*, pp. 272–85.

179. "General W. Sikorski's Memorandum," 5 March 1942, in Hirszkowicz, "The Soviet Union and the Jews," pp. 78–82.

180. In mid-1942 Jews constituted slightly over 7 percent of the soldiers in the Fifth Division; Nussbaum, *VeHafach lahem leRo'ets*, p. 63. There was also no separate Jewish battalion formed in accordance with Revisionist wishes. This idea had been specifically rejected by Anders already in October 1941; see above, n. 119. The unit to which Sikorski referred was a labor brigade based in the village of Koltubanka in the Urals, which consisted of about 1,000 Jewish soldiers who had previously been dismissed from the regular army; see above, n. 129.

181. Minute by F. K. Roberts, 21 March 1942, in Hirszkowicz, "The Soviet Union and the Jews," p. 83.

182. Minute by R. M. Mack, 22 March 1942, PRO—FO 371/31099.C2853.

183. Minute by [Charles] Baxter, 23 March 1942, ibid.

184. A Polish translation of the memorandum, headed simply "Memorandum (tłomaczenie)," and dated 30 March 1942, is located in AIP—[EP], "Sprawy żydowskie," File: "Ministerstwo dla spraw polskiej emigracji polit." The English original has not been located. It was, however, referred to in a letter from Raczyński to Dormer, 17 April 1942, PRO—FO 371/31099.C4176. Frankowski also gave a written account of a meeting he had with Dormer on 30 March that in general tallies with the Polish text: "Notatka z rozmowy Min. Frankowskiego z Ambasadorem Dormerem," 30 March 1942, HIA-PG, Box 459, File 851/e. It thus seems virtually certain that the Polish document in question is an authentic and accurate translation of the memorandum given by Dormer to Frankowski.

185. "Notatka z rozmowy Min. Frankowskiego" (see preceding note); Raczyński to Dormer, 17 April 1942 (see preceding note). See also Dormer to Eden, 31 March 1942, PRO—FO 371/31099.C3538. Frankowski could not resist gently chiding Dormer over the British position, "since we have heard so often complaints directed at us about [our] antisemitic attitude."

186. For a different interpretation of the parallel between Polish and British interests in the matter of the Jewish evacuation, see Litwak, "Shittuf Pe'ulah Polani-Briti," pp. 7–12.

187. See cable, A. Clark-Kerr, British Embassy, Kuibyshev, to Eden, 31 July 1942 (no. 1095), PRO—FO 181/969/8. The same situation was reflected in a letter from E. B. Boyd, British Colonial Office, to Joseph Linton, Jewish

Agency, London, 31 July 1942 (no. 75113/54/42), YVA—M2/326: "As regards the suggestion that provision should be made for a further influx of refugees into Teheran . . . , a great deal has already been done by the British authorities in Persia for Polish refugees, and there is, I am afraid, little hope of extending the scope of these arrangements at the present time."

188. For the texts of various orders by Anders concerning restrictions on the evacuation of Jews, see Nussbaum, *VeHafach lahem leRo'ets*, pp. 66–67.

189. See cable, Anders to Polish commander-in-chief, 4 August 1942 (no. 1050), AIP—KOL. 11/24; "Memoriał w sprawie żydowskiej" (see above, n. 145).

190. The Polish military leadership evidently did indeed apply a much stricter standard regarding the eligibility of Jewish candidates for evacuation than mandated by the Anders-Zhukov agreement of 31 July; see Nussbaum, *VeHafach lahem leRo'ets*, pp. 66–69.

191. According to Rudnicki, the Poles seem to have tried this approach in one instance. Jenicz purportedly submitted to Zhukov, through Jewish leaders, a list of 557 Jews whom the embassy certified as eligible for departure, thus in effect placing the potential onus for denying evacuation on the NKVD. In any event Zhukov expressed no objection, stating that he would consent to the transfer of anyone who possessed an entry visa into an Allied country. It seems, though, that the Poles had built a safeguard against such a Soviet response into their maneuver: Jenicz stipulated that evacuations from this list would not be at the expense of places allocated to Poles. Rudnicki to Jewish Agency, 8 September 1942 (see above, n. 156); see also "Edut miPi haRav Hager" (see above, n. 163).

192. Terry, *Poland's Place in Europe*, pp. 243–44, 284–98.

193. Untitled memorandum, YVA—O55/2.

194. T. Kiersnowski, "Pro Memoria," 7 October 1942 (No. 4985/Ia/42), AIP—PRM. 88/2. Kiersnowski also explained his reasons for initiating discussions with Palestinian Jewish leaders: "I began from the premise that everything that our official propaganda does in this matter [of the eastern border] . . . can always be branded as partisan. Those ill-disposed toward us can always say that . . . 'Polish imperialism' is coming into play here. . . . On the other hand, if the Jews speak out in defense of our eastern territories . . . they will be an unimpeachable party, against whom no one can put forth the above arguments. . . . I point out in addition that Palestine is a propaganda point of the first order, as correspondents from all English and American newspapers are there. . . . Jews throughout the entire world orient themselves in Polish-Jewish affairs according to Palestinian opinion, for the central representation of Polish Jews . . . is there."

195. Banaczyk seems to have forgotten the pogroms of the late 1930s.

196. "Konferencja z p. Prezesem Banaczykiem," 23 September 1942, CZA—J25/2.

197. The reference is unclear. No telegram from Gruenbaum and Schmorak to Kot that would meet the specifications of the document in question has yet been found. On the other hand, it is certain that Palestinian Jewish cir-

cles communicated with government leaders around the end of August 1942 suggesting that the Polish government could take steps to increase the number of Jewish evacuees. See Reprezentacja to Sikorski, 21 August 1942, CZA —J25/2.

198. Cable, Kot to Polish Consulate-General, Jerusalem, for Gruenbaum and Schmorak, 30 August 1942, AIP—KOL. 25/24. When this telegram was sent, the evacuation was still going on.

199. Engel, "HaSichsuch haPolani-Sovieti," in press.

200. Ostensibly, the purpose of Kot's visit was to rest. He had stepped down as ambassador to the USSR following the completion of the second round of evacuations, publicly claiming ill health, but actually for political reasons, and had been reassigned to the post of government delegate in the Middle East; see Kot, Listy z Rosji, pp. 56–57. However, as his cable to Gruenbaum and Schmorak indicated (see above, n. 198), he had long planned to meet personally with Jewish leaders. At one point he even told Gruenbaum that he hoped to meet "a person or Jewish circles with whom he could come to a general understanding and who would represent the Jewish people as the ally of the Polish Government"; "Wyjątek z protokołu z posiedzenia Egzekutywy Agencji Żydowskiej dla Palestyny," 24 January 1943, HIA-Anders, Box 70, Document 156. It is true that, following his arrival in Palestine, Jewish leaders contacted him before he contacted them; see Reprezentacja, Sprawozdanie, pp. 51–52; Moshe Shertok, Jewish Agency, to Kot, 5 November 1942, CZA—Z4/14752. However, in his very first discussion with a Jewish representative (Eliyahu Epstein of the Jewish Agency Political Department) on 10 November, he asked whether Zionist leaders in the United States would be willing to intervene with U.S. political figures on behalf of Sikorski's program for a postwar East European federation; Epstein to Shertok, 10 November 1942, CZA—Z4/14752. See also Engel, "HaSichsuch ha-Polani-Sovieti," in press.

201. At one point Kot lamented to Gruenbaum that although he had gained the impression that it might still be possible for the government to come to an agreement with the Zionist movement over certain specific political issues, he had not found any individual or body among the Palestinian Jewish community whom he could regard as the government's firm ally. "Wyjątek z protokołu" (see preceding note).

202. "Streszczenie rozmowy p. Ministra Kota z Ben Gurionem . . . ," 3 December 1942, YVA—O55/2; Reprezentacja, Sprawozdanie, pp. 67–72. See also "Reprezentacja Żydów Polskich," 5 December 1942, HIA-PG, Box 700, File: "Mniejszości Żydzi."

203. In his response Moshe Kleinbaum pointed out, among other things, the irreconcilability of these two characterizations. Reprezentacja, Sprawozdanie, pp. 76–77.

204. Reprezentacja, Sprawozdanie, pp. 67–72.

205. "Protokół z audiencji udzielonej przez p. Ministra Profesora Kota przedstawicielom prasy palestyńskiej," 5 December 1942, HIA-PG, Box 700, File: "Mniejszości Żydzi"; "Protokuł [sic] konferencji," 6 December 1942,

ibid. Present at the latter meeting were, among others, Ben Gurion, Schmorak, Chief Rabbi of Palestine Yitshak Herzog, Agudas Yisroel Chairman Rabbi I. M. Levin, and *Palestine Post* editor Gershon Agronsky. Subsequently Abraham Stupp of the Reprezentacja asked Kot why he had become so ardent a defender of Anders, when it was known that the two did not get along. Kot replied that former Sanacja supporters enjoyed strong influence in the Polish military, so that if Anders (an Endek) were not in command, his place would likely be taken by a Piłsudskist such as Sosnkowski. Wishing to avoid this change, Kot had resolved to refrain from any action that might discredit Anders or endanger his position. "Rozmowa z Min. Prof. Kotem," 13 January 1943, CZA—J25/2.

206. "Rozmowa z Min. Kotem," 19 January 1943, CZA—J25/2. The Reprezentacja would not consider this demand, and only Rosmarin's intervention persuaded Kot to drop it.

207. Reprezentacja, *Sprawozdanie*, p. 76.

208. See ibid., pp. 45–51, for the testimony of the group's chief spokesman, Ya'akov Kurc. The story of the arrival of the eyewitnesses and their impact upon Palestinian Jewry is told also in, among others, Laqueur, *The Terrible Secret*, pp. 190–94; Gilbert, *Auschwitz and the Allies*, pp. 88–92; Beit-Tsvi, *HaTsiyonut haPost-Ugandit*, pp. 68–72. These works also consider the problem of the general disbelief of previous reports. The last of them, a highly tendentious and frequently inaccurate study, challenges the statement that the question of rescue preoccupied Jews in Palestine and the West from late 1942 on. The most detailed and reliable investigation to date of the response of Palestinian Jewry (or at least of its central institution, the Jewish Agency Executive) to the Holocaust has not yet appeared in published format: Porat, "Helkah shel Hanhalat haSochnut." See especially pp. 17–34, including the account of the reception of the eyewitnesses, pp. 31–33.

209. "Protokuł [sic] konferencji" (see above, n. 205).

210. Epstein to Shertok, 10 November 1942, CZA—Z4/14752. On the federation concept, see Terry, *Poland's Place in Europe*, passim.

211. "Wyjątek z protokołu" (see above, n. 200).

212. "Protokuł [sic] konferencji" (see above, n. 205).

213. "Protokół z audiencji udzielonej przez p. Ministra Profesora Kota . . . przedstawicielom 'Agudat Israel' . . . ," 5 December 1942, HIA-PG, Box 700, File: "Mniejszości Żydzi."

214. "Protokół z audiencji udzielonej . . . przedstawicielom prasy palestyńskiej" (see above, n. 205).

215. "Reprezentacja Żydów Polskich" (see above, n. 202). This account of the meeting, evidently prepared by a Polish official, presents Kot's response more harshly than the account in Reprezentacja, *Sprawozdanie*, p. 72. For additional examples of Kot's attempts to use the slaughter of Polish Jewry as a lever for influencing the political behavior of the Jews of the free world, see Engel, "HaSichsuch haPolani-Sovieti," in press.

216. "Wyjątek z protokołu" (see above, n. 200). Gruenbaum did indicate, though, that if the postwar Soviet regime proved to be similar to the prewar

one, Jews would oppose the attachment of any of the eastern Polish territories to the USSR. His implication was that at the moment it was simply too early for the Jewish Agency to commit itself.

217. Reprezentacja, *Sprawozdanie*, p. 88. The statement was made in Kot's presence at his farewell banquet on 19 January 1943. Immediately thereafter, however, Reiss added, "On one matter there are no differences of opinion between us—that is when it comes to the freedom and independence of the Polish state." It should be stressed that at no point did any Jewish leader express himself in opposition to the renewal of Polish independence; to this extent virtually all Jews wholeheartedly backed the Polish cause. The sole bones of contention were the question of borders and the character of the regime's Jewish policy.

218. "Rozmowa z panem Kotem," 13 January 1943, CZA—J25/2.

219. Reprezentacja, *Sprawozdanie*, p. 86. Kot did eventually recommend to the government that it issue such an assurance, although he had not yet done so at the time he made this statement to the Jewish spokesmen; see cable, Kot to Polish Foreign Ministry, 9 February 1943 (no. 70), YVA—O55/3. It does not appear, however, that he regarded this as a terribly significant commitment. For one thing, he believed it to be implicit in the government's previous declarations on the Jewish question; see Engel, "HaSichsuch ha-Polani-Sovieti," n. 104. For another, as he explained to the delegation of religious leaders on 5 December, he did not believe that any Jews would be let out of Poland; see above, n. 213.

220. Reprezentacja, *Sprawozdanie*, p. 55; "Protokuł [sic] konferencji" (see above, n. 205). In the end, reported Kot, the Germans shot both the Poles and the Jews.

CHAPTER V

1. On German behavior and policy toward Poles under occupation, see, among others, Gross, *Polish Society*, pp. 29–109; Pobóg-Malinowski, *Najnowsza historia*, vol. 3; Broszat, *Nationalsozialistische Polenpolitik*; Madajczyk, *Polityka III Rzeszy*. On German behavior and policy toward Polish Jews during the first two years of the occupation, see, among others, Eisenbach, *Hitlerowska polityka zagłady Żydów*, pp. 129–267; Hilberg, *The Destruction of the European Jews*, pp. 125–74; Adam, *Judenpolitik im Dritten Reich*, pp. 247–58.

2. There are several serious studies which hold that the exploitation of Polish slave labor was merely "a residual goal" and that "extermination was the ultimate goal" for Poles as well as for Jews. Gross, *Polish Society*, pp. 50, 75; see also Madajczyk, "Mahanot haRikkuz haNatsi'im," pp. 45–46. There is indeed strong evidence that this possibility was seriously considered in leading Nazi circles. However, it is questionable whether it ever became accepted official policy. There is, in fact, considerable evidence that such a policy was ultimately rejected; see Tal, "On the Study of the Holocaust and Genocide," pp. 38–41. See also below, n. 6.

3. Broszat, *Nationalsozialistische Polenpolitik*, pp. 18–25, 38–48, 182–87; Madajczyk, *Polityka III Rzeszy*, 1:83–93.

4. Madajczyk, *Polityka III Rzeszy*, 2:119–64; Gross, *Polish Society*, pp. 75–78. According to Governor-General Hans Frank, the only educational opportunities that Poles might enjoy should be those which "show them the hopelessness of their national fate." Quoted in Bracher, *Die deutsche Diktatur*, p. 446.

5. On the deportations, see Madajczyk, *Polityka III Rzeszy*, 1:306–38. Gross, *Polish Society*, gives a figure of 1.5 million deportees. The incorporated regions comprised the Polish parts of Pomorze and Śląsk, with the cities of Poznań, Kalisz, Łódź, and Katowice, and a small salient around the town of Suwałki between East Prussia and Lithuania. They covered an area of over 35,000 square miles and were inhabited by more than 10 million people, including 8.9 million Poles, 600,000 Jews, and 600,000 Germans. All of the other areas west of the Ribbentrop-Molotov line constituted the Generalgouvernement. The legal status of this territory was somewhere between that of a client state (such as Slovakia) and a protectorate (such as Bohemia-Moravia); sovereignty was exclusively German, and Poles were excluded from the administration entirely; but the area was treated by the Reich as a foreign country, with its own currency and customs collection.

6. It should be pointed out that the theoretical distinction between the two groups was not always consistent; indeed, Poles too were frequently referred to as "subhumans [*Untermenschen*]." It seems, however, that this usage was more a reflection of the generally loose and constantly changing formulation of racial concepts that prevailed in Nazi ranks than a conscious equation of the racial quality of Jews and Poles. On this matter, as on the appellation *Gegenrasse*, see von zur Mühlen, *Rassenideologien*, pp. 236–44. Even though the distinction was not always clearly articulated, it does appear to have been understood by those who needed to use it as a guide for action. Thus, although at various stages in the war consideration was given to the possibility of a campaign of total murder of the Polish population similar to that being carried out against the Jews, such suggestions often appear to have been rejected on the grounds that the Poles were, after all, human. On the ideological denial by the Nazis of human status to Jews alone, in contrast to its application, however grudging, to Poles, see Tal, "On the Study of the Holocaust and Genocide," pp. 39–40. Moreover, though it was acknowledged that certain Poles, especially those who physically resembled the Nazi's ideal Nordic type, could be bearers of German blood and thus eligible for "re-Germanification [*Wiedereindeutschung*]," no official of the Nazi regime would have made the same acknowledgment concerning any Jews, no matter how blue their eyes or blond their hair. On the concept of *Wiedereindeutschung*, see Gross, *Polish Society*, pp. 195–98; Tal, "On the Study of the Holocaust and Genocide," pp. 31–32. For additional comparisons of the status of Jews and Poles in Nazi ideology, see Mosse, *Toward the Final Solution*, pp. 220–22; Bauer, *The Holocaust in Historical Perspective*, pp. 33–36.

7. The Einsatzgruppen were armed mobile units of the Security Police. They were established shortly before the launching of the invasion of Po-

land; their task was to follow the invading troops and "to overcome all elements hostile to the Reich and the German people." In this capacity, they were primarily responsible for the mass killings of the Polish intelligentsia in 1940. Following the invasion of Russia, they were to become the first executors of the final solution. See Buchheim, "Die SS," pp. 71–75.

8. "Instructions by Heydrich on Policy and Operations Concerning Jews in the Occupied Territories," 21 September 1939, in *DH*, pp. 173–78. In the introduction to the memorandum, Heydrich referred to the "final aim" with regard to the Jewish question, to which, he stressed, the steps he was about to outline were preliminary. He did not state explicitly what this final aim was, but he did speak later in the document of the need to bring about "the emigration of the Jews." This comment is in line with what seems to have been the prevailing Nazi attitude at the time about what ought to be done with Europe's Jews. In 1939 and 1940 two plans for solving the Jewish question dominated German thinking: one involved creating a large Jewish reservation in the Lublin region; the other, transporting all Jews under Nazi domination to the island of Madagascar. On these programs see, among others, Eisenbach, *Hitlerowska polityka zagłady Żydów*, pp. 465–82; Adam, *Judenpolitik im Dritten Reich*, pp. 253–57; Friedmann, "The Lublin Reservation and the Madagascar Plan," pp. 155–77; Browning, *The Final Solution and the German Foreign Office*, pp. 35–43. It is most unlikely that at this point Heydrich had in mind the systematic murder of all Jews as the "final aim"; see Bauer, "Genocide," pp. 35–45.

9. About 100,000 Jews were deported from the incorporated areas to the Generalgouvernement by March 1940; at that point further deportations were stopped because of the objection of Governor-General Frank, who did not wish to absorb more Jews (or Poles) into his domain. Ghettos were established in the larger Polish cities between October 1939 (Piotrków) and March 1941 (Kraków); the most populous were in Warsaw, with between 400,000 and 450,000 Jews (established November 1940), and Łódź, with some 160,000 Jews (established May 1940). Most of the larger ghettos were in fact far more restrictive than the Heydrich order had envisioned: they were virtually sealed off from the outside world, to the point where they constituted in effect, as one German official explained, "temporary concentration camp[s to be maintained] until the moment when the Jews can be removed." *Judenräte* were formed in Jewish communities throughout Poland in late 1939 and early 1940, in some cases even before Frank had legally mandated their creation in an order of 28 November 1939. During the same time an apparatus was set up for effecting systematically the confiscation of Jewish property and its redistribution to Aryans; much personal as well as real property was expropriated.

10. "Identifying Marks for Jews in the Government-General," 23 November 1939, in *DH*, pp. 178–79.

11. "Ban on the Use of the Railroads by Jews in the Government-General," 26 January 1940, in *DH*, p. 182.

12. See [Kaplan], *Scroll of Agony*, pp. 81–82; Hilberg, Staron, and Kermisz,

Diary of Czerniaków, pp. 89, 98, 145. See also Neshamit, *Ma'avako shel haGeto*, p. 41.

13. Hilberg, *The Destruction of the European Jews*, p. 157; see also "Przepisy specjalne dla ludności żydowskiej," n.d., HIA-PG, Box 921, File N55. The official rate of exchange at the beginning of the war was 5 zł. = $1.00. The value dropped quickly with the German conquest; by spring 1940 it had been halved. A black market also existed, in which the price of the dollar was several times greater than the official rate; see Bauer, *American Jewry and the Holocaust*, p. 70. The purchasing power of the sum available to Jews was steadily eroded under occupation. Taking 100 as the standard for July 1939, the overall cost-of-living index in Warsaw had risen by May 1942 to 1,932, and that of the cost of food to 2,791; Madajczyk, *Polityka III Rzeszy*, 2:66. On inflation of food prices in the opening months of the war, see Gutman, *Yehudei Varshah*, pp. 42–43.

14. In 1941 Germans were allotted 2,310 calories daily, Poles 654, and Jews 184. The cost per calorie for Germans was .003 zł., for Poles .026 zł., and for Jews .059 zł. Madajczyk, *Polityka III Rzeszy*, 2:226.

15. In March 1941 an average of 7.2 Jews occupied each available room in the Warsaw ghetto, as compared to 4.1 inhabitants per room on the so-called Aryan side. The density of population in the ghetto during the same month was 342,308 per square mile, as compared to 17,261 per square mile outside the ghetto. In the Łódź ghetto the situation was only slightly better: in September 1941 the density of population was around 90,000 per square mile, and there were an average of 5.8 Jews inhabiting each room. Hilberg, *The Destruction of the European Jews*, p. 152.

16. The difference was reflected in the occupiers' terminology: Poles were subject to *Arbeitspflicht*, Jews to *Arbeitszwang*. See "Wiadomości o położeniu Żydów w Polsce," 7 February 1940 (Nr. 2235/32), YVA—O25/73. On the distinction between the two terms see Neumann, *Behemoth*, p. 127. Sometimes the *Judenräte* undertook to pay Jewish forced laborers; see Hilberg, *The Destruction of the European Jews*, p. 164.

17. Often Jews entrusted their property and businesses to Poles for safekeeping, in order to avoid confiscation by the Germans. Frequently, though certainly not always, these unofficial Polish trustees expropriated the property de facto themselves. See Ringelblum, *Polish-Jewish Relations*, p. 77. The status of such property was to constitute a thorny problem for the government-in-exile toward the end of the war.

18. The commander of the *Wehrmacht* in Poland, Generaloberst Johannes Blaskowitz, complained to his commander-in-chief, Walter von Brauchitsch, in the early days of the war that anti-Jewish violence merely aroused Polish sympathy for Jews. Madajczyk, *Polityka III Rzeszy*, 2:215. Blaskowitz was in general, though, an opponent of the terror tactics of the Einsatzgruppen; see Hilberg, *The Destruction of the European Jews*, p. 127; Gross, *Polish Society*, pp. 69–70.

19. On German observation of Polish attitudes toward Jews in the years 1936–39, see Korzec, "Documents on the Jewish Problem," pp. 115–48.

20. Engel, "Early Account of Polish Jewry," pp. 12–13. See also [Kaplan], *Scroll of Agony*, pp. 113–14: "Since the conquest of Poland the conqueror has become the 'father and patron' of the Polish people, and he is saving the country from the Jews. . . . It is as if the Nazis were saying: 'We have taken your political independence away from you; but in its place we will give you economic independence. . . . Under our rule the Jews will be eliminated from all their occupations and you will take their place."

21. See Goldstein, *Finf Yor in Varshever Geto*, pp. 131–32: "Every law which treated Jews exceptionally was duly translated and interpreted for the Polish population . . . : 'Jews are dangerous parasites, dirty mangy pigs; they spread epidemics and bring disaster to those who live close to them. . . . Every place where Jews live is a stinking nest for all sorts of noxious effluvia and bacilli—a mortal danger to all its neighbors; therefore, the Jews must be completely isolated, like lepers separated from everyone else by a thick wall. . . .' Every Pole [thus] received his daily dose of Jew-poison."

22. *I Saw Poland Suffer*, p. 23.

23. Ibid., p. 24. The report does not mention Warsaw; the location is clear, however, from a parallel account by Czerniaków. See Hilberg, Staron, and Kermisz, *Diary of Czerniaków*, pp. 103, 114–15.

24. Engel, "Early Account of Polish Jewry," p. 7 (emphasis in original).

25. [Kaplan], *Scroll of Agony*, pp. 134–35.

26. Gutman, *Yehudei Varshah*, pp. 46–48.

27. See "Meldunek Nr. 15 o sytuacji wewnętrznej," 15 March–2 April 1940, in *AKD*, 1:194; see also Goldstein, *Finf Yor in Varshever Geto*, p. 134; Ringelblum, *Polish-Jewish Relations*, pp. 45–46.

28. Gutman, *Yehudei Varshah*, p. 51.

29. Republic of Poland, Ministry of Information, *The German Attempt to Destroy the Polish Nation*, p. 96. See also *The Persecution of Jews in German-Occupied Poland*, p. 7; *I Saw Poland Suffer*, pp. 24–25. The Polish government attached such importance to the propagation of this image that some of its highest officials at one point actually prepared a falsified version of a report from the underground that presented a much different picture. See Engel, "Early Account of Polish Jewry," pp. 3, 14.

30. [Kaplan], *Scroll of Agony*, p. 114.

31. Ibid., p. 82. In October 1939, however, he had written that "animosity toward Jews continues to grow . . ."; cf. pp. 46–47, 53.

32. Goldstein, *Finf Yor in Varshever Geto*, pp. 132–33.

33. "Report on the Jewish Situation in Europe," 10 December 1941, WL—K4b HEC.

34. "Bericht aus Warschau," 7 November 1939, HIA-Mikołajczyk, Box 12, File: "Jews in Occupied Poland, 1939–1944."

35. "La situation des Juifs en Pologne occupée par les Allemands," n.d., HIA-PG, Box 469, File: "Sprawy uchodźce, PCK i inne."

36. Gutman, *Yehudei Varshah*, pp. 47–48. See the assessment of Moshe Kleinbaum: "The attitude of the Polish population toward the Jews is not uniform. In critical moments both the diabolic and the angelic find expres-

sion in the human soul. Among the Polish masses there are many who are eager to assist in the plunder and persecution of their Jewish fellow citizens. In contrast, a revision—in the positive sense—in their attitude toward the Jews is noticeable among the Polish intelligentsia." Kleinbaum, "El Dr. N. Goldmann," p. 560.

37. [Kaplan], *Scroll of Agony*, p. 135. Kaplan may, however, have been referring to the German authorities who did not move to stop the riots; it is not entirely clear from the text.

38. Ringelblum, *Polish-Jewish Relations*, pp. 52–53. See also Landau, *Kronika lat wojny*, 1:369–70: "Today antisemitism is not a spontaneous phenomenon —it is clearly and unmistakably sown by the Germans, who aim at fanning the antagonisms between the Christian and Jewish populations. The guilt of the [Polish] community—if it is possible to speak at all of guilt in such matters—lies rather in the fact that it allows itself too easily to fall in with these currents, [that it] does not resist them sufficiently." Then again, Goldstein claimed that "the underground socialist and democratic press reacted sharply to the pogroms"; *Finf Yor in Varshever Geto*, p. 137.

39. Engel, "Early Account of Polish Jewry," p. 10.

40. Ibid., pp. 10, 12–13. On the other hand, he commented elsewhere in the report that "the Polish population does not yet at any rate reveal a disposition toward relations with the Jews along the lines of the methods and atmosphere being established by the Germans" (p. 8).

41. "Raport Ambasady RP w Bukareszcie: Żydzi," 19 April 1940, HIA-PG, Box 921, File N55. See also above, chapter II, n. 80.

42. "Stosunek do mniejszości narodowych," n.d. (handwritten date: 6 February 1941), HIA-PG, Box 920, File N18.

43. "Postawa Polityczna Społeczeństwa: Raport o sytuacji wewnętrznej," 1 February–31 March 1941, HIA-Komorowski, Box 5.

44. See "Wyciąg z rozmowy z panem Z. S. . . . ," 18 January 1940, HIA-PG, Box 921, File N55; "Stosunek Niemców do Polaków w okupacji," n.d. (beginning: "Drugim sposobem poróżnienia społeczeństwa polskiego . . ."), ibid.

45. "Stosunek Niemców do Polaków w okupacji," n.d. (beginning: "Gnębienie Żydów przez Niemców . . ."), ibid.

46. "Sytuacja w Warszawie i w Generalnym Gubernatorstwie," signed "Mersin," 31 December 1940, HIA-Komorowski, Box 3.

47. See Bartoszewski and Lewin, *Righteous among Nations*, pp. 37–38, 41–42, 116–19, 211, 244–45, 277–78, 287–96, 307; Iranek-Osmecki, *He Who Saves One Life*, pp. 119–33.

48. See Ringelblum, *Polish-Jewish Relations*, p. 38; [Kaplan], *Scroll of Agony*, p. 46.

49. See also the description of Polish attitudes by Roman Knoll (above, p. 65). Such an impression was no doubt strengthened by simultaneously arriving reports of hostility between Poles and Jews in the Soviet zone.

50. Engel, "Early Account of Polish Jewry," p. 13.

51. Ibid.

52. See Polish Interior Ministry to Sosnkowski, 7 April 1941 (L. dz. 581/41), HIA-Komorowski, Box 3.

53. Unfortunately, the Polish officials who read the various dispatches from the homeland that spoke of the extent of Polish anti-Jewish feeling did not as a rule record their reactions to these reports in orderly fashion (unlike their British counterparts, who attached minutes to virtually every document that circulated among them). It is thus impossible to prove beyond doubt that such was, in fact, the prevailing conclusion within the Polish government. It seems inconceivable, however, that in the face of the predominance of reports of anti-Jewish feeling that the government received, it could have concluded otherwise.

54. This tendency was undoubtedly reinforced by the vigorous complaint from the homeland that the government received following the Stańczyk declaration of November 1940. In this case, though, the government's statement concerned not the manner in which Poles should relate to Jews under German occupation but rather the status of Jews in the future independent Poland. About this matter there seems to have been much less ambivalence among most Poles than about the former issue; hence the strong reaction.

55. See "Uchwały Komitetu Ministrów dla spraw Kraju," 12 December 1939, in *AKD*, 1:24–26; "Skrót instrukcji Nr. 5 dla ob. Rakonia," 8 July 1940, ibid., 1:266–69. These two fundamental statements of the government's attitude regarding the scope and methods of resistance to the occupiers made no mention of the Jewish situation. To be sure, in March 1941, the military organization of the Polish underground, Związek Walki Zbrojnej, published an appeal, ostensibly "on behalf of the Polish Government-in-Exile," calling upon Poles to refrain from volunteering for service as guards in Jewish labor camps. In the text of the appeal the organization stated that "the Polish Government-in-Exile as early as last year issued an order to refrain from all manner of cooperation, even illusory, with the Germans in their anti-Jewish actions." Archival corroboration for the issue of such an order by the government in 1940, however, has not yet been adduced. The text of the appeal is in Bartoszewski and Lewin, *Righteous among Nations*, pp. 648–49.

56. On the government's concern with the evacuation of Polish political leaders from Wilno, see "Uchwała Komitetu dla Spraw Kraju . . . w sprawie ewakuacji działaczy politycznych z terenow Wilenszczyzny i Litwy Kowień-skiej," 17 April 1940, in *AKD*, 1:222. A number of Jewish political leaders also escaped through Wilno during the first two years of the war, but research on their escape has so far not noted any involvement of the Polish government. See Bauer, "Rescue Operations through Vilna," pp. 215–23; Bauer, *American Jewry and the Holocaust*, pp. 107–28; Porat, "Rikkuz haPelitim haYehudi'im beVilna," passim.

57. Funds, food parcels, medicines, and other supplies from abroad were distributed to Polish Jews by the Jüdische Soziale Selbsthilfe (JSS, or, in Polish, Żydowska Samopomoc Społeczna), a sort of federation of the various Jewish welfare agencies that had operated in Poland before the war. In May 1940 this body was granted legal recognition by the German occupying au-

thorities and permitted to receive shipments from foreign sources. At the same time the Germans mandated the creation of similar bodies for Poles and Ukrainians; when these were established, all three organizations were united under the auspices of a general welfare council known as Naczelna Rada Opiekuńcza. This overarching council received funds and supplies in large measure from the American Commission for Polish Relief (led by former President Herbert Hoover) and from the American Red Cross and was responsible for determining how they should be distributed among the three component ethnic bodies. After much debate, it was decided that the Jewish organization should receive 17 percent of all such donations; this figure represented a compromise between the initial Jewish view, which held that because of the especially severe conditions to which they were subject, Jews should receive 30 percent of the donations in Warsaw and 25 percent elsewhere, and the Polish view, which sought to limit the Jewish allocation to 8 percent (Jews constituted some 10–12 percent of the population in the Generalgouvernement). The allocation made up about one-half of the JSS budget; the rest came from funds supplied by the American Jewish Joint Distribution Committee.

Still, JSS found itself chronically short of funds, and it regularly turned for additional assistance to Jewish communities in the West. Copies of some of the appeals sent to these communities were apparently obtained by the Polish Ministry of Information in London; on 17 January 1941 Minister Stroński distributed one such letter, which he termed "highly characteristic," to the members of the Polish cabinet. In his cover letter he indicated that he regarded this as "an authentic document of the enormous poverty and exceptionally harsh conditions of life in which the Jewish population of the Generalgouvernement has found itself of late." However, Stroński's purpose in distributing this document seems to have been mainly propagandistic. Indeed, it does not appear to have aroused serious discussion in government circles of how the government ought to respond to what Stroński had acknowledged as an exceptional situation. On the other hand, the government was at the same time involved in the regular transfer of funds to the underground for use for civilian purposes among the Polish community. See Stroński to Polish foreign minister, 17 January 1941, plus attachment, E. Tisch to Jewish community, Lisbon, 20 December 1940, HIA-PG, Box 455, File: "Mniejszości Żydzi," Subfile: "Różne." On JSS and its sources of funding, see Weichert, *Yidishe Aleynhilf,* pp. 12–15, 133–39, 158–60; Bauer, *American Jewry and the Holocaust,* pp. 84–92. On Polish government financing of social welfare activities for Poles through the underground, see Gross, *Polish Society,* pp. 242–48.

58. Engel, "Early Account of Polish Jewry," p. 9 (emphasis in original).

59. "Raport z Rzymu," 26 April 1940, HIA-PG, Box 921, File N55. The charge was leveled at the Jews in the towns of Kutno, Łowicz, Sochaczew, and Błonie, all of which are located within 75 miles of Warsaw on the main highway west to Poznań. In Kępno, about 60 miles southwest of Łódź, on the other hand, "no instance in which Jews harmed Poles" was noted.

60. "Sprawy żydowskie," 15 October–20 November 1940, AIP—A.21/5/1; "Zeznanie p. Druchowskiego," 24–25 May 1940, HIA-PG, Box 921, File N55.

61. See above, chapter II, n. 82.

62. "Bericht über die Lage in Warschau," 27 October 1939, HIA-Mikołajczyk, Box 12, File: "Jews in Occupied Poland, 1939–1944."

63. See "Raport z Kraju," 25 November 1939, HIA-PG, Box 921, File N55; "Akcja przesiedleńcza," 3 January 1940, HIA-PG, Box 918, File N3; "Raport z Rzymu," 12 January 1940, ibid. There were, however, exceptions, which clearly described the Jews' situation as worse; see "Prześladowanie Żydów przez Niemców w Polsce," 10 January 1940, HIA-PG, Box 921, File N55.

64. See "Raport za czas od 5.II do 11.II.1940: Deportacje i przesiedlenia," 12 February 1940, HIA-PG, Box 918, File N3; "Raport z Kraju," March 1940, HIA-PG, Box 921, File N55; "Raport sytuacyjny," n.d., HIA-Mikołajczyk, Box 9, File: "Committee on Occupied Poland. Correspondence, September–October 1940"; "Sprawy żydowskie" (see above, n. 60); "Sprawy żydowskie," 20 November–20 December 1940, YVA—O25/89; "Stosunek do mniejszości narodowych" (see above, n. 42). See also Gross, *Polish Society*, pp. 185–86.

65. See "Raport z Kraju," 4 January 1940, HIA-PG, Box 921, File N55; "Raport z Kraju," March 1940, ibid.

66. Engel, "Early Account of Polish Jewry," pp. 9, 12 (emphasis in original). It should be pointed out that this evaluation also appears in some Jewish sources. See Kleinbaum, "El Dr. N. Goldmann," p. 561: "Anything can be had for money, or more precisely for gold, even at the highest ranks of the German occupation authorities. In the . . . Generalgouvernement, bribery has become . . . an everyday phenomenon. . . . On one hand, this has increased the arbitrariness and perfidy of the Nazi regime toward the Jewish population; but on the other hand, [the purchase of] rights for money is the sole means of rescue available to the Jews. . . ."

67. See Reiss to Gruenbaum, 8 October 1939, CZA—S26/1232: ". . . j'ai tout à fait l'impression que l'intérêt pour une . . . action d'assistance parmi la judaisme mondial n'est que très petit a rapport aux dimensions de malheur. Cet intérêt mediocre n'est pas comparable a la compassion que s'est montrée quand le régime hitlérien a été établi en Allemagne." Even here, Reiss was referring mainly to aid for refugees from Poland, in whom Jewish organizations generally tended to show more interest than in Jews remaining in the occupied homeland; see below, nn. 69, 70.

68. Gelber, "Zionist Policy and the Fate of European Jewry," pp. 196–200. This idea aroused in many Jewish organizations an ambivalence regarding the sending of relief to the Jews under Nazi occupation, in the belief that "every scrap of food sent into Europe . . . would merely serve to relieve German shortages, and would thereby postpone the day of Hitler's downfall." A. Leon Kubowitzki, "Survey of the Rescue Activities of the World Jewish Congress, 1940–1944," DRI—A1/112.1. For a highly captious description of the consequences of this attitude, see Beit-Tsvi, *HaTsiyonut haPost-Ugandit*, pp. 249–54.

69. See "Excerpts from the Annual Report of Dr. Stephen S. Wise . . . ," 11

February 1940, CZA—A243/71: "Even if American Jews were prepared to give a maximum of help to their fellow Jews in Central and Eastern Europe . . . that would not be enough. . . . Our service to them must not only embrace the tragic today but the more hopeful tomorrow. We are not to limit ourselves . . . to the business of supplying them with food and clothing and shelter. We are . . . to plan together with them for that morrow on which once again they will become free and re-enfranchised members of the human race, with their enslavement forever behind them." See also "Address by Dr. Nahum Goldmann . . . [at the] Inter-American Jewish Conference," 22–25 November 1941, DRI—A1/296: "To deal with the European Jewish problem means primarily to deal with the future of this problem. For the time being there is not much left of a Jewish problem in Europe in the [sic] terms of a political question." Arieh Tartakower maintained that the World Jewish Congress viewed relief operations as valuable only insofar as they served to further the congress's overall political program; see "Di Hilf-Arbet fun Idishn Velt-Kongres un Videroifboi fun idishn Lebn in Erope," ibid. The attitude of the Bund seems to have been similar; see "Memorial fun Ts. K. fun 'Bund' tsu der Poylisher Regirung," April 1940, YVA—M2/269.

70. See cable, Gruenbaum to Wise and [Abba Hillel] Silver, New York, 16 October 1939, CZA—S26/1232; cable, Gruenbaum to Dr. [Mordechai] Ehrenpreis, Stockholm, n.d. [October 1939], ibid. See also Barlas, Hatsalah biYmei Sho'ah, pp. 96–97.

71. "Protokol mehaYeshivah haPlenarit shel haVa'ad haKelali shel Yahadut Polin," 26 December 1940, CZA—J25/15.

72. Neither of the two major depositories of the government-in-exile's archives, AIP and HIA, appears to contain any significant correspondence with or about the Joint; nor does the relevant chapter in Bauer, *American Jewry and the Holocaust* (pp. 67–106), a book devoted entirely to the activities of the Joint during World War II, mention any Joint contacts with the Polish government. Such also seems to have been the case with RELICO, the Relief Committee for the War-Stricken Jewish Population of Europe, founded by Abraham Silberschein in Geneva during the first years of the war. See cable, Silberschein to Jewish Agency, 27 September 1939, CZA—S26/1232.

73. Noteworthy in this regard are the comments of Moshe Kleinbaum on the tasks of the World Jewish Congress vis-à-vis the Jews of Nazi-occupied Poland. Among Kleinbaum's recommendations for the congress's proposed Polish Division was "the establishment of a permanent link with the Jewish centers for refugees and émigrés from Poland, as well as with the most important centers of the Polish émigrés." On the other hand, he felt that the "difficult and honorable task of mediating between Polish Jewry and the Polish government" should be left exclusively to the Jewish representative on the Polish National Council, while the congress should "establish a bridge between Polish Jewry and world Jewry, as well as concern itself with the link between the Jewish world and the Polish agencies." Kleinbaum, "El Dr. N. Goldmann," p. 575.

74. *The Persecution of Jews in German-Occupied Poland*, pp. 7–8; see also Re-

public of Poland, Ministry of Information, *The German Attempt to Destroy the Polish Nation*, pp. 96–106; "Działalność władz okupacyjnych na terenie Rzeczypospolitej Polskiej," 1 September 1939–1 November 1940, pp. 166–69, HIA-MSW, Box 4.

75. *The Persecution of Jews in German-Occupied Poland*, p. 12.

76. Ibid., pp. 20–26; "Działalność władz okupacyjnych," p. 166 (see above, n. 74).

77. Already at the beginning of December 1939, for example, a question had been asked in the House of Commons concerning reports of German plans to establish a "Jewish reserve" in the Lublin area. The Polish government took careful notice of this question; see "Sprawa 'Rezerwatu Żydowskiego' w parlamencie angielskim," 3 December 1939, HIA-PG, Box 921, File N55.

78. This was the pamphlet entitled *The Persecution of Jews in German-Occupied Poland*, issued under the auspices of *Free Europe*.

79. Republic of Poland, Ministry of Information, *The German New Order in Poland*, pp. 213–48.

80. Prior to that time allusion to the Jewish situation had been made in the *Polish Fortnightly Review* only sporadically and in passing, and it had been neglected in discussions of subjects where it might reasonably be expected to have been raised. In a five-page article entitled "A Year of Occupation" in the issue of 1 September 1940, for example, Jews were mentioned in only two sentences, on pp. 8 and 9. In the next issue (16 September), an article titled "Recent News from Poland" referred to Jews only by pointing out that they were not deported for forced labor to Germany proper and that as a result, in order to escape from German press gangs, many Poles were seeking to rent Jewish identification armbands from their owners for a daily charge of 10–50 zł. On 1 November 1940 an eight-page issue devoted entirely to "The German New Order in Poland" did not mention the Jews. On 15 December 1940, in a seven-page issue entitled "Warsaw under the German Occupation," a short section on the newly established ghetto appeared on p. 4. And on 1 March 1941 an issue entitled "The German Economy in Poland" made no comment upon the economic oppression of the Jews. Specifically, in comparing the respective food rations allocated to Germans and Poles, it failed to point out that Jewish rations were in turn but a small fraction of the latter.

81. "Notes on the Situation of Poland under German Occupation," HIA-US, Box 33, File 2.

82. "Działalność władz okupacyjnych" (see above, n. 74). The report was first distributed in February 1941.

83. Ibid., p. 169.

84. See "Wyciąg z Komunikatu Nr. 8 Sztabu Naczelnego Wodza, Oddział II," 15 February 1941, AIP—KOL. 30/I/2: "In the present situation there is no parallel between the aims of Poland and those of any of the ethnic groups operating in Poland's territories. The only exception is a certain portion of

the Jewish community, namely the bourgeoisie and the most highly assimilated sections of the intelligentsia."

85. There is a controversy among historians about whether at the time of the invasion of Russia the murder of the Jews in all of Europe, or only of those in the former Soviet territories, was contemplated. This issue in turn is part of the larger debate over whether the so-called final solution was imminent in Hitler's world view long before he came to power or whether it was essentially an improvised solution to a set of problems confronted by the German leadership in the course of the war. For varying positions see, among others, Bauer, "Genocide," pp. 42–43; Adam, *Judenpolitik im Dritten Reich*, pp. 303–16; Krausnick, "Judenverfolgungen," pp. 297ff; Fox, "The Final Solution"; Broszat, "Hitler und die Genesis der 'Endlösung' "; Browning, "Zur Genesis der Endlösung"; Fleming, *Hitler and the Final Solution*, including the introduction by Saul Friedländer, pp. vii–xxxiii. Whatever the case, however, it is certainly reasonable in retrospect to view the murder on the eastern front in the summer and fall of 1941 as the first stage in the total biological annihilation of European Jewry that has infelicitously come to be known as the Holocaust.

86. Hilberg, *The Destruction of the European Jews*, pp. 177–90.

87. Figures compiled from Gilbert, *Atlas of the Holocaust*, pp. 67–69, 76–77.

88. On the deportation from Lublin, see especially Blumenthal, *Te'udot miGeto Lublin*, pp. 62–76.

89. Krakowski, "Avedot Yahadut Polin baSho'ah," pp. 231–37. See also Arad, " 'Mivtsa Reinhard,' " pp. 168–90.

90. "Rundschreiben Nr. 33/43g," 11 July 1943, in *DH*, p. 343.

91. Laqueur, *The Terrible Secret*, p. 109.

92. Ibid., p. 110.

93. "Meldunek Nr. 96 (o sytuacje na wschodzie . . .)," HIA-Komorowski, Box 4.

94. Gilbert, *Auschwitz and the Allies*, pp. 16–17. The Polish diplomat quoted here mentioned a figure of 1.5 million missing Jews. This figure was exaggerated; cf. Krakowski, "Avedot Yahadut Polin baSho'ah," pp. 232–33.

95. Ministerstwo Spraw Wewnętrznych, "Sprawozdanie Nr. 3/42," 15 August–15 November 1941 (issued April 1942), HIA-MSW, Box 1; *Dziennik Polski*, 5 May 1942 ("Z polskich Ziem Wschodnich"). See also "Gen. Rowecki do Centrali . . . ," 19 May 1942, in *AKD*, 2:265–66.

96. "Raport Bundu w sprawie przesladowań Żydów," May 1942, HIA-Mikołajczyk, Box 12, File: "Jews in Occupied Poland." The Polish text is reprinted, together with an English translation, in Bauer, "When Did They Know?" pp. 51–58; an English translation, only, appears in Bartoszewski and Lewin, *Righteous among Nations*, pp. 216–18. See also Laqueur, *The Terrible Secret*, pp. 104–5; Gilbert, *Auschwitz and the Allies*, pp. 39–42. It is noteworthy that over two months earlier the Bund had dispatched a longer report that had also clearly noted mass shootings in the east and gassings in the west at some length: "List Bundu . . . ," 16 March 1942, HIA-Mikołajczyk,

Box 12, File: "Jews in Occupied Poland." When this report was received, however, is not known. In any case, even if it did arrive before the May dispatch, it exerted no impact.

97. Raczyński interview.

98. This theme has been treated extensively in, among others, Gilbert, *Auschwitz and the Allies*, and Laqueur, *The Terrible Secret*.

99. Untitled, undated document with handwritten annotation: "Omówiony z F. Savery, 18.XII.41," AIP—KOL. 39/4.

100. See *Dziennik Polski*, 19 November 1941 ("Ghetto we Lwowie"), 22 January 1942 ("Mniejszość ukraińska we Lwowie"), 3 February 1942 ("Z Wilenszczyzny").

101. The Yiddish-language bulletins, bearing the English title *A News Bulletin on Eastern European Affairs*, are located in DRI—A1/1711. This series was initiated on 28 August 1941, replacing a previous English-language series (of the same title) that ceased publication three weeks earlier; see Stefan de Ropp to S. H. Rasmunsej, n.d., HIA-Polskie Rządowe Informacyjne Centrum, Box 61. In the Yiddish series see the issues of 18 September 1941 ("Nayes fun Mizrekh Galitsie") and 2 October 1941 ("Yidishe Nayes fun Natsi-Poylen").

102. Ministerstwo Spraw Wewnętrznych, "Sprawozdanie Nr. 3/42" (see above, n. 95).

103. *Dziennik Polski*, 5 May 1942 ("Z polskich Ziem Wschodnich").

104. See *News Bulletin on Eastern European Affairs*, 9 January, 12 March, 21 May, 28 May 1942.

105. Inter-Allied Information Committee, *Punishment for War Crimes*.

106. Quoted in Kubowitzki, "Survey of the Rescue Activities of the World Jewish Congress" (see above, n. 68).

107. Gilbert, *Auschwitz and the Allies*, p. 19.

108. "Notatka," Michał Potulicki, 20 July 1942, HIA-PG, Box 459, File 851/e. In a memorandum of 14 August 1942 Kraczkiewicz noted that Britain and other countries would object to the admission of a nongovernmental body to a committee defined as intergovernmental. He noted, however, that a suggestion had recently been made to create a parallel, nonofficial, interorganizational body on which Jews might be represented. "Notatka dla P. Ministra [Spraw Zagranicznych] . . . ," 14 August 1942, HIA-PG, Box 700, File 851/e, Subfile: "Ratowanie Żydów." Kraczkiewicz ignored the fact that the World Jewish Congress had asked not for membership on the committee but merely for observer rank.

109. According to Tadeusz Ullman, director of the Political Department of the Interior Ministry, the Poles had not been permitted by the British and American governments to send food packages to the Jews in the ghettos because this action would violate the Allied blockade on shipments to enemy territory. Ullman claimed that Sikorski had met with British and American officials in the hope of overcoming their objection and that he had obtained agreement for shipment of medical supplies through the Red Cross. Ullman to chief of Civil Chancellery, Office of the Polish President, 26 May 1942 (L.

dz. 1408/42), AIP—A.48.10/C1. A record of such interventions has not yet been found. Raczyński did tell Lord Selbourne on 17 June 1942 that the Polish government was interested in any scheme that might be devised to assist the ghettos, but this appears to have been a statement pro forma, and it was offered merely as a passing comment. See below, n. 125. On the unwillingness of the National Council to take special notice of Jewish needs in matters of relief, see below, n. 124.

110. Quoted in Iranek-Osmecki, *He Who Saves One Life*, p. 186. The recommendation was explained on the basis of "reasons of principle, and political ones, as such [anti-Jewish] action [by the Polish population] would be bound to make it terribly difficult for the government to profit from the situation in the international field."

111. "General Directive," n.d., HIA-Mikołajczyk, Box 10, File: "Radio Station ŚWIT, London: Correspondence, April–December 1942."

112. Ibid.; see also "Notatka z rozmowy z p. Leeperem," n.d., ibid.; "Heads of Policy for Research Units," n.d., ibid. In a handwritten draft of the last document, the sentence "Assume that in the reorganisation of Poland they [the Jews] will have equal rights" was crossed out. Indeed, the government had a powerful reason for wishing to discourage the station's listeners from making such an assumption. Reports from the underground continued to indicate strong anti-Jewish feelings among the Polish populace. A letter to the interior minister written in November 1941, for example, noted that "for all of the human compassion over the fate of the Jews, there is hardly anyone in Poland who would not demand a program [of action] with regard to the Jewish question, especially in the area of replacing them with Poles in their role in economic life." The document cautioned further that "without even such a minimal program . . . no Government will be able to rule in Poland peacefully and for a long time." "Ryszard" to minister for home affairs, 8 November 1941 (L. dz. K.3708/41), YVA—O25/89. See also "Sprawozdanie Kościelne z Polski za czerwiec i połowe lipca 1941," ibid.; "Radiogram NO. 266KK od Wacławy," 4 July 1941, HIA-Komorowski, Box 3; "Radiogram Nr. M. 80 A i B: Meldunek Nr. 80," 10 December 1941 (L. dz. 3743/tj. 41), ibid., Box 5.

113. Cf. *Dziennik Polski*, 10 June 1942 ("Rząd RP protestuje przeciw zbrodniom niemieckim . . .").

114. Laqueur, *The Terrible Secret*, p. 116, suggests that policy for ŚWIT was determined primarily by the British Foreign Office, and not by the Polish government, "because though the station employed Poles it was a British station." In fact the ŚWIT policy guidelines were signed by Sikorski and Interior Minister Stanisław Mikołajczyk. In one document it was specifically stated that "outlines of external policy are decided by agreement in advance between General S[ikorski] and the [Political Intelligence] Department"; that "questions of internal policy are for the decision of General S[ikorski], and an outline of policy will be supplied to General [Harold] Osborne [of the Political Intelligence Department, who directed the day-to-day operations of the station] to serve as a general directive"; and that "on important inci-

dents, where interpretation of policy may not be covered unambiguously by the general outlines, Mr. Osborne will ascertain the views of General S[ikorski] through Mr. [Mieczysław] T[hugutt, the Polish government official in charge of communication with the homeland]." The decisive influence in formulating station policy thus seems in most cases to have been Polish rather than British. Document headed "R. U.," HIA-Mikołajczyk, Box 10, File: "Radio Station ŚWIT, London: Correspondence, April–December 1942."

115. "Rząd RP protestuje przeciw zbrodniom niemieckim" (see above, n. 113). Subsequent quotations are from this broadcast.

116. As printed in *Dziennik Polski*, the speech discussed Jewish matters in 13 out of 236 lines.

117. Fox, "The Jewish Factor in British War Crimes Policy," pp. 82–89.

118. *Dziennik Polski*, 11 June 1942 ("Apel Rady Narodowej do Parlamentów Wolnych Państw w sprawie zbrodni niemieckich w Polsce").

119. Ibid.; see the typewritten copy of the text in YVA—M2/4.

120. Fox, "The Jewish Factor in British War Crimes Policy," p. 89.

121. *Polish Fortnightly Review*, 1 July 1942.

122. Ibid., 15 July 1942.

123. *Dziennik Polski*, 10 July 1942 ("S.O.S. Polski: Domagamy się represji przeciw narodowi niemieckiemu"); ibid., 11 July 1942 ("Sprawozdanie Ministra Mikołajczyka, złożone w Brytyjskim Ministerstwie Informacji"). Mikołajczyk added significant information that had not appeared in the Bund report, an indication that the government was continuing to receive news from other sources. In particular, he mentioned that the deportees from Lublin had been killed at Bełżec by poison gas; the Bund report had not spoken of Bełżec at all. In fact, the Poles had known about the executions at Bełżec at least since late June, when the Polish Information Center had released a short item on the murder of Polish Jewry (thirteen lines on p. 3 of a four-page bulletin) to the Jewish press in America; *News Bulletin on Eastern European Affairs*, 25 June 1942 ("Massen-Morden iber Iden in Poylen"). Mikołajczyk also spoke of executions of Jews by gas taking place at another location as well; according to the account in *Dziennik Polski*, this was Treblinka, whereas according to the *Polish Fortnightly Review*, 15 July 1942, it was Trawniki. Both readings are problematic. Most of the available evidence indicates that the Treblinka gas chambers began their operation with the arrival of the first deportees from Warsaw two weeks after Mikołajczyk's speech. Trawniki, on the other hand, was a labor camp, at which no installations for gas killings were erected. It is thus not clear to what Mikołajczyk was referring, or where he got his information.

124. "Sprawozdanie Komisji Prawno-Konstytucyjnej w przedmiocie wniosku . . . Zygielbojma i kol. w sprawie traktowania ludności żydowskiej w ghettach na równi z jeńcami wojennymi," YVA—M2/4. During June and July the cabinet had also devoted much attention to "German crimes against the Polish nation" but had considered the Jewish situation only peripherally; see "Protokół posiedzenia Rady Ministrów," 6 June, 6 July, 15 July 1942, and appendixes, AIP—PRMK. 102/48b-c.

125. See Raczyński to the earl of Selbourne, 17 June 1942, HIA-PG, Box 459, File 851/e. Raczyński added that "the Polish Government are of course highly interested in any scheme that could be devised with a view toward extending a measure of relief, however small and insignificant, to the suffering people of the ghettos." Selbourne replied that "deeply as I sympathise with the sufferings inflicted by the enemy on their [the Council of Polish Jews'] unhappy co-religionists in Poland, there is little we can do for them in the way of immediate aid while the enemy remains able to deprive them of all subsistence." Selbourne to Raczyński, 25 June 1942, ibid.

126. Gilbert, *Auschwitz and the Allies*, pp. 42–43.

127. Ibid., pp. 43–44. Zygielbojm's broadcast was in Yiddish; evidently this was the first time the language had been employed by the BBC.

128. Ibid., p. 43.

129. Quoted in Laqueur, *The Terrible Secret*, p. 112. See also "Uwagi ogólne," n.d. (L. dz. K.2385/42), HIA-Mikołajczyk, Box 9, File: "Committee on Occupied Poland. Correspondence, 1942–43."

130. See Gilbert, *Auschwitz and the Allies*, p. 47.

131. "BBC Home Service Nine PM News," 10 July 1942, WL—WMF 002.

132. Gilbert, *Auschwitz and the Allies*, p. 46.

133. Bracken went on to declare: "They will be treated as common murderers, which they are, and those gangsters will be punished with the utmost rigidity of the law. . . . The Government of Great Britain and all the Governments of the United Nations are in complete agreement on this question, that every care should be taken to secure the names of the persons responsible for these crimes; that they should be brought speedily to justice . . . ; and that their punishment will fit their crimes. . . . In view of the crimes committed by the Germans, the punishment will be in many cases the most severe known to any law. . . ." The entire statement was broadcast the next day over the BBC; see above, n. 131. Bracken's declaration was followed on 21 July with a statement by Franklin Roosevelt, made at a mass protest rally held at Madison Square Garden, that "those who carry out the crimes will be called to account on the day of revenge." Gilbert, *Auschwitz and the Allies*, p. 53.

134. For a detailed account of the deportations, see Gutman, *Yehudei Varshah*, pp. 217–47.

135. Sereny, *Into That Darkness*, pp. 150–52. The actual message has not been located, so that it is impossible to be certain of its specific content. See also Arad, " 'Mivtsa Reinhard,' " pp. 181–82.

136. Bór-Komorowski, *The Secret Army*, p. 99.

137. Korboński, *W imieniu Rzeczypospolitej*, p. 253.

138. "Pro memoria o sytuacji w Kraju w okresie 1–25 lipca 1942 r.," SPP—56/113.

139. Cable, Schwarzbart to [World] Jewish Congress, 27 July 1942, YVA—M2/534. In order to allow for comparison with other sources, the text of the cable is given here in full: "Officially informed Germans have begun mass murder in Warsaw ghetto. Posters appeared ordering deportation 6,000 to

East. Two trains left already feared execution. Despair suicides. Polish police removed. Lithuanians Latvians Ukrainians brought in. Shooting in streets and houses. Professor Raszeja of Poznan University also killed while attending Jewish patient. Inform Government." See also Laqueur, *The Terrible Secret*, p. 115.

140. Quoted in Gutman, *Yehudei Varshah*, pp. 271–72.

141. Significantly, Schwarzbart's diary contains no entry between 24 July and 10 August 1942.

142. Specifically, it cannot be determined whether Mikołajczyk's knowledge was derived from the situation report for the period ending 25 July or from some other source—such as, for instance, the cables mentioned by Korboński and Bór-Komorowski in their memoirs. Laqueur, *The Terrible Secret*, p. 114, reports that "copies of the many signals mentioned by Bór-Komorowski and Korboński have not been located" in either AIP or SPP. Recently a message from Korboński sent on 26 July has been located in AIP and quoted in Lukas, *The Forgotten Holocaust*, p. 156: "The Germans have begun the slaughter of the Warsaw Ghetto. The order concerning the deportation of 6,000 people was posted. One is allowed to take 15 kg. of luggage and jewelry. So far two trainloads of people were taken away to meet certain death. Despair, suicides. Polish police [Blue police] have been removed, their place was taken by the *szaulisi*, Latvians [and] Ukrainians. Shootings on streets and in houses. Professor of Poznan University Raszeja was killed during a medical consultation, together with another physician and Jewish patients" (Lukas's translation). A search through the most likely files in HIA-PG, -Mikołajczyk, -Komorowski, -Korboński, and -Karski has failed to turn up any earlier signals. The materials in all of these archives, however, are vast and often not fully registered, so that future searches could conceivably turn up such signals in hitherto unexamined files. In the meantime, the earliest datable dispatch from Warsaw is the report quoted in the text, which could not have been sent before 25 July. This report could have reached London within two days if it was dispatched by radio. However, it cannot be established whether it was in fact sent in this fashion; on this see Laqueur, *The Terrible Secret*, pp. 102–5, 111. Significantly, no incoming date is inscribed on the message. Thus it appears to be anyone's guess exactly what Mikołajczyk knew on 27 July.

143. *Palestine Post*, 28 July 1942 ("Warsaw Jews Threatened: Believed Executions Will Follow Exile"); *HaArets*, 28 July 1942 ("6,800 Yehudim miGeto Varshah—laHoreg?"); *HaBoker*, 28 July 1942 ("HaNatsim Hehelu beGerush haYehudim miGeto Varshah"); *HaTsofeh*, 28 July 1942 ("Hehel haGerush miGeto Varshah"); *Manchester Guardian*, 28 July 1942 (cutting in WL—PC 210).

144. The text given here is the English text as it appeared in the *Palestine Post*. There are slight variations in the versions published in the other newspapers.

145. *JTA Bulletin*, 28 July 1942 ("Pogrom in Warsaw: Mass Deportations to the East").

146. *HaMashkif*, 29 July 1942 ("Pogrom beGeto Varshah").

147. *New York Times*, 29 July 1942 ("Yugoslavia Driving Axis from Bosnia. . . . New Warsaw Curbs Due. Nazis Said to Plan Wiping Out of 600,000 in Ghetto").

148. The *Guardian* did introduce its account of the deportations with the words "according to the Polish Government in London," but it was the only one of the five newspapers carrying the Reuter's dispatch to do so. *HaBoker*, on the other hand, spoke merely of "Polish circles in London." In light of the discussion below, it seems most reasonable to conclude that the *Guardian's* attribution was inaccurate. Indeed, it was evidently not uncommon for British newspapers to identify Polish informants erroneously as government officials; see *Dziennik Polski*, 12 January 1942 ("Sprostowanie").

149. In Polish: "Dotychczas wywieziono już bez wieści 2 pociągi na stracenie." The syntax and word choice give the sentence an ambiguous quality.

150. *Dziennik Polski*, 29 July 1942 ("Żydzi z Warszawy wywożeni na Wschód"). The report appeared at the bottom of p. 2. The newspaper's lead article of the same day ("Dramatyczne wieści z kraju: Masowe egzekucje Polaków i Żydów") spoke of increased German terror against Poles and repeated information already released about shootings of Jews in the east and the gassing of 2,500 Jews from Lublin at Bełżec. It also mentioned that eighteen Jews in Warsaw had been murdered.

151. Gutman, *Yehudei Varshah*, p. 230.

152. *News Bulletin on Eastern European Affairs*, 4 August 1942 ("Shreklikhe Grisen fun Varshever Geto").

153. In Yiddish: ". . . di Daytshen *vilen* likvidiren dos Varshever geto" (emphasis added).

154. *News Bulletin on Eastern European Affairs*, 14 August 1942.

155. *JTA Bulletin*, 29 July 1942 ("The Warsaw Pogrom: 'Deportations' Only Pretext for Wholesale Mass Murder—Says Member of Polish National Council").

156. "Gen. Rowecki do Centrali . . . ," 19 August 1942, in *AKD*, 2:298 (received 25 August 1942). See also "Depesza z Kraju," 31 August 1942, SPP—56/117. A dispatch from Korboński on 11 August recently uncovered by Lukas mentioned that 7,000 Jews were being "taken away daily for slaughter" and that Czerniakow had committed suicide. There was, however, no mention of Treblinka. Lukas, *The Forgotten Holocaust*, p. 157.

157. See Hilberg, Staron, and Kermisz, *Diary of Czerniaków*, p. 23.

158. *Dziennik Polski*, 19 August 1942 ("Samobójstwo Czerniakowa").

159. *News Bulletin on Eastern European Affairs*, 20 August 1942 ("Zelbstmord fun Prezident fun Iden-Rat in Varshe").

160. *Times* (London), 17 August 1942 ("Suicide by Mayor of Warsaw Ghetto"). Associated Press, Reuter's North American associate, picked up the dispatch in London, and on 15 and 16 August the news appeared in several metropolitan dailies in the United States.

161. Unfortunately, it cannot be determined with certainty how this news reached a Reuter's correspondent in Switzerland. It is known that on 14 August 1942 a non-Jew who had just arrived in Switzerland from Poland

delivered to Richard Lichtheim, the Jewish Agency's representative in Geneva, some rather fragmentary information about the liquidation of the Warsaw ghetto. This person, described by Lichtheim as "eine sehr vertrauenswürdige und bekannte Persönlichkeit," could have spoken with someone from the Reuter's agency as well. However, Lichtheim's report of his conversation with this individual made no mention of Czerniaków; see the untitled document dated 15 August 1942, CZA—L22/83. There were apparently several other people from Poland who passed through Switzerland during the period of the deportations, and some written communications about the deportations were also evidently received by Lichtheim; see Lichtheim to L. Leder, 23 September 1942 (Nr. RL/LU/A2-13-4c-4d), CZA—L22/378. Any of these could likewise have been possible sources for the Reuter's dispatch.

162. The text of the article is reprinted in Bartoszewski and Lewin, *Righteous among Nations*, pp. 662–63. On the reaction in the ghetto, see [Kaplan], *Scroll of Agony*, pp. 384–85.

163. See *JTA Bulletin*, 17 August 1942 ("7,000 Jews Taken Daily from Warsaw Ghetto for Mass Execution: President of Warsaw Jewish Community Commits Suicide"). This release named Zygielbojm as an informant and noted that the authenticity of the information "is vouched for by the Polish Government."

164. "Notatka," Tadeusz Ullmann, 18 August 1942, AIP—A.48/10/C1.

165. Gutman, *Yehudei Varshah*, p. 230.

166. Sikorski's declaration is contained in a letter from Retinger to J. Zarański, 24 August 1942, HIA-PG, Box 700, File 851/e, Subfile: "Ratowanie Żydów." The declaration was apparently sent over the objection of Stroński, who believed that the date 1 September should be devoted exclusively to commemoration of the German attack against Poland in 1939. Handwritten annotation to cable, Rosmarin to Polish Foreign Ministry, 14 August 1942, ibid.

167. "Treść audycji radiowej z dnia 10 wrzesnia 1942 r. tajnej stacji krajowej dla Polaków zagranica . . . ," HIA-Mikołajczyk, Box 10, File: "Radio Station ŚWIT, London: Correspondence, April–December 1942."

168. *Jewish Chronicle*, 6 November 1942 (" 'Blackest Pages in History' "); *JTA Bulletin*, 30 October 1942.

169. Reprezentacja, *Sprawozdanie*, p. 44. At the time there were actually no more than 55,000 in the ghetto. Gutman, *Yehudei Varshah*, p. 231.

170. Cable, Rosmarin to Polish Foreign Ministry, 10 November 1942 (no. 74), HIA-PG, Box 700, File 851/e, Subfile: "Ratowanie Żydów."

171. Cable, Pilch, Polish Legation, Stockholm, to Polish Foreign Ministry, 12 November 1942 (no. 139), ibid.

172. Cable, Raczyński to Polish Consulate, Tel Aviv, 23 November 1942, ibid. The text of the cable was evidently prepared on 14 November; there is an annotation in Kraczkiewicz's hand bearing that date which reads, "As per understanding with Interior Ministry, which is referring this by telegraph to the homeland organization to verify the information."

173. Laqueur, *The Terrible Secret*, p. 118. Earlier, on 31 August, Bund leader

Leon Feiner (Berezowski) in Warsaw had sent a ten-page letter to Zygielbojm spelling out the situation in Warsaw and elsewhere in detail. However, this letter was long in arriving and was forwarded to the Foreign Ministry only on 12 December. "Do p. Zygielbojma . . . ," HIA-PG, Box 700, File 851/e; Zygielbojm to Polish Foreign Ministry, 12 December 1942, ibid.

174. Polish Foreign Ministry distributing cable no. 202 from Istanbul, 15 October 1942, AIP—A.48.10/C1.

175. Cable, Schwarzbart to World Jewish Congress, 18 November 1942, YVA—M2/534. Schwarzbart's note that this news was "not for publication before my obtaining Government's permission" strongly suggests deliberate government suppression of information. Laqueur, *The Terrible Secret*, p. 115, fixes the date of this cable at 16 November.

176. Karski had made one additional attempt, in June 1940, when he had been captured by the Germans and rescued by the underground. See Karski, *Story of a Secret State*, pp. 135–91.

177. Ibid., pp. 320–54. It should be pointed out that, as on his earlier mission, the conveyance of information about Jewish matters was incidental to Karski's primary task, which was to report on the relations between the Government Delegacy in the homeland, the Home Army command, and the various underground political parties. See the text of his report to Sikorski, HIA-Karski, Box 1.

178. The text of the Jewish Agency announcement is printed in Beit-Tsvi, *HaTsiyonut haPost-Ugandit*, pp. 68–69.

179. Gilbert, *Auschwitz and the Allies*, pp. 93–95. Easterman and Sidney Silverman passed the report on to the British Foreign Office on 26 November.

180. "Uchwała Rady Narodowej RP z 27 listopada 1942 r.," YVA—M2/5. The subsumption of the protest against the murder of Polish Jewry within a more general motion was, according to Schwarzbart, the only way that such a motion would have been considered. Schwarzbart Diary, 27 November 1942, YVA—M2/770. Schwarzbart also noted in his diary that twelve members of the council, including Mikołajczyk, did not sign the motion.

181. Cable, Raczyński to Polish Consulate General, Tel Aviv, 30 November 1942, HIA-PG, Box 700, File 851/e, Subfile: "Ratowanie Żydów."

182. Cable, Rosmarin to Polish Foreign Ministry, 22 November 1942 (no. 78), ibid. The Reprezentacja submitted the text of the cable to Rosmarin on 19 November; see Reprezentacja, *Sprawozdanie*, pp. 45–46.

183. See Raczyński to Mikołajczyk, 27 November 1942 (Nr. 245/IV.Z/42), HIA-PG, Box 700, File 851/e, Subfile: "Ratowanie Żydów."

184. Engel, "HaSichsuch haPolani-Sovieti," in press.

185. An overview of the correspondence directed by Jewish leaders and organizations to the Polish government between June and late November 1942 (i.e., the period between receipt of the Bund letter in London and delivery of the eyewitness testimonies of Karski and the exchangees) reveals that the major Jewish concerns during this time remained the status of the Jews in postwar Poland, the persistence of inequitable treatment of Jewish sol-

diers in the Polish Army and government offices, and discrimination in the treatment of Polish Jewish refugees in the Soviet Union and elsewhere.

186. *News Bulletin on Eastern European Affairs*, 28 November 1942 ("Dayt-shen Shekhten Ois Hunderter Toizender Iden in Poylen"); *Polish Fortnightly Review*, 1 December 1942 ("Extermination of the [*sic*] Polish Jewry: What Happened in the Warsaw Ghetto").

187. Ministerstwo Spraw Wewnętrznych, "Sprawozdanie Nr. 6/42," July–December 1942 (released 23 December 1942), HIA-MSW, Box 1.

188. According to statistics compiled by the SS in early 1943, almost 1.3 million Jews had been killed in the Generalgouvernement alone. If the annexed provinces and eastern territories are included, the figure may have exceeded even 2 million; see Laqueur, *The Terrible Secret*, pp. 14–15. The figure of 2 million was used in a memorandum prepared by the British Section of the World Jewish Congress on 27 November: "Mass Massacre of European Jewry," 27 November 1942, YVA—M2/5.

189. Republic of Poland, Ministry of Foreign Affairs, *The Mass Extermination of Jews in German Occupied Poland*. See also Gilbert, *Auschwitz and the Allies*, pp. 96–101.

190. Gilbert, *Auschwitz and the Allies*, p. 103.

191. Raczyński to Stroński, 26 November 1942, HIA-PG, Box 700, File 851/e, Subfile: "Ratowanie Żydów."

192. Stroński to Raczyński, 28 November 1942, ibid.

193. When ŚWIT finally took notice of the mass murder of the Jews of Poland, at the end of December, it did so only in passing, in order to emphasize the extent to which the Germans were capable of unprecedented brutality. Although it stated clearly that "after the mass extermination of the Jews comes the mass annihilation of the Poles," the broadcast issued no call for solidarity between the two peoples. Rather it concentrated upon urging the Ukrainian population not to cooperate in German anti-Polish actions. "Remember!" it exhorted Ukrainian listeners, "yesterday the Jews were murdered, today the Poles are being murdered, tomorrow the Germans will be murdering you." It seems that according to ŚWIT the Jews were already beyond help. Text of broadcast beginning, "Polacy! Wiadomości które Wam dzisiaj podajemy . . . ," n.d., HIA-Mikołajczyk, Box 10, File: "Radio Station ŚWIT, London: Correspondence, April–December 1942." The late December date is established by the fact that much of the information in the broadcast parallels the content of a note about new persecutions of Poles submitted by Raczyński to Churchill on 25 December 1942; see Gilbert, *Auschwitz and the Allies*, p. 106.

194. "Pro memoria o sytuacji w Kraju w okresie 11 października–15 listopada 1942," SPP—3.16.

195. See "Report on Conditions in Poland," 27 November 1942, HIA-US, Box 29, File 2. The Poles may, in fact, have had such information much earlier. Two Polish members of the Auschwitz underground had escaped in May and June 1942, and they had made contact with the Home Army in Warsaw. Garliński, *Oświęcim walczący*, pp. 107–9. In July 1942 a statement by

the government on the situation in the homeland was included in a brochure on conditions in occupied Europe presented by the overrun countries to the Vatican. It indicated that Poles and Russian officers had been killed at Auschwitz using poison gas, but included no mention of Jews. In fact, Jews were not mentioned in the statement at all; it opened rather with the sentence "Après deux ans et demi d'occupation allemande, il ne peut y avoir de doute que le Reich tend systématiquement vers l'extermination de la nation polonaise." "Situation dans les pays occupés par l'ennemi," July 1942, AIP—A.44/129/29.

196. See "Raport o sytuacji wewnętrznej. . . . Teror i bezprawia okupantów," 30 January 1941, in *AKD*, 1:431–33; "Pro memoria w sprawie sytuacji w Kraju," 16 March–15 April 1942, SPP—3.16. See also Garliński, *Oświęcim walczący*, pp. 19–75.

197. Ministerstwo Spraw Wewnętrznych, "Sprawozdanie Nr. 6/42," July–December 1942 (released 23 December 1942), HIA-MSW, Box 1. The reference to Jews at Auschwitz is on p. 71, at the end of paragraph 7.

CONCLUSION

1. See the evaluation by Anshel Reiss: "Poland did not spare efforts to arouse world opinion against the Nazis. It did this—at least this is how I understand its behavior—with full seriousness and full energy in order to convince the world of the truth about the barbaric actions of the Nazis, since it was quite interested in arousing resistance and hatred toward Germany; and the Jewish issue offered good material which it could exploit to its benefit. . . . However, they [the Poles] never raised their efforts [concerning the Jews] to the level of personal concern, which would have obligated the Poles to help their Jewish neighbors—wherever this was possible, of course." Reiss, *BeSa'arot haTekufah*, p. 236.

2. See S. Zamoyski to chief of staff for Polish commander-in-chief, 17 January 1941 (L. dz. 78/41), with attached correspondence from Richard Peirse, 15 January 1941 (No. RECP/DO/56), HIA-Komorowski, Box 2. The first underground report about conditions in the camp that has thus far been located was dispatched from Poland on 30 January 1941 and reached London only on 18 March. *AKD*, 1:431–33; see also Garliński, *Oświęcim walczący*, p. 64. There must, however, have been earlier reports; hence the prior request to bomb the camp.

3. It is significant in this regard that Schwarzbart, who virtually alone among the Jewish leaders continued to believe in the efficacy of politics, felt himself, with much justification, an outcast within the Jewish leadership.

4. Korzec, *Juifs en Pologne*, p. 282.

BIBLIOGRAPHY

The following is a list of the sources cited in the notes, and not of all materials consulted in the preparation of this study.

ARCHIVES

1. Archives of the Israel Labour Movement, Tel Aviv
   519 IV   V-League
2. Archiwum Instytutu Polskiego (formerly General Sikorski Historical Institute), London
   A.5   Rada Narodowa
   A.9   Ministerstwo Spraw Wewnętrznych
   A.12   Ambasada RP w Londynie
   A.21   Ministerstwo Prac Kongresowych
   A.44   Ambasada RP przy Watykanie
   A.48   Kancelaria Cywilna Prezydenta RP
   [EP]   Eaton Place Deposit (uncataloged)
   KOL.5   Tadeusz Romer (microfilms of originals
               at Public Archives of Canada)
   KOL. 11   Władysław Anders (formerly KGA)
   KOL. 25   Stanisław Kot
   KOL. 30   Stanisław Paprocki
   KOL. 39   Jan Wszelaki
   PRM.   Prezydium Rady Ministrów
   PRMK.   Prezydium Rady Ministrów, Kancelaria
3. Central Zionist Archives, Jerusalem
   A127   Yitshak Gruenbaum
   A243   Stephen S. Wise (photocopies of originals at Brandeis
               University)
   J25   Reprezentacja Żydostwa Polskiego
   L22   Jewish Agency for Palestine, Geneva
   S26   Jewish Agency for Palestine, Rescue
               Committee
   Z3   Zionistisches Centralbüro, Berlin
   Z4   World Zionist Organisation, London
4. Diaspora Research Institute, Tel Aviv
   A1   Institute for Jewish Affairs, New York
5. Histadrut Archives, Tel Aviv
   Minute Books, Executive

6. Hoover Institution Archives, Stanford, California
   Władysław Anders
   Tadeusz Komorowski
   Lt. Colonel Borkowski
   Jan Karski
   Stefan Korboński
   Stanisław Mikołajczyk
   Poland. Ambasada US
   Poland. Ambasada USSR
   Poland. Konsulat Generalny New York
   Poland. Ministerstwo Spraw Wewnętrznych
   Poland. Poselstwo Portugal
   Poland. Rada Narodowa
   Polish Government
       Akta Ambasady RP w Londynie
       Akta Ambasady RP w Paryżu
       Akta Ministerstwa Informacji i Dokumentacji
       Akta Ministerstwa Spraw Zagranicznych
   Polish Research Centre
   Polskie Rządowe Informacyjne Centrum

7. Jabotinsky Institute, Tel Aviv
   G4   New Zionist Organisation, Presidium, London
   G5   New Zionist Organization, Presidium, New York

8. Public Record Office, Kew, London
   FO 181   British Embassy, USSR
   FO 371   Foreign Office. General Correspondence, Political
   FO 954   Lord Avon [Anthony Eden] (photocopies of originals at University of Birmingham)

9. Studium Polski Podziemnej, Ealing, London
   3.16   Obozy koncentracyjne niemieckie
   56   Ministerstwo Spraw Wewnętrznych

10. Wiener Library, Tel Aviv
    Doc. 548   Wilfried Israel
    K4b   Persecution of Jews, Third Reich
    PC 210   Press Cuttings. Polish Government-in-Exile
    W6b   Polish Jewry, 1919–39
    WMF 002 BBC Home Service (microform)
    X3f   Antisemitism, Poland

11. Yad Vashem Archives, Jerusalem
    M2   Ignacy Schwarzbart
    O25   Michael Zylberberg
    O55   Alexander Bernfes

INTERVIEWS

Jan Karski, San Francisco, 18 April 1982
Count Edward Raczyński, London, 17 November 1983

NEWSPAPERS AND PERIODICALS

HaArets—Tel Aviv
Biuletyn Klubu Narodowego—London
HaBoker—Tel Aviv
Cavalcade—London
Congress Weekly—New York
Contemporary Jewish Record—New York
Daily Herald—London
Davar—Tel Aviv
Dziennik Polski—London
Evening Standard—London
Free Europe—London
Jestem Polakiem—London
Jewish Chronicle—London
Jewish Frontier—New York
JTA Bulletin—New York
Jüdische Rundschau—Berlin
Keesing's Contemporary Archives—
   London
Lebensfragen—Wilno
Manchester Guardian
HaMashkif—Tel Aviv
*The Monthly Future: A Polish-
   American Forum*—New York

Myśl Niepodległa—Warsaw
New Review—London
*News Bulletin on Eastern
   European Affairs*—New York
New Statesman and Nation—London
New York Times
HaOlam—Jerusalem
Opinion—New York
Palestine Post—Jerusalem
HaPo'el haTsa'ir—Tel Aviv
Polish Fortnightly Review—London
Prawda Robotnicza—Warsaw
Przyszłość—Paris, London
HaShilo'ah—Odessa
Times—London
Der Tog—New York
HaTsofeh—Tel Aviv
Tsukunft—New York
Unzer Tsayt—New York
Zionist Review—London

OTHER PRIMARY SOURCES

Anders, Władysław. *Bez ostatniego rozdziału: Wspomnienia z lat 1939–1946.* Newtown, England, 1950.
Armia Krajowa w Dokumentach. 3 vols. London, 1970–.
Babiński, Witold. *Przyczynki historyczne do okresu 1939–1945.* London, 1967.
Bendow, Josef [Jozef Tenenbaum]. *Der Lemberger Judenpogrom.* Vienna, 1919.
Bielski, Lucjan. *Głos z Kraju, czyli uwagi Polaka o ustroju przyszłej Europy.* London, 1941.
Blumental, Nachman, ed. *Te'udot miGeto Lublin: Yudenrat lelo Derech.* Jerusalem, 1967.
Borski, Jan. *Sprawa żydowska a socjalizm: Polemika z Bundem.* Warsaw, 1937.
Bór-Komorowski, T. *The Secret Army.* New York, 1951.

Bujak, Franciszek. *The Jewish Question in Poland*. Paris, 1919.

[Cadogan, Alexander.] *The Diaries of Sir Alexander Cadogan, 1938–1945*. Edited by David Dilks. New York, 1972.

Cang, Joel. "The Opposition Parties in Poland and Their Attitude towards the Jews and the Jewish Problem." *Jewish Social Studies* 1 (1939).

Chasanowitsch, L. *Die polnischen Judenpogrome in November und Dezember 1918: Tatsachen und Dokumente*. Stockholm, 1919.

Churchill, Winston S. *The Second World War*. Vol. 1, *The Gathering Storm*. Boston, 1948.

Ciechanowski, Jan. *Defeat in Victory*. New York, 1947.

Cohen, Israel. *The Jews in Poland*. London, 1936.

———. *A Report on the Pogroms in Poland*. London, 1919.

Dmowski, Roman. *Polityka Polska i odbudowanie państwa*. Hanover, 1947.

Documents on the Holocaust: Selected Sources on the Destruction of the Jews of Germany and Austria, Poland, and the Soviet Union. Edited by Yitshak Arad, Yisrael Gutman, and Avraham Margaliot. Jerusalem, 1978.

Documents on Polish-Soviet Relations. 2 vols. London, 1961–67.

Dziennik Ustaw Rzeczypospolitej Polskiej.

[Ehrlich, Henryk, and Alter, Wiktor.] *Henryk Erlich un Wiktor Alter: A Gedenk Bukh*. New York, 1951.

Engel, David. "An Early Account of Polish Jewry under Nazi and Soviet Occupation Presented to the Polish Government-in-Exile, February 1940." *Jewish Social Studies* 45 (1983): 1–16.

Feldstein, Hermann. *Polen und Juden: Ein Appell*. Vienna, 1915.

Foreign Relations of the United States, 1941. Washington, D.C., 1958.

Glicksman, Georges. *L'aspect économique de la question juive en Pologne*. Paris, 1929.

Głuchowski, K. *Na marginesie Polski jutra*. New York, 1940.

Goldmann, Nahum. *Staatsmann ohne Staat*. Cologne, 1970.

Goldstein, Bernard. *Finf Yor in Varshever Geto*. New York, 1947.

Goodhart, A. L. *Poland and the Minority Races*. London, 1920.

Górka, Olgierd. *Naród a Państwo jako zagadnienie Polski*. Warsaw, 1937.

Gruenbaum, Yitshak. *Milhamot Yehudei Polaniah, 1913–1940*. Jerusalem, 1941.

———. *Milhamot Yehudei Polin, 1906–1912*. Warsaw, 1922.

Haftka, Aleksander. "Działalność parlamentarna i polityczna posłów i senatorów żydowskich w Polsce Odrodzonej." In *Żydzi w Polsce Odrodzonej*, edited by I. Schipper, A. Tartakower, and A. Haftka, vol. 2. Warsaw, n.d.

———. "Ustawodawstwo Polski Odrodzonej w stosunku do żydowskiej mniejszości narodowej." In *Żydzi w Polsce Odrodzonej*, edited by I. Schipper, A. Tartakower, and A. Haftka, vol. 2. Warsaw, n.d.

———. "Żydowskie stronnictwa polityczne w Polsce Odrodzonej." In *Żydzi w Polsce Odrodzonej*, edited by I. Schipper, A. Tartakower, and A. Haftka, vol. 2. Warsaw, n.d.

Halicki, Wacław. *Chrześcijaństwo, Komunizm, a Żydostwo*. Lwów, 1933.

Hilberg, Raul; Staron, Stanislaw; and Kermisz, Josef, eds. *The Warsaw Diary of Adam Czerniaków: Prelude to Doom*. New York, 1979.

Hirszkowicz, Lukasz. "The Soviet Union and the Jews during World War II: British Foreign Office Documents." *Soviet Jewish Affairs* 3 (1973).

Hołówko, Tadeusz. *Kwestia narodowościowa w Polsce.* Warsaw, 1922.

Inter-Allied Information Committee. *Punishment for War Crimes: The Inter-Allied Declaration Signed at St. James's Palace London on 13th January 1942 and Relative Documents.* London, 1942.

Inwazja bolszewicka a Żydzi: Zbiór dokumentów. Warsaw, 1921.

I Saw Poland Suffer, by a Polish Doctor Who Held an Official Position in Warsaw under German Occupation. Translated by Alcuin [pseud.]. London, 1941.

Jabotinsky, Ze'ev. *HaMediniyut haTsiyonit.* Jerusalem, 1946.

Jędrzejewicz, Wacław, ed. *Poland in the British Parliament, 1939–1945.* 3 vols. New York, 1946.

Kahn, Alexander. *Condition of the Jews in Poland.* New York, 1937.

[Kaplan, Haim.] *Scroll of Agony: The Warsaw Diary of Chaim A. Kaplan.* Edited by Abraham Katsh. London, 1966.

Karski, Jan. *The Story of a Secret State.* Boston, 1944.

Kleinbaum, Moshe. "El Dr. N. Goldmann—Tazkir al Matsavah shel Yahadut Mizrach-Eiropah beReshit Milhemet haOlam haSheniyah." *Gal-Ed* 4–5 (1978).

Kleinman, I. A. *Miezhdu Molotom i Nakovalnei.* St. Petersburg, 1910.

Korboński, Stefan. *W imieniu Rzeczypospolitej.* Paris, 1954.

Korzec, Paweł. "Documents on the Jewish Problem in Poland on the Eve of World War II." *Michael* 6 (1980).

———. "General Sikorski und seine Exilregierung zur Judenfrage in Polen im Lichte von Dokumenten des Jahres 1940." *Zeitschrift für Ostforschung* 30 (1981).

Kot, Stanisław. *Listy z Rosji do Generała Sikorskiego.* London, 1955.

———. *Rozmowy z Kremlem.* London, 1959.

Kowalski, S. *Żydzi chrzczeni.* Warsaw, 1935.

Krasnowski, Zbigniew. *Światowa polityka żydowska.* Warsaw, 1934.

Kruszyński, Józef. *Dążenia żydów w dobie obecnej.* Włocławek, 1921.

Kukiel, Marian. *Generał Sikorski.* London, 1970.

———. *Six Years of Struggle for Independence.* Newtown, England, 1947.

Kutrzeba, Stanisław. *La question juive en Pologne.* Kraków, 1919.

Kwiatkowski, Michał. *Rząd i Rada Narodowa RP.* London, 1942.

Landau, Ludwik. *Kronika lat wojny i okupacji.* Warsaw, 1962.

Laudyn-Chrzanowka, Stefania. *Sprawa światowa—Żydzi, Polska, Ludżkość.* Poznań, 1923.

Levin, Shmarya. *In Milkhome Tsaytn (Bleter fun a Tage-Bukh).* New York, 1915.

Materiały w sprawie żydowskiej w Polsce. 4 vols. Warsaw, 1919.

Memorials Submitted to President Wilson concerning the Status of the Jews in Eastern Europe and in Palestine, by Representatives of the American Jewish Congress on March 2, 1919. New York, 1919.

Mitkiewicz, Leon. *Z Generałem Sikorskim na obczyźnie.* Paris, 1968.

National Polish Committee of America. *The Jews in Poland: Official Reports of the American and British Investigating Missions.* Chicago, n.d.

Nossig, Alfred. *Polen und Juden: Die polnisch-jüdische Verständigung zur Regelung der Judenfrage in Polen.* Vienna, n.d.

Olszer, Krystyna, ed, *For Your Freedom and Ours: Polish Democratic Thought through the Ages.* New York, 1981.

Papajski, Leon. *Rola Żydów w dziejach Polski.* Kraków, 1937.

The Persecution of Jews in German-Occupied Poland. London, 1940.

Pol'iaki i Yevrei: Materialy o pol'sko-yevreiskom spore po povodu zakonoproyekta o gorodskom samoupravlenii w Pol'she. Odessa, n.d.

Polonsky, Antony, ed. *The Great Powers and the Polish Question: A Documentary Study in Cold War Origins.* London, 1976.

Pryłucki, Noah. *Mowy.* Warsaw, 1920.

_____. *Redes oif Varshever Shtot-Rat.* Warsaw, n.d.

Raczyński, Edward. *In Allied London.* London, 1962.

Reich, Leon. "La situation des Juifs en Pologne et leurs revendications." In *Les droits nationaux des Juifs en Europe Orientale: Recueil d'etudes.* Paris, 1919.

Reiss, Anshel. *BeSa'arot haTekufah.* Tel Aviv, 1982.

Reprezentacja Żydostwa Polskiego. Sprawozdanie z działalności w latach 1940–1945. N.p., n.d.

Republic of Poland, Ministry of Foreign Affairs. *The Mass Extermination of Jews in German Occupied Poland.* London, 1942.

Republic of Poland, Ministry of Information. *The German Attempt to Destroy the Polish Nation.* London, 1940.

_____. *The German New Order in Poland.* London, 1940.

Retinger, J. H. *All about Poland.* London, 1941.

[_____]. *Memoirs of an Eminence Grise.* Edited by John Pomian. Sussex, 1972.

Ringelblum, Emanuel. *Polish-Jewish Relations during the Second World War.* Edited by Joseph Kermish and Shmuel Krakowski. Jerusalem, 1974.

Rosenfeld, Max. *Polen und Juden: Zeitgemässe Betrachtungen.* Berlin and Vienna, 1917.

_____. *Die polnische Judenfrage: Problem und Lösung.* Vienna and Berlin, 1918.

Rybarski, Roman. *Program gospodarczy.* Warsaw, 1937.

Scherer, Emanuel. *Polska a Żydzi.* New York, 1942.

Segal, Simon. *The New Poland and the Jews.* New York, 1938.

Snopek, Kazimierz. *Zmienianie nazwisk.* Warsaw, 1935.

Sprawozdanie stenograficzne z posiedzeń Sejmu Ustawodawczego. Warsaw, 1919–22.

Tartakower, Arieh. "HaPe'ilut haMedinit lema'an Yehudei Polin al Ademat Amerika beMilhemet haOlam haSheniyah." *Gal-Ed* 6 (1982).

Tenenbaum, J. *La question juive en Pologne.* Paris, 1919.

Waldman, Morris. *Conditions Up to Date in Poland.* Chicago, 1927.

Wasilewski, Leon. *Die Judenfrage in Kongreß-Polen: Ihre Schwierigkeiten und ihre Lösung.* Vienna, 1915.

Weichert, Michael. *Yidishe Aleynhilf, 1939–1945.* Tel Aviv, 1962.

[Weizmann, Chaim.] *The Letters and Papers of Chaim Weizmann.* Series A: Letters. Jerusalem, 1968–80.

Węgierski, Dominik [pseud.]. *September 1939.* London, 1940.

Wildecki, Tadeusz. *Niebezpieczeństwo żydowskie.* Poznań, 1937.
Zaderecki, Tadeusz. *Tajemnice alfabetu hebrajskiego.* Warsaw, 1939.
Ziemiński, Jan [Jan Wagner]. *Problem emigracji żydowskiej.* Warsaw, 1937.

SECONDARY SOURCES

Abella, Irving, and Troper, Harold. *None Is Too Many: Canada and the Jews of Europe, 1933–1948.* Toronto, 1982.
Adam, Uwe Dietrich. *Judenpolitik im Dritten Reich.* Dusseldorf, 1972.
Arad, Yitshak. " 'Mivtsa Reinhard': Mahanot haHashmadah Bełżec, Sobibor, Treblinka." *Yad VaShem: Kovets Mehkarim* 16 (1985).
Avital, Zvi. "The Polish Government-in-Exile and the Jewish Question." *Wiener Library Bulletin* 33/34 (1975).
Barlas, Haim. *Hatsalah biYmei Sho'ah.* Tel Aviv, 1975.
Bartoszewski, Władysław, and Lewin, Zofia. *Righteous among Nations: How Poles Helped the Jews, 1939–1945.* London, 1969.
Bauer, Yehuda. *American Jewry and the Holocaust: The American Jewish Joint Distribution Committee, 1939–1945.* Detroit, 1981.
————. *From Diplomacy to Resistance: A History of Jewish Palestine, 1939–1945.* Philadelphia, 1970.
————. "Genocide: Was It the Nazis' Original Plan?" *Annals of the American Academy of Political and Social Science* 450 (July 1980).
————. *The Holocaust in Historical Perspective.* Seattle, 1978.
————. "Rescue Operations through Vilna." *Yad Vashem Studies* 9 (1973).
————. "When Did They Know?" *Midstream* (1968).
Beit-Tsvi, Shabbetai. *HaTsiyonut haPost-Ugandit beMashber haSho'ah: Mehkar al Gormei Mishgeha shel haTenu'ah haTsiyonit baShanim 1938–1945.* Tel Aviv, 1977.
Bell, Daniel, and Dennen, Leon. "The System of Governments-in-Exile." *Annals of the American Academy of Political and Social Science* 232 (March 1944).
Benari, Y. *Tochnit haEvaku'atsiyah shel Jabotinsky veHazoto et Goral Yehudei Polin.* Tel Aviv, 1968.
Bertish, Roman. "Pezurat Yehudei Polin beMilhemet haOlam haSheniyah: Hithavutah veYahasah shel haMemshalah haPolanit Eleha." *Gal-Ed* 1 (1973).
Bracher, Karl Dietrich. *Die deutsche Diktatur: Entstehung, Struktur, Folgen des Nationalsozialismus.* Frankfurt, 1969.
Bronsztejn, Szyja. *Ludność żydowska w Polsce w okresie międzywojennym: Studium statystyczne.* Wrocław, 1963.
Broszat, Martin. "Hitler und die Genesis der 'Endlösung': Aus Anlaß der Thesen von David Irving." *Vierteljahrshefte für Zeitgeschichte* 25 (1977).
————. *Nationalsozialistische Polenpolitik, 1939–1945.* Stuttgart, 1961.
Browning, Christopher. *The Final Solution and the German Foreign Office: A Study of Referat DIII of Abteilung Deutschland, 1940–43.* New York, 1978.

————. "Zur Genesis der Endlösung: Eine Antwort an Martin Broszat." *Vierteljahrshefte für Zeitgeschichte* 29 (1981).

Buchheim, Hans. "Die SS—das Herrschaftsinstrument." In *Anatomie des SS-Staates*, vol. 1. Munich, 1982.

Bunzl, John. *Klassenkampf in der Diaspora: Zur Geschichte der jüdischen Arbeiterbewegung.* Vienna, 1975.

Canin, M. "HaYehudim baTsava haPolani." In *Entsiklopediah shel Galuyot: Varshah*, vol. 2. Jerusalem, 1959.

Chmielewski, Edward. *The Polish Question in the Russian State Duma.* Knoxville, Tenn., 1970.

Chojnowski, Andrzej. *Koncepcje polityki narodowościowej rządów polskich w latach 1921–1939.* Wrocław, 1979.

Cholawski, Shalom. *Al Neharot haNieman vehaDnieper: Yehudei Byelorusiah haMa'aravit beMilhemet haOlam haSheniyah.* Jerusalem, 1982.

Coutouvidis, John. "Lewis Namier and the Polish Government-in-Exile, 1939–40." *Slavonic and East European Review* 62 (1984).

Davies, Norman. *God's Playground: A History of Poland.* 2 vols. Oxford, 1981.

Duraczyński, Eugeniusz. *Kontrowersje i konflikty, 1939–1941.* Warsaw, 1977.

————. *Stosunki w kierownictwie podziemia londyńskiego.* Warsaw, 1966.

Eisenbach, Artur. *Hitlerowska polityka zagłady Żydów.* Warsaw, 1961.

Engel, David. "HaBerit haNichzevet: HaTenu'ah haReviziyonistit uMemshelet Polin haGolah." *HaTsiyonut.* In press.

————. "HaSichsuch haPolani-Sovieti keGorem beHityahasutah shel Memshelet Polin haGolah laSho'ah." *Shvut.* In press.

————. "The Polish Government-in-Exile and the Deportations of Polish Jews from France in 1942." *Yad Vashem Studies* 15 (1983).

Fein, Helen. *Accounting for Genocide: National Responses and Jewish Victimization during the Holocaust.* Chicago, 1979.

Feinberg, Nathan. *La question des minorités à la Conference de la Paix.* Paris, 1929.

Fleming, Gerald. *Hitler and the Final Solution.* Berkeley and Los Angeles, 1983.

Fox, John P. "The Final Solution: Intended or Contingent? The Stuttgart Conference of May 1984 and the Historical Debate." *Patterns of Prejudice* 18 (1984).

————. "The Jewish Factor in British War Crimes Policy in 1942." *English Historical Review* 92 (1977).

Friedmann, Philip. "The Lublin Reservation and the Madagascar Plan: Two Aspects of Nazi Jewish Policy during the Second World War." *Yivo Annual of Jewish Social Science* 7 (1953).

Garliński, Józef. *Oświęcim walczący.* London, 1974.

Gelber, N. M. *Toledot haTenu'ah haTsiyonit beGalitsiyah, 1875–1918.* Jerusalem, 1958.

Gelber, Yoav. "Zionist Policy and the Fate of European Jewry (1939–1942)." *Yad Vashem Studies* 13 (1979).

Gilbert, Martin. *Atlas of the Holocaust.* London, 1982.
_____. *Auschwitz and the Allies.* New York, 1981.
Golczewski, Frank. *Polnisch-jüdische Beziehungen, 1881–1922: Eine Studie zur Geschichte des Antisemitismus in Osteuropa.* Wiesbaden, 1981.
Gross, Jan Tomasz. *Polish Society under German Occupation: The General-gouvernement, 1939–1944.* Princeton, 1979.
Grudzińska-Gross, Irena, and Gross, Jan Tomasz. *War through Children's Eyes: The Soviet Occupation of Poland and the Deportations, 1939–1941.* Stanford, 1981.
Gutman, Yisrael. "Jews in General Anders' Army in the Soviet Union." *Yad Vashem Studies* 12 (1977).
_____. *Yehudei Varshah, 1939–1943: Geto, Mahteret, Mered.* Tel Aviv, 1977.
Heller, Celia. *On the Edge of Destruction: Jews of Poland between the Two World Wars.* New York, 1977.
Hilberg, Raul. *The Destruction of the European Jews.* Chicago, 1961.
Holzer, Jerzy. *Mozaika polityczna Drugiej Rzeczypospolitej.* Warsaw, 1974.
_____. *PPS, szkic dziejów.* Warsaw, 1977.
Iranek-Osmecki, Kazimierz. *He Who Saves One Life.* New York, 1971.
_____; Lichten, Joseph L.; and Raczyński, Edward. "The Polish Government-in-Exile and the Jewish Tragedy during World War II." *Wiener Library Bulletin* 37/38 (1976).
Izek, Hersch. "Roosevelt and the Polish Question, 1941–1945." Ph.D. dissertation, University of Minnesota, 1980.
Johnpoll, Bernard. *The Politics of Futility: The General Jewish Workers Bund of Poland, 1917–1943.* Ithaca, N.Y., 1967.
Kacewicz, George. *Great Britain, the Soviet Union, and the Polish Government in Exile, 1939–1945.* The Hague, 1979.
Kagan, George. "[The] Agrarian Regime of Pre-War Poland." *Journal of Central European Affairs* 3 (1943).
Kedem, Menahem. *Haim Weizmann beMilhemet haOlam haSheniyah: Weizmann vehaMediniyut haTsiyonit baShanim 1939–1945.* Jerusalem, 1983.
Kieniewicz, Stefan. *Historyk a świadomość narodowa.* Warsaw, 1982.
Korboński, Stefan. *The Polish Underground State: A Guide to the Underground, 1939–1945.* New York, 1978.
Korpalska, Walentyna. *Władysław Eugeniusz Sikorski: Biografia polityczna.* Wrocław, 1981.
Korzec, Paweł. "Der Block der Nationalen Minderheiten im Parlamentarismus Polens des Jahres 1922." *Zeitschrift für Ostforschung* 24 (1975).
_____. "Heskem Memshelet W. Grabski im haNetsigut haParlamentarit haYehudit." *Gal-Ed* 1 (1973).
_____. *Juifs en Pologne: La question juive pendant l'entre-deux-guerres.* Paris, 1980.
_____. "Polen und der Minderheitenschutzvertrag (1919–1934)." *Jahrbücher für Geschichte Osteuropas* 22 (1975).

———. "Der Zweite Block der Nationalen Minderheiten im Parlamentarismus Polens, 1927–1928." *Zeitschrift für Ostforschung* 26 (1977).

Krakowski, Shmuel. "Avedot Yahadut Polin baSho'ah—Ha'arachah Statistit." *Dappim leHeker Tekufat haSho'ah* 2 (1981).

———. "The Fate of Jewish Prisoners of War in the September 1939 Campaign." *Yad Vashem Studies* 12 (1977).

Krausnick, Helmut. "Judenverfolgungen." In *Anatomie des SS-Staates*, vol. 2. Munich, 1982.

Landa, Moshe. "Gush haMi'utim (1922)—Machshir Behirot o Etgar Medini?" *Gal-Ed* 4–5 (1978).

———. "Hafichat Mai 1926—Tsipiyot beYahadut Polin liTemurah Medinit veTahalich Hitbadutan." *Gal-Ed* 2 (1975).

———. "Mekomah shel ha'Ugoda' (miShenat 1925) beMa'arechet haYahasim haHadadiyim haPolanim-Yehudim." *Zion* 37 (1972).

Laqueur, Walter. *The Terrible Secret: Suppression of the Truth about Hitler's Final Solution.* Boston, 1980.

Levin, Dov. "Berit haMo'atsot veHatsalat haYehudim—Be'ayot veUvdot." In *Nisyonot uFe'ulot Hatsalah biTekufat haSho'ah: Hartsa'ot veDiyunim baKinnus haBeinle'umi haSheni shel Hokrei haSho'ah*, edited by Yisrael Gutman. Jerusalem, 1976.

Lifschütz, E. "HaPogromim beFolin baShanim 1918–1919: Ve'adat Morgenthau uMisrad haHuts haAmerikani." *Zion* 33–34 (1958–59).

Lipiner, Elias. "A Nova Imigracão Judaica no Brasil." In *Breve História dos Judeus no Brasil*, edited by Henrique Iusin. Rio de Janeiro, 1962.

Litwak, Yosef. "HaYehudim biTseva'o shel haGeneral Anders." *Shvut* 5 (1977).

———. "She'elat haEzrahut shel Yehudim Yotse'ei-Polin biVerit haMo'atsot (1941–1943)." *Behinot* 7 (1977).

———. "Shittuf Pe'ulah Polani-Briti liMeni'at Yetsi'atam shel Pelitim Yehudim im haTsava haPolani miBerit haMo'atsot biShenat 1942." In *Divrei HaKongres haOlami haShevi'i leMada'ei haYahadut: Mehkarim beToledot haSho'ah*. Jerusalem, 1980.

Lukas, Richard C. *The Forgotten Holocaust: The Poles under German Occupation, 1939–1944.* Lexington, Ky., 1986.

———. *The Strange Allies: The United States and Poland, 1941–1945.* Knoxville, Tenn., 1978.

Lundgreen-Nielsen, Kay. *The Polish Problem at the Paris Peace Conference: A Study of the Policies of the Great Powers and the Poles, 1918–1919.* Odense, 1979.

Madajczyk, Czesław. "Mahanot haRikkuz haNatsiyim keMachshir leDikkui haOchlusiyah haKevushah." In *Mahanot haRikkuz haNatsiyim—Mivneh uMegamot, Demut heAsir, haYehudim baMahanot: Hartsa'ot veDiyunim baKinnus haBeinle'umi haRevi'i shel Hokrei haSho'ah*, edited by Yisrael Gutman and Rahel Manber. Jerusalem, 1984.

———. *Polityka III Rzeszy w okupowanej Polsce.* Warsaw, 1970.

Mahler, Rafael. *Yehudei Polin bein Shetei Milhamot haOlam: Historiyah Kalkalit-Sotsiyalit le'or haStatistikah*. Tel Aviv, 1968.

Marcus, Joseph. *Social and Political History of the Jews in Poland, 1919–1939*. Berlin, 1983.

Melzer, Emanuel. "HaDiplomatiyah haPolanit uVe'ayat haHagirah haYehudit baShanim 1935–1939." *Gal-Ed* 1 (1973).

_____. *Ma'avak Medini beMalkodet: Yehudei Polin, 1935–1939*. Tel Aviv, 1982.

_____. "Mifleget haShilton OZON vehaYehudim beFolin, 1937–1939." *Gal-Ed* 4–5 (1978).

_____. "Relations between Poland and Germany and Their Impact on the Jewish Problem in Poland." *Yad Vashem Studies* 12 (1977).

Mendelsohn, Ezra. *Class Struggle in the Pale: The Formative Years of the Jewish Workers' Movement in Tsarist Russia*. Cambridge, 1970.

_____. "The Dilemma of Jewish Politics in Poland: Four Responses." In *Jews and Non-Jews in Eastern Europe*, edited by Bela Vago and George Mosse. Jerusalem, 1974.

_____. "The Politics of Agudas Yisroel in Inter-War Poland." *Soviet Jewish Affairs* 2 (1972).

_____. *Zionism in Poland: The Formative Years, 1915–1926*. New Haven, 1981.

Micewski, Andrzej. *Z geografii politycznej II Rzeczypospolitej*. Warsaw, 1966.

Mishkinski, Moshe. "HaSotsializm haPolani uShe'elat haYehudim erev Yissud PPS ve-SDKP (II)." *Gal-Ed*. In press.

Mosse, George L. *Toward the Final Solution: A History of European Racism*. New York, 1978.

Neshamit, Sarah. *Ma'avako shel haGeto*. N.p., 1972.

Netzer, Shlomo. *Ma'avak Yehudei Polin al Zechuyoteihem haEzrahiyot veha-Le'umiyot, 1918–1922*. Tel Aviv, 1980.

Neumann, Franz. *Behemoth: The Structure and Practice of National Socialism*. Oxford, 1944.

Nowogrodzki, Emanuel. "HaBund bein Shetei Milhamot haOlam." In *Entsiklopediah shel Galuyot: Varshah*. Jerusalem, 1959.

Nussbaum, Kalman. *VeHafach lahem leRo'ets: HaYehudim baTsava haAmami ha-Polani biVerit haMo'atsot*. Tel Aviv, 1984.

_____. " 'Legyon Yehudi' o Ahizat Einayim?" *Shvut* 10 (1984).

Pinchuk, Ben-Cion. *Yehudei Berit-haMo'atsot mul penei haSho'ah: Mehkar beVa'ayot Haglayah uFinnui*. Tel Aviv, 1979.

Pobóg-Malinowski, Władysław. *Najnowsza historia polityczna Polski, 1864–1945*. 3 vols. London, 1967.

Polonsky, Antony. *Politics in Independent Poland, 1921–1939*. Oxford, 1972.

Porat, Dina. "Helkah shel Hanhalat haSochnut biY'rushalayim baMa'amatsim leHatsalat Yehudei Eiropa baShanim 1942–1945." Ph.D. dissertation, Tel Aviv University, 1983.

_____. "Rikkuz haPelitim haYehudi'im beVilna baShanim 1939–1941: Ma'amatsei haYetsi'ah." M.A. thesis, Tel Aviv University, 1973.

Próchnik, Adam. *Pierwsze piętnastolecie Polski niepodległej: Zarys dziejów po-*

litycznych. Warsaw, 1983.

Redlich, Shimon. "Jews in General Anders' Army in the Soviet Union, 1941–1942." *Soviet Jewish Affairs* 2 (1971).

_____. "The Jews under Soviet Rule during World War II." Ph.D. dissertation, New York University, 1968.

_____. *Propaganda and Nationalism in Wartime Russia: The Jewish Antifascist Committee in the USSR, 1941–1948.* N.p., 1982.

Robinson, Jacob; Karbach, Oscar; Laserson, Max; Robinson, Nehemiah; and Vichniek, Mark. *Were the Minorities Treaties a Failure?* New York, 1943.

Rothschild, Joseph. *East Central Europe between the Two World Wars.* Seattle, 1974.

Schechtman, Joseph. *Fighter and Prophet: The Vladimir Jabotinsky Story—The Last Years.* New York, 1961.

_____, and Benari, Yehuda. *History of the Revisionist Movement.* Tel Aviv, 1970.

Schleunes, Karl. *The Twisted Road to Auschwitz: Nazi Policy toward German Jews.* Urbana, Ill., 1970.

Schwarz, Solomon. *Di Yidn in Sovetn-Farband: Milkhome un Nokhmilkhome-Yorn, 1939–1965.* New York, 1967.

Sereny, Gitta. *Into That Darkness: An Examination of Conscience.* New York, 1974.

Shapira, Anita. *Berl.* Tel Aviv, 1980.

Shatzky, Jacob. *Yidishe Yishuvim in Latein-Amerike.* Buenos Aires, 1952.

Shlomi, Hana. "Yehudei Polin biVerit haMo'atsot beMilhemet haOlam haSheniyah—He'arot veHavharot." *Shvut* 11 (1985).

Shohat, Azriel. "Parashat haPogrom beFinsk beHamishah beApril 1919." *Gal-Ed* 1 (1973).

Tal, Uriel. "On the Study of the Holocaust and Genocide." *Yad Vashem Studies* 13 (1979).

Tartakower, Arieh. *Nedudei haYehudim baOlam.* Jerusalem, 1947.

Tec, Nechama. "Righteous Christians: Who Are They?" In *Proceedings of the Eighth World Congress of Jewish Studies.* Jerusalem, 1982.

_____. *When Light Pierced the Darkness: Christian Rescue of Jews in Nazi-Occupied Poland.* Oxford, 1986.

Terry, Sarah Meiklejohn. *Poland's Place in Europe: General Sikorski and the Origins of the Oder-Neisse Line.* Princeton, 1982.

Tomaszewski, Jerzy. *Rzeczpospolita wielu narodów.* Warsaw, 1985.

Viefhaus, Erwin. *Die Minderheitenfrage und die Entstehung der Minderheitenschutzvertrag auf der Pariser Friedenskonferenz 1919.* Wurzburg, 1960.

Wandycz, Piotr. *The Lands of Partitioned Poland, 1795–1918.* Seattle, 1974.

Wapiński, Roman. *Władysław Sikorski.* Warsaw, 1978.

Wasserstein, Bernard. *Britain and the Jews of Europe, 1939–1945.* Oxford, 1979.

Wynot, Edward. "A Necessary Cruelty: The Emergence of Official Antisemitism in Poland, 1936–1939." *American Historical Review* 76 (1971).

Yahil, Leni. "Madagascar—Phantom of a Solution for the Jewish Question." In *Jews and Non-Jews in Eastern Europe*, edited by Bela Vago and George L. Mosse. New York, 1974.

Zabiełło, Stanisław. *O rząd i granice: Walka dyplomatyczna o sprawę polską w II wojnie światowej.* N.p., 1970.

Zechlin, Egmont. *Die deutsche Politik und die Juden im Ersten Weltkrieg.* Göttingen, 1969.

zur Mühlen, Patrik von. *Rassenideologien: Geschichte und Hintergrund.* Berlin, 1977.

INDEX